MYOPIC GRANDEUR

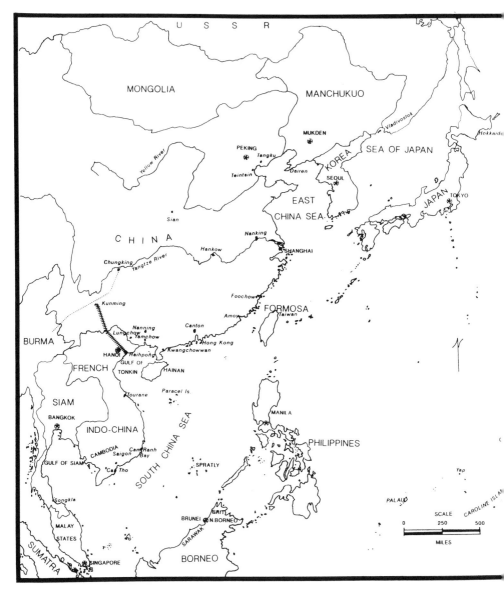

East Asia 1939

MYOPIC GRANDEUR

The Ambivalence of
French Foreign Policy toward the
Far East, 1919–1945

John E. Dreifort

THE KENT STATE UNIVERSITY PRESS
Kent, Ohio, and London, England

© 1991 by The Kent State University Press,
Kent, Ohio 44242
All rights reserved
Library of Congress Catalog Card Number 91–11434
ISBN 0–87338–441–5
Manufactured in the United States of America

Library of Congress Cataloging-in-Publication Data

Dreifort, John E.
Myopic grandeur : the ambivalence of French foreign policy toward
the Far East, 1919–1945 / John E. Dreifort.
p.   cm.
Includes bibliographical references and index.
ISBN 0–87338–441–5 (alk. paper)
1. East Asia—Foreign relations—France.   2. France—Foreign
relations—East Asia.   3. France—Foreign relations—20th century.
4. Indochina—History.   5. Great powers—History—20th century.
I. Title.
DS518.2.D74   1991
327.4405—dc20   91–11434

British Library Cataloging-in-Publication data are available.

To Todd, Darren, and Kimberly
who make life rich

Contents

Preface

Several years ago, while initiating preliminary research for this study in the archives of the French Foreign Ministry, I discovered a document that appeared to provide an important clue to understanding French foreign policy toward the Far East during the 1920s. The memorandum, like so many others in the collection, contained little evidence about its destination or its origin other than a signature. Unfortunately, the signature was an indecipherable scribble. In the vain hope that the archivist might be able to provide a clue as to the identity of the author, I showed her the document in question. She could not identify the author from the signature. "But," she said, "feel this paper. It is definitely from the Ministry of Defense." The memorandum had obviously come from a person in that ministry. Little did I realize at that time how prophetic this incident would prove to be. Not only would I find myself "feeling my way" through the documentation, I would also find myself "feeling my way" through the vagaries of French foreign policy-making and implementation as it related to the Far East between 1918 and 1945, a task made more difficult by the incomplete state of the documentary record available.

The background to World War II in the Far East has drawn the attention of many outstanding historians during the past couple of decades. Most studies, however, have focused upon the activities of the United States, Great Britain, or Japan, and particularly with reference to the decade between the Manchurian crisis of 1931 and the attack on Pearl Harbor in 1941. The French role in the crisis of the region during the interwar years has been given little attention—certainly none in such detail as accorded other major powers with interests in the area. This has occurred for several reasons. For the most part, Frenchmen as well as historians have tended to view the period through European lenses. The belief persisted that the period 1919 to 1939 was simply a twenty-year armistice between France and Germany. Therefore, the major crises produced by German and

Italian aggression have drawn the most attention. Moreover, when the war became worldwide with the attacks in the Far East in 1941, much of the fighting was conducted by the Americans and the British, in stark contrast to the apparently abject surrender of Vichy French leaders. Finally, and perhaps most important, the events that unfolded in the Far East between 1919 and 1945 clearly were linked to the subsequent inglorious dismantling of the French Empire, a substantial portion of which lay in the Far East, and a concomitant reduction of France's traditional great-power status to that of a second-rank regional power. Such a limited role for the heirs of Louis XIV and Napoleon has been hard to accept. Yet, there is no doubt that there was a direct line from Manchuria in 1931 to Dien Bien Phu in 1954. In fact, the threat to France's great-power status came not only from its European neighbors but from a potentially hostile, ambitiously expansionistic power on the other side of the world.

The Orient, generally perceived by Westerners as a place of mystery and inscrutable leaders, was an area that few people in France, other than the handful of specialists, gave any sustained attention. One needs to search long and hard in the *souvenirs* of leading policymakers of the period—men such as Briand, Bonnet, Daladier, Paul-Boncour, Herriot, Flandin, Reynaud, or de Gaulle—to find more than passing references to Far Eastern affairs. Unsurprisingly, they focused upon the more immediate points of high crisis in Europe—the post–World War I security and reparations issues, the role of the League of Nations, the birth of Nazi Germany, Italian aggression in Abyssinia, the Spanish Civil War, and the succession of German violations of the Treaty of Versailles all seized the attention of French officials, the media, and the public. Historians of French foreign policy have reflected this European preoccupation.

This does not mean, however, that all French leaders entirely neglected the Far East or that they failed to realize the importance of developments in the area. Whether they wanted to or not, they found themselves progressively enmeshed in the problems of the region, and the opening of the French archival and documentary records of the period reveal the depth and extent of the concern displayed by French policymakers that has been unappreciated heretofore. Against a backdrop of domestic turmoil, military weakness, crumbling collective security, and world crisis, French leaders attempting to formulate their policy in the Far East faced a series of disquieting dilemmas that soon revealed the great disparity between French aspirations and resources. France's Far Eastern policy had to be considered in the global context of commitments worldwide—at home, in

Europe, and elsewhere in the empire. Continuous Japanese pressure on a chaotic China infected by a growing nationalism threatened to inflame the whole Far Eastern region and to destroy the substantial interests of the Western imperial powers. French commercial and cultural interests in China and its most important colony in Indochina stood directly in the path of Japanese expansionism.

Furthermore, the myth of French superiority that had created and sustained the empire in the region now stood the danger of being laid bare. The French chiefs of staff insisted that a renascent Germany would absorb all of France's defensive capacity and that its military capability in the Far East would remain woefully inadequate to the task of taking a leading role in restraining Japan. The depression of the 1930s exacerbated the problem of military funding, supplies, and personnel in the area and altered an already-difficult situation to one that was impossible for France to meet. If the resources of the empire were concentrated for the defense of French interests in China, Indochina, and the Pacific, Germany might seize the opportunity to attack in Europe. On the other hand, by focusing its attention and resources in Europe, France ran the risk of providing Japan with an opportunity to expand in the Far East at French expense. Psychologically unprepared to abandon its role in the Far East, but with its resources dwindling relative to the challenges presented by German, Italian, and Japanese aggression, France had to find some less expensive way to overcome the long-term incompatibility of its aims and resources. It resorted to skillful diplomacy as the only means at hand to defend its interests and salvage its great-power status as a major player in Far Eastern affairs.

French diplomatic efforts calculated to reduce tensions in the Far East, while simultaneously seeking support from potential allies, were viewed as being vital to continued French presence in the Far East. But nothing proved harder to accomplish. Pressure on China to accede to Japanese demands threatened to produce another xenophobic outbreak that could jeopardize Chinese goodwill essential to continued French commercial, political, and missionary activities in that vast, divided country. The United States, which had significant interests in the region, initially appeared unconvinced about the Japanese threat and, in any case, remained dominated by isolationist sentiment. Great Britain had even greater interests threatened by Japan's aggressive imperialism, but its traditional suspicion of France and its frequently contradictory actions and vacillating policies, both in Europe and in the Far East, confused the situation still further. The Soviet Union, also threatened by potential Japanese aggression, was viewed with mistrust by conservative French politicians and with doubt by the military men. Effective Franco-Soviet cooperation was thus ruled out. With few viable alternatives available, therefore, an incredible amount of vacillation and indecision, lack of coordination, and missed opportunities characterized French handling of the Far Eastern situation prior to 1939.

Even after the outbreak of war in Europe, France found itself unable to ignore completely the situation in the Far East, although it was placed at the bottom of the list of priorities. With the debacle of 1940, it became even more imperative in the minds of patriotic Frenchmen that they defend and retain all vestiges of former greatness. But, of course, the disaster in Europe simply encouraged Japan to pursue more aggressively its southward expansion. While this policy ultimately brought the United States into an active role in the Far East, something the Western powers had been unable to achieve throughout the interwar period, for France it appeared to be a mixed blessing. American goals and French aspirations concerning the postwar Far East differed sharply and consequently produced a strained relationship during and after World War II.

Given the considerable span of time examined by this study, an attempt to review the whole history of French foreign policy toward the Far East within the confines of a single volume would be extremely difficult and not very meaningful. Clearly, therefore, some topics are more thoroughly discussed than others. Indeed, some facets of concern unquestionably receive less attention than they deserve. This is not a study of French colonialism or of French colonial policy, although the Far Eastern possessions provided the basis of France's presence and concern. Neither is it an examination of French military policy, although French military debilitation laid bare France's vulnerability. Rather, it is a study of the diplomatic efforts of France to protect its substantial interests, tangible and intangible, in the Far East. Certainly, matters of colonial and military policy will be discussed, for they obviously had a significant impact upon those who formulated and implemented French foreign policy in the area. But there will be no effort made to retrace the steps covered by other outstanding scholars of those particular facets of the twentieth-century French experience. It should be noted, too, that coverage of French diplomatic efforts concerning the Far East will be uneven from the standpoint of period. I have necessarily focused on the periods of high tension and crisis, so that the events of the 1930s and World War II receive the greatest attention. But by no means were developments during the relatively peaceful transitional period of the 1920s, for example, unimportant. Indeed, the period from 1919 to 1945 needs to be considered as a whole in order to appreciate the nature of the problem that confronted France and to understand its failure to devise suitable solutions to problems in the Far East. Ultimately, any study of this nature that ranges far and wide in time and space will leave significant gaps. Indeed, this study must be viewed as a beginning rather than an end to our understanding of France's foreign policy in the Far East during the period. It is hoped, therefore, that this study, rather than closing the door on the subject, will open the possibilities for additional fascinating areas for historians' inquiry and analysis. In this way, understanding might be gained about a facet of international relations during the twentieth century that has not been given the attention that it deserves, particularly in light of postwar developments and misery suffered by millions.

In the course of the past decade during which the work on this study occurred, I have accumulated many debts that I wish to acknowledge. The archives of the French Ministry of Foreign Affairs, the British Foreign Office, and the United States Department of State form the basis of this volume. Therefore, my debt of gratitude is considerable to the staffs of the Quai d'Orsay archives in Paris, the Kew Gardens branch of the Public Record Office in London, and the National Archives in Washington, D.C. My thanks also go to the staffs of the following libraries and institutions in which I have worked while preparing this work: Bibliothèque de Documentation Internationale Contemporaine and Bibliothèque Nationale Foundation Nationales des Sciences Politiques in Paris; British Museum Reading Room; Cambridge University Library; Churchill College Library, Cambridge; Franklin D. Roosevelt Library, Hyde Park, New York; Houghton Library, Harvard University; Institute of Historical Research and Senate House Reading Room, University of London; Library of Congress; and the Wichita State University Ablah Library. The thorough, unfailingly courteous assistance provided by the staffs of these institutions helped to ease the task of investigating the primary materials essential to this study. I am particularly grateful for the proficient support of Thoburn Taggart and his interlibrary-loan staff of the Ablah Library at Wichita State University.

Inadequacies in the documentary record were in part offset by interviews and correspondence with the following persons, who were extraordinarily generous with their recollections: Suzanne Bidault,

Georges Bonnet, Henri Bonnet, Charles Corbin, Anthony Eden, Robert Luc, and Robert Murphy. I am grateful for the insights and nuances that they provided; those cannot be gleaned from the official record.

Insofar as I have been able to develop a broader perspective about Far Eastern issues in the context of the global affairs of the period, much is owed to early discussions about this study with Christopher Thorne and William Roger Louis. Their important studies of related aspects of the period are models of scholarship. I am indebted to my colleagues at Wichita State University, J. Kelley Sowards and William E. Unrau, who read the manuscript and made helpful suggestions and provided stimulation through their prolific scholarship. Special thanks, too, are due to John L. Harnsberger, who supported and encouraged my efforts during the long period of gestation required for this work. Anthony P. Gythiel skillfully rechecked the notes with meticulous care. Fran Majors typed the manuscript with remarkable precision and made valuable stylistic suggestions.

Research conducted in France, Britain, and the United States was made possible by two generous grants from the Penrose Fund of the American Philosophical Society. A grant from the Eleanor Roosevelt Institute made it possible to carry out research in the archives of the Franklin D. Roosevelt Library. I am grateful to the Faculty Research Committee and the Office of Research Administration of Wichita State University for extensive financial aid which helped to defray the cost of travel and research materials.

Finally, I wish to thank numerous friends, students, and colleagues for their understanding, patience, and courtesy over these many years as I frequently sought to juggle too many professional projects and activities. Most of all, I thank my wife, Carol, who has shared the frequent frustrations, cheered my enthusiasms, endured with me the long absences, and made possible the entire endeavor. As must be the case in the end, however, whatever limitations of fact and judgment that may exist are my responsibility alone.

MYOPIC GRANDEUR

one

FRENCH INTERESTS IN THE FAR EAST

PRIOR to the start of the Washington Conference on the Limitation of Armaments in 1921, the French Foreign Ministry surveyed the general situation in the Far East and the great power relationships in the area since the end of World War I. The Quai d'Orsay's analysis focused on some of the difficulties facing French policymakers in the area and concluded, "France cannot play a principal role in the Far East. Its policy must draw its inspiration from defending its acquired interests while trying to conciliate the international rivalries or appeasing if possible the causes of civil troubles, for we cannot remain indifferent to an aggravation of the situation which would be likely to affect Indochina."[1] The desire to maintain the status quo in the Far East and thereby protect French interests would remain the salient feature of French policy for the entire period between the conclusion of World War I and the end of World War II. But such a policy, so simple to define, would become increasingly difficult to sustain in the face of political, economic, and social malaise at home, the German threat in Europe, rising Asian nationalism overseas, and general diplomatic isolation. To understand the concerns of French policymakers as they sought to maintain the French position in the Far East, one must first sketch the nature of France's interest—both real and perceived—in the region and trace briefly the evolution of its relationships with the area prior to the end of World War I.

French presence in Asia and the Pacific had been achieved by a remarkable series of imperial conquests that occurred in the last quarter of the nineteenth century, when the Third Republic acquired an empire second only to that of Great Britain. Attempts by historians to analyze the reasons for the tremendous overseas expansion by a host of other powers during the same period seldom agree, and so it is for French imperial activity. What is clear, however, is that such expansion did not result from sustained government policy or from enthusiastic public support. Perhaps one student of the Third Republic came the closest to the mark when he observed that it was "the work of a few dedicated missionaries, soldiers, and administrators, who literally carved out the French Empire behind the back of the people."[2] Be that as it may, however, it does not tell us what motivated this handful of imperialists.

During the first half of the nineteenth century, France, like most of Europe, languished in a state of imperial apathy. Exhausted after the Napoleonic grab for power and glory, much of France focused its attention upon domestic issues. The scattered remnants of her once-great overseas empire remained largely neglected. To be sure, a few territories were added, including Tahiti and a handful of Pacific archipelagoes in the Far East, and there began some very tentative initiatives along the banks of the Mekong River. But nothing seemed to presage the tremendous outburst of colonial expansion that characterized the last quarter of the century.

Undoubtedly, a variety of motives can be attributed to this expansionist activity. Surely, much of the fervor displayed by Europe's most Catholic country reflected its hopes of Christianizing and civilizing backward peoples. Many of those imbued with the notion of a *mission civilisatrice* would have thrilled to the charge of the French vice-counsul in Shanghai, Louis Charles de Montigny, who argued, "The moment has come for France . . . to play the first role in the Far East. An occasion more favorable will never be offered to us. Faithful to the mission that Divine Providence has confided to us, we will once again show ourselves [to be] the champions of humanity."[3] Others may have been simply the bored heirs of a generation of revolutionaries and adventurers of the fitful nineteenth century who were driven by a psychological need to carve out their own niche through a search for glory.[4]

More ardent have been those who have emphasized economic motivation for the French colonial surge. Jules Ferry, usually linked most closely with renewed French imperial activity, is frequently cited as having promoted the idea that colonies were necessary for France's economic development. They would provide new sources of raw materials, vast potential markets, and outlets for French investors. However, there is simply too little evidence to support a theory that the economic drive for empire became paramount in France. Compared to Britain, France's economic need for colonies was slight.

Industrialization had developed more slowly in France than in Great Britain, and the economy remained basically self-sufficient. Consequently, its foreign trade remained relatively small and concentrated on the continent. Moreover, French industry did not develop the ravenous hunger for raw materials that characterized British industry. Neither did it produce large stocks of manufactured goods for the overseas market. Commerce with the underdeveloped colonies remained only a small part of the French economy, and the nation's businesses took slight interest in it. French farmers, tending to regard overseas commodities as competition, hardly sympathized with colonial enterprise. Finally, only a tiny fraction of French foreign investment went into the economic development of the colonies. Cautious French investors preferred to invest in safe government bonds or in Russian industry. Indeed, while only 10 percent of France's overseas investment found its way to the colonies, Russia may have received as much as 25 percent.[5] Private enterprise certainly flourished in some centers of the empire—in Algiers, Saigon, and Hanoi—but the balance sheet of the French colonial experience prior to World War I suggests that the economic advantages of the empire were more than offset by the cost of administration and defense of such far-flung interests. Ironically, in fact, France did not attempt to reap full economic advantage from its possessions until it was too late. One must therefore conclude that economic arguments were primarily used either as the ex post facto justification or as preliminary assurance intended to rally a reticent French population. As Raymond Betts has suggested, "Ferry's most famous utterance—'colonial policy is the daughter of industrial policy'—would have made better economic sense if it had been expressed in English."[6]

What, then, explains the French rush to empire? In the final analysis, one must agree with Henri Brunschwig's verdict that while British imperialism may have been commercial, French overseas expansion resulted from a search for prestige wherein patriotic rather than economic drives dominated. The argument that French imperialism was economically profitable was "nothing more than a myth. . . . The real cause of French colonial expansion was the spread of nationalist fever, as a result of events which had taken place in 1870 and 1871."[7] In a similar vein, John Cady has persuasively argued, "The taproot of French imperialism in the Far East from first to last was national pride—pride of culture, reputation, prestige, and influence. . . . The basic considerations behind French policy in the Far East from the time of Louis XIV to that of Louis Napoleon and Jules Ferry were more political than economic."[8] The same Ferry declared to the Chamber of Deputies in 1885, "To shine without acting, without taking part in world affairs . . . is, for a great nation, to abdicate, and, faster than you might believe, it is to descend from the first rank to the third or the fourth."[9]

3

With the defeat of 1870, France had been forced to surrender the hegemony that she had held on the continent since Louis XIV. Her prestige fell to its lowest ebb since 1815. If, as became increasingly apparent, immediate *revanche* was out of the question, to some French patriots it seemed logical that the acquisition of a colonial empire would restore French national prestige and provide resources that would strengthen France for an eventual return match with Germany. Certainly, not all French nationalists were persuaded. Led by Georges Clemenceau, many resisted any attempt to divert their attention from "the blue line of the Vosges." The Duc de Broglie fulminated before the Senate, "To suppose that an essentially continental and European power like France can . . . find compensation for her lost strength in distant expeditions is to go against both history and common sense."[10] Some plainly saw it as a Bismarckian tactic to divert France from regaining Alsace and Lorraine and from resuming her proper role in Europe. Paul Déroulède, the rightist poet and political agitator, cried, "I have lost two children and instead you offer me twenty domestics."[11] On the other hand, along with Ferry, other leaders with considerable prestige supported, at least spasmodically, the French imperial efforts. Léon Gambetta and Théophile Delcassé, for example, believed that the Empire could complement the French hand in Europe. Eugène Etienne, leader of the *groupe colonial* in the Chamber of Deputies and one of the most active and passionate French imperialists, summed up the belief of many: "We had to prove to Europe that we were not finished."[12] In the final analysis, then, one must agree with the conclusion of one study that French involvement in the imperial scramble was "predicated on a simple patriotism and on a reaction to the shame of 1870."[13] Economic considerations and arguments became useful ex post facto rationalizations or preliminary assurances designed to placate the economically conservative bourgeoisie who remained cautious about pocketbook matters. Even the most ardent imperialists realized that Frenchmen would accept the costs necessary to build and maintain an empire only if they could be led to believe that a profit might be reaped from it. Only then could the potent *revanchist* forces of Clemenceau be brought to tolerate, however grudgingly, the imperial efforts. Thus, one could argue the existence of a symbiotic relationship between prestige and economic justification as a way to revitalize the French position in Europe prefatory to eventual *revanche*.[14]

Yet these activities abroad and at home on behalf of the French Empire were conducted by a relative handful of people. General public interest in the Empire and empire building, although increasing by the end of the century, remained relatively slight. Except for rare occasions, as Ferry, *le tonkinois,* would attest, the halls of the Chamber of Deputies and Senate did not ring with colonial debate. Of course, if few Frenchmen fervently sought an empire, virtually none demanded that the nation hand it back to the indigenous peoples.[15] Consequently, by World War I, largely as a result of a long quest for a resurrection of French glory and prestige, the French found themselves in possession of a vast empire. Paradoxically, in the end the liquidation of the French Empire would prove a more traumatic and costly task than its acquisition. Nowhere was this more true than with its Far Eastern Empire.

France's greatest colony in the Far East—indeed, some believed it to be France's most valuable possession anywhere—was its "balcony on the Pacific," Indochina. In 1923, Albert Sarraut, colonial minister and onetime governor-general of Indochina, unabashedly described Indochina as "from all points of view, the most important, the most developed and the most prosperous of our colonies."[16]

French interest in Southeast Asia had been of long duration, stretching back to the reign of Louis XIV and recurring spasmodically during the eighteenth and early nineteenth centuries. The expansionism of Napoleon III and the Second Empire naturally increased the French aggressive posture in the Far East, beginning in 1858 with the annexation of part of Cochin-China. This was France's opening wedge in the region that came to be labeled and administered as Indochina. By 1870, in a series of easy campaigns, the Mekong delta area had been conquered and the colony of Cochin-China established. Consequently, the fledgling Third Republic inherited a toehold on the Asian continent, which, during the next generation, it used as a springboard to establish military, legal, and political protectorates over Annam, Tonkin, Cambodia, and Laos. In 1873, an expedition led by the young naval officer Francis Garnier seized Hanoi, the capital of Tonkin, and in the following year negotiated treaty rights to establish a vague protectorate over Tonkin and open the Red River to French trade. As the French continued to expand in Indochina, they came into conflict with the Chinese, who regarded the area as a tributary state. Annamese appeals to China for protection led in 1883 to a second Tonkin war against Annam and China. This placed the second ministry of Jules Ferry in an awkward situation, for French public opinion remained unwilling to support a war in such a far-off place. Nevertheless, Ferry pressed ahead and, with a relatively minor force, was able to subjugate Annam. By the Treaty of Tientsin of 1884, France established a protectorate over the whole of Annam.

China refused, however, to accept the treaty and dealt French forces a temporary reversal on the Chinese border at Langson in the following year. Ferry, who had gambled on a quick victory over China, was discredited and forced to resign, but the weak Manchu government in Peking decided that its remote tributary was not worth the cost and agreed to give up its claims to suzerainty over Annam. With this obstacle removed, France invoked the treaty negotiated earlier with Annam. Thereafter, the remainder of Indochina quickly fell in line. By 1893, Cambodia and Laos had also been brought into the French colonial fold.[17]

It was largely as a result of its Indochinese empire that France came to be considered a major power in the Far East. While French conquest of Indochina may be largely attributed to concern for national prestige, honor, and glory, France ultimately came to develop significant cultural, economic, and political interest in the colony that made continued control over it appear to be increasingly important.

With an area one and a third times greater than that of France, and with a population of some 24,000,000 by 1940, Indochina was the largest and most populous of France's overseas possessions. But the colony had no physical or ethnic unity and no political cohesion apart from that imposed by the French administration. Indeed, the history of the region prior to the French conquest had been fraught with constant warfare. Responsibility for French control over the colony resided with the Colonial Ministry in Paris, which generally kept tight reign on the local governor-general. The ministry was also assisted by the Conseil Supérieur des Colonies, composed of former governors and other persons with colonial administrative experience or with important colonial interests. The Conseil, however, was unwieldy in size and remained generally unconsulted. Reflecting its centralized political system, the bulk of the colonial legislation was enacted by the French Chamber of Deputies in Paris or issued by ministerial decree.

Hanoi became the seat of the French Indochinese Government General and was headed by the governor-general, who was appointed by the French cabinet but took his orders from the minister of colonies. Theoretically, he held extensive powers, but in practice he remained greatly restricted. The men who served as governors-general were of quite uneven quality. Few of them had previous experience in Indochina, although some had seen service in other colonies. Some were simply politicians who had lost favor in France. Others—Paul Doumer, Albert Sarraut, and Alexandre Varenne—had been men of first rank in French public life and rendered excellent service in Indochina. Unfortunately, many of their accomplishments were nullified by incompetent successors or hampered by obstruction on the part of permanent officials and by hostility of the French community in Indochina, who could effectively lobby in Paris. The situation was exacerbated by the lowly status in the ministerial lineup of the fledgling and ineffective Ministry of Colonies. The colonies did not attract the best personnel that France had to offer, generally being thought of as places for government employees, merchants, or idlers who had failed to succeed at home. Who else in his right mind would leave *la patrie* for such faraway backwaters of the world! Certainly, Indochina was no exception. As D. W. Brogan observed, "The French clerk who was willing to exile himself to further Asia for a salary of less than [$1,000] a year was seldom, either by character or attainments, an impressive representative of the ruling race."[18] Moreover, the average tenure of office of a governor-general was only two to three years. "By the time the titular governor has taken stock of the situation and settled down to apply his formula, he is unceremoniously removed because he has offended some potentate in the colony or in Paris, or because he has not immediately wrought miracles, or because there has been a change in the French political lineup."[19]

French colonial policy toward Indochina was generally described in terms of assimilation—the making of Frenchmen out of Indochinese. Only gradually did the French begin to see the folly of trying to force French customs and institutions upon peoples of such dissimilar historical, political, and cultural traditions. In any event, the granting to the Indochinese the full political status of a *citoyen français* was strictly limited to natives who could show that they had special qualifications, such as marriage to a French woman or a period of ten years in public service. Consequently, a few natives became French citizens. Nevertheless, the ideal died hard that overseas colonies should be simply overseas *départements*. Eventually "assimilation" was replaced by the idea of "association," a policy which implied that the colonies, while remaining under the general control of Paris, would enjoy a degree of local political and economic autonomy. Such a change was brought on by a successful resistance among Indochinese to assimilationist theories.[20] The experience of the two world wars also hastened the modification of French colonial theories. Frenchmen came to see their colonies not only as places providing jobs for incompetents who could not make good at home but as sources of military manpower, economic aid, and national prestige. The realization of the necessity of granting local autonomy came too late to head off disaster.

Certainly, France made many mistakes, and its rule in Indochina was characterized by an uncertainty and fickleness made more objectionable by blunders and excesses committed by unfit civil servants. While the effects of many of these mistakes were never eradicated, the French did, particularly after World War I, achieve a great deal in Indochina. Despite difficulties of terrain and climate, they provided the colony with a system of roads and railways that compared favorably with those in neighboring British colonies. The development of such a transportation and communications system enhanced the distribution of food from Cambodia and Cochin-China to the overcrowded lowland areas of Tonkin and Annam. It also facilitated the trade and industrial and agricultural exploitation of the colony by French entrepreneurs. French engineers also built a system of dykes in Tonkin that Virginia Thompson described as "one of the greatest systems in the world."

Undoubtedly, the French cultural contribution to Indochina suffered from the defect, inherent in the assimilationist policy, of transplanting French institutions and ideas without sufficient regard to the very different social milieu and cultural tradition of the region. Moreover, in the areas of education and medicine, for example, the French effort was frequently hampered by a shortage of funds, low expectations, and a corresponding lack of modern equipment. On the other hand, while the French did not attempt to eradicate the teaching of Annamite or other local languages or history, there existed among the native intelligentsia considerable demand for and popularization of Western studies. As a result, the frequently indiscriminate Westernization was not wholly the fault of the French. In higher education, all distinction between purely French and indigenous institutions gradually vanished, and the standards and diplomas of such institutions were recognized as equivalent to those of similar schools in France. Indochina shared with Algeria the distinction of being the only colony whose medical degree equaled that of France. By the outbreak of World War II, the French could claim that they had established more than 7,100 public schools in Indochina. Nevertheless, it has been estimated that only about 15 percent of all school-aged children received some kind of schooling and that about 80 percent of the population remained illiterate.[21]

Thus, there was sufficient reason for conflicting views of the Indochinese venture. While exalted notions of the inherent validity of the French *mission civilisatrice* led some sentimental Frenchmen to exaggerate the nature of French interests in Indochina, others ultimately came to believe that France stood to reap tremendous economic advantages from the colony. Albert Sarraut was not alone in his belief that Indochina was France's most important and prosperous colony. Grasping at any straw in light of the economic dislocations created by World War I and the subsequent depression, many Frenchmen concluded that the Empire, including the Far Eastern holdings, would prove to be an important factor in curing France's economic ills. It did not matter, as most recent studies have proven, that the myth of economic importance was just that—a myth. What mattered was that many believed otherwise and exaggerated the importance of Indochina in their minds. One student of the area has noted that "European observers and participants regarded Indochina as an outstandingly successful endeavor in imperial rule, as well as a matchless source of wealth for France."[22]

In fact, Indochina was far from worthless economically, even though the French did not maximize their opportunity there. The colony held tremendous potential as a valuable source of foodstuffs and raw materials. The third most important exporter of rice in the world, it also exported corn and rubber. It had vast reserves of timber and minerals such as coal, tin, iron ore, phosphates, and tungsten. Indeed, with its steadily expanding trade, it was one of the few French colonies to export more than it imported.

French awareness of the economic potential of Indochina came years after the conquest of the area. Only at the end of the nineteenth century, through the initiative of Governor-General Paul Doumer, did the systematic exploitation of Indochina's vast economic potential begin, with the aim of monopolizing Indochina's raw materials and markets for French industries. Most French investment went into those areas rather than into promoting local industry that might prove to be competitive with industries at home. Only very belatedly, confronted with the Japanese threat and a realization that Indochina might be cut off from France during World War II, did the French government, spurred by the military, begin to promote industrial growth in Indochina. But such development was only in its infancy by 1940. Joseph Buttinger writes that French colonial policy "exploited but did not develop Vietnam." But one must be wary of crediting to the French a systematic economic or colonial policy, even if exploitive. In fact, as Bernard Fall has suggested, until the post–World War I period French policy was quite haphazard. With new tariff rates introduced in 1921, foreign imports became prohibitively expensive and could not compete with the free-traded French goods.

9

By the 1930s, French trade had achieved a virtual monopoly throughout the empire. Stephen H. Roberts, a contemporary observer, described the situation as the "conspicuous triumph of French colonization, unrivalled economically in the French Empire."[23] Protectionist barriers established after World War I reflected the belief among many that an economic policy based upon mercantilistic principles would be advantageous. Yet Indochina's closer economic ties with France proved to be a mixed blessing. France provided a more stable market for the colony's staple exports than did neighboring Far Eastern countries, which produced competing rather than complementary commodities. Moreover, Japan was not a particularly good customer for most of the period, while the Chinese demand fluctuated greatly. Indochinese rubber—which was high-priced, even if higher in quality—would have found it hard to compete outside the French protective tariff barrier. On the negative side, most of the economic progress benefited only the French, and not the Indochinese. The French large landowners and entrepreneurs grew wealthy, but the peasant's lot steadily deteriorated. As a result, although nearly 60 percent of all imports into Indochina came from France, the colony remained too poor to become a large market for French industry. Even so, Indochina's trade with France exceeded its trade with the other countries of the Far East.[24]

Alfred Sauvy, in his masterful study of the French economy during the interwar period, noted that the strong favorable balance of trade enjoyed by Indochina can be explained by investments made in the colony.[25] Indeed, during the interwar period, as the French franc steadily depreciated, the stability of the Indochinese piaster became attractive to many French investors. About ten billion francs, or 95 percent of foreign investment in Indochina, came either from French investors at home or from French residents in the colony itself. Most government loans supported public-works projects and administrative expenses. Private investment went into rubber plantations, mining, transportation, or industries devoted to the processing of local agricultural commodities. For example, the rapid postwar expansion of the automobile industry gave a large financial bounce to Indochina's rubber industry as large-scale corporations such as the Michelin Tire Company invested heavily in new plantations in the area. Saigon developed into the "Paris of the Orient," complete with paved streets, sidewalk cafés, and Western architecture dominating new, modern residences and office buildings. Roadways, railroads, and waterways connected the city with the French plantations surrounding it. Nevertheless, it has been estimated that the return on

French investments in Indochina during the period may have been only a meager 2.3 percent.[26]

Another factor in France's increased appreciation of the empire after World War I was the realization that the colonies would be able to aid the defense of *la partrie* in the face of a resurgent and dynamic Germany. With a generation of leaders decimated between 1914 and 1918, with a decline in the birthrate that would eventually produce a thin "waist" in the pool of available military labor during the later 1930s, and with a need for strategic raw materials in the event of another war, the colonies were viewed as a potential, though partial, solution to the problems confronting the motherland. Indochina clearly figured in the French thinking. Nearly 100,000 Vietnamese had participated in the European war as riflemen or as laborers, and the colony had, along with other colonial sources, subscribed to several million francs in war loans.[27] With further planning and development, an even greater contribution might be expected in the future.

On balance, perhaps as important as considerations of amour propre and economics, Indochina served as a base from which French influence could be exerted throughout the Far East. To be sure, as one observer noted, it was the only French colony that resembled in any way Britain's prosperous dominions of Australia and Canada. But more than a source of influence, it was a base from which France could establish a belt of imperial control and influence from South China across the South Pacific.[28] Its loss would be a heavy blow to French national prestige and glory, and these, after all, had been the touchstone of French imperial expansion from the beginning.

While French possessions in the South Pacific were not as extensive as the holdings of other colonial powers in the area, they were substantial, attractive, and strategically located. The French territories consisted of island groups scattered over an immense area of the South Pacific, but administered in two groups: New Caledonia, with its center being the Grand Terre—the second largest island in the Pacific next to New Zealand—around which a series of small islets and the Loyalty Archipelago are clustered, comprised one unit. Politically, economically, and culturally, the city of Noumea clearly dominated. The second area, known as French Polynesia, consisted of more than 120 islands included in five archipelagoes. The most important of the islands was Tahiti, whose major city of Papeete contained more than half of the territory's population and served as its administrative capital.

French interest in New Caledonia emerged in 1843, when the Marist Fathers established the first Christian mission there. But a formal protectorate had been deferred for fear of antagonizing the British, who had similar designs in the area. Napoleon III, probably prompted by his rivalry with England, annexed the island in 1853. Over the next few years, perhaps following the British example in Australia, the French turned the island into a penal settlement governed by naval officers. Between 1860 and 1894, more than 40,000 prisoners, ranging from common criminals to the political prisoners from the ill-fated Paris Commune of 1871, were sent to the island.[29] Many of the prisoners served as a cheap source of labor and were used to develop public works on the island. When freed, many subsequently remained on the island and were helped by the government to secure farmland.

Eventually, the value of New Caledonia became based upon the extraordinary range of minerals found there. By the turn of the century, New Caledonia became the world's largest producer of cobalt, nickel, and chromium. Nickel and chrome mining remained the mainstays of the island's economy, but by 1905 it had lost its leadership in nickel mining to Canada, and in 1921 it lost out to Rhodesia in the production of chrome. Even so, during the thirties Germany and Japan continued to buy large quantities of nickel ore. Indeed, Japanese miners, who came to the island along with earlier Japanese settlers, became an increasingly important element in the commercial life of New Caledonia.[30]

A direct economic link with Indochina was established because of the need for cheap Asiatic labor for the New Caledonian mines. The rebellious indigenous population, whose numbers declined rapidly due to their confinement on reservations by the French, refused to work underground. Turning elsewhere for laborers, mine owners brought in Chinese and Japanese workers. But the best source of hard-working and docile laborers proved to be Tonkinese. More willing to cope with the crude working conditions, as many as 5,000 Tonkinese contracted—for a few francs a day plus board—to go to the colony to sweat in the mines and keep New Caledonian low-grade ores reasonably competitive with those of other producers.

For the most part, the New Caledonian economy remained dependent upon France because of the mother country's policy of attaching its colonies to the metropolitan economy and because of the fluctuations of world demand for New Caledonian resources. France provided a reasonably steady market for New Caledonia, and the colony was largely reserved as a market for French produce.[31]

By 1939, the island had become unique in the South Seas. Noumea, its capital, had grown rapidly and had acquired a Francocosmopolitan appearance; nickel and chrome mines dotted the mountainsides; coffee plantations and cattle ranches sprawled across the landscape; sawmills penetrated the extensive forests, removing valuable timber; populations native to the island lived, or perhaps endured, in reserves set aside in remote areas of the island; some 17,000 Europeans dominated the political, economic, and social life of the colony, which they regarded as their home. If not completely idyllic, many Frenchmen had good cause to believe that the colony was an asset that should be protected.[32]

French Polynesia, formally called the Etablissements Français de l'Océanie (EFO) but generally known to the world as Tahiti because of that island's incredible natural beauty, consisted of some 120 islands scattered over five archipelagoes spread out over two million square miles of the south Pacific.[33] This dispersion and isolation of the islands, compounded by considerable neglect by the French government, allowed the islands to develop in their own manner and thus preserve their own cultural characteristics to a greater extent than many other French Pacific colonial holdings. The islands had been haphazardly gathered between the 1840s and 1880s, but because they held little importance strategically or economically, the French had done little to develop them. Even the long-awaited opening of the Panama Canal in 1914 did not demonstrably enhance the significance of the Etablissements. Although some mining and tourism developed, the basis of their economy remained subsistence agriculture, with vanilla and copra being virtually the only cash crops. Even the import-export trade of the islands was only loosely tied to France, for the bulk of the islands' trade remained linked with the West Coast cities of the United States and with New Zealand. By World War I only about a thousand Frenchmen lived on islands.

Clearly, then, the islands were not economically or strategically vital to France. Yet that fact did not make the nation any more inclined to surrender the Etablissements to the encroachments of any other power. The islands helped to legitimize France's entrée into any discussions and negotiations concerning the status of the Pacific basin, such as those held in Washington in 1921–22. Ultimately, however, one must agree with one study of the area that concluded, "The real value of the Etablissements by 1900 appears to have resided almost wholly in the almost intangible and in any case highly negotiable romantic appeal of 'Tahiti,' both in terms of scenery and la douceur de vivre, in a tradition established by [Louis-Antoine de] Bougainville long ago and so assiduously propagated by a long line of others since."[34]

The last colonial holding in the Far East to be formally organized within the French Empire was the New Hebrides. Here the situation was complicated by an intense Anglo-French rivalry. In the 1870s, some thought had been given to utilizing the New Hebrides as a source of labor for the New Caledonian mines. Although the French government had agreed with Britain to respect the independence of the islands, local Frenchmen continued to press French claims and alarmed the British and their Australian and New Zealand colonies. Eventually, the two governments agreed in 1887 to form a mixed naval commission to protect the interests of both powers in the New Hebrides. This commission was replaced in 1906 by an agreement that established a permanent Anglo-French protectorate over the New Hebrides.[35] These islands, like the others, made no substantial economic contribution to France, although French influence emerged as dominant because French law favored the expansion of plantations and the importation of thousands of Indochinese laborers. Of the nearly one thousand Europeans in the islands, nearly three-fourths were French. By 1939, the number of the native population had been reduced sharply to about forty thousand, whose activities and identities ranged from those of the cannibals on the outlying islands to those of the Westernized copra plantation workers.[36] A classic case of "preemptive colonialism," the main reason for France's maintaining its presence in the islands appears to have been to prevent other powers, mainly the British, from annexing them to the detriment of French prestige in the Pacific.

Though the colonies were important, French interests in the Far East were not confined to them alone. China and Japan had long held an attraction for French business and cultural interests, and while the French stake in those nations was not as large as Britain's or, eventually, that of the United States, it was substantial and was expected to grow larger. French interest in China dated back to the reign of Louis XIV, but it was not until the nineteenth century that anything more than sporadic contacts developed. While the British East India Company had dominated trade with China, French commercial activity remained slight. Beginning in 1840, with the British success in the so-called Opium War, the French moved to obtain advantages in China similar to those negotiated by Britain. By the Treaty of Wampoa of 1844, France gained Chinese recognition of equal status with the other major powers in their commercial and missionary rights at the five treaty ports. For the remainder of the century, although their rivalry raged in Europe, the major European powers frequently cooperated with each other in China to press their common interests.

While France ultimately came to pursue missionary activity more than commercial enterprise, it found itself, along with Britain, often resorting to armed force to protect and expand its influence. Next to the British, the Chinese came to regard the French as the "most crafty" of all the Western barbarians.[37] The French colonizing activities in Indochina during the Second Empire had brought them into direct conflict with the Chinese, who viewed themselves as protectors of Annam and Tonkin. It had been the undeclared Franco-Chinese war of 1884–85 and the French defeat at Langson that had brought about Ferry's defeat at home. But the Chinese decision to come to terms in 1885 by the Second Treaty of Tientsin finally assured French dominance over Indochina. More than that, however, it gave France access to the neighboring Chinese provinces of Yunnan, Kwangsi, and Kwangtung, where many French imperialists believed that tremendously rich mines awaited exploitation. Indeed, by the end of the century and as a result of the scramble by the imperial powers for extraterritorial privileges in China, France was able to carve out a large sphere of influence in southern China. Moreover, during the course of the century, France had won concessions at the ports of Canton, Hankow, Tientsin, and Shanghai. Many Frenchmen viewed such holdings to be a means of access to the rich Chinese market. Although the dream of the wealth to be earned from the Chinese market had not been realized prior to World War I, many believed that it would materialize eventually. Besides, the economic dislocations caused by the war and the uncertainties that lay ahead in the postwar era meant that no potential market should be ignored.[38]

The French economic stake in China, while not as large as the British, Japanese, and American, firmly established her as a major economic power in the eyes of the Chinese.[39] France's share of China's foreign trade remained at less than 5 percent, although the figures improved somewhat when Indochina's trade with China was included. The usual French export items were not in high demand in China. Still, in the interwar period such companies as the Renault automobile company saw China as a market of some potential. Renault sold a variety of its World War I tanks and heavy auto chassis to China, although the market never developed into a major outlet for its products.[40] Since international trade after World War I failed to regain its prewar levels, even such paltry figures as those of Sino-French trade could not be lightly dismissed, especially since Asia as a whole continued to increase as a net importer during the interwar period.

Because of the importance of Paris in the nineteenth century as a financial capital second only to London, French investments in China became substantial and grew rapidly prior to 1914. During that period, French loans to the Chinese government represented more than half of the total foreign loans to that country. China had resorted to overseas borrowing to pay for large indemnities imposed by the Japanese after their victory over China in 1895 and by the Western powers after the Boxer Rebellion of 1900. Moreover, between 1898 and 1911 China raised significant loans abroad to finance large-scale railroad construction. By 1914, either by itself or through international consortiums, France held approximately $111,400,000 in Chinese government obligations. While this amount dropped during the postwar period, it was more than offset by increased private business investment in China. Indeed, after negotiating her sphere of influence in South China in 1895, France had quickly moved to exploit the area by obtaining railroad concessions. The Yunnan Railway, begun in 1904 and opened in 1910, starting at Kunming and running through Lao Kai and then on to Haiphong, was completely French-constructed and French-owned. Through an eighty-year lease, the railroad was legally the property of a French corporation that received subventions from the government of Indochina and was partially controlled by the French government. Since the railway was the only easily accessible route from the South China seaboard into Yunnan, it became the chief vehicle for expanding French influence in South China. Nothing could be transported over the railroad without French permission, and French goods naturally enjoyed an advantage over other foreign articles traveling on the route. Consequently, nearly 60 percent of Yunnan's imports were French.[41]

In Shanghai, French investments in land and public utilities such as light, electricity, and transport reached approximately $38.9 million by 1930. The French made similar but less extensive investments in their concessions at Tientsin and Hankow.

Another large category of French investment consisted of property held by the Roman Catholic missions under protection of the French government. Such missions had long enjoyed extensive privileges in China, both in and outside the treaty ports. The income from such missions supported their educational and missionary programs. Although difficult to estimate accurately, such holdings probably amounted to about $21.6 million by the 1930s. Moreover, as their influence and activity increased, the accumulated wealth of the missions grew correspondingly. In fact, one estimate was that the value of the Shanghai missions had increased more than five times since the turn of the century.[42]

Ogier Ghiselin de Busbecq wrote in the sixteenth century that "religion supplies the pretext and gold the motive." While this relationship did not fully describe the French situation in China, there is no doubt that France used its position as the greatest Catholic power to enhance its status and prestige in China. During its great imperial rivalry with Britain in the nineteenth century, France assumed the role of protector and champion of the Roman Catholic missions in China to offset the great economic predominance of Britain in the area. It was the French who, during treaty negotiations concluded in 1860, successfully pressed for the right of Catholic missionaries to proselytize anywhere in the Chinese Empire. During the periodic outbreaks of antiforeign violence that occurred thereafter, the French government stood firm in their defense and, as in the Tientsin massacre of 1870, negotiated restitution for damages suffered. Even after the French separation of church and state in 1905, France continued to show interest in defending Catholic rights in China. Clearly, such republican efforts on behalf of the church were not due so much to religious zeal as to political prestige and influence that accrued from such activities. The political benefits of such cultural influence were not measurable, but something to be sustained as long as possible.[43]

The French also sought to maintain influence in the Chinese military establishment. A former French military attaché in Peking was recruited by the Chinese in 1912 to reorganize their army. Advanced graduates of the Foochow Navy Yard occasionally were sent to France for additional training. Other educational activities in China, such as Aurora University at Shanghai, established by the Jesuits, and the local mission schools frequently flourished and provided France with considerable influence. Indeed, it was an influence that France probably hoped would replace that of her chief rival in Europe—Germany—in post–World War I China. In any event, such educational activities, combined with the proselytism of the missionaries, helped to justify to intellectual skeptics at home the value of far-flung French interests overseas, including China.[44]

French interests in Japan were neither long-standing nor extensive. France had not figured in the early Western attempts to open Japan, and its first modest effort to penetrate the islands off the coast of East Asia came with missionary and naval activities in the Ryukyu Islands. But this initiative ultimately collapsed by 1848. The visit of Commodore Perry to Japan in 1853, and subsequent American and British initiatives to open Japan to Western trade, forced France to act lest it be left behind in its chronic rivalry with Britain. As Meron Medzini has observed, "The 'Grande Nation' could not stand by while England continued to extend her influence throughout the world. . . . England, with her vast trading interests, sought a commercial treaty with Japan; hence France, despite her modest commerical interests, had to have one, too."[45] Although a commercial treaty was concluded and trade relations established in 1858, Franco-Japanese trade continued to be relatively insignificant. Nevertheless, the French continued to cooperate with the other major powers in defending their treaty rights against the occasional anti-Western outbreaks generated by Japanese nationalists.

Although the United States played a dominant role in the Westernization of Japan, the Japanese frequently looked to the prestigious great powers of Europe as economic, military, and institutional models. Japan turned to France for technical advice in modernizing its army. Ernst L. Presseisen concluded that "to the French . . . must go the distinction of having been the founders of the modern Japanese army." Eventually, during the 1880s, German influence came to supplant that of the French, but the latter had laid a solid foundation for later reforms by teaching the Japanese how to organize, train, and command its military units; demonstrating the value of field artillery; establishing an officers' academy; and helping Japan's industrial development by promoting locally manufactured military equipment.[46]

The modern educational system established by Japan, while incorporating features from several different countries, most closely resembled the French organizational structure. Like the French system, the country was divided into eight university districts which were then subdivided into middle-school and elementary-school districts. Detailed regulations governed age, qualifications, and compensation of teachers at all levels.[47]

The French economic stake in Japan remained small. As previously indicated, French trade never assumed major proportions. In 1866, for example, after considerable effort had been made to gain access to Japanese silkworm production, the French share of the Yokohama trade reached only 14 percent, compared with nearly 68 percent for Britain. The French emphasis on silk continued down to the eve of World War II, when French silk imports amounted to 193 million francs out of an import total from Japan of 338 million francs. France found very early that its exports to Japan—chiefly luxury items such as wines, jewelry, glassware, and toys—were subjected to prohibitive customs duties and could not balance its silk imports. Even after World War I, when Japan began importing more French iron, steel, and chemical products, French imports from Japan more than doubled exports to that country. The picture was somewhat brightened by increased Japanese imports from France's Far Eastern colonial holdings, especially Indochina, which supplied large quantities of rubber, and New Caledonia, which supplied nickel to Japan.[48]

French investment in Japan remained miniscule. Prior to the Sino-Japanese War of 1894–95, Japan had distrusted foreign investors and abstained from contracting foreign loans. Indebtedness caused by her wars with China and Russia forced her to change her attitude, and during the decade prior to World War I she started to borrow more freely in the world money markets, including that in Paris, to finance her national development. But the borrowing impulse proved to be short-lived, for by 1914 Japan had become a capital exporter. Moreover, the bulk of French foreign lending during the period continued to find its way to Central and Eastern Europe and the Middle East.[49]

While not wishing to appear to do so, because of its limited economic stake in Japan, France tended to follow the lead of the other major powers, especially Britain, in diplomatic dealings with Japan. Striking an independent posture in Japan was clearly not worth antagonizing its European neighbors. Consequently, when Japan's imperial appetite threatened to get out of hand after its victory over China in 1895, France joined with Russia, Germany, and Britain to pressure Japan into returning the Liaotung Peninsula to China, much to the disgust of the Japanese. It has been persuasively argued that the conclusion of the Anglo-Japanese Alliance of 1902 paved the way for the Entente Cordiale between France and Britain in 1904 because of British fears of being dragged into a Russo-Japanese conflict.[50] When its European ally, Russia, suffered its humiliating defeat at the hands of the Japanese in 1905, considerable concern swept through France about Japanese intentions. France's passive support of Russia had not won friends in Tokyo. Therefore, when Japan sought to float a post–war loan in the Paris money markets, France quickly moved to tie it to political negotiations that culminated in the Franco-Japanese Agreement of 1907. The two nations agreed to respect each other's interests in China and promised to support each other in maintaining peace and security in those areas of China adjacent to the territories where they held autonomy. In essence, the two powers recognized each other's spheres of influence—Japan's in Korea, Manchuria, and Fukien; France's in Indochina and the South China provinces of Yunnan, Kwangsi, and Kwangtung.[51] With the Anglo-Russian

Entente of August 1907, a system of agreements existed in Europe and East Asia that seemed to complement each other. From the French viewpoint, such a situation would have the desirable effects of stabilizing the Far Eastern situation, protecting French interests in the area, and allowing France to retain her attention on the more immediate problems in Europe.

French interests in the Far East at the end of World War I, if not as vast as Britain's, were nevertheless substantial. In addition to her colonial possessions in Indochina and the Pacific, France had significant economic, strategic, and cultural interests in China. Already, before World War I, it had become evident that the only way to safeguard such distant and far-flung interests—both existing and potential— would be by diplomacy. The cost and dislocations caused by the war clearly exacerbated an already-difficult situation.[52] But the war also seemed to prove to many Frenchmen the value of their overseas possessions and interests, including those in the Far East. To a France spilling its life's blood in Europe, the Empire had contributed over half a million soldiers and nearly two hundred thousand laborers. Raw materials vital to the war effort, such as New Caledonian nickel and Indochinese rubber, helped achieve victory.[53] Therefore, after the war the belief that France should remain an imperial power with worldwide commitments became widely accepted. The postwar period witnessed growth in colonial commerce, and increased interest in the colonies was reflected in the miniature empire created on the outskirts of Paris for the Colonial Exposition of 1931, which drew nearly thirty-four million visitors. More importantly, however, as the insecurities of the economic depression began to affect France, and as alarm grew over the Nazi threat, the economic and military value of France's widespread interests and possessions seemed increasingly obvious. By 1939, over half of the Frenchmen surveyed in an opinion poll believed that the loss of a piece of the Empire would be as painful as the loss of a piece of France. So the empire that had been backed into, almost crablike—indeed, a motion of 1885 for the evacuation of Tonkin had been defeated by only one vote in the Chamber of Deputies—had now become "a buttress for France's 'great power' status."[54] But the realities of maintaining and defending such interests, especially in such far-off places as in the Far East where the French presence had always been based more upon myth than power, would soon become painfully apparent as it fell to a war-weary generation to defend the increasingly indefensible.

two

VERSAILLES AND AFTER

A T the Paris Peace Conference ending World War I, the primary concerns of the Clemenceau-led French delegation were security and reparations. In the months following the termination of hostilities, as the long lists of names accumulated on the monuments to the war dead of small villages, as row upon row of white crosses sprang up in military cemeteries, and as the reserved seats for crippled servicemen rapidly appeared in subway and railway cars, it became clear that security had become the most important peace aim of France. The fact was that France had paid a frightful price for victory.[1] Moreover, the gnawing anxiety persisted that the defeated Germany remained potentially stronger than victorious France in terms of resources, population, and organization. The prospect of Germany eventually renewing the struggle at an advantageous moment haunted French leaders. Clemenceau's main attention, then, was directed toward devising a scheme that would guarantee the security of France, a depleted nation of less than forty million, against the potential aggression of a strong Germany of over sixty million whose nationalists refused to accept defeat. Complicating the problem was the fact that the war-weary French population refused to make any additional financial sacrifices for postwar reconstruction. Instead, they were determined to make the Boche pay the full costs through reparations. Naturally, as recent studies have proved, the security and reparations issues were not divorced in the minds of either the French or the Germans. As Stephen Schuker has correctly observed, "France's insecurity about the long-term prospects informed the whole direction of its postwar policy."[2]

Because of its preoccupation with the German problem, it is not surprising that France paid scant attention to the Far Eastern issues that arose during the conference. Yet, although the French delegates did not play a vital role in the dispute that quickly degenerated into a United States–Japanese confrontation, it would be wrong to assume that they were not aware of the problems and prospects that the Far East held for France. The voluminous correspondence between the French representatives in the Far East and the Quai d'Orsay, including numerous memoranda by the French foreign minister, Stephen Pichon, reveals a lively interest that simply had to take a back seat to more pressing concerns closer to home. Nevertheless, the concerns evinced, attitudes expressed, and policies pursued during the war and immediate postwar period shed additional light on the French Far Eastern problem as it subsequently developed.

The outbreak of war in Europe had created a widespread feeling that it represented the "opportunity of a thousand years"[3] for Japan to fulfill its goals of preeminence in East Asia and recognition as a major imperial power. Accordingly, within a month of the outbreak of the hostilities in Europe, Japan had entered the war against Germany after Berlin ignored an ultimatum that it turn over its important naval base at Kaiochow. Within three months, Japan had forced the surrender of German forces in their leased areas in Shantung province. This was followed by Japan's takeover of German-occupied islands north of the equator and the destruction of Germany's Pacific fleet. Japan also took advantage of the European powers' preoccupation to advance its interests in China at the expense of a series of weak Chinese governments. In early 1915, Tokyo presented to China its so-called Twenty-one Demands, to which, under threat of force, China acceded. The clumsily presented demands required the transfer of all German rights in Shantung to Japan and established the preeminence of Japanese interests in Manchuria and northern China. The extent of the demands created a storm of international controversy, but during the remaining years of the war Japan proceeded to consolidate its legal and diplomatic hold over its wartime gains. In September 1918, the Japanese negotiated with China substantial railway and mining concessions as security in return for large loans required by the unstable Peking government. The continuing hostilities in Europe forced European recognition of the Japanese gains. Formal agreements were concluded with France, Britain, and Russia in February 1917, binding the European Allies to support at the postwar peace conference the Japanese claims to former German rights in Shantung and the German islands in the North Pacific. Moreover, by the Lansing-Ishii agreement of November 1917, the United States recognized that Japan had "special interests" in China because of its geographical proximity, and both powers promised to observe the territorial integrity of China and to maintain the Open Door policy. Consequently, Japan attended the postwar peace conference in physical control of the former German territories, and as Arthur L. Link put it, legally "Japanese claims at the Paris conference were nearly impregnable."[4]

French relations with Japan had been generally friendly ever since the conclusion of the 1907 entente, by which the two powers agreed to support each other's interests in the areas of China adjacent to those territories in which they held extraterritorial or sovereign rights.[5] France had been impressed with Japan's display of military prowess, and with the outbreak of war in 1914 she made several attempts to secure Japanese military intervention in Europe. Consequently, Paris was willing to turn a blind eye to Japanese aggression in China. Working through their mutual ally, Great Britain, the French proposed to allow Japan an expanded interest in China as long as Tokyo promised to maintain China's integrity. Essentially a reiteration of the old Open Door, it offered Japan the freedom to expand in China as compensation for support in Europe. But Japan, dominant in East Asia, was extremely reluctant to involve itself in faraway Europe. Its main objective remained the strengthening of its position in East Asia, so that after the war it would be able to compete successfully with the Western powers. Undaunted, many Frenchmen, including Georges Clemenceau even before he became premier, maintained a high regard for Japan and continued to agitate for closer ties with her. Such an attitude, combined with the desperate wartime needs of France, led the government to maintain a discreet silence when Japan issued its Twenty-one Demands.[6] Although Japan maintained its determination not to send troops to Europe, it did ultimately expand its role in the war by undertaking increased naval responsibilities, thereby releasing additional British ships for European waters. But the Western powers had a price to pay. When the German submarine campaign began to peak in 1917, Japan was asked to expand its patrols. In return, Tokyo asked for Allied support for its claims to Shantung and the German Pacific islands at the postwar peace conference. Although the British initiated the negotiations, the French were quickly asked to lend their support. In February 1917, Aristide Briand, the French foreign minister, relayed his government's willingness to support Japan's claim to both Shantung and the German islands. But his quid pro quo revealed a doubt about Japanese designs. Briand required that Tokyo give assurances of its disinterest in Yunnan province by reaffirming its commitment to the 1907 agreement.[7] Japan's consent assured her of another secret accord to wield at an appropriate moment at the ensuing peace conference, for as the French correctly judged, Tokyo was anxious to avoid having its gains undermined in case China belatedly entered the war and won admission to the peace conference.[8]

Nevertheless, France retained some sympathy for China for a variety of reasons, but especially for important economic and political concerns. Unimpeded access to the potentially large Chinese market would be important in a world in which traditional markets and trading patterns had been disrupted by war.[9] More immediately, the French found Chinese laborers to be most useful to the war effort in Europe by digging trenches and in making and transporting ammunition. Eventually, after China's entry into the war in 1917, the year the Chinese indicated that they would be willing to send troops, the French enthusiastically supported the enterprise and in January 1918 prevailed upon the Supreme War Council to agree. Moreover, some French officials, including Clemenceau's foreign minister, Stephen Pichon, clearly distrusted what they perceived as a Japanese tendency to favor the German military regime, which more closely approximated Tokyo's own autocratic inclinations. For these reasons, France wished to support Chinese interests where possible, but without alienating Japan or, worse, driving her into German arms. Therefore, French officials encouraged an agreement between China and Japan that might provide the basis for a general accord between the Japanese and the Western Allies and which would include the United States in an active role.[10]

With the end of the war in Europe, Japan went to the Paris Peace Conference determined to retain her wartime acquisitions. She had achieved the status of a first-class power, leadership in East Asia, and physical possession of Shantung province and all the German islands north of the equator. All of this had been reinforced by assurances from France and Britain that they would support Japan's claim to the transfer of German rights in those areas. With Japan, France, Australia, New Zealand, and Britain all clinging together, the question of the islands was disposed of quickly. The former German islands north of the equator were assigned to Japan as C-class mandates of the League of Nations, while Australia and New Zealand split those south of the equator.[11]

The issue of Shantung, however, developed into a major crisis between the powers. Japan based its claim to the leased territory in Shantung on the fact that Germany's expulsion from Shantung had been primarily due to the effort of Japanese troops. Therefore, the surrender of German rights in Shantung would be made to her. Tokyo ultimately promised that it would restore the leased territory to China, but it continued to insist upon German unconditional surrender first. Japan promised to retain for itself only Germany's purely economic privileges in the area. It was a matter of amour propre, not simply a matter of form over substance.[12] The Chinese delegation fiercely resisted Japan's claim. They argued that the Japanese treaties with China of 1915 and 1918 had been extorted by threat of force, and that, in any event, China's belated entry into the war in 1917 made null and void all treaties with Germany and that the German leased territories would revert to China. Moreover, the Chinese expressed grave doubts about Japanese promises to restore sovereignty in the area to China. Indeed, they argued, the substitution of Japan for Germany in Shantung posed a greater meanace than before, because of Japan's geographical proximity.[13]

President Wilson warmly sympathized with the Chinese position as part of his endeavor to establish the principle of self-determination. Such sentiments reflected also his long-standing interest in and sympathy for China. On the other hand, Wilson remained wary of the Japanese, who he believed were "very ingenious in interpreting treaties." In fact, the situation was out of his hands. In the end, the Japanese held the trump cards that forced Wilson to capitulate. The assurances of 1917 that Tokyo had received from France and Britain were revealed, and both Clemenceau and Lloyd George told the Chinese that their governments would honor their treaty obligations. Moreover, the Japanese shrewdly timed their demands for Shantung in April 1919. The crisis climaxed just after the Italians had left the conference in a huff over the issue of Fiume. Belgium threatened to do likewise over reparations. General dissatisfaction existed among the small powers at Paris about the way the Council of Four dominated the decisions. Yet, with the German delegation due to arrive and learn the terms of the treaty, it seemed essential to present them with a united front. In the midst of these developments, the Japanese threatened to leave the conference and not join the League of Nations unless her Shantung demands were met. Without Japan, the formation of Wilson's cherished League of Nations would have been endangered, so he compromised his principles in order to save the League. The best that he could do for the Chinese was to promise that the League forum would be a place where their grievances might be successfully aired, and he extracted from the Japanese an oral promise that they would restore full sovereignty to Shantung. A frustrated Wilson lamented the settlement, "the best that could be got out of a dirty past."[14]

The position of the French during the crisis, while not decisive, was interesting and instructive. As noted earlier, and as a memorandum prepared by the Political Intelligence Department of the British Foreign Office recognized in February 1919, the French saw the conference "spending its time for weeks upon abstract questions like the League of Nations which . . . scarcely interests them at all, and of remote questions like those of the Pacific and of the African colonies which appear to be of very secondary importance."[15] All of this was further aggravated by a pressing sense that France had suffered far more during the war than any of the Allies. French attention remained riveted to the German problem. As a result, except for his role as president of the conference, Clemenceau played only a minor role in the Shantung controversy. The "Tiger" was reportedly "indifferent or patiently tolerant" toward the Japanese. Even though the Marquis Saionji was regarded as a personal friend dating back to the 1870s, when Saionji had been a student in Paris, Clemenceau viewed the Japanese with suspicion, once commenting that he would "never trust the Japanese too far while I think I could do honest business with the Chinese. Of course no Occidental can ever fully penetrate the Oriental mask, but to me the Japanese are cunning and avaricious, while the Chinese apparently are the opposite."[16] In fact, the French premier expressed some doubts about the validity of Japanese participation in the inner circles of decision makers. At a meeting of the Supreme War Council on 12 January 1919, in an impassioned outburst he rather bitterly recognized that "Japan participated in the war in the Far East, but who can say that in the war she played a part that can be compared for instance to that of France? Japan defended its interests in the Far East, but when she was requested to intervene in Europe, everyone knows what the answer of Japan was. The account that has to be settled is not one alone of money; there is an account for the blood shed that has to be settled also; the blood which France has shed gives France an indisputable right to raise her voice."[17]

Clemenceau rarely relied upon his Far Eastern experts, such as Jean Gout, who was chief of the Asiatic section of the Ministry of Foreign Affairs, although Stephen Pichon, the French foreign minister and a former minister in Peking, may have had some influence upon his premier.[18] The French Foreign Ministry archival records reveal that Pichon was kept fully informed on Far Eastern affairs, and his frequent memoranda suggest that he took considerable personal interest in the area. Nevertheless, the records of the Council of Four on this topic indicate that Clemenceau had virtually nothing to say about the Shantung issue. Clemenceau probably felt that Britain's interests were most affected by the Far Eastern discussions, and therefore he was prepared, as Lord Hankey put it, to leave "the running mainly to

Mr. Lloyd George." Generally, Clemenceau confined himself to supporting the British prime minister's arguments that the wartime
agreements with Japan could not be treated as mere scraps of paper,
and Wilson grudgingly had to admit that such commitments were
valid.[19] Surely, from Clemenceau's viewpoint, it would have set a
dangerous precedent for the future of the Versailles Treaty if the
Germans could be shown that treaty commitments need not be
fulfilled.[20]

Nevertheless, the Japanese remained skeptical as to whether France
and Britain could withstand determined American pressure in favor
of the Chinese claims.[21] In fact, French archival records reveal that in
the French case, at least, the Japanese fears were justified. Just as the
debate over the Shantung question was about to heat up, Pichon reminded his ministry of the French agreement with Japan of March
1917, in which France had promised to support Tokyo's postwar
claims. He also reiterated that the French position from the beginning
of the war had been to remain in accord with Japan. But he went on
to state, "If the United States and England take the decision to oppose henceforth the development of Japanese action in China . . .
France must also modify its policy." Such a change in policy would be
rationalized on the basis of self-determination and the respect for the
sovereignty of all states, and in such matters France could not allow
itself to appear less liberal than its allies.[22]

Consideration of such a policy shift was stimulated by what some
French diplomats viewed as a conflict of British and American interests in China with those of Japan. These circumstances, especially
combined with President Wilson's pro-Chinese sympathies, might
lead to a softening of British support for Japan, thus leaving France
alone and exposed to Chinese pressure. Nevertheless, the French ultimately stayed in step with Britain in Far Eastern matters, even to
the point of opposing Wilson. Had Wilson insisted upon his point of
view, such action could have created a difficult dilemma for France.
But Wilson, of course, through British prodding, had to admit to the
validity of the Anglo-French treaties with Japan as well as the Sino-
Japanese Treaty of 1918, freely negotiated by China, and his ultimate
acquiescence to the combined Franco-British-Japanese pressure took
France off the hook.

The chaotic situation in China during the period may have also increased French reluctance to side with her during the negotiations.
Under pressure from the United States, the rival Peking and Canton
regimes had patched up their differences for the purpose of sending a
united delegation to Paris. But the continuation of the north-south

rivalry and the near anarchy that prevailed in the countryside worried many Westerners. Philippe Berthelot, secretary-general at the Quai d'Orsay, sought to warn the Peking regime that renewed civil war "would produce a deplorable effect upon the spirit of the representatives gathered in Paris." A Foreign Ministry report prepared for the Banque de l'Indochine, which conducted considerable business in China, concluded that "the central government is impotent" and that complete anarchy reigned in areas occupied by the rival armies.[23]

Aware of the acute Chinese disappointment should the position not be sustained, the French tried to assuage sensitivities by assuring the Chinese that France had no selfish interests in China, only a desire to see China resolve its disputes and to be reunited and prosperous. Moreover, Paris professed to believe in Japan's commitment to restore to China its sovereign rights to Shantung and that, moreover, France, confronted with the valid wartime agreements, could do little else.[24] Clemenceau relayed to the Chinese delegation the opinion of the Council of Four that the whole issue of special rights in China had not arisen from the war and did not therefore properly fall within the province of the peace treaty. Instead, such matters should be brought to the attention of the League of Nations when it began to function.[25]

If the Allies felt that such a proposal would make the Chinese feel that they had received justice at the hands of the conferees, they were quite mistaken. When word got back to China that her great hopes had not been fulfilled, a great explosion of nationalist sentiment broke out, especially among the intellectual community. The revolutionary May Fourth Movement, initially organized to protest against the decisions of the conference, created more problems for the shaky Peking regime, which was accused of collaborating with Japan and of failing to remodel the Chinese political and social structure in order to compete with the West. Alarmed by the violence at home and perceiving considerable sympathy for their cause abroad—especially in the United States—the Chinese refused to sign the Treaty of Versailles. Although broadly antiforeign initially, as the strikes and demonstrations spread to other Chinese cities, especially to Tientsin and Shanghai, increasingly they took on an anti-Japanese focus. Encouraged by the American opposition to the treaty and fearful of domestic opposition, the Chinese rejected compromise offers by Tokyo, and widespread boycotting of Japanese goods occurred.[26]

Along with opportunities, the situation presented the French with some problems. When rumors swept through the Chinese press that France and Japan had agreed to a formal alliance in order to share zones of influence in China, the Quai d'Orsay quickly issued a formal denial.[27] On the other hand, the French ambassador in Tokyo urged his superiors to take advantage of the disruption of Japan's trade with China caused by the boycott to move in, especially with Indochinese products that could replace goods that had been formerly supplied by Japan. Moreover, he argued, Japanese dissatisfaction with the United States due to the treaty negotiations might allow some French substitution for American goods in Japan.[28]

In the end, there is no evidence that the French tried overtly to capitalize on the fluctuating fortunes of the Far East during or after the Paris Peace Conference. Clearly, they saw disadvantages in identifying France too closely with either side in the Sino-Japanese dispute. In any case, the attention of most policymakers remained riveted on the German question as the French Assembly embarked on the treaty ratification process. Indeed, a study of the debates concerning the treaty reveals that little discussion occurred about overseas matters; that which did take place tended to focus upon the advantages gained in Africa from acquisition of the former German colonies there. None of these debates took on the virulent nature of those that accompanied the European-related issues. During the six weeks of debate leading to ratification in October 1919, colonial and other French overseas interests failed to concern the deputies to the extent that they felt any compulsion to shout down Clemenceau or to follow the ministers back to their seats and, as in the case of Pichon, to shake fists in their faces, as they did when stimulated by the German issue.[29]

Nor did French public opinion pay much attention to the Far Eastern clauses of the treaty. The French press focused upon the questions concerning Germany, reparations, and the League of Nations and devoted little space to the Far Eastern issues. Indeed, major studies of public opinion during the conference do not even mention the Shantung issue.[30] Additionally, when the American ratification process began to turn the settlement sour in the mouths of Frenchmen, a great round of accusations occurred, virtually a who-lost-French-security? debate that further distracted most attention from the Far Eastern settlement.

Nevertheless, some farsighted French observers predicted that if certain fundamental questions were not resolved in the Far East, "they reserve for the world in the future new and grave difficulties."[31] As future premier and foreign minister Pierre-Etienne Flandin later lamented, one of the gravest errors of the Treaty of Versailles was that it "furnished to the Empire of the Rising Sun the means of its future expansion in China and in the Pacific. The Japanese fleet could maneuver in the shelter of the Far Eastern waters, where neither the American nor the British could intervene with equal force. . . . Hong Kong, the Philippines, and even Singapore risked . . . being dangerously isolated and falling quickly into Japanese hands."[32] From the French viewpoint Indochina was obviously just as vulnerable, if not more so. Moreover, as A. P. Thornton has pointed out, if World War I had been fought to prevent German domination in Europe, all other kinds of domination were equally "wicked and wrong." And, "If it had been right and proper for China to abrogate in wartime the extraterritorial rights there of Germany and Austria, why should it not be so for it to abrogate everybody else's in peacetime?"[33] Surely, there were those in France who realized the dangerous possibilities in such thinking. Surely, too, many recognized the storm clouds gathering just over the horizon.

Nevertheless, the next few years saw little serious interest in Far Eastern matters among most Frenchmen. An understandable desire to return to stability at home preoccupied them. The war had torn huge holes in the fabric of French society and had poisoned the political, social, and economic climate of the nation. The demographic losses had been catastrophic. Much of the industrial and financial infrastructure for French economic life had seriously deteriorated during the war. It is hardly surprising, then, that given such problems, especially when combined with a peace treaty that took little account of France's security needs, the mood of most Frenchmen allowed little room for attention to Far Eastern matters. As Stephen Schuker has aptly put it, "No amount of self-reassuring rhetoric about the totality of victory could relieve the anxiety felt by the overwhelming majority of Frenchmen at the thought that the struggle might have to be resumed . . . once the German colossus had reconstituted its military power." Because of this situation, it was natural for a nervous, tentative, war-weary French population to give added importance to European security, economic, and financial problems. The struggle with Germany resumed, but in the form of an economic cold war, as French politicians and civil servants made an abortive attempt to achieve economic hegemony in Europe. Indeed, the reparations issue became the means by which the Franco-German struggle was continued and therefore became "the pivotal issue in European diplomacy during the years after the war."[34] If Frenchmen thought at all about the East, their eyes did not wander beyond the Near East, where a sharp deterioration of relations with Britain had developed over the Chanak episode during Turkey's nationalist revolt and where the two erstwhile allies jockeyed for financial and diplomatic advantage over each other.

On the continent of Europe, economic chaos prevailed. Prewar trade patterns had been disrupted not only by the war but also by the establishment of new successor states with their new boundaries, new tariff barriers, and new currencies. Inflation was rampant, generated by postwar reconstruction and government deficits. Worn-out and obsolete plants and equipment, high unemployment, and huge domestic and foreign debts all complicated the domestic economic scene.

Despite all of this, most Europeans still considered Europe the center of the world, and Frenchmen considered Paris to be the center of Europe. It was developments in Europe that mattered. Traditional European rivalries attracted far more attention than the continuing Sino-Japanese controversy, which was generally considered irrelevant and unimportant.[35] Nevertheless, noticed or not, events continued to unfold in the Far East that necessarily affected European interests there. Certainly, the fact that the United States and China did not ratify the Versailles Treaty meant that the Far Eastern issues would eventually be reopened.

Perhaps the salient feature of Far Eastern international relations in the immediate postwar period was the steadily deteriorating relationship between the United States and Japan. The Americans had remained very apprehensive about Japanese ambitions in China and the Pacific. Along with its substantial victories at Versailles, Japan utilized the immediate postwar years to consolidate its naval supremacy in the western Pacific and to maintain naval parity with the United States throughout the Pacific. Advocates of American naval superiority argued that Japan had designs for control over China and must be resisted. Britain, refusing to fall behind the United States in naval power, continued to add to its fleet after the war. The prospect of another runaway arms race, with its resultant sense of insecurity and further destabilization of the already-shaky postwar economies, brought a willingness to seek a solution in all three countries. A complicating factor, however, was the Anglo-Japanese alliance that had been renewed in 1911 and was due to expire in 1921. Japan had made great advances as a major power during the years since concluding the alliance and sought to have it renewed. Britain, while apprehensive about Japan's ambitions, favored a continuation of close ties with Japan. But the Commonwealth nations and, above all, the United States objected. Washington believed that the alliance actually encouraged Japanese expansionist tendencies. The Americans clearly expressed their reservations to the British, forcing them to choose between the United States and Japan. When confronted with such an unpleasant choice in light of American economic power and the prospect of an escalating naval race, Britain in 1921 expressed its willingness to compromise on the Japanese alliance and to accept parity in naval power.[36] The United States then took the initiative of calling upon the major Far Eastern powers to attend a conference in Washington to deal with the limitation of armaments as well as other Pacific and Far Eastern questions.

Despite Japanese reservations about attending and her attempts to keep the agenda limited, the conference took up a wide range of issues concerning the Far East.[37] Sweeping new arrangements for the area were made in attempts to reconcile the divergent interests of Britain, Japan, and the United States. In order to make the termination of the Anglo-Japanese Alliances as palatable as possible to Japan, the diplomatic device of a Four Power Treaty pledged the signatories—Britain, Japan, the United States, and France—to consult with one another concerning conflicts of interest and instances of aggression in the Pacific. The powers each agreed to the maintenance of the status quo of the area through respect of the others' rights and interests regarding their various insular possessions in the Pacific. Concomitantly, by the Nine Power Treaty all of the signatories pledged to respect the territorial independence and integrity of China and reaffirmed the Open Door principle. But only conversations, not specific sanctions, were provided for in the event of violation of the treaty provisions. Moreover, many Chinese grievances about existing foreign concessions and special privileges went unheeded. On the other hand, in a related settlement, technically negotiated outside the conference under the good offices of Britain and the United States, Japan finally agreed to return Shantung to full Chinese sovereignty, with certain guarantees for the protection of Japanese interests there.[38]

Perhaps the most difficult and emotionally charged negotiations were those regarding naval arms limitation. Dramatic American proposals at the opening of the conference included specific reductions in capital ships that would involve considerable scrapping of existing capital ships and leave the United States and Britain with about 500,000 tons each. The plans allowed Japan 300,000 tons and France and Italy 175,000 tons apiece. After long and at times acrimonious debate, a Five Power Treaty was concluded, essentially along the lines of the American proposal. Japanese reluctance was overcome only on condition that the status quo be maintained concerning fortifications and naval bases in the Pacific. This implied that no naval bases were to be built within operational distance of Japan—that is, no American base west of Hawaii and no British base east of Singapore. The practical effect of this was to guarantee Japan's home islands against naval attack and assure her of naval supremacy in the western Pacific. The American desire to extend the same ratios to auxiliary ships, especially submarines, was thwarted by French opposition. Concerning the issue of the reduction of land armies, French demands relegated the issue to a back burner from the very beginning.

Indeed, France stood practically isolated at the Washington Conference, generally misunderstood and thoroughly disgruntled.[39] In fact, in a memorandum circulated through the Quai d'Orsay the day after the announcement of the invitations to Washington, Louis Aubert cautioned that such a conference might be a two-edged sword for France. On the positive side, France could render a service to the United States by siding with her in her ongoing rivalry with Japan; for, he speculated, if Pacific issues were raised, the Americans would need support. French policy toward China meshed better with that of the Americans than with the Japanese policy. Moreover, Aubert reasoned, it was in France's interest to aid the United States because "it is necessary that a war in the Pacific not rekindle universal war, it is necessary likewise that the preoccupation with such a war not incline the United States to isolate itself from European affairs." Finally, the conference would give the French another "occasion to plead our cause anew and nearer this time to the ear and the heart of the senators and the American people, that is to say of speaking again of our situation, of our 'role' in the world." If the Americans could be persuaded about the French arguments regarding the Rhine and the importance of an Anglo-American guarantee, then the British would, by the very nature of things, be won over too.[40]

On the other hand, Aubert suggested some of the dangers of the conference, prophetically warning, "Beware the nation that will be decreed responsible before history of a failure of the Washington meeting!" His chief fear was that high hopes reminiscent of the pre-Versailles period existed in the United States. This would be exacerbated by the fact that the conference would be held right under the eyes of the American people and press: "At the Washington Conference, the principal American personage will be the people." He predicted that when the major maritime powers failed to negotiate a limitation of naval arms, public pressure to accomplish some limitation would lead them to focus upon land armaments. Because of its strength, the French army would be singled out, and it would naturally be seen as a tool for conquest rather than a mere means of enforcing the postwar peace treaties. But the French regarded its army as indispensable. So when France naturally resisted attempts to limit it, the wrath of the American people would be aroused, with repercussions for other issues such as war debts.

To Aubert, France was in a difficult situation that could be ameliorated only by a major and sustained propaganda effort prior to the opening of the conference. The purpose of such an effort would be an attempt to explain to important segments of the American population the difficulties of the French situation in Europe and to persuade Americans of France's goodwill: "Give them the impression of laying the cards on the table." It would be a campaign equal to that mounted during the war to secure American support. Aubert urged, "Let the American people judge our situation, its necessities and its obligations."

In the end, as feared, France found itself undeservedly labeled the intransigent conference spoiler. It has been widely argued that the French assumed that a deadlock would occur between the Anglo-American naval rivals and that such a situation would allow France to enter the picture as a mediator. At that point, the French would reintroduce the issue of a security guarantee to replace the one that the United States had reneged on after Versailles. As Briand told the Chamber of Deputies prior to his departure to lead the French delegation, "Let all guarantees be given so that France has nothing to fear. . . . France will not be the last to limit her armaments. However, we must have these guarantees; they are essential."[41] But when, to their disbelief, Britain quickly agreed to naval parity with the United States, the French tactic was foiled. In eloquent fashion, Briand then clearly spelled out the French position at the third plenary session of the conference on 21 November. After pointing out the continued German threat and reiterating that France had reduced the length of its military service by half, he argued, "to go beyond this . . . is impossible. . . . If someone said to us . . . 'We, as well as you, can see this danger; we understand it and we will share it with you; we will offer you all the means of security you could wish': immediately France would adopt a different course." He admonished the conference, "From the point of view on the ground, the danger is imminent—it surrounds us, it prowls, it hangs over our heads."[42]

Briand's hope of linking military guarantees and land-force reduction with naval-arms limitation proved to be a pipe dream. Secretary of State Charles Evans Hughes perceived the French intentions and quickly shelved the issue of land disarmament. France's platform disappeared, and she had little alternative bargaining power. The reduction of naval arms was to be discussed, but France had little to reduce. Far Eastern affairs were an important agenda item, but French holdings, although extensive, did not equal those of Britain and Japan, and her power did not rival America's. Besides, French hearts were simply not yet in such matters.

Nevertheless, the proposed naval agreement resulting from preliminary discussions between the three major naval powers, excluding France, provided a vehicle for the French to vent their frustrations. When presented with the figure of 175,000 tons for capital ships, French representatives became indignant. Such a figure clearly made them a fourth-rate naval power and, perhaps even more difficult to accept, reduced France to the same level as Italy. All this had happened when France had expected parity with Japan. Nevertheless, the French marshaled several justifiable arguments against their allotment. Undoubtedly, the war, with its demands for building an army, had reduced French naval expenditures sharply. By 1921, therefore, the overaged French fleet ranked significantly behind those of the Big Three naval powers in tonnage and effectiveness.[43] Was France to pay the price again for diverting its resources for the good of the Allied cause? Moreover, unlike Italy, which was a Mediterranean power only, France had two coasts to defend. Finally, France had an empire of more than sixty million inhabitants whose communications and security depended upon the French navy and who in time of emergency provided France with vital goods and services. Admiral Ferdinand de Bon of the French delegation was most vehemently critical of the limitations, contending that "France was willing to limit her armament, but she did not propose to disappear from the seas."[44]

A stalemate ensued that was broken only when Hughes put very heavy pressure on Briand, who had already left the conference. Secretary Hughes was frank: "The attitude of France will determine the success or failure of these efforts . . . . " Already facing bitter British antagonism over outstanding European issues, confronted by worsening relations with America, and dogged by increasingly difficult domestic economic and financial problems, Briand capitulated. But in doing so, he refused to consider the extension of the ratio to lighter ships and auxiliary craft, which the French considered defensive in nature and vital to the defense of and communications with its empire.[45] This led, however, to a major debate with the British concerning submarine limits. To the French, burdened by the expense of a large army and deprived of the prospect of sufficient capital ships, the inexpensive submarine offered to be an equalizer. But while the French argued that it would be used as a defensive weapon, the British remembered the vast tonnage lost to such weapons during the war. Tempers again flared on both sides. In a fit of paranoia, Britain's officials and media alike speculated that France aimed to build a fleet of submarines to be directed against her. Briand retorted that the submarines no more threatened England than the latter's capital ships operating in the English Channel menaced France.[46] When the French grimly held fast to their position regarding submarines, the British refused to consider reductions of aircraft carriers and auxiliary craft such as destroyers. Nevertheless, it was the French who were blamed for the breakdown of the arms negotiations.

With regard to the negotiations concerning the Far East, France played only a small role. Because of American insistence, perhaps put forth to assuage French sensitivities concerning the issue of the capital ship ratios but more likely to assure that Britain and Japan could not unite to outvote the United States in a future conference, France was included in the Four Power Pact. Secretary of State Hughes undertook the task of drafting the document, and the French delegates were only informed of their inclusion. Nevertheless, they were delighted, and legend has it that René Viviani, France's chief delegate after Briand's departure, displayed his Gallic enthusiasm by kissing the startled Hughes when the latter presented the draft accord.[47] To be sure, whatever the American motivation, the pact recognized the fact that France was indeed a major Far Eastern power, and, at a time when European issues remained of paramount concern to the French, the pact would provide stability in the Pacific and thus assure greater security for French possessions in the area without significant additional cost. On the other hand, when the French sought to have Indochina covered by the agreement, the Americans and British resisted on the grounds that Japan would insist on similar status for Korea.[48]

The negotiations leading to the Nine Power Treaty, which reiterated the sanctity of the Open Door doctrine and respect for the territorial and administrative integrity of China, were dominated by the United States, Britain, and Japan.[49] France did, however, make a proposal that created a flurry of excitement. The Chinese, who had been kept at arm's length during the negotiations, bitterly criticized the continued possession of Western leaseholds in China, which they claimed constituted "serious invasions upon China's territorial and administrative integrity . . . [and] contribute materially to the military weakness of China." The Chinese, therefore, wanted termination of such leases. Although it had been widely speculated that China would raise the issue, there was general surprise when the French delegation proclaimed that it "welcomes the claims of China with the greatest favor." The French then declared themselves "ready to join in the collective restitution of territories leased to various powers in China" by returning Kwangchow-wan to Chinese sovereignty. But the French added conditions to their proposal: all private rights must be respected, and, most significantly, France could not be the only power to relinquish its leased territory.[50]

Although the British expressed their willingness to surrender their lease to Wei-hai-wei, they would not give up Kowloon. When Japan adamantly refused to consider surrendering Port Arthur and Dairen in Kwangtung province, the French argued that since their conditions had not been fulfilled, they would have to reconsider their situation. Despite efforts by Hughes to get the French proposals reconsidered, it quickly became clear that none of the powers was interested in altering its position, and France let its offer drop.[51]

The French motivation for making such an offer must remain a matter of speculation. Clearly, there were those in the government who adamantly opposed opening negotiations over the leased territories for fear that it would ultimately lead to a complete surrender of rights in those areas. Consequently, they adopted an attitude of uncompromising hostility toward the notion. Many, as Viviani argued when he made the French offer, believed that France had brought great progress to their leasehold at considerable cost and, consequently, that those territories should not be gratuitously turned back to China. It seems clear, then, that the French proposal was nothing more than a bit of grandstanding, with a twist of the lion's tail thrown in for good measure. Its proposition involved a general abandonment of leased territories that it must have known would be unacceptable to the other major powers involved. Therefore, France had nothing to lose by making a dramatic gesture (which Viviani demanded be released to the press), appearing to support the Chinese cause but knowing quite well that it would not have to fulfill its offer. Moreover, at a time when the debate concerning the ratios of capital ships was heating up, the opportunity to make the British and Japanese squirm a bit might have appealed to French statesmen who thus far had been obliged to take a back seat at the conference. In the end, of course, the French proposal did nothing to ease strained Franco-British relations. The latter were clearly disinclined to surrender their leased territories, for as Victor Wellesley, assistant secretary in the British Foreign Office, put it, "there is nothing to be gained by making gratuitous concessions to China."[52] Additionally, although Hughes claimed that America held an attitude of "benevolent disinterestedness" in the issue because it held no leased territories, the French proposal piqued his interest. But he was only to see the French drop it easily when opposed by Britain and Japan. In the end, the proposal may have given the French some temporary satisfaction, but it could only have reinforced the belief of many that France's main interest was in behaving as the conference spoiler.

The French delegation had fully realized the importance of "leaving its footprints" in the record of the conference, if only for the edification of the French press and public opinion. In fact, the conference received a widespread but generally unfavorable press in France.[53] With the close of the conference, most French press analysts viewed the agreements as a defeat for France. They devoted the greatest attention to the naval accord, which was widely viewed as a capitulation signaling the demise of the French navy, and paid little attention to the Far Eastern settlement. But the limited analysis devoted to that area suggested that little would change, especially given the chaotic condition of China.[54] Many lashed out at the unjustifiable attacks that they felt France had suffered at the conference, but they simultaneously blamed the French government for its shortsightedness and tactical diplomatic mistakes. The government and the treaty fared little better in the French Assembly, where Briand received a very chilly reception when the accords were introduced for ratification. His longtime parliamentary nemesis and soon his successor, Raymond Poincaré, caustically wrote in the *Revue des Deux Mondes,* "Briand returned from Washington; he opened his valise and faithfully showed that it was empty." Although the assembly ultimately ratified the treaty, the debate, which again focused mostly on the naval accords, was long and difficult, as Briand's government was vigorously criticized for mishandling the French case.[55]

Undoubtedly, the French committed some grave errors of tact and substance during the conference. They misread the status of Anglo-American relations by assuming that the two would find themselves at loggerheads over the naval disarmament issue. They then overreacted to what they perceived as Anglo-American collusion. They should not have demanded a large number of battleships when, in fact, economic reality dictated that they could not pay for such a fleet. Their demand for the right to build a large submarine fleet, while economically justifiable, inevitably struck a sour chord with the British, who could not share the view that such vessels were defensive in nature. When it is all said and done, however, none of these miscalculations justified the severe criticism of the French by the Americans and British. Nor should they have contributed to the apparent determination of John Bull to convince himself that France constituted a threat to the European balance of power and therefore a danger to the security of Britain.

In any event, having become part of the naval disarmament scheme of the period did not affect the French Far Eastern situation in the short run. Even if she had wanted to revitalize her fleet for the protection of her interests in that area, the economy simply could not support such a naval program at a time when great effort and wealth were being poured first into the reconstruction of war-torn territories and then into the construction of the Maginot Line fortifications. The latter reflected the continuing "Europe-first" concerns of the nation and its decision makers. Even the construction of these frontier fortifications was eventually limited by a lack of money, so although Admiral François Darlan eventually began a successful modernization program in the thirties, it is inconceivable that adequate funds could have been allocated for developing a fleet that could play a significant role in the Far East. Even if an adequate fleet had been built, France had no major naval base in the area to service it. To build such a facility would have meant additional cost; not to build one meant that any French fleet would be based too far away to be of use in defending French interests in the Far East. Therefore, one of the fundamental problems confronting French policymakers during the period under consideration was that they lacked the means by which they could unilaterally protect their interests in the Far East. Consequently, France had to build a policy based upon a fragile foundation of British power, American support, and Japanese restraint. This meant that if protection of its Far Eastern possessions, access to the area's markets, and the maintenance of France's status as a major world power were considered important goals, they would have to be achieved by diplomatic rather than military means. But time would reveal that Britain's alleged power in the Far East was nearly as mythical as France's, and the United States was simply uninterested in sustained involvement in the affairs of the area. Consequently, given the daunting outlook at home and in Europe, together with Britain's increasing military unpreparedness and American passivity, it made sense for France to pursue a path of caution in the Far East.

Fortunately for the French, while the Washington settlement encountered noisy opposition in Japan, especially in military and nationalistic circles, for the remainder of the 1920s Japan appeared content for the time being to abandon its expansionist ambitions. Economic problems, political instability, and other domestic concerns tended to divert Japanese attentions from foreign affairs. Moreover, feeling somewhat isolated after the Washington settlement, Japan was reluctant to strain her remaining international ties.[56] As a result, relations between the major powers with interests in the area remained relatively quiet during the period of the late 1920s—a lull before the storm.

On the other hand, the Far East remained a region of flux and uncertainty, stimulated by a great swirl of change that engulfed China during the postwar period. China continued to be wracked by ceaseless and confusing rounds of protracted civil war. These were laced with eruptions of antiforeign incidents—such as in Shanghai in 1925 and in Nanking and Hankow in 1927—as Chinese nationalism asserted itself and forced Western agreement to restore Chinese tariff autonomy by 1929. But antagonism persisted over such issues as extraterritoriality, the status of foreign concessions, and the extent of shipping rights.[57]

Although they steadfastly opposed the relinquishment of extraterritorial privileges in China,[58] the French generally followed cautiously in the wake of the other major powers of the area, especially Britain. Wishful thinking persisted about the economic potential of the area, especially the possibilities of tapping the large China market by utilizing Indochina and France's concessions in China as a foot in the door. On the other hand, the continued chaos generated by China's protracted civil war caused concern. French representatives in China felt frustrated by the waves of antiforeign violence, and policymakers in Paris fretted about the role of the Soviet Union and the Comintern in taking advantage of the strong Chinese nationalist agitation against the treaty powers to spread their communist ideology. The correspondence between Paris and French representatives in the Far East during the period clearly revealed a French concern about the danger of a spillover of such propaganda and agitation across the border into Indochina.[59] Indeed, legitimate cause for concern existed; for, inspired by the infiltration of revolutionaries and their ideas from southern China, violent nationalist outbreaks occurred in the colony with disconcerting regularity. Try as they might, the French succeeded only in driving the Indochinese communists underground; they could not completely crush them.[60] Yet such problems were difficult to measure. To many Frenchmen the danger to French interests was not clear and present and, therefore, constituted no compelling reason for France to involve itself in a leading capacity in the affairs of the area. Some French officials complained that the French legation in China too often supported the most reactionary elements in the country while forgetting the Chinese masses—indeed forgetting the very spirit of the French Republic. But to others the Chinese government was a useful fiction with which the West could deal, and perhaps in the long run it might provide the basis for a truly united China.[61]

Yet there existed no confusion in many French minds about the relative status of Japan and China in the Far East. For example, during one of the annual reviews for the Japanese emperor's birthday, the Chinese assistant military attaché fell off his horse, which was quietly gathered up and led off by a Japanese officer, followed by the Chinese rider on foot. At that point, the French attaché, General Raoul Voruz, leaned over to his English counterpart and whispered, "We have seen a parable." Indeed, the Quai d'Orsay believed that Japan sought hegemony in China and was prevented from achieving it only by the opposition of the United States. As Charles-Arsène Henry, the French ambassador in Tokyo, acknowledged, while Japan would continue its intrigues to keep the Chinese pot boiling and thereby profit from China's weakness, Tokyo would remain "extremely prudent" in order to avoid provoking the Americans.[62]

The Japanese rivalry with the United States and the cooling of its relations with Britain, as signaled by the Washington Conference, presented France with an opportunity to strengthen its ties with Japan. With some Japanese prodding, French representatives in Tokyo had repeatedly urged their superiors to send a high-level political or military mission to Japan to capitalize upon France's postwar prestige—the victorious France of Foch and Clemenceau.[63] Paul Claudel in Tokyo urged Premier Raymond Poincaré to take advantage of the Japanese feeling of isolation and the cordial state of Franco-Japanese relations to negotiate a rapprochement with Japan. The advantages accruing would be several: French industries, particularly in military-related areas, would benefit from contracts that would otherwise go to Britain or Germany; Japan might lend support for the French position at various international conferences where the French often found themselves isolated; rapprochement might help safeguard French rights in China and strengthen French opportunities to mediate in Sino-Japanese disputes; it would allow a closer link within the Japanese officer class; and, finally, it would increase the security of Indochina and the internal tranquility and prosperity of the colony by increasing its trade with Japan.[64]

No sense of emergency existed in Paris, however, where a string of more pressing negotiations concerning matters closer to home consumed most of the consideration and imagination of policymakers. The Dawes Plan, the Locarno Pact, the Briand-Kellogg Pact, coupled with the interminable domestic squabbling, an endless succession of ministries, and abortive economic and social schemes sufficed to divert French attention. Besides, few saw Japan as a threat to French interests. Even Claudel remarked, "I am persuaded that Japan has been baking its bread for several generations in the immediately neighboring regions and that it will feel no temptation to burn its fingers with the rice of our deltas."[65] For much of the period prior to 1931, therefore, it seemed wise not to provoke Japan and thus endanger French interests, but neither did there seem to be a compelling need to move closer to Japan.

Nevertheless, time was running out in affairs both near and far. The Washington Conference had afforded breathing space, but the settlement had not been designed as a permanent solution to Far Eastern issues. As *Le Temps* had observed in 1922, "The edifice is weak, and this weakness is the only excuse for the numerous emergency exits which the builders have arranged for themselves."[66] The signatories displayed little interest in building a reinforced superstructure, and so a new system failed to emerge that could guarantee long-term peace, prosperity, and stability in the area. Consequently, by the time the Great Depression erupted, the situation remained insecure and still fundamentally based upon Japanese restraint. In 1931, after experimenting with cooperation with China in the late 1920s,[67] Japan threw off its inhibitions and launched an attack against Manchuria, an act that ripped off the thin veneer of order that had constituted the Washington system. Like it or not, France, try as she might, simply could no longer lie low in the hopes that the other Western powers would bear the brunt of the winds of change that swept the Far East. For, as Christopher Thorne has observed, "anything that threatened France's hold on Indo-China threatened also to diminish further her status as a major world power. Indifference would scarcely be possible."[68]

three

THE MANCHURIAN CRISIS:
FROM MUKDEN TO SHANGHAI

B Y the fall of 1931, almost unnoticed in the West, where a depression of unparalleled severity increasingly absorbed attention, the situation in East Asia had reached the boiling point. The condition of China remained unsettled and confused. In 1928, the Kuomintang forces of Chiang Kai-shek had taken Peking, and the government had been transferred to Nanking. But peace and order did not ensue. Communists controlled Kiangsi and Fukien and maintained an active underground movement throughout much of China. Semiautonomous warlords continued to dominate large areas of the country, including Manchuria. The Kuomintang continued to tear itself apart by internecine conflicts. Perhaps as a device to unite these factions behind him, Chiang had tried to focus nationalist sentiment against foreign interests in China. Issues of extraterritoriality and tariff autonomy had been the focal point of Chinese foreign policy. While there had been some successes in negotiations with the West, Chiang had been severely stung when he tried to force Soviet interests out of northern Manchuria. Despite this setback, or perhaps because of it, Chiang next focused his attention on Japanese influence in southern Manchuria, attempting to undermine the value of Japan's treaty rights by building railways to parallel Japan's South Manchurian Railway. Chinese settlers were encouraged to emigrate to Manchuria, and beginning in the summer of 1931, Japanese products were boycotted throughout China. Robert Butow has suggested that "whereas the British had previously been the chief object of anti-foreignism stimulated by China's new nationalistic fervor, the Japanese now suddenly became the focus of Chinese hatred."[1] Chiang's timing could not have been worse.

The Chinese actions greatly exacerbated a Japanese political crisis that had been brewing for some time. Throughout the 1920s, Japan had been plagued by a series of social and economic problems that the liberals of the period had been unable to resolve. Increasing expectations could not be met by economic performance. The war had left Japan with an inflated cost structure, and the violent fluctuations of the international economy of the 1920s had disastrous effects on the rice and silk markets. The agrarian interests in Japan, which included more than half the population, felt a nagging recession and a decline in their standard of living. Concomitantly, however, Japanese industry grew and greatly increased its dependence upon imported raw materials, resulting in persistently adverse balance of payments. All of this was aggravated by the onset of the Great Depression in 1929, which engulfed Japan by 1931. After the price of silk had already dropped by a third by 1929, in one year the export of silk plunged by another half. The struggling liberal government, with its very shallow roots, was far less able to withstand opposition pressure than those of the Western democracies, several of which did not fare so well either.

Increasingly, it began to be advocated that the solution to Japan's economic, demographic, and political problems lay in extending the empire on the Asian mainland. The Washington system, however, had been predicated upon cooperation with the great powers. But there were elements on the Japanese political scene that resisted the limitations on Japan that had been included in the Washington and London naval ratios. This policy had been attacked by military leaders, who found the ratios humiliating, and by the nationalists, who resented any limitations on Japanese treaty rights in China.

Various patriotic societies had long been the promoters of a Greater East Asia movement. Disappointed with the results of World War I and the postwar mandate arrangements, they fretted over American efforts to limit Japanese economic influence in China, and they generally opposed the moderate and conciliatory foreign policy of Baron Shidehara Kijuro, foreign minister for most of the period between 1924 and 1931. Increasingly, the patriotic societies turned to the right wing and the military for support. The army responded eagerly. Its prestige was at low ebb, military appropriations had been cut, and equipment and rations were poor and in short supply. Contemptuous of the civilian government, the military had begun to circumvent it by appealing directly to the people in order to prevent additional cuts at the forthcoming world disarmament conference. Many junior officers began to feel that simply maintaining the status quo was unacceptable. They became convinced that a bold stroke was needed to restore the army's prestige.

It was against this background of the devastating effects of the depression, the crippling ineffectuality of the civilian government, the fanaticism of the nationalists, and the grumbling of the military that many in Japan began to view with greater seriousness the Japanese position in Manchuria. As a semicolonial area, it offered an opportunity for Japanese economic growth and an outlet for Japan's burgeoning population; it offered imperialist glory for the aggressive nationalists; and it offered salvation for the army. Ominously, the aggressive anti-Japanese policies pursued by the Chinese appeared to jeopardize Japan's prospects in the area. Therefore, the Japanese Kwantung Army, with the complicity of general-staff officers in Tokyo, determined that it must take the initiative to protect Japan's vital interests in Manchuria.[2]

On 18 September 1931, Japanese army officers in Manchuria forced the hand of the government in Tokyo by fabricating an incident in the South Manchurian Railway zone near Mukden.[3] After setting off an explosion on the Japanese-owned and -operated railroad in order to accuse the Chinese of sufficient provocation, the Kwantung Army launched a rapid, well-coordinated attack against Chinese forces, capturing Mukden within hours. Two days later, Japanese reinforcements moved out from Korea to expand the area of Japanese control in Manchuria, quickly securing control of the southern part of the province. Overwhelming popular support in Japan favored the army's initiative. Only with great difficulty did the government of Premier Reijiro Wakatsuki and Foreign Minister Shidehara, with little support in their own cabinet, manage to restrain, if only temporarily, further advances by the Kwantung Army. Clearly, if some favorable settlement did not occur quickly, the government would lose whatever feeble influence it retained. Indeed, the very tenuous control of the politicians in Tokyo was further revealed when, on 8 October, the Kwantung Army again took the initiative and Japanese planes attacked Chinchow, well along the railway toward Peking.[4]

In China, meanwhile, Chiang Kai-shek took advantage of the situation to create, though only temporarily, national unity to meet the Japanese aggression. On 21 September, Chiang's Nationalist government appealed to the United States as a signatory of the Kellogg Pact and to the League of Nations. But he appealed under Article Eleven of the Covenant, which did not require League action, rather than under Article Ten or Article Sixteen, either of which would have forced some action by the League against Japan.[5] At Geneva, both the Council and Assembly were in session, and considerable sympathy existed on behalf of the beleaguered Chinese, who, in fact, had just suffered the loss of thousands of lives from severe floods. But Western governments that dominated the organization were very cautious about

overreacting to the Chinese plea. Confronted with disastrous economic problems at home and questions of disarmament, reparations,
and war-debts payments on the international scene, the conventional
wisdom of the wishful thinkers amounted to the belief that the
Japanese extremists were only temporarily out of control and that the
Tokyo government would soon bring them back into line. Japanese
reassurances to the League that Japan had no territorial designs in
Manchuria struck a responsive chord in the ears of the major powers.
Besides, nobody knew for sure what was actually happening in that
remote region of the world. So the League merely invited both parties to "hasten the restoration of normal relations between them" and
adjourned, hoping that the situation would resolve itself.[6]

Nevertheless, despite Tokyo's assurances to the contrary, the
Kwantung Army continued to expand its operations in Manchuria
against the Chinese "bandits." By the time the League Council met
again in mid-October, Japanese control had been extended considerably. At this time, with an American observer in attendance, the
Council passed a resolution urging Japanese withdrawal to the railway zone within three weeks. But since Japan voted against the
resolution, it was not binding, and as the November deadline approached, it became clear that the Japanese had no intention of abiding by the moral wishes of the League. So when the Council
reconvened in Paris in November, it was confronted with an ever-
worsening situation. Chaos prevailed in China, while in Japan the civilian government became increasingly powerless to control the
military, whose advances had captured public enthusiasm. Indeed, civilian leaders who argued for moderation lived under threat of assassination. By the time the Council met, Japan had, for all intents and
purposes, conquered northern Manchuria and gave every appearance
of launching an attack southward toward the Great Wall and China
proper. Consequently, Japan rejected Chinese offers of arbitration.
Having had its authority openly flaunted, the embarrassed League resorted, at its meeting of 10 December, to establishing an investigating
commission that would investigate on the spot. The commission,
headed by Lord Lytton, would be composed of representatives of the
four major European powers and the United States. Pending the report of the commission, Japan promised not to aggravate the situation further. But the civilian government in Tokyo, clearly unable to
control the situation, resigned on 11 December, and subsequently the
new government decided on what amounted to an occupation of all
of Manchuria. In the frigid cold of late December, the army launched

its move against the city of Chinchow, taking it by 3 January. Japan, in effect, was the master of Manchuria.[7]

But in France this was of very little note. The conflict in Manchuria seemed inordinately distant to most Frenchmen. Consumed by political upheaval and economic crisis at home and issues of reparations, war debts, and disarmament on the international scene, the French had precious little time or inclination to pay much attention to the Sino-Japanese clash in the autumn of 1931.

France had enjoyed, perhaps too well, the ephemeral and superficial return to normalcy from 1926 to 1931. A measure of prosperity had returned, unemployment had nearly disappeared, the devastated areas had been rebuilt, and an influx of immigrants, including the American expatriates, had partly offset the population decline. It had been a period when one could enjoy the good life, in a Paris that once again reigned as the capital of Europe, and the "spirit of Locarno" was felt by many to be the harbinger of continued peace. But in the midst of this optimism, storm clouds had gathered. The Wall Street crash of 1929 soon sent shock waves throughout the international economy. Although France was one of the last Western nations to feel the effects, by 1931 many worrisome developments had occurred to seize French attention. President Herbert Hoover had forced a moratorium on German reparations payments, while at the same time insisting upon payment of French war debts. In Germany, the severe economic crisis had generated an ever-deepening political crisis for the tottering Weimar regime. Indeed, shortly after the last French troops pulled out of the Rhineland in 1930, the Nazi party made its first significant electoral breakthrough in the Reichstag. In the spring of 1931, a dreaded Anschluss with Austria had been attempted in contravention of the Treaty of Versailles, only to be thwarted by vigorous French opposition. Hard on the heels of this, however, the Austrian financial structure disintegrated with the collapse of the Credit Anstalt Bank. The financial panic that ensued in central Europe soon rocked the West, and in September 1931 England was forced off the gold standard, and the Bank of England had to be supported by France and the United States. When the world's financier was so badly shaken, things must be serious indeed. Now, too, France, *"l'île heureuse,"* despite its devalued franc and its well-balanced and seemingly well-cushioned economy, began to feel the pinch. From 1931 onward, French trade began to decline at an alarmingly accelerating pace as the luxury goods, which formed an important part of the French export trade, suffered and economic activity

47

slowed down. Unemployment, although less serious in France than in other industrialized countries, began a slow, relentless climb, reaching 260,000 by 1932, while production dropped by a quarter. It is no wonder, then, that when the Far Eastern crisis hit in September 1931, most French attention was focused elsewhere. As André Tardieu put it, Manchuria was a long way off.[8]

The convergence of all of these problems dissolved all vestiges of consensus that may have existed in France. After the departure of Poincaré in 1928, no man, no party, no segment of society could impose itself or its ideas. Instead, the demands of extremists and special-interest groups on all sides became increasingly strident and uncompromising. Indeed, as one student of the period has observed, "The Republic's last decade constitutes the most controversial, turbulent, and pathetic in its history."[9] The socioeconomic impact of the depression and the worsening international situation fused to produce widespread and violent opposition to the government. The threat of the Communist party on the Left, with its slavish subservience to Moscow, was met with the growth of a scurrilous, paranoiac Right, with a concomitant weakening of the center. Street brawls between the hoodlums of both sides were nearly matched by incredible behavior in the Chamber of Deputies. All of this activity eventually climaxed with the infamous riots of 6 February 1934, which seemed to threaten the very existence of the Republic. While it is not the intent of this study to examine in detail the domestic difficulties of France during the period, it is of the utmost importance to keep fully in mind the unrelieved shabbiness of the internal situation when considering the government's response to external crises, especially in far-off Manchuria. In fact, as events unfolded in East Asia between 1931 and 1933, France went through six ministries, and five different men held the portfolio of minister of foreign affairs. In the midst of these ministerial shufflings, the profound socioeconomic discontent led to a new leftist coalition, the Cartel des Gauches, sweeping into power as a result of elections in the spring of 1932. This significant shift of power from the Right did not resolve the fundamental economic problems of the country, and it provoked a new wave of antiparliamentarianism from the Right. Moreover, as Nathanael Greene has suggested, "the degree to which internal stresses influenced the conduct of foreign affairs is considerable."[10] No doubt, the chronic instability of internal conditions in France explains in considerable degree the frustrations encountered in the formulation and implementation of its foreign policy. This proved to be no less true of its policy toward the Manchurian crisis than toward problems in

Europe—no less true for the period from 1931 to 1933 than for the remainder of the decade both in Europe and the Far East. The initial French reaction to the Manchurian crisis is somewhat difficult to ascertain with any degree of certainty. It seems probable, however, that the first impulse was to minimize the significance of the conflict and to hope that the Washington system would be strong enough to reestablish the peace before matters got out of hand. In his authoritative study of the West and the Manchurian crisis, Christopher Thorne concluded, "In the first ten months of the Far Eastern crisis, it appears that little was attempted in the Quai d'Orsay in the nature of a long-term analysis of the Far Eastern scene."[11] Such a judgment makes good sense because of the domestic and European problems that appeared more urgent.

The direction of French foreign policy during the first phase of the Manchurian crisis, which ran from September until the end of 1931, was in the hands of Briand. But as foreign minister in Pierre Laval's first government, he was widely distrusted among the nationalists for his avowed faith in the collective security of the League of Nations. His ill-advised attempt at the presidency in the summer of 1931 had revealed his weakened political position, even though his public support remained strong enough to prevent Laval from dumping him from the cabinet, at least temporarily. Still, advancing age and debilitating illness prevented him from effectively manipulating what Thorne called the "creaking apparatus" of the Quai d'Orsay.[12] Furthermore, his desire to see the League participate actively in the crisis as well as his role as president of the League's Council beginning in October necessarily diverted his attention from the formulation of French policy. But in Geneva, too, Briand was a mere shadow of his former figure. When ill health forced him to move the League's Council meetings to Paris in October, one observer was astounded at his infirmity: "He cut a pathetic figure. He could hardly speak. He was overcome by a continuous fit of coughing and could continue his speech only by sipping Evian after every few words, and gasping for air. . . . He was like the dying symbol of forlorn hopes." When Laval seized an opportunity to reorganize his cabinet in January 1932, he excluded Briand. When the latter died a few months later, Herriot eulogized him as "the pacificator" who died as "an exile in his own country." If, as James Barros has concluded, "French policy in this question largely depended upon Briand's leadership," that policy was bound to be indecisive.[13]

This was particularly the case because Briand enjoyed little support from the permanent officials of the Quai d'Orsay. Probably the staunchest champion of his policy supporting the League was René Massigli, chief of the League of Nations section at the Quai d'Orsay and a member of the French delegation at Geneva. Hugh Wilson, the American minister to Switzerland, described Massigli as the "right hand man of the French delegation," whose intelligence and negotiating experience gave him "a competence and authority in League discussions out of all proportion to his official position in France." But Massigli was in Geneva, while back home in Paris, where policy was established, leading officials remained unenthusiastic about League initiatives in the Far East. Philippe Berthelot, longtime secretary-general of the Quai d'Orsay and a principal formulator of French policy until his retirement in 1933, remained obsessed with the European situation and was regarded by some observers as "more or less frankly pro-Japanese." Alexis Léger, besides being Briand's *chef de cabinet,* was an expert concerning Far Eastern matters, having served in Peking from 1916 to 1921. Like Berthelot, he was a protégé of Briand and, in fact, upon Berthelot's retirement in 1933, Léger assumed the position of secretary-general. Because of his presumed status as an "insider," other observers believed that particular attention should be paid to his views. But while personally loyal to Briand, he, too, was inclined to favor Japan.[14] Although the precise attitude of Emile Naggiar, head of the Quai d'Orsay's Far Eastern Department, is uncertain, comments he made to one diplomat early in the crisis concerning Briand's probable position may well have been more reflective of his own opinion. Naggiar indicated that while Briand would first of all keep in mind the League's interests, he would not forget that the crisis was not the same as if occurring between two European countries. It must be remembered—and here it is likely that Naggiar began inserting his own bias—that "several powers had the right, by treaty or by custom, to send troops to China and ships of war into the Chinese ports and rivers. . . . In the action which they had . . . taken, the Japanese had perhaps gone too far. None the less their action could not be treated as an act of war. . . . If the Council allowed itself to be influenced too greatly by the letter of the Covenant, it might wreck the whole League organization."[15] Although, as Anthony Adamthwaite suggests, such officials as Berthelot and Léger may have appeared to dominate policy-making more than was actually the case, it nevertheless is true that Briand's old control over his subordinates had loosened considerably. Shortly after Briand's dismissal in January 1932, one British observer noted, "No doubt is entertained [in Washington] regarding the sincerity with which M. Briand spoke for the League as the representative of France . . . but it is believed here that the France that speaks at Geneva and the France which speaks through the Quai d'Orsay and, by the way of the Metropolitan press, to the French opinion, are not entirely the same."[16]

In the sensitive diplomatic posts overseas, the attitude of French representatives hardly differed from those in Paris. In Tokyo, French Ambassador Damien de Martel had wide experience in the Far East, having also served in Peking. Considered to be affable but intelligent and incisive, during the crisis he remained frank and cooperative with his Western colleagues in Tokyo. But while not considered pro-Japanese, Martel believed that the Chinese had brought the attack upon themselves through their intense propaganda in Manchuria. Reportedly, he wired Paris that the "Chinese deserve all they have got." In fact, he suggested that Japanese action would be to the advantage of all foreign interests in China. The poet-diplomat Paul Claudel, a favorite of Berthelot's, and French ambassador in Washington since 1924, was also openly sympathetic toward Japan. In October, he admitted that although the Japanese had gone too far, they had "endured almost more from the Chinese in Manchuria than was humanly endurable." Moreover, he felt confident that the civilian authorities in Japan would regain control before matters got out of hand.[17]

The French public initially reacted tentatively to the Manchurian crisis. Most attention remained focused upon other issues. But gradually, as with most other issues of the period, opinion reflected the political persuasion of the individual or group. On the Left, as typified by *Le Populaire* and *La Lumière,* the press generally supported League action, although skeptical about whether it was worth antagonizing Japan. After all, was it worth wrecking the League in order to solve the Far Eastern crisis? On the Right, *Action Française* and *Figaro* sympathized with Japan and scoffed at the League. On balance, however, many papers, and perhaps the public at large, tended to view Japan as a longtime friend and defender of order and Western values in the Far East. Perhaps *Le Temps* best typified this view by running a series of articles favorable to Japan. One such piece clearly tied Japan to French Far Eastern interests:

> Japan, civilized nation, our loyal wartime ally, who alone represents and defends in the Orient the social order and peace of the world against a savage anarchy, who, alone, for the moment, has the power to bar the bloody surge of bolshevism, is for us French one of the invisible ramparts of our Indochina.[18]

La Lumière might bemoan the depths to which *Le Temps* had sunk in its defense of aggression and the discrediting of international procedure, but *Le Temps,* as was customary, mirrored in its editorials the main lines of government and public opinion, a view that changed little for the first few months of the crisis. As Christopher Thorne has observed, "domestic uproar awaited any French government which tried to go so far as to take a prominent part in attempting to coerce Japan."[19]

A summary review of government actions during the first phase of the crisis reveals that it contemplated no such action. Despite the obvious and leading role that Briand played with the League, French policy remained markedly cautious. Formal support for the League was displayed, and French diplomats in Tokyo, Paris, and Geneva joined those of other nations whenever it was necessary for the Western nations to register their protests to the Japanese. But the dilatoriness of such French actions prompted considerable skepticism and, in fact, irritation among the British, who came to feel that the French would be quite willing to drop over the horizon and leave Great Britain holding the bag.

Early in the crisis, Franco-British misunderstanding brought the two nations to loggerheads. After suggesting on 22 September the possibility of sending Western military attachés to act as foreign observers in Manchuria, on the following day Massigli apparently told the British delegation that France was sending instructions to her ambassador in Tokyo to concert with his British, German, and Italian colleagues with a view to separate representations "drawing Baron Shidehara's attention to the gravity of complications which might ensue from a prolongation of the present situation" and to remind Japan that as a member of the League's Council it had a "moral responsibility that is all the greater." Based on this initiative, London instructed its ambassador to take similar action to that of the French ambassador.[20] But as Massigli admitted later, he had the authority only to *suggest* such a representation. The Foreign Ministry in Paris, either because of the influence of Léger or the infirmity of Briand, was indecisive and slow in formulating French policy. Martel in Tokyo received no instructions to protest to the Japanese. The British ambassador, Sir Francis Lindley, acting beyond his instructions to concert with his French colleague, spoke to the Japanese foreign minister on the twenty-fifth, conveying an *aide-mémoire* essentially along the lines suggested by Massigli. Having thus isolated and exposed himself, Lindley was told by the Japanese foreign minister that although Japan was aware of the gravity of the situation, she could not allow League of Nations observers into Manchuria. Placing responsibility for the proposal at the feet of the British, he pointed out that such an attempt would lead to a public anti-British outburst. In the meantime, learning of such hostility to a League attempt, the French informed Martel that the necessity for League action had passed. Ultimately, modified instructions were sent to Martel that amounted to little more than counsel of moderation. When the British Foreign Office began to put bits and pieces of the puzzle together, the officials were outraged. Robert Vansittart, permanent undersecretary, concluded that Britain had been

> maneuvered into isolated action in Tokyo which could only be interpreted by the Japanese Government as inspired by a less friendly feeling towards them than other countries cherished. . . . We are entitled to some explanation. It looks like a choice between incompetence or ill-faith somewhere as an interpretation. I am quite willing to believe in the former; but I am not willing to be "led up the path" like this and then let down without a word of warning or explanation. . . . If they were going to run out it is elementary fair play that we should have been told. . . . We might have been let in for a most invidious position.[21]

One pugnacious member of the Foreign Office Far Eastern Department, Douglas MacKillop, wrote to his chief, "the French really cannot get away with an extremely pro-Japanese attitude at Tokyo and a very firm attitude toward Japan at Geneva, while we are to speak firmly to the Japanese!"[22]

In the end, the British ambassador became convinced that it had not been as much a matter of bad faith on the part of France as a problem of indecision and confusion at the Quai d'Orsay and with the French delegation at Geneva. Moreover, rumor in Paris had it that the Japanese had deliberately exploited the situation.[23] Nevertheless, such breakdowns in communications made it difficult for the two major enforcers of League policy to collaborate, either inside or outside the auspices of the League. While Franco-British suspicions of bad faith were of a long-standing nature and had been further intensified by their differing attitudes concerning the nature of postwar security, it is clear that many in Britain, as well as in France, believed that France sought to make a deal with Japan behind the backs of the other Western nations. The rumored understanding between France and Japan involved France accepting a Japanese advance into Manchuria, where French interests were slight. The quid pro quo from Japan would be support for the French position at the forthcoming disarmament conference. Japan was the only member of the League's council who openly supported the French theory that a strong army, navy, and air force provided the best guarantee of security unless adequate security pacts were negotiated before disarmament. This suspicion of a Franco-Japanese agreement, even going so far as to include a military understanding, continued to plague France's relations with the other Western countries well into 1932.[24]

In fact, the archives of the Quai d'Orsay reveal that no discussion of such an agreement occurred at the Foreign Ministry until January 1932, when senior officials, in response to American press allegations, rejected the idea. Moreover, apparently Martel in Tokyo received no instructions to pursue such an agreement. Instead, it was the Japanese, who would later make a secret démarche in the late summer of 1932, exploring the possibility of such an agreement. As Christopher Thorne astutely suggests, if there had been an existing Franco-Japanese agreement, it would have been unnecessary for Japan to make such an approach later. In fact, it is clear that French policymakers, especially during the initial phases of the conflict, were determined to avoid becoming involved in an anti-Japanese movement and thus diverted from more pressing problems at home and in Europe. Seeking instead to appear more evenhanded, Massigli was instructed on 24 September that any League initiative must be directed to China as well as to Japan. French policy generally reflected this attitude in the months that followed.[25]

If French policy was so cautious, why was France so distrusted and maligned in the eyes of other Western statesmen and the press? It seems clear that as in many other foreign-policy issues of the interwar period, Washington, and especially London, completely misread the basic intentions and policy of Paris. In this case, there existed a willingness, perhaps even an eagerness, to believe that France still harbored ambitions of increasing her colonial holdings in the Far East, conceivably to include the annexation of the troublesome Yunnan province of China adjacent to Indochina. Constantine Brown, writing in *Asia* magazine, gave expression to these views when he speculated that in return for France's not opposing Japan in Manchuria, Tokyo would allow France a free hand in Yunnan: "With Yunnan in their power and with the oil resources [within easy reach], the French would be able to consolidate their Asiatic possessions and boast of an empire second to none. In order to be able eventually to put into force French ideas in the southern part of Asia, it is essential to support, even if indirectly, Japan's plans in North China." Although this may have been a particularly extreme expression, its main thrust was not unique among statesmen and journalists of the time. Unfortunately, even serious scholars have subsequently picked up and passed along such nonsense in attempting to explain French policy.[26] In fact, the time was long past when France seriously sought to expand its colonial holdings, especially those in the distant Far East. Rather, France had become more concerned with simply maintaining the status quo in the area so that she might be able to retain those territories already acquired. The fallacious perception of French objectives, undoubtedly aggravated by confusion in Paris, clearly damaged France in the eyes of the other major Western powers involved in the crisis. Only Briand's role at Geneva, where he doggedly labored to bring Japanese adherence to the League's resolutions, prevented more open criticism of France during the initial phase of the crisis.

Following the failure of Japan to withdraw from Manchuria in accordance with League resolutions of 30 September and 24 October, the Council decided on 10 December to appoint a commission of inquiry to investigate the circumstances threatening the peace in East Asia. But if the major powers believed that the situation would remain stable while the Lytton Commission undertook its work, they were to be sadly mistaken. Within forty-eight hours of the League's action, the Japanese government fell, driven out by extremist factions in Tokyo. With it went all hopes of conciliation with China. The new government was far more aggressive and determined to support the expansionist goals of the Kwantung Army. Within a few weeks, Japanese forces resumed their drive southward in Manchuria. With the capture of Chinchow on 2 January 1932, they destroyed the last major center of Chinese authority in Manchuria. As Japan consolidated its control, however, an effective anti-Japanese boycott spread throughout China. As tension rose, outbreaks of fighting occurred between Japanese and Chinese civilians, especially in Shanghai. The Japanese reacted by demanding reparations and by strengthening their garrison in the city's International Settlement. Ultimately, open hostilities between the Japanese and Chinese forces in the city ensued, thereby initiating a new and more dangerous phase of the Far Eastern crisis. For France and the other major powers with interests in Shanghai, the new escalation in fighting now involved their interests in a more direct fashion than had been the case in Manchuria.

The situation became more complicated with a significant shift in the attitude of the United States, which, under the active leadership of Secretary of State Henry Stimson, sought to exert pressure to stop Japan's expansion. When the League began its deliberations in October, the American consul at Geneva, Prentiss Gilbert, had been instructed to sit in on the Council's meetings as an observer and to participate only in discussions relating to the Kellogg-Briand Pact and Japanese and Chinese obligations as signatories. Thereafter, Washington had tended to follow the League at a distance, avoiding anything that might involve a unilateral American action. But continued Japanese advances led to increased concern among American policymakers, and the completion of the conquest of Manchuria in the early days of 1932 stripped their illusions about the ability of Japan's moderates to control the situation. Moreover, to many Americans, including Stimson, Japan's seizure of Manchuria represented a threat to American economic interests in the area. With its flouting of the League and other treaty obligations, Japan threatened the peace system that had been hoped would keep the world, including the United States, at peace. By early January 1932, Stimson and President Hoover had become convinced that the United States had to act to reinforce the treaty structure and thereby preserve the stability of the world. In this connection, then, they sought to replace military and economic pressure with moral pressure to mobilize world opinion and persuade Japan to back off. On 7 January, Stimson issued his famous note to Japan and China in which he proclaimed that the United States "does not intend to recognize any situation, treaty, or agreement which may be brought about by means contrary to the covenants and obligations of the Pact of Paris."[27]

The policy of nonrecognition, or the Stimson Doctrine, as it came to be labeled, was broadly framed so as to allow other like-minded nations to follow suit. For this reason, the Kellogg-Briand Pact had been specifically mentioned rather than the Nine Power Pact dealing only with China. The United States hoped that the statement would call attention to the fact that Japan's action posed a threat far greater than its danger to China alone. International peace was at stake. Stimson and Hoover anticipated that the two most important leaders of the League's efforts—France and Britain—would issue similar statements of nonrecognition. Britain did not take Stimson's statement very seriously and responded quite coolly by indicating that it could not act independently of the League and that Japan should be allowed the opportunity to display its good faith and continued adherence to the Open Door in China. Moreover, through a faux pas at the Foreign Office, the British response was released to the newspapers before being transmitted to the State Department. This premature revelation greatly irritated Stimson, who felt he had been let down, and it initiated a period of considerable Anglo-American misunderstanding, animosity, and distrust.[28]

In Paris, the new Japanese advances in Manchuria had led Foreign Minister Briand to contemplate the nature of an appropriate response and to inquire about the American attitude. Stimson had revealed to Claudel as early as 2 January that he contemplated sending his note of nonrecognition to Japan and had outlined its substance. Stimson indicated that it would add to the influence of the statement if France and Britain would support it. Claudel did nothing to discourage Stimson, indicating that he regarded the occupation of Chinchow as a "slap in the face" of the Western nations.[29]

Meanwhile, the French ambassador in Tokyo was instructed to coordinate with his British and American colleagues concerning a response to the Japanese action. It was anticipated that such a representation would call Japan's attention to the League's resolution of 10 December and Japan's commitment to refrain from resuming the initiative in Manchuria.[30] But the Americans did not favor making such a démarche under the League's resolution, arguing that they were not part of the League and must therefore utilize treaties to which the United States belonged. Accordingly, Stimson sent his nonrecognition note to both China and Japan and expressed his hope that Britain and France would take similar action. The French immediately approached the British to ascertain their response. The cool attitude in London did not encourage a vigorous response from Paris. Victor Wellesley, deputy undersecretary of state for foreign affairs, and a major formulator of British Far Eastern policy during the crisis, indicated to Aimé de Fleuriau, the French ambassador in London, that any action taken might be premature and only cause additional irritation in Japan. Fleuriau agreed with such an assessment.[31]

At the Foreign Ministry in Paris, Naggiar, head of the Far Eastern Department, indicated that if Britain could not associate itself with Stimson's initiative, then certainly France could not do so. Instead, Briand continued to wrestle with developing an appropriate League response, one he hoped would be tied to the League's resolution of 10 December.[32] In fact, however, Briand had reached the end of his line. Premier Laval had been looking for a way to dump the dying old man. Consequently, when André Maginot, the minister of war, died of food poisoning on 7 January, the same day that Stimson issued his statement, Laval used the opportunity to reshuffle his cabinet and replace Briand. On Briand's resistance, a political crisis ensued, leading Laval to ask for the resignation of the entire Council of Ministers. For several days, then, Laval attempted to broaden his government, even offering the post of foreign minister to Edouard Herriot, a longtime political opponent. When Herriot refused, Laval assumed the post himself. Unsurprisingly, the attention of most Frenchmen within and outside the government was riveted upon the domestic situation.[33] Furthermore, by the time Laval pieced together his second government, on the fifteenth, other foreign-policy issues had erupted.

On 9 January, Chancellor Heinrich Bruning revealed that Germany could not continue its reparations payments. The German action brought the issues of reparations and war debts to the forefront in the French press, and undoubtedly in the Foreign Ministry. The seriousness of the German action in the minds of many Frenchmen was revealed in the calling up of key reservists and the consideration given to mobilizing the army in order to force German compliance with the reparations agreements. Although such thinking was ultimately abandoned, the crisis had the effect of torpedoing a conference to be held at the end of January in Lausanne to deal with the adjustment of intergovernmental debts.[34]

The domestic state of affairs and the governmental crisis, combined with increasing attention on the long-awaited League of Nations disarmament conference due to begin on 2 February, meant that Stimson's statement received little attention in France. For that matter, the entire Far Eastern situation was of little note. And so it would remain for a while, for when Laval replaced Briand at the Quai d'Orsay, he replaced Briand's broader world geopolitical vision and concern for the League's role in the Far East with a more Eurocentric viewpoint. Indeed, Laval's new government led a troubled and short-lived existence, barely lasting a month before its fall on 16 February. During that brief period, Laval had little opportunity, and probably little inclination, to address the Far Eastern situation, its implications for France, or French policies toward the area. Consequently, French policy toward the Sino-Japanese crisis continued to drift.

Unfortunately, events in the Far East did not continue to drift. Indeed, the situation took quite a turn for the worse, as the violence spread from Manchuria to Shanghai. As Japan had extended its control over Manchuria, an anti-Japanese boycott swept through China. In Shanghai, the boycott had a significant impact upon Japanese trade. This was met with a carefully orchestrated escalation of tension and violence perpetrated by Japanese street thugs. Japanese army and naval commanders, under no firmer control in Shanghai than in Manchuria, became determined to make their own grab for glory. The opportunity came on 18 January, when the Japanese command apparently conspired to have five of its own nationals beaten up by workers from a local Chinese towel factory.[35] Despite an apology by the Chinese mayor of Shanghai, the Japanese naval commander in Shanghai, Admiral Koichi Shiozawa, took advantage of the situation to present the Chinese with a list of demands that included the closing down of the boycott associations. Even though the Chinese complied with the Japanese ultimatum on 28 January, Shiozawa sent his marines into the Chinese suburb of Chapei ostensibly to protect Japanese subjects living there. When they were met by determined Chinese resistance, the Japanese launched what amounted to a full-scale attack, complete with artillery barrages, aerial bombardment, and significant reinforcements amounting to nearly 50,000 troops by the time the fighting ended five weeks later. To a world not yet accustomed to the mass killing of indiscriminate aerial bombardment, the attack on Shanghai produced an international public outrage. The photographs and luridly descriptive accounts of journalists, who now found it fairly easy to get to the battlefront, helped convey the brutality of the fighting. As one correspondent wrote, "For terrifying ghastliness the aerial bombardment of Chapei is . . . appalling beyond appreciation . . . ."[36]

Consequently, while the Manchurian crisis had not previously aroused a great international public outcry, the Shanghai bombings evoked a strong reaction. Moreover, for the first time many Europeans began to realize that Western interests were at stake. In Shanghai, simply because the International Settlement and the French Concession existed, there was a greater concentration of Western economic and cultural interests and population than there had been in the whole of Manchuria. Shanghai had the largest international settlement in all of China, with great numbers of British, Japanese, American, and French citizens. It was generally regarded as the greatest port in Asia, as well as the industrial and commercial center of China. Despite profuse reassurances to the contrary, should Japan manage to gain control of the city and close the Open Door, as it showed signs of doing in Manchuria, Western business would incur significant losses. Perhaps the entire Western position in China would be undermined by a deadly combination of Japanese arrogance and Chinese xenophobia. The Western attitude of relative indifference now turned to outrage mixed with alarm at Japan's intentions and China's response.[37]

As with the outbreak of the Manchurian fighting, the civil authorities in Tokyo found themselves scurrying to catch up with the military initiatives. Surprised and perhaps embarrassed by the new turn of events, the government was concerned about the possibility of an armed clash with the Western powers with interests in Shanghai. Therefore, on one hand it urged moderation upon the army. On the other hand, for domestic political reasons, it could hardly disavow the actions of the military. Consequently, it sought to resolve its dilemma by promoting a quick, decisive military victory in Shanghai, followed by a moderate diplomatic peace settlement. The hope was that this would allay any fears Western powers might have about Japan's intentions regarding their interests, but that it would show the Chinese that Japan would act to defend its own interests in China.[38] Since Japan intended to pursue a negotiated settlement, and since China's immediate response was an appeal for League assistance, a flurry of diplomatic activity concerning the crisis developed.

The League Council took action at Geneva as well as in Shanghai, where a committee of consular officials representing the Western nations with interests in Shanghai, including France, worked to find a solution. Simultaneously, the American secretary of state, Stimson, worked aggressively to bring American pressure to bear against Japan. Additional warships were authorized to go to Shanghai, and additional American marines were landed. When Japan asked for the use of the good offices of the United States to end hostilities, Stimson and British foreign secretary John Simon set forth a series of terms: cessation of violence, no further mobilization, withdrawal of belligerents from points of mutual contact, establishment of a neutral zone to be patrolled by neutrals, and settlement of *all* outstanding issues between China and Japan. Since Tokyo apparently sought such early negotiations as a means of preventing unfavorable effects on Japan's position in Manchuria, it rejected the last point. Manchuria was not a matter to be settled in the presence of neutrals, since it was a purely Sino-Japanese problem.[39] Stimson then reverted to an attempt to revive his nonrecognition doctrine based upon violations of the Nine Power Pact of 1922 and the Kellogg-Briand Pact. If Japan refused to cooperate, the Western powers would then have the right to impose an embargo on Japan. As with his original nonrecognition statement of 7 January, Stimson sought the support of the other major Western powers for his position. Especially crucial was the support of London. But the British hesitated. They found themselves on the horns of a dilemma: should they risk antagonizing the Japanese by cooperating with the United States, or should they risk further alienating the United States by refusing to pressure the Japanese? While Stimson fretted impatiently, the British wavered and procrastinated for several days. Simon ultimately fell back on Britain's responsibility as a member of the League as well as a signatory of the Nine Power Pact and avoided any blunt rejection of Stimson's démarche. Neither he nor the rest of the cabinet was willing to expose Britain to Japanese animosity by climbing out on a limb with the United States in condemning Japan's aggression. Instead, Simon managed to push through the League Council on 16 February a doctrine of nonrecognition along with references to the Nine Power Treaty and the Kellogg Pact. Although it included a good deal of Stimson's substance, the Council carefully diluted his intention of bringing heavy moral pressure to bear against Japan when it avoided any references to Manchuria or Shanghai and pronounced no verdict against Japan. Stimson was angered by the decision of Britain to seek safety in a "flock" of nations rather than assert itself with the United States to force Japan to back off. But in London, Simon contended, "it was impossible for this country to assume the burden of Japanese resentment."[40]

Stimson, however, fired a final salvo in the round of negotiations. On 23 February, he expressed the American position in an open letter to Senator William Borah, chairman of the Senate Foreign Relations Committee. The letter contained an appeal for world nonrecognition of situations arising from violations of the Kellogg-Briand Pact and Nine Power Treaty. He reaffirmed the American commitment to the idea that China had the right to modernize free from outside interference. Moreover, Stimson went far beyond his original statement of 7 January by indicating that Japan's violation of the Nine Power Treaty would negate the other part of the Washington Treaty system—that is, the naval accords limiting naval forces and fortifications in the Pacific. Here was a clear warning that Japan's actions in China would free the United States from the limits placed on the size of its battle fleet and that it no longer felt obliged to abide by the self-denying nonfortification agreements negotiated at the Washington conference.[41]

Japan reacted bitterly to Stimson's initiative—indeed, a minor war scare swept the country, and the government discarded the idea of using American good offices to negotiate a settlement to the crisis.[42] Although the impact of Stimson's letter appeared minimal in the West, the principle of nonrecognition finally achieved broader support on 11 March, when, through the efforts of Simon and pressure by the small European states, the Assembly of the League passed a resolution adopting the nonrecognition policy. Moreover, a Committee of Nineteen, composed of the representatives of the Western nations with interests in China, was established to find a basis for resolving the crisis.[43]

The struggle over Shanghai simmered unabated for the next month and a half before cooling down as the Committee of Nineteen, led by British ambassador Miles Lampson and including French Minister Auguste Wilden, slowly and painfully negotiated the basis for a complete Japanese withdrawal. In fact, the Japanese were eager to conclude the Shanghai affair, but not under circumstances that would cause them to lose face. The navy wanted to avoid any action that might directly threaten Western interests and provoke an armed response against Japan. The army preferred not to be diverted from its objective of consolidating control over Manchuria. By early May, after a major offensive had finally cleared the Chinese resistance from a zone around the International Settlement, the two sides finally reached an uneasy truce. The Sino-Japanese armistice agreement of 5 May, negotiated by the League's Committee of Nineteen, managed to secure the removal of the nearly 50,000 Japanese troops without incident.[44] Japanese face had been saved, and Tokyo could claim that it still held control over the military. But the hostile international climate that resulted from the Shanghai crisis and the statements of nonrecognition from Washington and Geneva showed that it was a Pyrrhic victory.

Throughout the weeks of the Shanghai affair, French policy hewed very closely to that of Britain. Clearly, the attack on Shanghai struck close to the economic and financial interests of France. Moreover, those who had engaged in the considerable missionary and educational activity in northern China were aghast at the reports that filtered out of Shanghai concerning the severity of the Japanese attack and the extensive damage to the city. But if the Japanese bombing produced an anti-Japanese attitude generally, consistent with earlier reaction to events in Manchuria, the bulk of public attention turned only sporadically to the Shanghai crisis. In the leading metropolitan newspapers, news of the East Asian developments only occasionally made the front pages. Little sense of direction appeared from the commentary as the sense of dilemma confronting the Western powers in the Sino-Japanese dispute prevailed. Edouard Herriot, who would subsequently have to deal with the Far Eastern situation upon becoming premier in June, reflected French ambivalence in *L'Ere Nouvelle:* "We are presently neutralized between an international policy in this case sterile, and a national policy impossible for anyone wishing to respect loyally. M. Paul-Boncour finds himself . . . in a most difficult position faced with nearly irreconcilable contradictions."[45] Some commentators, including François Coty's *Figaro* on the Right and Edouard Daladier's *La République* on the moderate Left, argued that to participate in the crisis in an active way might invite trouble in Indochina. As Herriot reminded his own readers, "We are and we must remain friends of the yellow race. Now, China has more influence in our Far Eastern colonies than France itself." Other leading papers tended to lay blame upon the Chinese, urging that a local solution be found and that the great powers should stay out of the crisis. Indeed, in *L'Echo de Paris* French journalist Pertinax (André Géraud) criticized the United States for abandoning its earlier aloofness and ridiculed the League for its continued "clumsy intervention." When the crisis broke, *Le Temps* quickly urged restraint on the part of Britain and the United States when it was rumored that they might cooperate in economic sanctions against Japan. It would be dangerous to make the Shanghai episode an international problem: "In reality, the Shanghai affair, like the Mukden affair, is a local conflict, which must be settled on the scene by the parties involved."[46] As the conflict continued, the paper's position changed little. It warned that Japan could not be held in check, for it was not only a question of prestige but of vital economic interest. To be sure, the conflict provoked great international concern, but China should not expect direct intervention by the Western powers or the League and thus transform the local character of the crisis. In this context, the newspaper tried to play down Stimson's letter to Borah by surmising that Stimson merely wanted to call attention to existing treaties and their relationship to the crisis. It was neither a threat to Japan nor a mark of a new American policy. Neither Washington nor London wanted to engage in an adventurous policy and thereby risk jeopardizing the possibility of offering their good offices to resolve the conflict. *Le Temps* warned, however, that "those who would like to intervene by means of sanctions risk provoking general complications." In the end, however, many probably sympathized with the observation made by Pertinax that the victory of Japan in Shanghai boiled down to "a simple question of fact. . . . Let us not forget that in the Far East Japan is the master, since no power wants to launch in the game the smallest ship or the least soldier."[47]

The French response on the diplomatic front reflected the caution expressed in public circles. Ambassador Martel in Tokyo urged Paris to tread softly with Japan, especially in view of the disarmament conference. Christopher Thorne has noted that this advice met "with sympathy by officials in the Quai d'Orsay." René Massigli probably reflected the general position of the government when he told Naotake Sato, Japan's representative in Geneva, that the League Council would probably not take any action until the Lytton Commission had reported. Certainly, the fear existed that if the Council undertook an investigation of the crisis under Article Fifteen of the

Covenant, it could provoke on the part of Japan "an ill-considered reaction such as its resignation from the League of Nations."[48]

Nevertheless, the government recognized that the fighting around the International Settlement in Shanghai could easily spill over into the French Concession. Therefore, France had already reinforced her garrison there and sent the cruiser *Waldeck Rousseau* from Saigon to Shanghai.[49] Additionally, they dutifully joined with the other Western nations in urging restraint upon Tokyo. When, for example, London expressed its concern that Japan do nothing to jeopardize the international character and status of the settlement, the French instructed Martel to act similarly.[50] No doubt, the French were keenly aware of the danger posed for their own concession adjacent to the International Settlement. Moreover, they were cognizant of the necessity of maintaining solidarity among the Western powers. Therefore, the Laval government kept in step with the other interested powers in urging moderation upon Tokyo and in pointing out the importance that they attached to maintaining the international character of Shanghai. On the other hand, the French feared the repercussions in both China and Japan should the excited state of public opinion get out of hand or be directed against the Western powers. Consequently, they sought to avoid the use of any language that had a threatening ring and sought to influence the others in a similar sense.[51]

This belief was probably enhanced by the feeling among Western diplomats by mid-February that little could be done to resolve the crisis until one side or the other—most likely the Japanese—could achieve a substantial victory. Only then would the Japanese be willing to consider negotiations seriously.[52] It was in this context that France responded quite coolly when Stimson made a proposal on 11 February to apply his nonrecognition doctrine to violations by Japan of both the Nine Power Treaty and the Kellogg-Briand Pact. Just as Stimson hoped to gain the support of Britain for his policy, French adherence might have induced other countries to support the nonrecognition doctrine and stimulate a strong opposition to Japanese actions in China. But just as the British held the American initiative at arm's length, so did the French. For a week they evaded and procrastinated, responding only when, on 18 February, the American secretary of state pointedly asked Claudel about their position. Even then, no official government statement could be made, but Claudel argued that the difficulty with Stimson's approach remained that both Japan and China were convinced that none of the Western powers would fight to enforce the provisions of the Nine Power Treaty. Therefore, in the words of the Chinese proverb, it was "a case of straw guns and snow swords." In any event, when the two sides did settle their dispute, Claudel feared that it would be at the expense of the West.[53]

The thoughts that dominated the decision makers' minds in Paris are not clear, for the available records on this point are silent. But it is probable that many of the same reservations held in London also predominated in Paris. Indeed, Simon stopped through Paris on his way from Geneva and met with Laval. Although a record of this meeting apparently does not exist in the archives of either Britain or France, it is probable that the two leaders consulted on the issue and expressed their mutual aversion to Stimson's proposal.[54] A glimmer of French reasoning can be ascertained in a conversation between Claudel and Stimson nearly a month later, on 10 March. The Frenchman argued that resorting to economic sanctions had been generally futile in the past. Besides, Japan would ultimately fail in her aggression, because she did not have the resources to carry it through. Japan was a poor country that was trying to maintain a position of economic and political privilege in Shanghai, which was the London and Paris of the East. Dominance over commerce of the Yangtze Valley was of considerable importance to a poor Japan. But this did not mean that Japan sought to establish a protectorate over all of China, which was too big to control. Compounding the problem for Japan was the fact that it suffered from mediocre leadership whose minds did not go "beyond that of a military officer." All of this had produced considerable discontent in Japan that might ultimately generate revolution.[55]

Although this point was never articulated to the Americans, the French undoubtedly felt that since they were members of the League, they held a different position from that of the United States. Surely, they did not want to appear to be abandoning the League over an issue so far away. Such an act by one of the League's most important members might have a serious impact upon the organization's status and, therefore, its ability to assure collective security closer to home in Europe. Clearly, the French found themselves on the horns of a dilemma: they did not wish to abandon the League; yet they did not want to alienate the Americans by failing to support Stimson's initiative. In his memoirs, Joseph Paul-Boncour suggested that the League should have frankly told the United States, "Without you we can do nothing. If we act, what will you do?"[56] If one reads "France" instead of "the League," it is possible to gain a clue to the thinking of some policymakers. As in London, there was undoubtedly some confusion about just what Washington's policy statements meant. This was mixed with a large dose of suspicion as to Washington's unwillingness to back up its statements of moral condemnation. Undoubtedly, the French had a strong suspicion that they and the British would, as Simon put it, "assume the burden of Japanese resentment."[57] Therefore, it seemed the better part of wisdom to continue to be cautious, keep a low profile, and prevaricate. As Laval told the Chamber of Deputies when questioned on 9 February about the Far Eastern conflict, France sought to maintain steady and impartial pressure to reestablish normal Sino-Japanese relations. Indeed, French "impartiality" was emphasized by Laval. Insofar as the provisions of the League Covenant, the Nine Power Agreement, and the Kellogg Pact could be implemented, they had been, and France had used all of its influence to counsel moderation.[58] Obviously, France sought to avoid alienating either China or Japan in this matter.

In the end, they found it comfortable to go along with a British compromise. The League Council would be pressed to make a public declaration referring to the Covenant, the Nine Power Treaty, and the Kellogg Pact. The appearance of cooperation with the Americans would be maintained, but the declaration could be worded vaguely enough to avoid alienating Tokyo any further. Indeed, the document shepherded through the League Council by Simon and adopted by the Assembly on 11 March included references to the Kellogg-Briand Pact and the Nine Power Treaty. But it also included some substance of Stimson's proposal by endorsing the principle of nonrecognition. Nevertheless, Stimson's accusatory ring was ameliorated by framing the document in the form of a friendly appeal in which no verdict was assessed against Japan.[59]

After a round of self-congratulatory messages between the powers, the situation in Shanghai gradually sputtered to a halt on 5 May, under the pressure of the efforts of the League's Committee of Nineteen and dogged negotiations undertaken on the spot under the steady hand of Sir Miles Lampson, the British ambassador in China. Although the French had representatives in both groups, there is no indication that they played a particularly significant role. More important, however, was the short-term damage to Franco-American relations caused in part by the apparent French unwillingness to support Stimson's proposals concerning the Shanghai crisis. The bitterness that the American secretary of state held toward Simon and the British is well known. Stimson clearly felt that Britain had let America down and had sought to "take refuge in the inconspicuousness of . . . action" among a "flock of Nations." Indeed, Stimson developed nearly a personal fixation about British failure to support his proposals that he still carried with him in 1935, when he launched a bitter broadside at the British in his book, *The Far Eastern Crisis,* that precipitated British countercharges of American impatience.[60]

As for France, Stimson and the rumor mill sought to explain its reticence in terms of a Franco-Japanese deal negotiated behind the backs of the other Western powers. In fact, as indicated above, rumors of Franco-Japanese cooperation had been current in Washington and London for some time but had become more widespread since the beginning of the year. In the United States, the Hearst newspapers vigorously asserted that this was the reason for the French failure to cooperate more openly with the other powers. The trade-off, they suggested, was Japan's support for the French position at the Disarmament Conference, which prevented any meaningful disarmament measures.[61] In London, *The Times* reported that responsible circles assumed that a Franco-Japanese agreement existed. In the Foreign Office, opinion was divided between those who suspected that some arrangement existed and others who simply attributed French reluctance to support Stimson's initiative to "caution and correctness."[62] The charge also circulated that the arms industry in France was manipulating the press and government contacts on its behalf. The fact that the stock values of arms industry giants such as Hotchkiss and Creusot rose sharply on the French stock exchange, the Bourse, in February seemed to lend additional credence to the accusations.[63]

Under instructions from the Foreign Ministry, French representatives in Washington, London, Nanking, and elsewhere "categorically denied" that such an agreement existed.[64] Stimson was initially disinclined to believe that the rumors were anything more than mere gossip and appreciated French helpfulness in providing information from their representatives in the Far East through Claudel.[65] At other times, however, in his outrage over Japanese acts, the secretary of state seemed to lend more credence to the accusations. In the aftermath of his failure to obtain French adherence to his proposal of February, he launched an attack against France, citing his understanding that the French press and government were pro-Japanese, that there was a secret agreement, and that the French had even advanced money to Japan.[66] Although this attack on the French seems to have been an aberration, the fact is that such rumors did plant the seeds of doubt and helped to color the relations between the two nations.

There is little doubt that French policymakers were unenthusiastic about the prospects for the Disarmament Conference and were interested in anything that would make agreement doubly impossible. Yet there is no evidence now and none existed then to suggest that an agreement existed with Japan, or even that an approach was made to Tokyo. This is not to say that the Japanese did not express their interest in such an agreement. Ever since the termination of the Anglo-Japanese Alliance in 1922, Japan had been interested in inducing France to take Britain's place in some form of alliance.[67] Indeed, as will be seen, another Japanese démarche in the late summer of 1932 indicated Japan's interest, but it also revealed that no such prior agreement existed.

On balance, such an agreement in 1932 was as undesirable for France as it had been in 1922. To be sure, a community of interest between the two powers did exist that probably helped to fuel the skepticism that greeted French denials. On the other hand, France's interests were still centered in Europe, and her interests in the Far East were simply not comparable to those of Britain. The risks and dangers engulfing the Far East seemed likely to persist for a long time to come. Given its concerns in Europe, it would have been very unwise for France to become entangled in the area by an agreement with Japan. Still, France did not relish the thought of jeopardizing those interests that it had in the area. So it did not wish to be pushed into the forefront of an anti-Japanese campaign. At the same time, Paris recognized that Japanese flouting of the fulfillment of treaty obligations was a dangerous precedent that could affect France's own national security. As Premier André Tardieu stated to the Foreign Affairs Commission of the Chamber of Deputies on 4 March, the "special characteristics of the events" in East Asia determined and made more difficult the French response. The distance of the events from Geneva, the complexity of the treaty relationship between the two belligerents, the internal disruption in China, the preponderant interest of the United States, which was not a League member, and the necessity of coordinating League efforts with conventional diplomacy all posed new, complex considerations for French policymakers.[68]

In the end, the French maintained an essentially "correct" position during the Shanghai crisis. The French minister in Peking, Auguste Wilden, collaborated closely with Lampson during the latter's negotiations to bring about a Sino-Japanese settlement. The French representatives at Geneva displayed no pro-Japanese bias. Ambassador Martel in Tokyo continued dutifully to associate France with the protests lodged by the representatives of the other powers. France sought to play an even hand in the crisis and promoted a démarche that included China as well as Japan. It certainly remained reluctant to seek trouble for the sake of the Nine Power Treaty or the Kellogg Pact.

While such a policy had short-term advantages for France, Stimson and others, especially in the United States, undoubtedly felt as let down by the fickle French as by the unreliable British, and there is little doubt that subsequent American coolness reflected this attitude. Unfortunately for France, however, there is little indication that any officials thought seriously about the changes occurring in Japan's policies and goals and therefore failed to realize the long-term impact Tokyo's designs would have on the Far Eastern situation. Policy formulation continued to be based upon shortsighted considerations of the moment, which, in turn, produced a strong tendency to procrastinate and follow in the wake of others, especially the British. But this delaying pattern also generated considerable suspicion in Washington, as the relations between the United States and Britain were strained by their differing perceptions of the problem and by the differing responses to it. Undoubtedly, a bolder policy in Paris would not have altered the course or the outcome of the Shanghai crisis, but it might have led to a more serious analysis of the general situation in the Far East and a fuller appreciation of the future dilemma of simultaneously defending France's interests in that area and in Europe.

four

THE MANCHURIAN CRISIS:
MANCHUKUO AND BEYOND

W HILE the simmering Shanghai crisis continued to divert Western attention during the spring of 1932, events continued apace
in Manchuria, where the new state of Manchukuo had been proclaimed on 9 March. Clearly, the Japanese held undisputed control
over the new state through its puppet regent, Henry Pu-yi. Nevertheless, perhaps because of the high pitch of the Shanghai crisis in
early March, "the founding of Manchukuo had created scarcely a rip-
ple in France." On the Right, the press argued that the action must be
regarded as a fait accompli, while the Left judged the move to be of
little concern to France.¹ The government's position hewed closely to
that of Britain. Premier André Tardieu wired Ambassador Martel in
Tokyo that it would be "premature" to invoke any treaty regarding
the status of Manchuria, but that if such a step became necessary,
France would not hesitate. Meanwhile, "should the occasion present
itself," Martel should recall to the Japanese the pertinent clauses of
the League Covenant as well as the Nine Power Treaty, which stipulated the maintenance of the status quo for Manchuria as for the
other Chinese provinces.²

By the late spring of 1932, the unstable political situation in France
that had existed throughout the fall and winter began to unravel at
an ever-increasing pace. Having formed his new ministry without
Briand on 13 January, Laval found himself thrown out of office barely
a month later. Although Tardieu patched together another center-
right coalition, taking the Ministry of Foreign Affairs himself, it was
generally believed that he could not hold on for long. From mid-
March, therefore, the major attention in France turned toward speculation about the general elections to be held in May, with
concomitant interest in forthcoming German elections. The elections
in France resulted in a victory for a coalition of the Left led by radical
socialist Edouard Herriot, who became premier for the second time.
The Leftist coalition, which found it easier to combine for the elec-

toral victory than to agree upon and implement programs, was quickly confronted with increasingly difficult problems and an increasingly vitriolic opposition. Financial irresponsibility by its predecessor now came to nag a government that could not agree upon a common policy for solving the problem. In foreign affairs, it inherited several crucial problems that demanded policy consideration: the Disarmament Conference; the question of reparations undertaken by the Lausanne Conference that convened in June 1932; and the war debts controversy with the United States.[3] Under these circumstances, it is not strange that little attention was focused upon the Far East.

The French hoped to bolster the League but at the same time to cooperate with the United States and Britain. Most of all, however, they sought to protect their interests in China by keeping a low profile and avoiding unnecessary controversy with either Japan or China. As seen above, concerned about problems in Europe, beset by domestic difficulties, and doubtful about American dependability, the politically precarious French leadership hardly wished to assume a bold stance or undertake daring initiatives in the early phases of the Sino-Japanese dispute. Fortunately, the late spring and summer of 1932 proved to be a period of relative quiet, while the major powers concerned with the Sino-Japanese conflict waited for the report of the Lytton Commission, which continued its investigations in the Far East. This did not mean, however, that all diplomatic activity came to a halt. In fact, a coordinated Japanese initiative in early July put the new Herriot government squarely on the spot. Convinced that France had no large interest in Manchuria but, like Japan, had considerable interest in preventing the spread of Chinese nationalist demands, Tokyo believed that an entente could be negotiated with France that would serve the interests of both nations. In light of the increasing German challenge in Europe, Japanese planners believed France would be interested in such a Franco-Japanese rapprochement. For Japan, such an agreement might induce Britain to adopt a more favorable view of Japan's policy toward China. Japanese planners thought that by granting the French a privileged investment opportunity in Manchuria and by extending a guarantee of Indochinese security, they could arrange a Franco-Japanese entente.[4]

Accordingly, in Tokyo on 8 July, General Kuniaki Koisso, Japan's vice-minister of war, approached Ambassador Martel and indicated that Japan, in order to make the most of its rights in Manchuria, needed financial assistance that France was alone able to provide. He pointed out that both France and Japan had "every interest in a

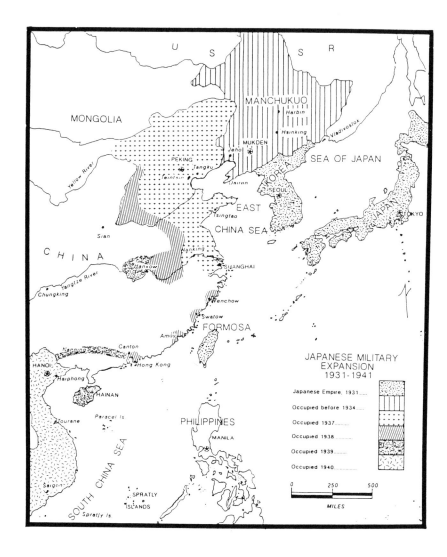

JAPANESE MILITARY
EXPANSION
1931-1941

Japanese Empire, 1931	
Occupied before 1934	
Occupied 1937	
Occupied 1938	
Occupied 1939	
Occupied 1940	

rapprochement that would facilitate in the Far East the reestablishment of a balance of forces and, consequently, a political stabilization." Martel believed that Koisso's démarche should be given considerable weight, because he represented the most vigorous element of Japan's ruling military clique.[5] The next day, Colonel Junichiro Kobayashi, military advisor to the Japanese delegation at Geneva, made a similar but blunter approach. He suggested that if the Lytton Commission report proved to be unfavorable to Japan, his country would withdraw from the League. But such a development would be quite a remote possibility if a unanimous decision could not be reached on the Commission. Kobayashi went on to recite the long admiration of Japan for France and to suggest that, given such a feeling in Japanese military circles, perhaps the time had come for a rapprochement with France. He pointed out that such a rapprochement would be advantageous to France, for it would give France a valuable guarantee against Russia; it would "assure the security of Indochina against communism . . . . " Japan would recover the alliance in Europe that it had lost by the Washington treaty system. Then Kobayaski went on to ask—and perhaps the most important thing on his mind—whether the French government would issue instructions to its representative on the Lytton Commission, General Henri Claudel, presumably to support the Japanese position and thereby prevent a unanimously anti-Japanese report from being achieved. Massigli politely recalled the French interest in collaborating with Japan in the largest possible questions. He argued that Japan could be assured of French support at Geneva for "legitimate interests of Japan." On the other hand, while he was in no position to commit the French government in such policy areas, he believed that it would be premature for his government to express an opinion regarding a solution to the crisis until the commission made its report and recommendations. With regard to Claudel, Massigli evaded by arguing that Claudel was a member of a League commission and that "he does not represent to any degree the French government which has no right to give him instructions." Furthermore, while profusely indicating French feelings of friendship toward Japan, Massigli declared that at a time when the war debts question was being debated, "our relations with America are for us of supreme importance, and the French government will certainly not want to undertake any engagement which . . . will risk being interpreted by American opinion as being directed against the United States." Finally, Massigli pointed out that as a member of the League, France was legally prohibited from concluding such pacts. Despite such arguments, Kobayashi insisted that Massigli pass along the proposal and elicit an official response.[6]

Despite Alexis Léger's immediate reaction, "Unacceptable; avoid any response,"[7] the Japanese persisted. Twice, on 12 and 20 July, the Japanese ambassador in France visited Herriot to broach the subject, and Koisso returned to the charge in Tokyo by seeing Martel again.[8] Not long thereafter, Matsuoka Yosuke, soon to be Japan's representative at Geneva, made a similar approach to the French consul in

73

Harbin.[9] In September, in a conversation with Admiral Berthelot, the French military commander-in-chief in the Far East, General Sadao Araki himself seized the opportunity to present the Japanese position. After expressing his admiration for the valor of the French army and people during World War I, the war minister unequivocally stated that the Japanese position regarding Manchuria was "unshakable." Japan was driven not by the desire for conquest, but simply the determination to assure its legitimate rights. "The recognition by Japan of the new state of Manchukuo is firmly decided. The imperial government, the army, the navy, and all the Japanese people are agreed on this point, and nothing will be able to change this decision." While other nations opposed Japan's action because of their ignorance of the situation, the French government and people, as epitomized by General Claudel, had displayed a clear understanding of the facts and a "perfect sense of the realities." Moreover, no significant conflict of interest existed between the two countries. In light of all of this, the general concluded, "I think that . . . a closer and closer rapprochement, more and more intimate, between the two countries would be natural to serve our common interests, as well as an element in world peace." Wanting to be as certain as possible about Araki's statement, Admiral Berthelot had the statement carefully retranslated both in French and Japanese before answering. His response was flatteringly noncommittal, but he promised to transmit the proposal to Paris.[10]

The French response to the repeated Japanese feelers was, as Herriot put it, "courteous evasion." The leaders took great care to avoid creating any ambiguity in the Japanese minds about France's commitment to the League of Nations and the Nine Power Pact. On the other hand, they emphasized France's continuing desire for friendship with Japan, while noting that French financial assistance was impossible to grant because of the needs of France itself.[11]

Undoubtedly, the American attitude influenced considerably the position taken by Herriot. As indicated, considering the deteriorating French economic situation and the unstable conditions in Germany, Herriot believed that good relations with Washington remained paramount, and Secretary of State Stimson was increasing his pressure on France to take a strong stance against Japan. So, with growing pressure from Tokyo and Washington, France began to be dragged reluctantly onto center stage along with Britain.

In Washington, Stimson had become more and more exasperated with his failure to bring Japan to heel by his policy of firmness and protest. Indeed, he had probably succeeded only in unleashing a virulent anti-American phobia in Japan. It seemed clear that the brief

burst of European resolve in March had been dissipated and that neither France nor Britain would act without American prodding. As
Stanley Hornbeck advised his chief, "We can count on no other great
power as a firm 'ally' or associate."[12] Despite widespread pressure to
the contrary, Stimson remained determined to issue a strong statement of American policy that "would help tremendously over in
Europe at this time." Consequently, in a well-advertised speech before the prestigious Council on Foreign Relations in New York on 8
August, the secretary of state lashed out at Japan. After voicing support for the Kellogg Pact and the League, he stated, "Hereafter when
two nations engage in armed conflict . . . we can no longer treat
them with the punctilio of the dueller's code. Instead we denounce
them as lawbreakers." Under such circumstances, the United States
had an obligation to consult with other signatories of the pact. Then,
in a thinly veiled condemnation of Japan, he said, "A nation which
sought to mask its imperialistic policy under the guise of defense of its
nationals would soon be unmasked."[13]

Not surprisingly, the address generated considerable debate at
home and abroad, where many felt it presaged a significant shift in
American policy away from its traditional isolationism. In Paris,
most important newspapers commented favorably upon the speech.
Even the right-wing press, which had been supportive of Japan as a
bulwark against the spread of communism in the Far East, was
attracted by the prospect of American support against "lawbreakers"
in Europe—a resurgent Germany, for example.[14] Calmer French
analysts remained unconvinced. Jules Henry, the French chargé
d'affaires in Washington, reflected these ambivalent feelings. To be
sure, Stimson had pressed for closer cooperation with Europe.
Clearly, he realized that the maintenance of peace in the world
through such consultation and cooperation was a vital interest for the
United States. Since this also held true for France—indeed, for France
"the consequences of a conflict would be more injurious than for any
other [country]"—it was in the French interest to promote such an
American position. But, Henry warned, "Stimson is not free to act
as he personally wishes." President Hoover, burdened and controlled
by domestic considerations and Senate opposition to an increased
American role in the world, would not allow Stimson to get entirely
carried away.[15]

In fact, Stimson's statement scarcely daunted the Japanese coalition
government led by Admiral Saito Makato, for the Japanese also did
not believe that he would be able to go beyond words and fight for
China. If anything, Stimson's discourse strengthened Japanese resolve

to defy the West. Four days after his speech, the Japanese cabinet decided to recognize Manchukuo, regardless of what the Lytton Commission might recommend. On 15 September, Japan formally recognized the new state of Manchukuo and assumed the role of its guardian and advisor, which essentially involved taking control of its defense, foreign affairs, and important economic assets.[16] By refusing to wait, as promised, for the Lytton Commission report, Japan generated considerable outrage in the West. In France, many former sympathizers or neutrals attacked the action. *Le Temps* decried the act as discourteous and compared it to contempt of court. Herriot, far more pro-League than his predecessors and far less sympathetic to the Japanese situation in East Asia, took steps to halt loans being floated for Japan and Manchukuo by small French banks.[17]

Meanwhile, the French government developed its own policy, submitted by the Quai d'Orsay on 11 September, regarding recognition of Manchukuo. The document argued that Japan had isolated itself diplomatically by the conflict that it had provoked. Suffering from an economic crisis and "driven to inflation by a costly policy of prestige, Japan is anxiously seeking to consolidate, with the regime that it has established for its own benefit in Manchuria, a political, economic, and social situation already compromised." France would not recognize the Manchukuo regime for several reasons: (1) such an action would prejudice the decision of the League of Nations and would be a repudiation of existing agreements, such as the Assembly's declaration of 11 May 1932, that recognition would not be granted to changes in the status quo brought about by means of force; (2) under Article Ten of the Covenant of the League, France, along with the other members, was bound to respect and maintain the territorial integrity of League members—including China; (3) as a signatory of the Nine Power Pact, France had undertaken to respect the sovereignty and independence of China, just as Japan had; (4) by the Open Door provisions of the Washington Treaty, France was obligated to uphold equal opportunity in China; and (5) Article Two of the Washington Treaty provided for the respect of the sovereignty, independence, and territorial and administrative integrity of China. In other words, by virtue of its treaty obligations France could not recognize the change of status in Manchuria, and to do so would prejudge the conclusions that the League might reach.[18]

From Washington came word that Stimson remained preoccupied with the Far Eastern situation and that continued French adherence to the doctrine of nonrecognition would be "greatly appreciated."[19] Even from unofficial circles, the French were warned about the importance Stimson attached to holding the line over Manchuria. The syndicated columnist Walter Lippman, who was on particularly good terms with Stimson and who, himself, had supported the secretary's doctrine of nonrecognition, warned Jules Henry that American public opinion toward France was very "hostile." The American attitude was affected by the questions of debts, disarmament, and the situation in the Far East. If France wished to remove the latter as a problem area—one around which rumors of a Franco-Japanese deal still occasionally surfaced—nothing would be so useful as continued adherence to the nonrecognition doctrine. "By a complete recognition of the Stimson doctrine, the French government would put an end to the legend according to which French policy in the Far East is pro-Japanese and anti-American. It would assure perhaps the future success of the policy of consultation proclaimed by Stimson. It would demonstrate that on this ground, France is on the side of America."[20] The message was clear. American support could not be expected on other issues if a quid pro quo failed to materialize regarding the Far East. Whether intentional or not, the linkage of the three outstanding issues in Franco-American relations could hardly help but influence French policymakers.

During the fall of 1932, the French went out of their way several times to reiterate their position to the Americans. Alexis Léger, director of political and commercial affairs at the Foreign Ministry, told the American ambassador in Paris, Walter E. Edge, that France agreed with the American position for several reasons. Stimson's nonrecognition policy accorded with the fundamental principle of the inviolability of treaties, which was the basis of French foreign policy. Therefore, French sympathies lay preponderantly with China. Of course, China's proximity to Indochina made it important that France not provoke hostilities with that country. Equally, France had no desire to antagonize Russia by assuming responsibilities in Manchuria. Finally, Léger expressed the French concern that the Lytton report might have significant repercussions on other issues such as disarmament and economic readjustment.[21] Subsequently, both Herriot and Philippe Berthelot, secretary general of the Quai d'Orsay, reiterated that two principles of French policy dictated that the American lead be followed: first, the necessity of the respect for treaties must be maintained, and Japan had violated this cardinal rule; second, it was necessary to secure the friendly cooperation of the United States and Great Britain in the fight against the reactionary forces of the world and those who believed that might makes right. On the other hand, they made it clear that France was willing only to follow. It would be unwilling in any way to take the lead. After all, they argued, American interests in the Far East greatly surpassed those of France.[22]

Undoubtedly, the firmer stance displayed by France in the fall of 1932 was prompted by a variety of considerations. Belief in the sanctity of treaties and the desire for American cooperation on a broad range of issues played the most significant roles, but other factors contributed as well. Clearly, Herriot held a view of Japan and its activities different from that of his predecessors. Representative of the more liberal end of the French political spectrum, the premier held an abiding concern for the health and vitality of international organization and cooperation as symbolized by the League. Therefore, he sought to do everything possible to support its decisions and maintain its credibility. He felt that the best guarantee of French security was close cooperation with the United States. To promote such cooperation, he emphasized French contributions toward disarmament by lowered defense budgets and by insisting that France continue to pay its war-debt installments. In fact, it was over this latter issue that his government fell from office in December 1932. Additionally, in order to gain British friendship, he surrendered France's reparations claims at the Lausanne Conference.[23] Perhaps the best glimpse of Herriot's concerns can be ascertained in an article he wrote in 1933 after being forced out of office. In it, he concluded:

> We are witnesses of a moving battle between the struggle for life and right as guaranteed by treaties.
> If realism and might prevail, if right is undefended, if the Treaty of Washington is violated, then all the efforts which have been made since 1918 will have been in vain. The reign of might will again be supreme. Signatures will be worthless. The League of Nations will be shown up as powerless. It is therefore important that the Advisory Committee in Geneva . . . oppose this savage revival of force with the continued action of wisdom, calm, and reason.[24]

Even if he could dismiss Japan's flouting of the League, in Herriot's mind Japan simply could not offer to France political security and economic advantages comparable to those offered by the United States.

Besides, conventional wisdom at the Quai d'Orsay held that Japan had bitten off more than it could chew, and increasing economic difficulties would probably force a settlement of the conflict.[25] It had become clear to many observers, however, that Japan would not be diverted from her course in the short run. Auguste Wilden, the

French minister in Peking, reflected this attitude. He reiterated the sacrifices that Japan had endured thus far and concluded that Tokyo would not be influenced by the recommendations of the Lytton Commission. Only superior force would bring Japan into line, but one would have to search in vain to find such force. Certainly, "it is necessary to recognize that the oratorical manifestations of Stimson have only, in exasperating Japanese pride, fortified Japanese resolve not to be deflected from the path that it has chosen. It appears therefore that the task of Western diplomacy must now content itself with trying to accept the faits accomplis in a form that will conceal the defeat."[26] From Tokyo came the assurance from Adrien de Lens, the French chargé d'affaires, that the Japanese government had not taken the decision lightly. The politically insecure Saito government, under pressure from public opinion and the military, had acted because it was convinced that the League would do nothing to stop it. Distracted by other international problems and realizing that the United States would not act beyond verbal condemnation, the League would continue to hesitate. De Lens warned that although many Japanese favored an understanding with the United States, others saw America as a competitor and a dangerous rival. Therefore, a latent hostility manifested itself in the attitude that the United States eventually would become an enemy who must be met by continued development of the Japanese navy. In the end, de Lens argued, peace in the Far East ultimately depended upon how Japan and Washington treated each other.[27]

In the meantime, the Lytton Commission had been hard at work investigating the situation in Manchuria. The Commission, created by a resolution of the League's Council on 10 December 1931, had, after considerable delay caused by the member-selection process, finally arrived in the Far East at the end of February 1932. Its chairman was the British representative, Victor Alexander George Robert Bulwer-Lytton, the second Earl of Lytton. He was a man of considerable distinction by virtue of both his title and his accomplishments. Son of a viceroy of India, a former governor of Bengal himself, a literary figure of repute, and a successful civil servant, Lytton cut an impressive figure, displayed a tremendous capacity for work, and left no doubt about his role as chairman. Furthermore, he clearly endeavored to support the ideals of the League of Nations. The antithesis of Lytton in virtually every respect was the French representative, General Henri Claudel. As George Blakeslee, an adviser to the Commission recorded, Claudel was "as characteristically French as the Earl of Lytton was characteristically British." A distinguished member of

the Conseil Superieur de la Guerre, recently inspector-general of colonial troops, Claudel alternated between displays of effusive geniality
and outbursts of emotional criticism: "Suddenly the fascinating smile
and winning expression would disappear, and grim, hard lines would
take their place, as if once again he were in some desperate battle in
the World War." If differences of personality, nationality, and language (Claudel spoke only French, which Lytton understood only
with great difficulty) created difficulties between the two men, their
perceptions of the Manchuria crisis were fundamentally antagonis-
tic. Blakeslee subsequently recalled that "as the days passed these two
men misunderstood each other more completely and the gulf between them continually widened."[28] Under the circumstances, the
remaining three members of the Commission—the German, Dr.
Heinrich Schnee, the Italian, Count Luigi Aldrovandi, and the American, General Frank McCoy—had to smooth over the differences
between Claudel and Lytton. Aldrovandi and McCoy proved themselves particularly adept as mediators.

During the spring and summer of 1932, the group traveled thousands of miles as they crisscrossed East Asia collecting evidence and
hearing testimony about the background to the crisis and the subsequent course of events. The writing of the Commission's report
turned out to be an extremely arduous process, complicated by the
recurring illness of Lytton, who nevertheless insisted on trying to
write most of the report himself, and by basic differences between
Lytton and Claudel. The latter, like all of his colleagues, agreed that
Manchukuo had been the creation of Japan and that it continued to
exist only because of Japanese support. But whereas Lytton tended
to indict Japan on virtually every charge while finding virtue in the
Chinese account, Claudel sought to soften any harsh wording that
smacked of condemnation of Japan. To him, the tone was nearly as
important as the conclusions. Consequently, many of Claudel's colleagues and their advisers incorrectly came to believe that Claudel
was under orders from Paris to prevent any condemnation of Japan.[29]
As the days and weeks passed, compromises were hammered out between the Lytton and Claudel positions as the Commission sought to
achieve a consensus. Even so, the recommendations provided in the
final chapter of the report came close to creating an irrevocable split,
with Claudel threatening to issue his own minority report. The general agreed with his colleagues that Japan's actions in Manchuria had
been unjustified. As he had wired Paris in early July, "Imagined
and developed by a group of Chinese-Manchuria autonomists and
Japanese individuals, the army, then the Japanese government consid-

ered making use of [Manchukuo] in order to maintain Japanese influence without resorting to a permanent occupation or an annexation . . . . "[30] Nevertheless, he argued to his colleagues on the Commission, although "Manchukuo is an illegitimate child, . . . we have it on our hands."[31] Therefore, with the support of Aldrovandi, he sought to make it possible that should a modified Manchukuo be organized in the future, it would be acceptable to the League. This, he believed, would take into account the realities of the situation in the Far East and allow for what appeared to be Japan's inevitable recognition of Manchukuo. Although the other commissioners refused to go along with Claudel's soft stance regarding the reorganization of Manchukuo, compromise language was finally agreed upon, after many tense moments, and the precious unanimity that Lytton sought was retained.

Claudel gave the Quai d'Orsay a glimpse of the report's essence on 3 September, the day before the commissioners affixed their signatures, although the complete text was to be kept secret until it had been received via the trans-Siberian railway. As transmitted through Auguste Wilden, the French minister in Peking, Claudel's final judgment was that the document treated China more favorably than Japan, but he reported that he felt successful in preventing Japan from being branded the aggressor. Nevertheless, he warned that if the League subsequently blamed Japan for the crisis, Japan was ready to leave that body. "I must add that, from the point of view of [Japan's] national defense, the strategic guarantees in Manchuria, which have preoccupied the Japanese so much, have been, in my opinion, only very insufficiently taken into consideration in the report."[32]

The Lytton Commission's report was finally made public on 2 October. As much as any report drawn up by committee can be, it was a model of thoroughness and moderation. It attempted to reconcile the conflicting interests of a dynamic Japan with those of a chaotic China, distributing blame over both nations but clearly assessing the greatest amount against Japan. It lauded Japan's contributions to Manchuria's economic development and acknowledged the damage that China's political and economic chaos had produced in the area. But on the critical question of responsibility for the events of September 1931, it found that the military operations of the Japanese troops that initiated the crisis "cannot be regarded as measures of legitimate self-defense." Moreover, it determined that the existing regime in Manchuria "cannot be considered to have been called into existence by a genuine and spontaneous independence movement." The existing administration owed its existence to "the presence of

Japanese troops and the activities of Japanese officials, both civil and military." The Commission realized that a return to the *status quo ante* would be impractical. Therefore, it recommended the restoration of Chinese sovereignty over Manchuria, but with considerable local autonomy for the area. Foreign advisers, including Japanese, would be allowed to plan for the governance of the area. Japanese economic rights would be protected, but Japan would not have the "right to control the country either economically or politically."[33]

In fact, as one student of Japanese policy during the period has concluded, the objectives of Japanese policy toward Manchuria had gone far beyond the "free participation of Japan in the economic development of Manchuria, approved by the Lytton Commission, and aimed, indeed, at the complete control of the country, militarily, economically, and politically."[34] Nevertheless, Tokyo wished to delay a final split with the League, and so it quickly asked for a six-week delay so that it could review the document. Thus began another series of delays that lasted into February 1933. When the League Council met in late November to consider the report, an impasse quickly developed, and it decided after a week's discussion to turn the matter over to the Assembly. When the Assembly met in early December, many of the smaller nations asserted themselves and urged immediate adoption of the report and its recommendations. They warned that the very existence of the League was at stake if it did not act to uphold the principles of the Covenant. But the larger members, as typified by Paul-Boncour's opening remarks to the Assembly, emphasized the complexities of the problem and sought to promote conciliation. In the end, the Assembly agreed to British Foreign Secretary John Simon's proposal to refer the issue to the Committee of Nineteen, which was empowered to invite the United States and the Soviet Union to join its deliberations. This committee subsequently devoted two months to finding some face-saving solution to the dispute, but intransigence on both sides made it a hopeless task. Japan was in no mood to compromise. Indeed, at the Assembly meeting in December the Japanese representative, Yosuke Matsuoka, announced that nothing would force the Japanese out of Manchuria, and he hinted that they would be willing to quit the League.

Moreover, during the delay following the presentation of the Lytton report, Japan had acted to strengthen its position in Manchuria. On 1 January 1933, following another railway accident, Japanese troops launched a drive south into neighboring Jehol province, which the Japanese claimed was part of Manchuria. By 4 March, they had successfully conquered most of the province, and the Chinese had once again been sent into a chaotic retreat. While the fighting may not have influenced the deliberations of the Committee of Nineteen, no clearer statement of Japan's uncompromising position could have been made.

By the middle of February, the Committee finally reached the inevitable conclusion that conciliation was impossible, and it presented its own report and recommendations to the Assembly. Essentially, it incorporated most of the Lytton report's findings as the basis for a settlement, while avoiding the condemnation of Japan as the aggressor. On 21 February, the Assembly finally met to consider the Committee's report. After three days of debate, on the twenty-fourth, the vote was taken in an atmosphere charged with anticipation. By a vote of forty-two of the forty-four nations present, the Assembly adopted the report and its recommendations. Only Japan, which voted against the motion, and Siam, which abstained, did not support the report. Matsuoka, after a brief statement expressing Japan's dismay at the League's inability to understand the real situation in East Asia, abruptly led the Japanese delegation from the chamber. As the Japanese delegation passed out in single file through the great doors of the Assembly Hall, a hush of doubt momentarily filled the room. Japan's intent became clear within a few weeks of this dramatic departure, when Tokyo formally withdrew from the League, thereby becoming the first great power to do so.[35]

The French role and policy during the unfolding of these events of the fall and winter was predictable. The publication of the Lytton Commission's report apparently did not occasion much of a stir among French policymakers beyond reassuring those who inquired that French policy remained committed to maintaining close ties with Britain and the United States and sustaining the strict respect for treaty obligations as they applied to the Far East.[36] But shortly before the League Council met in November to consider the report, the Quai d'Orsay undertook a serious review of available options and outlined a proposal that it believed might provide an alternative solution to that being contemplated by the League's Secretariat and supported by the British. Already, it was widely anticipated that the Council would pass the issue on to the Assembly for consideration. But rather than have the Assembly accept the report without its conclusions—that is, with only the historical recapitulation of the events—accompanied by a rejection of the recognition of Manchukuo, the French sought to maintain a mediation role for the League. The Assembly would "adopt" the report's description of the evolution of the conflict, and it would "approve" its conclusions.

Beyond that, however, a procedure analogous to that used to settle the Shanghai crisis would be established. The Assembly would invite those powers with special interests in the area (the nine powers plus Germany and the Soviet Union) to mediate locally between Japan and China along the lines of the Lytton report. To the French mind, this approach had the advantage of preventing another interminable delay and at the same time allowing the League to avoid the embarrassment of rejecting the recommendations of its own commission. Simultaneously, it would keep the other great powers, including the United States, in play, but without the dangers of a summit conference that would be opposed by Japan. Since it would be sponsored by the League, that body would not have to admit that it had reached the end of its line. Moreover, since the mediation would be undertaken by the Western powers, they could see to it that any settlement would not compromise Western interests in the area. The imponderable question was whether the Americans and Soviets would agree to participate.[37]

In the end, of course, the proposal never got off the ground and, in any case, probably would have foundered against the uncompromising positions of the Japanese and Chinese. But the proposal revealed continued concern in Paris about key elements of its policy: the credibility of the League and the necessity of maintaining its institutions and desirability of keeping the United States involved as much as possible. On the other hand, it also revealed that France remained unwilling to take the lead in actually finding a solution to the crisis.

The French tendency to sit back and wait was strengthened by the conviction in many quarters that the enormous problem of pacifying Manchuria and the attendant strains created for the Japanese economy might bring Tokyo to its senses. Consequently, although the Herriot government favored the earliest possible publication of the Lytton report, it did not object to the initial Japanese request for delay of the report's consideration until November. As Herriot pointed out, such a delay would help to avoid inflaming Japanese public opinion.[38] Others, such as Ambassador Paul Claudel in Washington, argued that by acting too vigorously against Japan, the League would merely bring about the downfall of that nation and with it the demise of Western influence in the Far East, perhaps opening the door for the advent of communism in Japan. Rather than throwing out the good with the bad, it might be best "to refuse to have any dealings with Manchukuo and then wait patiently to see how the matter will work out."[39]

As a result, when the League Council passed the Lytton report on to the Assembly for its consideration, concern developed in Paris that

84

the small powers, who dominated that body and who had nothing to lose, would simply press ahead, censure Japan, and not make any constructive suggestions.[40] Perhaps to head off such a development, Joseph Paul-Boncour, soon to become premier of France, urged the Assembly that its first "inevitable duty" was to find a solution through conciliation, using the Lytton report as the basis for such action, and that certain principles should first be established in order to facilitate an equitable solution.[41] Despite his emphasis upon conciliation, strongly echoed by Simon of Britain, who followed him to the rostrum, the small powers seized the bit in an effort to force the major powers to take effective action. Indeed, there must have been a heavy, collective sigh of relief in Paris when, failing to agree on any other course of action, the Assembly passed the Lytton report on to the Committee of Nineteen for its study and recommendation.[42]

Nevertheless, the cleavage between the small and great powers on the Committee of Nineteen continued to exist, with Czechoslovakia, Spain, Sweden, and Norway desiring to force the issue with Japan, while the French representative, René Massigli, along with his British and Italian colleagues, continued to stress conciliation and the need to avoid condemning either side. Massigli continued, however, to support the principles of the League Covenant and the League's resolution of nonrecognition of Manchukuo.[43] Still, it became increasingly apparent as the days passed and the year's end approached that the endeavor to settle the dispute would fail. Japan refused to budge on the fundamental issue of Manchurian autonomy and, as noted, resumed its military offensive shortly after the beginning of the new year.[44]

By the end of the year, Paul-Boncour, now head of his own short-lived government, recognized that little else could be done to avoid a final rupture, for "existing divergences leave . . . little hope about the chances for success of these negotiations." The negotiations had evolved to the point that a decision would have to be reached, either to give in to Japan's demand for direct negotiations with China or to follow the recommendations of the Lytton report. "It hardly seems possible [to go] further along the path of compromise." Since accepting the Japanese position would compromise the League's principles, Paul-Boncour correctly expected that the Committee of Nineteen would support the Lytton report and the Assembly would condemn Japan's actions. Expecting the worst reaction, the foreign minister directed the French representatives in Tokyo to reassure the Japanese of France's attempts to conciliate the situation. "The Japanese government must be assured . . . of the conciliating action that we have never ceased to exercise at the heart of the committees . . . ; this action has only been limited by the obligations of the pact that we ourselves must respect."[45]

At the Quai d'Orsay, those charged with responsibility for League affairs had come to the same realization that under the circumstances of Japan's uncompromising position, the League would have to act. Any further attempt at conciliation "risked being interpreted in Tokyo as proof of weakness, would be more prejudicial than a report which . . . has at least the advantage of maintaining intact the principles of the League of Nations and of safeguarding its dignity." France had no choice but to rally to the side of the general will of the League, "without taking any particular initiative that would put it in an exposed position vis-à-vis Japan."[46]

With the realization that events were moving inexorably toward a climax at Geneva that might have a significant impact on French interests and relationships in East Asia, the Far Eastern Department undertook another analytical review of the situation in January 1933 and reaffirmed already-entrenched beliefs. Review of the nature and extent of Franco-Japanese political, economic, financial, and cultural relations led to the conclusion that Japan did indeed face a demographic, economic, social, and political crisis. The solution pursued by its leaders was territorial expansion and imperialism in Asia. Such a policy resulted from Japan's adoption of modern Western technology, which, combined with ancient Japanese attributes, had produced a nationalist revival that remained unaffected by Western moral and intellectual discipline. On the other hand, it would be unjust and imprudent to lay total blame on Japan for the existing crisis. China's attitude toward foreigners, its political chaos, its administrative venality, and its boycott excesses undoubtedly taxed the patience of Japan. In fact, the report reminded, "it would be dangerous to encourage any solution that entailed the reorganization, with or without Japan, of a homogeneous and disciplined China, which would constitute an immediate danger to the very frontier of Indochina." It recognized the fundamental problem that "we possess important interests within reach of Japan, but greater interest still in maintaining the contractual system instituted since the war and in the respect of international obligations." If Japan persisted in its repudiation of its international obligations, France would have no choice but to support the League's action against it. But France should avoid becoming involved in any step that would exonerate China from the heavy responsibility that it should bear and that would "uselessly strike at Japanese self-regard and push them to extreme solutions."

86

The department concluded with the sanguine, familiar prediction that the crisis would "produce its own solution and that the economic and monetary realities must sooner or later bring around Japanese opinion to a more exact notion of the possibilities and a more just appreciation of the necessity of collaboration with the other great powers." French policy should be carefully directed toward bringing about such an evolution in Japanese thinking.[47] To do more would be useless, might provoke hostilities, and, above all, would expose France to the dangers of taking the lead. It would be better to move slowly rather than precipitously toward a resolution of the crisis.

Neither did the majority of the French public wish to become involved in the crisis in any significant way. Although the left-wing newspapers made a great deal of noise, urging the government to support the League and to denounce the Japanese aggression, those in the center and on the Right remained far more restrained. Like it or not, they argued, Japan was in Manchuria, and it would be unwise for the Western powers to force the issue in the face of obvious Japanese determination. As it had throughout the crisis, *Le Temps* promoted the idea of direct Sino-Japanese negotiations. Besides, as a result of the Chinese boycott, "Manchuria has become an indispensable field for Japanese expansion." The Radical Socialist newspaper, *La République,* added the sobering note, however, that if the League failed to take effective action in Manchuria, it would also fail when aggression occurred closer to home.[48] But on the whole, the public remained more concerned with problems closer to home and preferred to deal with the League's stature in European problems when the time came.

Meanwhile, although Pierre Cot, undersecretary of foreign affairs, had indicated as early as 8 January that the French delegation at Geneva would vote to support the League's position,[49] the American secretary of state, Stimson, even as part of a lame-duck administration soon to leave office, actively sought to keep France in line for the forthcoming vote. On 15 January, before the French delegation left for the reconvening of the League session, Theodore Marriner, counselor at the American Embassy in Paris, recalled to Cot the basic American position: the United States approved of the Lytton report's conclusions; the time had come for the League to "pronounce itself on the facts," although this did not mean sending forces to fight Japan. Marriner insisted that this also reflected the attitude of President-elect Franklin Roosevelt. Indeed, he predicted, "The new government will be probably even more anti-Japanese." Premier Paul-Boncour's annotations on the memo reflected his own approval of the Lytton report.

But he also noted, "the key will be to avoid the lead and that England move in the same sense."[50]

The concern that France not get ahead of the United States seemed justified in view of the estimates conveyed by the French representative in Washington. Paul Claudel warned that "America is very little disposed to act in the Pacific other than diplomatically . . . . " Even when the United States agreed with the other powers, it sought to maintain an independent stance. The sad state of the American navy prevented it from pursuing an aggressive policy. Any aid it could give Britain in the area would be insufficient. Anyway, Claudel wryly commented, "two weaknesses do not constitute one force. America possesses with regard to Japan a terrible weapon, which is the economic weapon, but it is little disposed to use it and thereby widen the radius of the zone devastated by the crisis." Finally, Claudel astutely noted that the recent vote by the Congress to grant the Philippines its independence and the attitude of the influential Hearst press indicated that "the American public takes less and less interest in Far Eastern affairs."[51]

While Stimson continued to profess his conviction that Japan's attitude regarding the League was in great part bluff, French observers in Tokyo and Geneva failed to perceive much bluff in the Japanese position. From Geneva, Massigli reported the various proposals that the Japanese made throughout January and February. But he noted that such proposals offered little hope, for they reflected little significant change in attitude by Tokyo, seeming instead to constitute a marking of time. The issue of the recognition of Manchuria remained the major point of difference over which neither Japan nor the members of the League's committee would compromise.[52] From Tokyo, de Lens offered an even more pessimistic assessment about the likelihood of a compromise solution. On 6 January, he reported that Arita, the Japanese vice-minister for foreign affairs, believed that the Committee of Nineteen could not succeed unless it were willing to take into account Japan's basic position of direct negotiations and the recognition of Manchukuo. De Lens warned that the Japanese government was so dominated by the military that it would "prefer to resign from the League of Nations rather than concede on the question of the independence of Manchukuo." His perception changed little over the next month and a half. On 14 February, he reported Japan's intent to leave the League if the Assembly approved the Lytton report. De Lens had no doubt that this was not a bluff, and he warned that if sanctions were imposed, the Japanese public, "always ready to let itself be guided by the nationalists and militarists, could be provoked

to war in which one could predict neither the extent nor the consequences." When Japan dramatically walked out of the League after
the vote of 24 February, de Lens warned, "it is certain that any attempt of the powers to resort to sanctions against Japan not only
would precipitate the complete rupture with the League of Nations
but also precipitate dangerous reactions on its part." With its military
preparations at a high level, Japan, the French chargé d'affaires
cautioned, was prepared for any eventuality.[53] From Geneva, however, Massigli was less pessimistic. He believed that Japan's cooperation with the League might not cease altogether. In any event, he
felt that Japan would continue to participate in the Disarmament
Conference and in the preparations for the forthcoming World Economic Conference.[54]

Massigli's reference to the disarmament and economic issues reflected the continued and considerably greater concern about those
issues in the minds of many Frenchmen. During the fall and winter of
1932–33, the Far East, the Lytton report, and associated developments could occupy only a secondary place in the minds of most
French statesmen, politicians, and public. No debate occurred in the
Chamber of Deputies concerning the Far Eastern situation or French
policy regarding it. French newspapers only occasionally addressed
the problem, but even then their concern focused more on the impact
that the crisis would have on the League or on the other international
developments of the period. Of the latter, there were plenty: the
Disarmament Conference, involving considerable planning and attention connected with a mutual assistance plan by Herriot and Paul-
Boncour; the war-debts dispute, with American rejection of French
requests for their suspension; the American presidential elections and
concomitant discussion about what the advent of the Roosevelt presidency would mean for France and international relations in general;
the signing of the Franco-Soviet nonaggression pact of November
1932 and the furious debate that began concerning ratification; and,
finally, tremendous attention remained riveted upon the unstable political situation in Germany, with the Reichstag elections of November, the machinations of Franz von Papen and Kurt von Schleicher,
and the appointment of Adolf Hitler as chancellor. As distracting as
these international developments seemed, the domestic political and
economic situation also produced raging controversy. With no party
able to command a majority in the Chamber, government by coalition continued, and the results proved to be dismal. As the depression
began to make itself felt more severely, the major issue became that of
dealing with the economy. Opposition to the deflationary policies of

Herriot became widespread, so that when he insisted on France making a war-debt installment despite the lack of reparations from Germany caused by the Hoover Moratorium, established to halt international debt payment for one year, he was overwhelmingly defeated in the Chamber. These developments, the senatorial elections of late October, and the inevitable speculation surrounding the formation of Paul-Boncour's first government kept the domestic pot boiling. In fact, Paul-Boncour's government barely lasted a month before he was turned out over a minor financial issue. Edouard Daladier followed in January 1933, forming his ministry the same day that Adolf Hitler was appointed chancellor of Germany. In light of these developments, there can be little wonder that news of the Far Eastern crisis was once again crowded off the front pages. Even though many newspapers, such as *Le Temps,* expressed their concern about Japan's withdrawing from the League,[55] most foreign news coverage was focused on developments across the Rhine, where the violence of domestic change immediately seized foreign attention.

Although some interest, but only faint support, arose over a subsequent, short-lived attempt by Britain to embargo arms shipments to Japan and China, the major concern that developed within the next few weeks was whether Japan and Germany, as two international outcasts, would be attracted to each other. In September 1932, after the Japanese démarche regarding an entente with France had been rebuffed, the Japanese military attaché in Paris, General H. Kasai, had declared to General Moyrand of the French General Staff, that "since politically Japan cannot remain isolated in the West, it will seek, if it loses the support of France, to draw closer to other Western powers; these powers can only be Germany and Italy." In the aftermath of the League's decision, considerable attention was focused upon a trip to Germany made by Matsuoka in early March 1933. The former Japanese representative to the League made something of a splash when he publicly emphasized to the German press the historical similarities of the two countries which were both fighting for recognition in the eyes of the world. At a subsequent reception, he stated that Japan was ready to collaborate with any nation, but especially with Germany, with whom Japan had no political differences and with whom her economic relations had always been excellent. While there was no substance to the French fear yet, astute observers had every reason to be concerned about a marriage of convenience between two powers who had a great deal to gain from the dismantling of the international order established after World War I. Indeed, cautiously and slowly the two states did begin to draw closer over the next several months, with a culmination on the formation of the Anti-Comintern Pact in November 1936.[56]

Although many studies of the Manchurian crisis find it convenient to conclude with Japan's departure from the League in February, the fighting continued until it came to a halt with the Tangku Truce at the end of May 1933. To be sure, many contemporary observers appeared eager to pronounce the conflict dead, or at least hoped that it would simply go away. In London, French Ambassador de Fleuriau's pronouncement, "But it is a finished affair, there is no longer war; in fact there are only those military operations . . . where one party advances and the other retreats without fighting,"[57] probably reflected the wish of many Westerners. Satisfied that the League had acted and that not much else could be done safely, they were content to sit back and allow events to run their course.

In fact, the League's action did not change Japan's plans. Indeed, the military launched a new campaign in the neighboring Chinese province of Jehol, where in a brief, brilliant campaign Japanese forces crossed the Great Wall itself as the Chinese armies virtually disintegrated. By early March, Japanese forces took the provincial capital of Chengteh. In the face of Chinese division and confusion, there seemed to be little to prevent the Japanese from moving all the way to Peking and Tientsin. Some doubt existed whether China could still be considered a united, sovereign state. But the Japanese paused momentarily, perhaps to consolidate their gains, but also because of considerable debate and ambivalence in Tokyo about the policy to be pursued. Proponents of caution seemed temporarily to gain the upper hand. But after some sporadic fighting along the Great Wall in late April, the Japanese launched a major new offensive in early May. They rapidly pushed into the open plains south of the Great Wall. No match for the Japanese, the remnants of China's army in the area collapsed, and Japanese airplanes appeared in the skies over Peking, where a direct attack was expected from Japanese troops that had penetrated to within fifteen miles of the gates of the city. But the assault did not come. The Chinese, recognizing the gravity of the situation, finally undertook the bilateral negotiations with Japan upon which Tokyo had always insisted. The Chinese had desperately sought to obtain British assistance in mediating the dispute, but when the latter poured cold water on the effort, little choice remained. Amidst very tight secrecy and security, negotiators from both sides finally hammered out a settlement on 31 May, called the Tangku Truce. Chinese military forces were to withdraw from the area between Peking, Tientsin, and the Great Wall, leaving the security of the area up to their police, which were to be "friendly" to Japan. Once satisfied that the area had been demilitarized, Japan would withdraw its own forces to the Wall. The effect of the settlement, however, was to leave a large part of the North China Plain open to renewed Japanese attack whenever Japan deemed such action necessary or desirable. This, in turn, gave the Japanese considerable political and economic leverage in the area. It was hardly a satisfactory solution to the hard-pressed Nanking government of Chiang Kai-shek, which had little alternative, and it bode ill for the future of Sino-Japanese relations.[58]

During the final phases of fighting prior to the Tangku agreement, most attention in France remained riveted on the situation close to home, where developments overshadowed the Far Eastern mess that many would just as soon forget. The most urgent matter for Frenchmen was the unfolding of Hitler's National Socialist revolution. The implications for French security and foreign policy, should the Nazis attempt to carry out their promised scrapping of the Versailles system, seemed obvious, and a war scare broke out. Concomitantly, the Disarmament Conference reconvened but seemed on the verge of collapse under the pressures of the new tensions in Europe and the long-standing divergences of viewpoint of France and Britain concerning the issue of security. Even as the debate went on concerning various disarmament schemes, rumors circulated that Hitler would soon announce German rearmament. The continuing economic crisis of the depression also vied for space in the headlines. With the new Roosevelt administration's economic reforms, interest reemerged about the problems of war debts, currency stabilization, and trade restrictions. Preparations were in full swing for the forthcoming World Monetary and Economic Conference to be held in June. The United States's abandonment of the gold standard at the end of April sent shock waves of concern through the French financial community. Negotiations for a rapprochement with Italy were initiated in March and ultimately produced the Four Power Pact, which was signed on the day before the Tangku Truce was initialed.[59]

On the domestic scene, coalition politics precluded any meaningful attempt to tackle the economic and social problems caused by the depression. Budgetary issues that had buried the Herriot and Paul-Boncour ministries were largely ignored by the new Daladier regime. By avoiding any substantive financial proposals to the Chamber of Deputies, he sought to survive as long as possible. But the result was a political stalemate that consumed inordinate quantities of energy and attention by the politicians and exasperated political commentators. The Socialists, led by Léon Blum, had become the largest party

in France in the elections of 1932, but they still adhered to their position of refusing to enter a government they could not control and
would only support it in the Chamber. But they could not agree with
Daladier's Radicals about an economic program, for they held fundamentally opposed views about who should bear the brunt of such reform. Daladier's preference for deflationary programs clashed head-on
with the Socialists' views. The resulting stalemate increasingly led
dissatisfied elements of the population to look for an alternative.
They found it in the large number of right-wing, antiparliamentary,
authoritarian organizations that began to emerge. As the quasifascist
ligues noisily turned up the volume of the political debate, France began heading down the path of political chaos that culminated in the
crisis of 6 February 1934, when the very Republic itself was shaken to
its roots. Unemployment continued to climb, and strikes by bureau-
crats, opposing proposed pay cuts, and by auto workers further damaged the economy.[60]

Nevertheless, members of the Far Eastern Department of the
Foreign Ministry, of course, continued to monitor closely the developments in East Asia. Reports from the area continued to be
pessimistic. From Tokyo, Ambassador de Martel reported the unwillingness of the Japanese to cooperate with the West over such issues as the Disarmament Conference. More and more, he suggested,
Japan's position regarding such issues would be determined according
to the concerns born out of its conflict with China and the potential
hostility of the Soviet Union. From Peking, the French minister,
Wilden, reported the growing confusion, defeatism, and division in
China's governing circles. Desperately, the Chinese were appealing
for financial and diplomatic support from anyone who would listen.
But Wilden admitted that despite the alarmingly deteriorating
conditions, the time was not yet ripe for the major powers to intervene on behalf of negotiations that would end the hostilities. From
Nanking, Philippe Baudet, the French representative, concurred that
Chiang Kai-shek was not yet ready to concede.[61]

In any event, in Paris the signs clearly discouraged any bold initiatives to end hostilities. Foreign Minister Paul-Boncour cautioned
French representatives in all of the pertinent capitals that any step
taken to facilitate a "suspension of hostilities" (as opposed, presumably, to the negotiation of a peace settlement) must be taken only
in conjunction with the British and Americans. Moreover, "if humanitarian considerations are of a nature to justify such an action on
our part, we must avoid any participation in an understanding that
would prejudice a delimitation of a frontier between China and

Manchukuo."[62] But by the middle of May the situation had deteriorated to such an extent that an alarmed Paul-Boncour instructed the
French representative at the Geneva disarmament negotiations to inquire "informally and discreetly" as to whether the other powers
might be disposed to undertake a mediation effort. Paul-Boncour had
finally begun to realize that the major powers could no longer afford
to remain indifferent to the events in East Asia. "Their silence could
be interpreted as a tacit acquiescence, susceptible of encouraging the
Japanese government in the work of disintegration that it pursues in
China, by means of force and in violation of its contractual obligations. In fact as in law, the development of such a situation is serious
for its repercussions in the international order and by the precedent
that it creates contrary to the very objective of our efforts in the European order." The French continued to see a linkage between their
security in Europe and the effect that the Far Eastern hostilities had
upon the credibility of the major powers and their resolve to uphold
the system of international commitments and organization that
would ensure that very security. On the other hand, French officials
remained chary of getting out in front of the other powers in any attempt to resolve the struggle. Paul-Boncour warned Massigli to
"take all necessary precautions in order that we not be left appearing
to bear responsibility for the initiative." The American attitude, however, likely had not changed significantly since 2 May, when Stanley
Hornbeck, chief of the State Department's Far Eastern Division, had
told the French ambassador in Washington of the American determination to proceed cautiously. It was not inclined to take any initiative
but would be willing to cooperate with an Anglo-French lead.[63]

In the end, of course, before Paul-Boncour's initiative could be carried out, the direct Sino-Japanese negotiations bore fruit with the
Tangku Truce. On the very day that the agreement was signed in the
Far East, the Far Eastern Department in Paris submitted its analysis
of the situation. While admitting that Japan's motives and goals for
agreeing to such a truce in spite of its favorable position militarily
were difficult to ascertain, the department predicted that it was "not
likely to result in a permanent settlement of the Sino-Japanese conflict." It suggested that some of the Chinese warlords of North China
had a vested interest in preventing the Nanking government from
reaching such a settlement, because the conflict meant that Chiang
Kai-shek could not concentrate his efforts on bringing them into line.
Therefore, it was likely that they would keep the pot stirred. As far as
Western interests were concerned, the report was pessimistic. Part of
the Japanese tactic in China had been designed to measure the nature

of Western response in defending their interests in the area. By allowing the establishment of a new order in North China as "bystanders
with crossed arms," the Western powers succeeded only in "dimin-
ishing their prestige and facilitating the elimination of the white race
from a domain where the latter had still made prodigious efforts and
realized a great achievement."[64]

This ominous warning of 1933 proved prophetic in the long run.
But over the short span of the next few years the situation in the Far
East quieted down considerably. Indeed, for the better part of the
next four years, from the spring of 1933 to the summer of 1937, peace
settled, if uneasily, over the area. To be sure, Japan utilized every opportunity to gain economic and political advantage in North China.
Consequently, as Chiang Kai-shek slowly began to get his government in order and a new vigor returned to Nanking, friction continued to build between the two states. In Japan, an active, vocal cadre
of opponents of the existing regime continued to complicate the
court-party-military web of intrigue that developed. Attacks against
the "bourgeois democracy" modeled along Western lines ebbed and
flowed during the period as ardent nationalists pressed for a "Showa
Restoration" based on a return to a benevolent imperial rule and a
more independent stance in international affairs. The armed forces remained influential in policy-making. Although divergences of opinion remained among and within branches of the armed forces, leading
to some bumpy times for the governing circles in Tokyo—most notably the Tokyo mutiny of 1936—the military remained generally
united on the need to carve out an autonomous national defense policy. Perhaps the clearest articulation of Japanese policy came in April
1934, when Foreign Ministry spokesman Amau Eiji warned that
Japan would oppose any foreign economic, technical, and military aid
to China. In effect, by the so-called Amau Doctrine, Japan sought to
establish its own version of the Monroe Doctrine, warning foreign
powers to keep their hands off China. Other foreboding notes
sounded at the end of 1934, when Tokyo abrogated the Washington
and London naval treaties, and again in 1935 when it withdrew from
the London Naval Conference. Japanese naval expansion could now
be undertaken without international restraints, and keels were
quickly laid for the world's two largest battleships.

On the other hand, although relations with the Soviet Union
steadily deteriorated, culminating with the Anti-Comintern Pact
with Germany in 1936, Japanese leaders had no intention of embark-
ing on a major war in the immediate future. Although war with
the United States and Britain was not discounted, it did not appear

imminent. With regard to China, the Japanese believed that Chiang Kai-shek would be unable to arrive at a permanent accommodation with his communist opponents. At home, the excited state of Japanese public opinion began to fade as more mundane daily concerns and pleasures diverted public attention. Economic reforms were instituted, unemployment began to decline, prices stabilized, and a favorable balance of trade was restored. A political equilibrium appeared in the offing and was symbolized by the accession of a young civilian nobleman, Prince Fumimaro Konoye, to the post of premier in June 1937. But ironically, just when prospects for peace and prosperity appeared brighter than they had for years, everything crumbled to dust with the advent of renewed fighting between China and Japan.[65]

French interest in Far Eastern affairs waxed and waned during the period, although on balance it remained at a low level, for, as during the Manchurian crisis, developments at home and in Europe preempted the attention of French public opinion and policymakers. Indeed, as is well known, events in Europe gathered momentum that accelerated with alarming speed during the period. Within five months of the end of fighting in China, Hitler took Germany out of the Disarmament Conference and out of the League. In October 1935, the Italo-Ethiopian War erupted. In March 1936, Germany reoccupied the Rhineland, and in July the Spanish Civil War exploded. With these new pressures on the tottering European security system, most attention was focused on staving off disaster there, not on the more distant and more subtle developments in the Far East. Only a handful of Frenchmen with special interests in or responsibility for that area paid it any sustained attention. The Far East could not be completely neglected given the extent of French interests there. But, again, those who paid the area any attention repeatedly found their hopes and aspirations dashed by events over which they had little control.

For a few months following the Tangku Truce, French observers expressed a cautious optimism about a stabilization in the area. De Martel felt that, barring some ill-conceived Chinese challenge, moderate elements in Japan might be able to reassert themselves. In China, French representatives felt the domestic situation had improved with the end of the fighting. Even American-Japanese relations seemed to have a chance for improvement under the new Roosevelt administration, though it was necessary to recognize the profound differences that still existed.[66]

When Japan issued the Amau Doctrine in April 1934, France reacted with predictable caution. Besides the fact that the circumstances
surrounding the statement were somewhat ambiguous, the French
had a good deal of sympathy for the motives of Japan. The Far Eastern Department pointed out that the Chinese had been quite successful in procuring foreign financial, technical, and military aid from a
wide range of Western countries. This had come at a time when increasing barriers had been erected against Japanese imports around
the world: "Is it any wonder, then, that Japan, impatient to affirm its
hegemony in Asia and meanwhile anxious at seeing the foreign powers taking advantage of Sino-Japanese hostility to establish more sol-
idly their influence in China, should want to create a diversion?" The
declaration simply gave Japanese policy a doctrinal basis. In any
event, it was subsequently noted, the Japanese action was not unprecedented. The American Monroe Doctrine and a four-power announcement in 1922 regarding the independence of Austria fell into
the same category. The Quai d'Orsay initially fell back on the Nine
Power Treaty, for Tokyo's action seemed to be a clear violation of
that document by which all contracting powers had agreed to respect
the sovereignty and independence of China. The Japanese declaration
came close to making China a protectorate. Thus, the nine powers
should be the ones to deal with the problem. On the other hand,
France did not want to be the one to initiate a call for such conversations. Consequently, it undertook to ascertain the American and
British attitudes. French representatives in those cities were warned,
however, that in their "*consultative* démarche, they should avoid anything that could make us bear the responsibility or the appearance of
an initiative normally incumbent upon the American government,
trustee of the treaty of 1922."[67]

But the Roosevelt administration was determined not to create additional friction with Japan. It, too, was willing to cooperate with
other powers but would not take the lead. When Britain could not
propose a plan and when France had clearly indicated that it would
not take the initiative, Washington issued a mild statement of its own
and tried to restrain the press from exacerbating the situation. The
Nine Power Treaty was not mentioned, and China was not defended.
As Ambassador André Lefebvre de Laboulaye suggested from Washington, the condition of the American navy did not permit the
United States "to run great risks in its relations with Japan."[68] Consequently, Paris remained equally reluctant to antagonize Tokyo. In
its subsequent note to the Japanese, France expressed satisfaction with

Japanese assurances that the Open Door policy in China would remain in effect, and it agreed with Tokyo's promise that Japan could not remain indifferent to interventions that might prejudice the maintenance of order and justice in the Far East. But the note reminded the Japanese that should problems occur in China, the proper method of resolving them would be through the procedures outlined in the Nine Power Treaty. Interestingly, the Quai d'Orsay sought to rationalize its tardy response in terms of wishing to be in accord with the policies of Britain and the United States.[69] In fact, of course, they wished to avoid being caught out front with a strong response that would not be supported in London and Washington, thus exposing Paris to the brunt of Japanese ire. Therefore, although initially desirous of claiming the Japanese statement to be a violation of the Nine Power Treaty, the French, when the United States assumed a mild stance, quickly followed suit and toned down their own response. But this was consistent with their policy throughout the period of the Manchurian crisis and beyond.

A major concern for France during the 1933–37 period was the evolving relationships between France and Russia and between Japan and Germany. This pair of bilateral relationships provided a clear linkage of European and Far Eastern affairs and posed severe complications for Franco-Japanese relations. Confronted during the period with an increasing German threat, France continued a general rapprochement with the Soviets. Following the negotiation of a nonaggression pact, ratified by the French Chamber of Deputies in May 1933, the two countries had continued to move closer together. French foreign minister Louis Barthou sponsored the Soviet entrance into the League of Nations, and after Barthou's assassination in 1934, Pierre Laval continued, although with less enthusiasm, to take steps to recreate the old Franco-Russian alliance of pre–World War I days. Ultimately, in May 1935, a Franco-Soviet Pact was signed, though watered down significantly from what had been anticipated and lacking a military convention necessary to give teeth to the pact. Even so, it aroused considerable animosity in France, in Europe, and in Japan. Indeed, as early as the fall of 1933, Emile Charvériat, undersecretary of the Far Eastern Department of the Quai d'Orsay, had warned of a negative Japanese reaction. Should Japan get into a fight with the Soviets, he argued, and should France find itself obliged by treaty to support Russia, Japan would consider this a hostile act and could threaten French possessions in the Far East. Charvériat, felt that it might be prudent not to go beyond the nonaggression pact.[70] As the treaty ratification process progressed during the spring of

1936, numerous Japanese interests showed considerable dissatisfaction. Almost unanimously, from the Foreign Ministry to the military, they argued that the pact had the effect of providing security for the Soviets in Europe and thereby would allow them to refocus their attention and reestablish their freedom of action in the Far East, where Soviet interests clashed with those of Japan. Consequently, the Japanese saw the pact as an act of hostility.[71]

The French sought to allay Japanese suspicions and fears by vigorously arguing that the Franco-Soviet Pact did not pertain to the Far East, denying that it would have any bearing on the situation there. They reiterated their long-standing friendship for Japan and pointed out that because of their friendship with both Japan and the Soviet Union, they could serve a uniquely useful role in resolving the differences between the two powers. Besides, they argued, the Franco-Soviet Pact would actually bring the Soviet Union back into the middle of European affairs and thereby act as a constraint on Soviet activities in the Far East.[72] These arguments apparently carried little weight with Tokyo, and the Far Eastern Department warned that the delicate Soviet-Japanese relationship might well affect the security of French possessions in the Far East, where French forces were "notoriously insufficient." This was doubly unsettling since it seemed clear that the United States was in no mood to oppose any Japanese expansionism. Jules Henry, the French chargé d'affaires in Washington, wired, "It is difficult to foresee at the present moment which new factors could lead Washington authorities to depart from this attitude of hope and bring them to define more boldly their attitude with regard to the problem created by the Japanese expansion in China and the collapse of the contractual system, built by the signatory powers of the accords of 1922, for the protection of Chinese national integrity."[73]

The worst French fears were realized with the negotiation of the Nazi-Japanese Anti-Comintern Pact in November 1936. To be sure, the existence of the Franco-Soviet Pact did not by itself bring about the Japanese act. To believe that it did, as some Frenchmen professed, simply attached more importance to Franco-Soviet relations than circumstances warranted. Yet it was true that the Franco-Soviet Pact, ratified in the spring of 1936, provided another disconcerting piece of evidence to Tokyo that its longtime rival on the East Asian mainland was maneuvering its way out of diplomatic isolation and had dramatically improved its political and diplomatic position since 1931. During the same time period, Japan's diplomatic isolation from the rest of the world had grown measurably. The French reaction was one of surprise and concern. Foreign Minister Yvon Delbos expressed his dismay, especially in view of France's reassurances regarding its relationship with Moscow and continued friendship for Japan. From Tokyo, Ambassador Albert Kammerer expressed a fear, undoubtedly shared by many others, that although the pact might not have much bearing on the Far East, even a declaration as limited as the Anti-Comintern Pact would have consequences for the European situation and therefore for France. When the French expressed their concerns about the Japanese action, Foreign Minister Arita dismissed them by telling them not to place much credence in rumors initiated by the Soviet Union, especially with regard to military aspects of the pact.[74] Again, however, when asked by the Chinese to join in making a declaration to counterbalance the effects of the Nazi-Japanese agreement, Paris declined, resorting to its favorite position that because of concern for its interests in the Far East, it must avoid taking an initiative in the matter, although it would be willing to join with other powers in a collective declaration.[75]

Nevertheless (as Colonel Charles Mast, the French military attaché in Tokyo, articulated), some Frenchmen were becoming increasingly worried about the deterioration of the French relationship with Japan. In four short years, Mast argued, France had lost the position of considerable prestige in Japan that it had enjoyed after World War I. The essential cause of this reversal of fortune was the Franco-Soviet Pact, combined with the obvious German successes in Europe and the concomitant crumbling of the French security system. Both of these developments had made a profound impression on Japan's military circles, which were increasingly dominated by Germanophiles. In order to reestablish the French position, Mast argued, it would be advisable to (1) utilize the French relationship with Japan and Russia to mediate the outstanding differences between the two powers; (2) court those military officers in Japan who remained favorably disposed toward France and thereby try to modify the pro-German attitude of the high command; (3) utilize all propaganda channels to emphasize conflicting German and Japanese interests in China; (4) finally, and most essentially, reestablish for Japan the credibility of French military power vis-à-vis Germany. Even taking into account Mast's position and obvious military bias, as well as the fact that the Franco-Soviet Pact had been widely opposed in French military circles (thereby helping to block Soviet efforts to conclude a military convention to the pact), his apprehensions were shared by increasing numbers of French. For example, Ambassador Kammerer fully supported the main points of Colonel Mast's analysis and recommendations, arguing that the harmful nature of the pact stemmed from the fact that it would not "reassure Japan of our pure and simple neutrality."[76]

While there is no evidence that Mast's recommendations were acted upon—indeed, some of them flew in the face of the government's general inclination to maintain a low profile in Far Eastern disputes—the evidence suggests that the French began to give more thought to Japan's long-term objectives and to French Far Eastern interests. In fact, six months earlier Kammerer's predecessor, Fernand Pila, had warned that Japan's expansionistic tendencies would soon impose a fundamental choice upon Japan's leaders—whether it should continue its active policy in north China or whether it should turn toward the south. Pila had presciently estimated that much would depend upon which military faction established its ascendancy—the northward-looking army or the southward-looking navy. In either case, the situation bore watching, but should the latter path be pursued, the consequences for French interests would be perilous. Subsequent speculation that Japan had designs on the Chinese-controlled island of Hainan in the Gulf of Tonkin, within striking distance of much of Indochina, provoked alarm in the Quai d'Orsay for the stability and security of the colony. Certainly, as the Far Eastern Department warned at the end of 1936, past experience proved the impossibility of correctly predicting the future of the situation in the Far East. Just the complexities of Chinese politics made it difficult to forecast an outcome. The most that France could do would be to follow closely the developments in the area, being careful not to align itself with either side, but always being ready to defend its own interests. The unwillingness of the French government to do more was still apparent in the spring of 1937. When the new French ambassador in Tokyo, Charles-Arsène Henry, suggested that it might be a propitious moment to revive peace negotiations between Japan and China, despite obvious difficulties, the notion was dismissed by a Foreign Ministry notation; "What contradictions!"[77]

This, of course, did nothing to resolve the fundamental differences between Japan and China, and warnings continued to flow into Paris from French posts in the Far East. On 30 June 1937, virtually on the eve of the next major round of fighting, Colonel Gabriel Sabbatier, the French military attaché in Peking, wired his concerns. Although he believed that the atmosphere in the area had relaxed somewhat, "this situation . . . could prolong itself for a long time yet but not indefinitely." Very basic differences continued to separate Japan and China: "By virtue of its dynamism, Japan tends to absorb China little by little, politically and economically. China, which is perfectly aware of the danger that menaces it, is decided to remain master of its destiny." Consequently, while war might not be in the offing immediately, "it is an eventuality to be considered seriously." Moreover, Sabbatier feared that a future conflict might well reveal the global implications of the struggle going on in the Far East. For France and its possessions—especially Indochina—such renewed conflict might have great consequences. In the event of a Japanese attack on Indochina, Tokyo would first want to secure control of Hainan as an indispensable base for operations. So France, he argued, must remain particularly alert about that island's fate. Moreover, France should not neglect any aid that China might be able to render in defense of the colony. As long as China did not become friendly with Japan, he believed, Indochina had nothing to fear from its northern neighbor. Indeed, it should view favorably the development of China's military power, for it would present an obstacle to continued Japanese expansion on the continent.[78] Sabbatier's sense of timing may have been incorrect, but as events soon proved, his sense of gloom was well grounded.

During the period from 1931 to 1933, the Manchurian crisis posed some fundamental questions for French foreign policymakers. For the first time, they were forced to consider the nature of French interests in the Far East and relate them to the alternatives and resources available to France in preserving those interests. To be sure, for much of the crisis the situation was not nearly so clear in the minds of the French statesmen. It could not be otherwise, considering the paucity of reliable information available concerning the situation in the area as well as the inability of key decision makers to focus on the issues involved. Consequently, policy remained muddled and was carried out in fits and starts. Domestic concerns related to the deepening economic depression had a significant impact. Although in retrospect it seems clear that the depression in France was not as severe as in other industrialized nations, it would have been hard to convince Frenchmen of that fact at the time. They felt on the verge of economic disaster. Anything that would divert the government's attention from this problem or any policy that risked exasperating the situation—for example, the loss of an overseas market by the use of sanctions— would not be tolerated. Additionally, any forceful action might stimulate a violent reaction from Japan (few seemed to doubt that Japan would fight if cornered), the consequences of which for the security of French possessions might be severe. This might not have been a problem if France felt confident about its military capabilities in the area. But in fact, of course, France was in no position on land or at sea to put up much resistance to a determined Japanese thrust. The lack of military wherewithal in the Far East, however, was largely dictated by the overriding French concern about developments in Europe. The unstable German situation, culminating with Hitler's advent to power, necessarily diverted French attention and resources. Indeed, French attention on events on the other side of the "blue line of the Vosages" was the single most important factor in France's determination to play it safe in the Far East.

Such considerations might have been less formidable if the United States and Britain had been willing to take forceful action. Without the support of those nations—indeed, without the support of even one of them—no action, whether economic or military could have been successful. But in the light of their own difficulties, the Americans were increasingly unable to do much more than some fitful posturing and moralizing. If the United States would not act, Britain surely would not. Indeed, the misunderstandings and acrimonious debate that developed between the two English-speaking states concerning the best path to pursue made it even more unlikely that they could develop a coordinated policy. Consequently, there may have been no small amount of posturing by France itself when it repeated its willingness to participate in collective action by the great powers. Knowing full well that neither America nor Britain was inclined to take the initiative, France could feel safe in making such an offer.

It must also be considered that there existed in France a good deal of residual sympathy for Japan. A former ally and longtime friend, the stability, achievements, and at least superficially Western attributes of Japan stood in stark contrast to the impression of chaos, division, and xenophobic condition of China. Moreover, through the use of troops to defend their interests, the Japanese in some ways appeared to be doing no more than what France and the other Western powers had repeatedly done in China in the past. To be sure, it remained to be seen whether Japan would continue to honor the Open Door as it had promised. On the other hand, Japanese development of Manchuria might actually improve trading opportunities there. In any event, distrust of Chinese intentions toward Western interests in the country prevented many from automatically assuming that a victorious China would remain friendly. Indeed, much evidence suggested the opposite.

In the end, with all of these factors in mind, it is not surprising that France pursued the path of caution. It seemed far wiser to allow the principals to resolve the issue between themselves, while taking care that the fighting be limited to the contested area. In fact, remaining uninvolved might be one way to guarantee that the conflict would not spread. It was not a bold policy, if indeed it was a policy at all, but given the overriding concerns and commitments of France elsewhere, it seemed to be a pragmatic one.

five

OPPORTUNITY LOST:
THE SINO-JAPANESE CONFLICT
THROUGH THE BRUSSELS
CONFERENCE

W HEN fighting broke out between Chinese and Japanese forces in
North China on 7 July 1937, the information reaching the
French Foreign Ministry was deceptively optimistic, and no sense of
emergency existed in Paris. The attention of most Frenchmen was
riveted on the Spanish Civil War, which was at its peak and had produced a severe Mediterranean crisis because of a sharp increase in attacks against neutral shipping in the area. From Paris, the American
ambassador, William C. Bullitt, observed, "The French Government
faced by its troubles in Europe is somewhat loathe to take any active
part with regard to matters in the Far East."[1] Initially, the French responded as usual to the renewed Far Eastern hostilities, instructing
their representatives in Tokyo and Nanking merely to express their
concern and to cooperate with any attempts by the British and American representatives to urge moderation and conciliation.[2] But as the
fighting escalated, it became clear that the problem could not be so
easily settled. Moreover, for France to remain detached from the
events of the area for long would prove to be impossible. Indeed, on
13 July, the Chinese ambassador in Paris, Wellington Koo, asked the
French foreign minister, Yvon Delbos, about the French reaction if
China took its case to the League of Nations. Delbos asked for time
to consider the question, but it is evident that he and other French
policymakers vigorously opposed such an appeal to the League. That
body could hardly refuse to take up such a request from one of its
members. But Japan obviously would reject any approach by the
League, and the "most dangerous of impasses" would develop.
Therefore, unless its members were willing to resort to sanctions under Article Sixteen of the Charter, as had happened during the
Abyssinian crisis, little could be done, and, in fact, the traditional impotence of the League would once again be demonstrated.[3] As Delbos
subsequently admitted to U.S. Ambassador Bullitt, the League had
become a cipher, and "the only result of a Chinese appeal would be

[that] the cipher would become the shadow of a cipher. The League still had some utility in Europe and he [Delbos] did not wish to see it made ridiculous."[4] The Quai d'Orsay warned that should the League impose sanctions, the risks for France would be twofold: first, such sanctions would be only marginally effective and would lead Japan to seek revenge against Western interests in the Far East, including the militarily vulnerable French Indochina; second, French policy had to focus on Europe, and if the authority of the League were further damaged by its inability to act favorably, the impact on Europe would be serious. Delbos advised Koo, "You might as well call on the moon for help as on the League of Nations."[5]

Instead, the French favored an appeal to the signatories of the Nine Power Treaty of 1922, which had pledged the powers to respect China's independence. As Delbos put it, "Taught by the experience of the Manchukuo affair, we must search for a method that puts the United States in the obligation of immediately taking their share of the common responsibility incumbent on all signatories of the Nine Power Treaty. The Quai d'Orsay feared that "the intervention of the League of Nations will furnish Washington with a convenient excuse to restrict American action to encouragements of a moral nature," under the pretext that it could not officially associate itself with the policy of the League.[6] While the United States was not a member of the League, it was a signatory of the Nine Power Pact.

The British Foreign Office poured cold water over the idea of a conference between the Washington signatories. The time was not right, the British argued, for the Japanese had consistently maintained the attitude that Sino-Japanese relations were a matter to be settled between the two countries alone rather than by the intervention of a third party. The Foreign Office recalled that even at the Washington Conference difficulties between Japan and China had been resolved outside the conference. Only if it became clear that a conference could be called "without wearing the appearance of putting joint pressure on Japan and so antagonizing her from the start," would Britain join in such a plan.[7]

Under pressure from the Chinese, who continued to threaten to take their case to the League, Delbos doggedly worked for a united Western démarche to the Japanese. Simultaneous, though not joint, approaches would be make by France, Britain, and the United States in which the powers would politely indicate that they had no intention of abandoning their rights and privileges in China, that the conflict was infringing upon those rights and privileges in China, and that China and Japan should attempt to negotiate a peaceful solution to the dispute.[8] Clearly, the paramount consideration in Delbos's mind remained the necessity for close French cooperation with Britain and the United States.[9] When China indicated at the beginning of September that it had decided to bring the dispute before the League, Delbos quickly urged the United States to send an observer to Geneva, as had been done during the Manchurian crisis, and thereby encourage the League to take strong action by condemning Japanese aggression. He also urged Washington to issue a parallel, though independent, condemnation. He admitted that such a censure by the League would not resolve anything, but it might be heartening to the Chinese and would help them gain the support of world public opinion.[10]

But the French foreign minister was not ready to concede that the issue necessarily had to be brought before the League. At a meeting of the League's Far Eastern Advisory Committee in September, Delbos took the initiative of suggesting to the American representative in Geneva that the matter be taken out of the hands of the Advisory Committee and be given to a subcommittee made up of representatives of those nations directly involved in the Far East.[11] Here would be a body that might be able to act decisively, just as a similar body at the Nyon Conference had recently acted to calm the sensitive Mediterranean crisis brought on by the Spanish Civil War. Perhaps such a step would mollify the Chinese, at least temporarily.

Whatever the vehicle utilized, the Quai d'Orsay suggested only two alternatives for resolving the crisis. The first would be to place responsibility for the conflict upon the Japanese, refusing to recognize any change in the status quo brought about by force of arms. The second would be to condemn the use of warfare against the civilian population and to offer immediate assistance to China. Of the two alternatives, the second appeared to be the less risky. It was the more moderate alternative, and it had the advantage of not furnishing Japan with an excuse for recriminations. The first option, on the other hand, had the drawback of humiliating and raising the rancor of Japan without actually helping the Chinese. Japanese hostility had been virulent enough when a similar situation had developed in Manchuria, where Western interests had been minimal. But it would be quite different in China proper where large French and British interests would be directly threatened. Such an act would serve only "to underline the weakness other than verbal" of the powers.[12]

French concerns intensified following a thinly veiled Japanese threat of 12 September. In a conversation with the French ambassador in Tokyo, Charles-Arsène Henry, the Japanese foreign minister, Koki

Hirota, warned of the possibly bad effect on French Far Eastern interests should France support China at the League session. Henry cautioned the Quai d'Orsay, "I have the clear impression that if at Geneva we overtly support China in an action which can have no practical result but which will nonetheless be very much resented by Japan, we will find her very worked up against us here in the Far East."[13] In spite of such fears, however, on 27 September the League proceeded to pass the Cranborne Resolution condemning the Japanese bombing. A few days later, the Assembly adopted two reports of the subcommittee which stated that Japan had violated its treaty obligations, expressed the Assembly's "moral support" for China, and urged its members to "consider how far they can individually extend aid to China." It further recommended that a conference of the Washington Treaty powers be held to consider how to end the conflict.[14] This was precisely what the Quai d'Orsay had feared—action strong enough to antagonize Japan but too weak to restrain her or to aid China effectively. On the other hand, the idea of a conference of the signatories of the Nine Power Treaty finally appeared on the verge of becoming reality. The United States, as one of the signatories, would be actively brought into the picture.

As the powers made halting progress toward setting up a nine-power conference to be held in Brussels in November, the French position became increasingly equivocal. Alexis Léger, the secretary general at the Quai d'Orsay, indicated that continued tension in Europe related to the Spanish Civil War would make it impossible for France to take part in any common action in the Far East, such as the application of economic sanctions against Japan, that might necessitate the use of armed force. France could not even spare additional forces that would be needed to defend its own vulnerable possessions in the event of a general conflict in the area. Léger lamented that "it was regrettable that this situation existed which served to facilitate aggression in the Far East but the situation was a fact and had to be faced."[15] Such concern reflected the increasingly difficult position in which France found herself in the Far East, and at the end of October France took a step to improve her position with regard to Japan and the upcoming Nine Power Conference.

France had extended considerable direct and indirect aid to Chiang Kai-shek's forces after the outbreak of fighting. Indeed, Indochina had become one of the major supply routes for the Chinese. Over a railroad running from Haiphong to Yunnanfu, a steady stream of badly needed war materiel flowed to the Nationalist forces. Initially, the Japanese had shown no great concern about such supplies being sent to China. But as the war dragged on, Japan made increasingly vigorous efforts to limit the flow of such materiel into China by harassing neutral shipping in the China Sea. France, along with the other powers, protested such activities, but Tokyo, while apologizing, refused to back down. They warned France that since the importation of such war supplies would undoubtedly enhance Chinese opposition to Japan, "future developments may compel the Japanese Government to devise more effective and suitable measures to stop all importations of arms and ammunition into China." Consequently, as the fighting in China spread southward, the French became more fearful that Japan might make a bold stroke to end the flow of supplies entering through Indochina by moving against Yunnan province adjacent to Indochina or by occupying Hainan Island in the Gulf of Tonkin. In either case, the security of Indochina, whose defenses were woefully inadequate, would be endangered.[16]

In fact, on 28 September, the Japanese warned that they would bombard the section of the railroad that ran through Chinese territory "if it were established that war materiel was transported by this line."[17] This warning sparked a reappraisal of French policy.

The Far Eastern Department of the Quai d'Orsay argued that prolongation of the conflict would endanger French commercial, financial, and cultural interests as well as the security of Indochina. It recalled that France had given considerable aid to and sympathy for the Chinese cause, but it now questioned "whether we could go further, without gravely compromising French interests in Indochina and in the Pacific." If France increased its aid to China, as the Chinese urged, Japan would be aroused to take measures against Indochina. The Far Eastern Department concluded, "We cannot hope to protect our positions in the Far East against Japan and at the same time allow these positions to serve as a base of operations to organize a massive resupply of China in arms, munitions, and planes." The "practical solution" to the problem would be to prohibit the transportation of all war materiel through Indochina. Thus, any pretext for Japanese intervention in Chinese territory where France held special interests would be removed.[18]

The fundamental problem, which had been considered earlier but kept at arm's length, had been laid before the government. How could France's sympathy for the Chinese cause be reconciled with the necessity of maintaining good relations with Japan for the purpose of protecting the security of Indochina? On 12 October, the Council of National Defense met to consider the situation. Apparently a division developed among the French ministers, with the

Socialists favoring continuation of arms shipments through Indochina and the Radical Socialists, perhaps excluding the minister of national defense, Edouard Daladier, arguing that such transit would risk retaliation from Japan.[19] The Radical Socialists succeeded in gaining the adoption of a policy that placed an embargo on the shipment through Indochina of any war materiel destined for China. In reviewing the decision afterward, the Far Eastern Department reiterated, "The abuse of the facilities for the resupply of China in our colony would risk, in effect, leading Japan to take preventive measures in the form of an occupation of Hainan Island or in military operations in the immediately surrounding area of the Indochinese frontier and the destruction of the French railroad in Yunnan, which would not fail to place a heavy mortgage on the security of our possessions in the Far East, or else even drag them into the orbit of the Sino-Japanese conflict." The French decision covered all materiel from French factories; it also prohibited the transit of such goods from other nations through Indochina.[20]

The response by the powers with significant interests in China and the Pacific was predictable. The Chinese protested that the decision ran contrary to the League's recommendation. Moreover, since war had not been officially declared in the Far East, the French were acting in violation of conventional international practice by prohibiting such shipments. The British, who feared that the Japanese would now be able to focus their attention on Hong Kong, the only other major channel of arms supply for Chiang's forces, considered the decision "unreasonable" and "pusillanimous." Alexander Cadogan, deputy undersecretary at the British Foreign Office, argued, "It is improbable that, if munitions of war were transported over the railways, the Japanese would risk involving themselves in international complications by attempting to attack the lines within French territory." President Roosevelt relayed his "purely personal" opinion that "this measure risks prejudicing China and placing that country in an unfavorable situation at the opening of the Brussels Conference." The Americans asked the French to reexamine their decision.[21] Under this pressure, the most important members of the French cabinet involved in foreign policy-making met on 22 October to reconsider the issue. Some members—mainly the Socialists in the government coalition— had never favored prohibiting the Indochinese transit and now wanted to lift the ban completely. Delbos, however, insisted that it should be maintained until the Brussels Conference met. Ultimately, the two sides struck a compromise that allowed a relaxation of some of the restrictions. French materiel ordered before 15 July 1937, or supplies that had been shipped before 13 October, would be allowed transit through Indochina.[22]

The French explained the decision to prohibit arms shipments through Indochina in what came to familiar terms. First, as Premier Camille Chautemps put it, the Japanese, "in a most polite way but letting him feel the iron," had indicated that they had long memories and that, should a European war break out, they would remember those who had committed unfriendly acts. Second, the Japanese had threatened not only to destroy that part of the French-owned Haiphong-Yunnanfu Railroad that ran through China but to seize the Chinese island of Hainan, a move that would allow them to dominate the Gulf of Tonkin and which further would place them in a good position to threaten the security of Indochina.[23] Simply put, French possessions and interests were too exposed to risk retaliation by Japan. While these arguments contained merit—for the Japanese had indeed threatened such action—when viewed in conjunction with other developments of the period, they are insufficient as motives that would explain fully the French action at this particular time.

With the Brussels Conference less than three weeks away, an objective appraisal suggests that the French would have delayed making such an important unilateral decision pending the outcome of the conference, and especially the clarification of great-power attitudes. Moreover, the decision came in the aftermath of President Roosevelt's sensational Quarantine Speech in Chicago on 5 October, in which he regretted the spread of "international lawlessness" and proposed that those responsible for it be "quarantined," just as one would isolate carriers of epidemic diseases. While Roosevelt's motives and meaning have remained matters of speculation,[24] the speech had a profound impact abroad. Little doubt existed that the statement had been aimed at Japanese activities in China. Perhaps, this time, Roosevelt had really sounded the tocsin and meant to take effective action. Jules Henry, the French chargé d'affaires in Washington, was cautiously optimistic. He warned that it would be premature to consider the speech a prelude to vigorous American cooperation—for the reaction of the American people and of the Congress had yet to be considered—and that "it is therefore important not to yield to conclusions that subsequent events did not justify." Yet he believed that the speech was the most important that Roosevelt had made on foreign policy since ascending to the presidency. In fact, no president since Wilson had make declarations of "such lofty moral impact."[25] When Secretary of State Cordell Hull struck a similar chord in a speech on 22 October, Henry enthusiastically wired Paris, "Hull wants to convince the countries who resort to warlike methods to achieve their claims, that they will sooner or later dearly pay the price for their errors."[26]

Why, then, given the apparent prospects for great-power action, did the French decide to end arms shipments? In view of the evidence, it appears that they sought to exploit their strategic position in the Far East to wring guarantees for the security of Indochina from Britain and the United States at the Brussels Conference. When Delbos informed the French ambassador in Tokyo of the government's decision, he indicated that it was a step that "the results of the Brussels Conference could eventually lead us to revise." When explaining the decision to the British and American representatives in Paris, he pressed home the same point. After meeting with Delbos, Eric Phipps, the British ambassador in Paris, informed the Foreign Office that the French would insist upon obtaining a general guarantee from the powers gathered at Brussels before allowing transit through Indochina to be restored.[27] American Ambassador Bullitt in Paris reported to the State Department that Delbos had indicated that France would permit the shipment of arms through Indochina "on condition that if Japan should attack French Indo-China France would receive physical support from the other members of the Brussels Conference in protecting Indo-China."[28] Given the hopeful signs of American action, the French wished to direct it in a way that would be most beneficial to their interests in the Far East. Their posture at the Brussels Conference confirms this analysis.

So much anticipation and planning preceded it that it is ironic that by the time the Nine Power Conference opened in Brussels on 3 November, few people in France—or elsewhere, for that matter—expected substantive results. As had been widely anticipated, Japan had announced that it would not attend the meeting. Tokyo claimed that it was simply defending its interests in China and alleged that as in 1931 Japan would not receive a fair hearing at the conference even if in attendance.[29] Jay Pierrepont Moffat, a member of the American delegation, observed upon his arrival in Brussels, "I have never known a conference where even before we meet people are discussing ways to end it," and from Paris, Ambassador Bullitt wrote to a friend at the State Department, Judge R. Walton Moore, "There is less than no interest in the Brussels Conference and the only idea of the French is to avoid any friction with the Japanese."[30] Nevertheless, almost immediately upon arriving in Brussels, Delbos, leading the French delegation, resumed his effort to push the United States to the fore and secure its firm commitment of support. At a preconference planning session on the afternoon of 2 November, with Norman Davis, the chief American delegate, Anthony Eden, leading the British delegation, and Paul-Henri Spaak, Belgium's foreign minister, Delbos made it clear that he opposed using the conference simply to educate public opinion. In fact, he opposed the idea of having any public sessions at all. Only in the face of united American-British pressure did he agree to a series of keynote addresses to initiate the conference. Davis interpreted this reluctance to hold public sessions as indicative of Delbos's desire to adjourn as quickly as possible.[31] He misread the Frenchman's intent.

As Delbos guessed, the keynote speeches the following day were lackluster. With many eyes focused upon the American position, Davis produced a disappointingly mild address, emphasizing conciliation and a peaceful settlement. Eden followed suit, and Delbos, still unconvinced of the usefulness of such a session, simply added his useful but "colorless" support. Although the Italian delegate, Count Luigi Aldrovandi, temporarily fired up the session, the mood was more graphically displayed when the assembled delegations roundly cheered the Portuguese delegate for the brevity of his minute-and-a-half speech.[32]

Late that evening, Delbos made his way to Davis's room, seeking to establish the French position in the type of private session that he preferred. In a free-swinging exchange in front of members of the British delegation, the two men argued their positions. Davis initiated the discussion by noting the recent French action with regard to the transit of arms through Indochina and asked whether France would be willing to take action should the conference fail to end the conflict or merely "hand over Indo-China to Japan." Delbos retorted that they would "prefer to give Japan the Philippines." Having temporarily checked the American delegate, Delbos seized the opportunity to express his viewpoint about the conference and the international situation. He pointed out that it might be desirable to adopt a firm line but insisted that the conferees must not utter any threats that they might not be able to carry out. He argued that it was futile to expect Japan to cooperate with the conference or to abide by the decisions of the powers assembled at Brussels unless Tokyo began to encounter military difficulty in China. Therefore, rather than attempting to impose sanctions against Japan, it might make more sense to extend aid to Chiang Kai-shek. Of course, such action might provoke an aggressive Japanese response. Japan might tighten its blockade of China, thus inevitably creating the possibility of incidents with the Western powers. But this might be overcome by

Western cooperation to protect the sea lanes, as had been done recently in the Mediterranean. A more serious problem would result if Japan reacted with direct reprisals against those governments aiding China that held Far Eastern possessions. The powers could be protected only by a mutual guarantee of security. The French foreign minister reminded Davis of the Japanese warnings against using Indochina for the transit of supplies to China. Delbos reiterated that "we do not want to confront them alone should the occasion arise." Although he did not ask for a guarantee for the French colony from the United States or Britain, he obviously planted the seeds for such a request by suggesting that contingency plans be discussed in case a Japanese attack occurred.

Davis refused to be drawn into a discussion of specific action, preferring to talk about moral pressure and mediation. When the American sought to link the Far East with general world conditions, Delbos forcefully invoked his case for a united front of democratic nations. In the face of outrageous aggression by the dictatorships, "civilization had been retreating." Only an organized front of free nations could stop the retreat, and the only leader who could organize such a "peace front" was President Roosevelt, who could call together a world conference. Until such an event could be organized, France, Britain, and the United States should work together as closely as possible with regard to the Far East. Delbos believed that his position enjoyed considerable support from the British, but Davis deftly parried his suggestions. The "woolly old man," as one senior British official labeled Davis, argued that it was impossible for his government to make precise commitments, especially in an area where America's direct interests were not so great as those of other powers who seemed reluctant to assume any risk in defending them. Moreover, if the Brussels Conference failed to solve the Far Eastern crisis, it would be highly unlikely that President Roosevelt could be convinced that a larger conference could resolve the many other complex problems confronting the world. Davis suggested that France, as well as Britain, actually faced two crises—one in Europe and the other in the Far East—and that "France must decide which could most readily be settled." American public opinion would not allow United States involvement in European affairs, but he held out hope that "in the Far Eastern one we might be able to help somewhat as we were numbers of the Nine Power Pact and had certain obligations."[33]

As Delbos later recalled, "I . . . tried to obtain at the very least a solidarity in the Far East." But, he must surely have had ambivalent feelings about the results of the meeting. If one were compiling points to determine the winner of the verbal sparring that had occurred, Delbos probably would emerge the victor. Unfortunately for him, there was no scorecard to record the victory. He had clearly made a pertinent point that the United States must not expect other nations to state what they were prepared to do while at the same time remaining uncommitted itself. But just as clearly, Davis had refused to alter his position. As Delbos lamented, "Any idea of international solidarity remains foreign to the conceptions of the American delegate." Conversely, Davis left the meeting disillusioned about French intentions. He wired Secretary of State Cordell Hull that France had "no interest in the Conference unless she can get assurances from Great Britain and ourselves of protection for her possessions in the Orient, or if the Conference will enable her to bring about a political front of the leading democratic nations." He subsequently complained over the telephone to Bullitt in Paris, "They are not willing to take any responsibility. The whole purpose is to push us out front."[34]

Over the next few days, Delbos continued to press Davis to consider alternatives to moral diplomacy and mediation as a means of resolving the crisis. Delbos may have been aware of the division within the American delegation as to the appropriate policy to pursue. The two chief advisers to Davis at the conference—Moffat, head of the European Division at the State Department, and Stanley Hornbeck, the department's political adviser on the Far East—held dramatically opposite views. Moffat opposed any American involvement in the Far East, while Hornbeck believed that the United States should act forcefully in the area.[35] If the point of view embraced by Hornbeck held any chance of becoming official American policy, Delbos undoubtedly wished to do whatever he could to encourage its adoption.

French hopes soared in the wake of a report from Jules Henry, chargé d'affaires in Washington, in which he described a meeting with President Roosevelt on 6 November. While visiting the White House with Jacques Stern, a former French minister of colonies, on rather routine business, Henry was suddenly reproached by Roosevelt about the French decision to stop the flow of arms through Indochina to China. Henry quickly defended the decision on the grounds that it had been motivated by considerations of national security. The president responded, "I am perfectly aware of your point of view. However, I have the impression that you have perhaps some unfounded fears. . . . " He followed up by telling Henry, "Besides, do they not clearly realize in France *that a Japanese attack against Hong-Kong, or Indochina or the Dutch Indies would constitute equally an attack against the Philippines?* [Italics Henry's.] In this eventuality, our common interests would be endangered and we would have to defend them together." Roosevelt went on to describe the isolationist sentiment in the United States but denied that any of the sentiment heard or the legislation passed had actually brought the American people the security that they sought: "By no means, for it brought about risks and can lead to dangerous situations, even war." The existence of such possibilities, he admitted, had led him to deliver his speech in Chicago. Henry enthusiastically noted, "In the course of this exceptionally cordial and frank meeting, Roosevelt gave me once more the impression that he was truly moved by profoundly friendly feelings toward France." On the other hand, Henry cautioned that these were purely Roosevelt's own personal ideas. Obviously, the press and Congress had demonstrated opposition: "These are the realities that it is necessary not to lose sight of." Henry concluded that Roosevelt "appeared determined to push as far as possible his policy of international collaboration, and to awaken [public] opinion." That being the case, with France being more favorably viewed than at any time since 1919, it behooved France to do all that it could to cultivate these feelings.[36]

Delbos must have been elated by Henry's report. But, surely, he was somewhat confused as well. As he asked Bullitt over the phone, who more correctly had ascertained American policy—Davis or Henry?[37] Clearly, what Roosevelt had said in Washington did not correspond to what Davis had said in Brussels, nor was it consistent with subsequent comments made by members of the State Department.[38] Consequently, on the evening of 9 November, Delbos wired directions to Henry that he should restate the basic French position to Roosevelt. He reiterated that "we are not in the presence of a vague and distant general threat, but of intentions and preparations as precise as they are immediate." He recalled the pattern of Japan's behavior in China and its thinly veiled threats against Indochina and the surrounding area. He reminded the president that France's decision to halt the transit of arms through Indochina had been conditional, depending upon the nature and extent of international cooperation that developed at Brussels. In that regard, he expressed his great disappointment with the attitude of Norman Davis thus far, as well as with the American delegate's refusal to recognize Indochina's vulnerability to Japanese reprisals. Surely, he suggested, Davis would not assume a position that was out of step with that of the State Department. Therefore, he gravely exhorted, as long as the American position remained the same, France, as desirous as it was of reaffirming "the policy of solidarity" as suggested in Chicago, "will be forced to observe in this question a particular prudence." Delbos admitted that he understood the difficulties Roosevelt confronted in leading a public that was far behind him in recognizing the threat. By the same token, however, Roosevelt must understand that in the presence of the threatening general situation, "the opinion of our country would legitimately fear seeing France expose itself, alone, to complications in the Far East which could bring about singular temptations for whoever would want to disturb European peace."[39]

The previous evening, Ambassador Bullitt had relayed a request from Davis that Delbos return to Brussels.[40] Upon his departure late on the evening of 9 November, following his wire to Henry, Delbos must have buoyantly expected that positive action would be taken by the conferees in Brussels. Roosevelt's statement to Henry fueled considerable hope that the Americans would finally take the lead, and Henry had been directed to reinforce such an inclination by reemphasizing the need for a direct, cooperative Western response to restrain Japan. Maybe Davis's invitation held promise in this direction.

Meanwhile, Premier Camille Chautemps took the occasion of a routine luncheon on 10 November to impress upon Bullitt the French position. He suggested that it was easy for the United States to view France and Britain as acting like "scared rabbits," but perhaps America was acting most scared, since no gun was pointed at her. He sympathized with America's desire to remain neutral in any conflict that might break out. "What I cannot understand," he argued, "is that you Americans from time to time talk as if you really intend to act in the international sphere when you have no intention of acting in any way that can be effective." He contended that if this were the case with regard to Roosevelt's speech in Chicago, it would have been infinitely better had the president said nothing. "Such a policy on the part of the United States merely leads the dictatorships to believe that the democracies are full of words but are unwilling to back up their words by force, and force is the only thing that counts today in the world." As Chautemps saw the situation, two courses of constructive action were open to the United States: first, it could announce its determination to oppose any aggressor by economic or military means; second, it could take an active, constructive role in attempting to establish world peace. Barring some action of this sort, "the world will rapidly enter the most horrible of wars." Although the Far Eastern crisis had given rise to the concerns of the moment, Chautemps revealed that the most intractable problem for France remained Germany. If the crisis in Franco-German relations were resolved, then all else would become possible. France would be willing to sacrifice a great deal, in its colonial empire, for example (although he offered no details), to achieve such a reconciliation. In any case, it could be accomplished only through the decisive influence of President Roosevelt. Chautemps concluded by repeating, partly for the benefit of Finance Minister Georges Bonnet, who had joined the conversation toward the end, "I believe the world is definitely doomed to war unless the United States either can take an engagement to enter war against an aggressor state or can take some effective action for peace, and I am convinced that the only way to peace in Europe and in other parts of the world is by way of reconciliation between France and Germany." To this, Bonnet added his complete concurrence.[41]

It is unlikely that his foreign minister would have approved of Chautemps's remarks about making colonial sacrifices to achieve a settlement with Germany. It manifestly smacked of the appeasement policy Bonnet would pursue during the following year after he became foreign minister. Certainly, the shifty Chautemps was quite inclined in that direction. Nevertheless, with regard to the crisis at hand—the Sino-Japanese conflict and the Brussels attempt to resolve it—the premier's points buttressed those that Delbos had sought to promote all along.

While these exchanges between Washington and Paris went on, the conference in Brussels had limped along. Upon the suggestion of Davis, the conferees had decided to issue a second invitation to Japan to attend, and, although virtually nobody expected a favorable response in view of previous Japanese statements, a major debate occurred over the wording of the document. Another major point of contention arose concerning the composition of a subcommittee that would attempt to work out a basis for mediation between China and Japan. After some hesitation, Delbos insisted that by virtue of being a great power with significant possessions in the Far East, France must be a member of the subcommittee. The French position opened a Pandora's box, for then Russia and Italy, among others, sought membership. Davis opposed expanding the subcommittee for fear of losing its effectiveness and having it appear to be a revival of the wartime alliance. Even after Delbos had returned to Paris on 5 November, the French delegation, now headed by François de Tessan, deputy undersecretary of state for foreign affairs, continued to maintain the attitude that they must be part of the negotiating subcommittee. Indeed, the issue apparently had not been resolved by the time Delbos returned to Brussels late on the ninth, and Davis tended increasingly to view this as typical French obstructionism.[42]

On 10 November, after his return to Brussels, Delbos hosted a luncheon for Eden, Davis, and their immediate advisers at the restaurant La Belle Meunière. It seems likely that Delbos expected considerable progress to be made at the meeting.[43] Initially, the main discussion focused upon the proper response to be made by the conferees should the Japanese, as expected, refuse the second invitation to participate in the conference. After considerable discussion about the nature of the declaration to be issued should the anticipated response occur, Davis went on to suggest that the good offices of the conference be offered to mediate the dispute. If nothing else, he argued, such an offer, if accepted by China and rejected by Japan, would place the regime of Chiang Kai-shek in a more favorable light in world public opinion and would emphasize Tokyo's intransigence. To Delbos, this must have smacked of more of the same thing he had opposed from the beginning of the conference, emphasis on a peaceful solution and the education of public opinion. He reacted vigorously, questioning the wisdom of such a mediation offer as an implication of a weakening of China's will to resist. Beyond that, however, the Frenchman was eager to get to the bottom line. "We should," he argued, "already begin to consider how far we would be willing ultimately to go." Delbos reiterated his familiar position that France was prepared to go as far as the United States, provided there was complete solidarity. Since she was deeply committed in China and confronted with stubborn resistance, "Japan had little stomach for risking hostilities with the Western powers if she knew that they were definitely united." If all of the powers could contribute something, even if only minor, the cumulative effect would be significant. He recounted France's position regarding munitions traffic through Indochina and revived the idea of a guarantee for that colony. Eden recorded that "Delbos said categorically that France was ready to co-operate to the utmost limit of her available resources and that just as she would undertake to do her share in protecting and helping any nation which might be victimized by Japan on account of its part in any collective action, so she would expect that any help and protection which might be necessary should be accorded her by the other Powers concerned." Indeed, although a bit more equivocal than Delbos, the British foreign secretary repeated his nation's willingness to go as far as the United States. Specifically, he suggested that although, in view of the Abyssinian episode, economic sanctions would not be popular in Britain, his government would be willing to follow the United States in such a course of action. An alternative might be a combined naval display of force in the Far East. Eden indicated his impatience, too, by arguing that the conferees could not stay in Brussels indefinitely and that the sooner they got down to brass tacks, the better.[44]

Davis temporized. He agreed that they could not delay much longer,[45] but he also indicated that when it came to considering questions of collective pressure on Japan, his government's hands were tied by neutrality legislation, which he hoped Congress might soon revise. "In the last analysis, public opinion would have to guide any decisions of the American Government." It was still too early to know what to do. Despite Davis's clear lack of enthusiasm for decisive action, or perhaps because of it, Delbos returned to the charge and concluded the meeting by arguing that he viewed a strong Western alignment as a deterrent to Japan as well as to the fascist nations. A strong policy in the Far East was justified as protection for possessions there, but also by the effect that it would have in Europe.

The three leaders resumed their discussions for an hour early that evening in Eden's suite, focusing upon further steps at the conference, should, as they assumed, Japan's reply prove unacceptable. They tentatively agreed on the tone and contents of a stiffer note to be sent to Japan in such an instance and on a timetable for working out a final resolution, although not on its contents. The normally cautious Davis, now straining at his own leash, allowed himself a short step out on a limb by indicating that they might consider the advisability of such acts as nonrecognition of Japanese conquests or the refusal to extend loans and credits to Japan. He repeated that these were his own suggestions and did not reflect the position of his government. Any significant change in policy would be dependent upon the attitude of Congress, which was due to meet the following week. Again, the implication that the neutrality laws might be revised (in Davis's case, the wish was undoubtedly the father to the thought) perked up the ears in the room. Delbos, reflecting his own impatience, remarked that if it had not been for the prospect of awaiting action by Congress, he would have strongly opposed proceeding as slowly as they had been doing.

The French foreign minister then repeated once more his very familiar position, but he added a couple of new twists. He indicated that he was still greatly preoccupied over the question of transit of war materiel through Indochina. He admitted that some of the pressure had been relieved by the decision to allow transit to any materiel already en route. He added that France "probably would always let airplanes through." This was an interesting admission that would assume considerably greater importance as the debate warmed up between France and Japan concerning exactly what goods constituted war materiel eligible for denial of transit rights. Delbos revealed that Indochina's nervous colonial authorities had been requesting additional ships and troops to strengthen the colony's defenses. The Frenchman came back to the dilemma confronting French policymakers: "France does not wish to back water in the affair. If she is not supported it would be necessary for her either to send more ships and men, which she cannot do as a result of conditions in Europe, or else she will have to close the railroad." Again, he argued that in the final resolution of the conference the powers could agree that in return for some form of "joint responsibility" France would keep the railroad open. France, in turn, would help keep Hong Kong open for the transit of goods to China.

When Davis indicated that he could not give any assurances or make any commitments along such lines, Delbos revealed his ace in the hole. He disclosed the substance of Jules Henry's meeting with Roosevelt on 6 November. Delbos emphasized that the president wanted to keep the railroad open and had indicated that an attack against Indochina "would create a community of interest and might even constitute a threat to the Philippines." On the basis of such discussions, Delbos believed that Davis would surely be receptive to the proposals he had suggested. Moffat recorded, "To this Mr. Davis made no response."[46]

Surprisingly, it appears that neither Davis nor the rest of his delegation had been apprised of the Roosevelt-Henry meeting. Even Acting Secretary of State Sumner Welles's attempt at qualifying the president's statements had not been shared with the delegation.[47] Certainly, Davis must have been surprised to learn of such an apparent shift of policy, especially from the French foreign minister. Upon reflection, however, skepticism probably dominated his thinking. Yet Davis, too, had become increasingly uneasy about the pace and direction of the conference. That very morning of the tenth, Davis had wired Roosevelt that prolonging it much longer, as the president had hoped, would be impossible in view of the conferees' inability to persuade Japan to cooperate. He urged a more active policy toward Japan, for "if moral pressure fails and we have to draw completely into a shell or to adopt a more positive policy we may find ourselves embarrassed or impotent." He advocated a revision of the neutrality legislation as it applied to Japan. "This would startle and worry Japan, encourage the Chinese and have a dynamic effect upon world opinion.[48] Given his own inclinations, Davis's noncommital attitude during his meetings on 10 November is amazing. More surprising still was his failure to report Delbos's revelations of the Roosevelt-

Henry meeting until 14 November. Perhaps, as John Haight suggests, since he had already made his appeal to Washington, he was prepared to sit back and await a response.[49]

The Brussels Conference had reached a critical stage. Both Delbos and Davis hoped for a breakthrough. The latter noticed and even commented that "the French attitude has improved appreciably of late and Delbos has been cooperative and helpful."[50] But the high expectations very quickly came crashing to the ground. Already, on the morning of 10 November, Henry called Alexis Léger at the Quai d'Orsay to relay some bad news. In a subsequent wire that Delbos received only at 9:00 P.M. that evening, after a hard but apparently effective day of negotiations with Davis and Eden, Henry spelled out disaster for Delbos's hopes. The previous evening, 9 November, Henry had met with Sumner Welles, acting secretary of state, who had received a wire from Bullitt reporting the different perceptions of the earlier Roosevelt-Henry talks. Welles wanted to set the record straight about the president's intent, for he believed that Bullitt's wire revealed that the French government could be "under the impression that in case of a Japanese attack against Indochina, the American fleet would participate in the defense of [the] colony." Welles pointed out that the president actually meant, "If the possessions of the powers in the Far East were the object of a Japanese attack, it would result in a world situation to which the United States could not remain indifferent." He emphasized the hypothetical nature of the situation discussed, not specific methods of handling it—a position Welles had assumed when he first learned of the meeting. Certainly, any idea of direct or indirect American protection for Indochina was to be dispelled. Henry repeated to Welles his conviction that he had heard the president correctly. Indeed, Henry and Stern had both been so struck by the president's words that they had compared notes afterward. Admittedly, the president had not spelled out just how Western interests could be defended (in fact, Henry did not claim that use of the American fleet had been considered).

Henry repeated to Delbos his conviction that he had accurately reported the essence of Roosevelt's views. Be that as it may, however, the fact remained that Welles had made a significant "rectification" of those views. The French chargé sought to explain the bewildering turn of events with a personal observation about Roosevelt's behavior:

It sometimes occurs to the president, whose temperament you know is impulsive, to express himself in terms that exceed his thoughts. He sometimes gives the impression of wanting to transform into acts intentions that he nurtures at one moment and which he is forced to abandon by the following. . . . Moreover, M. Roosevelt who, on the occasion of the current situation, is certainly far in advance of the ideas of the country and even of his own administration, finds himself in a situation delicate enough and it is difficult to foresee the possibility of development of the policy that he defined at Chicago.

With obvious disappointment, Henry concluded that, in view of this situation and the developments at Brussels, "We must manifest a great deal of prudence."[51]

When Henry met with Welles on the evening of the ninth, he had not yet received the full text of Delbos's wire of the same day urging the chargé to reiterate to the president the French position and to make certain of the positive American attitude that Henry had reported on the sixth. Welles's clarification of the American position to Henry had taken care of the latter concern, but the French chargé returned to see Welles on 10 November to relay the French position regarding the Far East and the Brussels Conference. Henry vigorously insisted that the dangers that threatened the security of Indochina were "neither as imaginary nor as distant" as officials in Washington and Brussels appeared to believe. As a result of such dangers, it would be impossible for France to change her position as long as the degree of cooperation that could be established at Brussels remained a matter of uncertainty. Obliquely alluding to Roosevelt's Chicago speech and subsequent statements made by Hull, Henry reminded Welles that in public as well as in private statements the American government had expressed its support for the democracies and its opposition to the aggression of the dictatorships. At that point, Welles interrupted to say that Henry knew full well the difficulty confronting the president given the state of public opinion and how much he must avoid the impression of taking sides. Henry retorted that such a problem did not escape his government. "But it appeared to us that in the present state of the world, and in view of the repercussions that Far Eastern affairs have on European affairs, any American moral call, any sympathetic gesture, even relative to questions of secondary importance, could only serve the common goals of our two countries such as the President himself had defined them in Chicago." Any other attitude would simply encourage those countries whose policies had been condemned by the United States. Henry believed that Welles was sympathetic, but of course nothing was promised.[52]

So it was that Delbos's short-lived hopes came to their abrupt end. Realizing that his cause was lost, he played an inconsequential role at another closed meeting of the major delegates on 11 November. He made no attempt to press Davis for additional commitments or to inquire about the American position. Davis, too, soon found his recommendations for stronger action against Japan quashed. On 12 November, Secretary of State Hull wired Davis that none of his proposals submitted on 10 November were acceptable to the Roosevelt administration. As Moffat delightfully recorded in his journal, the American delegation had been clearly informed by Hull, as well as by other messages from the State Department, that the administration "did not wish this Conference at least to take any positive steps."[53]

Events, previously snagged, now unraveled very quickly. On 12 November, Japan, flushed with the impending capture of Shanghai, sent the expected refusal of the second invitation to meet with the other signatories of the Nine Power Treaty. Tokyo reiterated its contention that the dispute concerned only Japan and China and therefore did not fall under the jurisdiction of the Nine Power Treaty. Since sanctions had been rejected in Washington—and therefore in Paris and London—little could be done. Consequently, when a general meeting of the Brussels Conference was held on 13 November, Delbos joined Davis and Eden in passively uttering platitudinous statements about the principles of international behavior, the sanctity of treaties, and the peaceful aims of the conference. Only the Chinese representative, Wellington Koo, interrupted the torpor, reminding the delegates that Japan had slapped them in the face. But his appeal for sanctions went ignored.[54] Ultimately, a declaration drafted by the American, British, and French delegations was submitted to the conference, and revisions of the text were hammered out.

The declaration was presented and adopted at a meeting of the conference on 15 November. The declaration reaffirmed that the conflict was indeed within the purview of the powers represented at Brussels, and it expressed the hope that Japan would confer with them. In a thinly veiled threat, it also stated that the powers would consider their "common attitude" toward Japan.[55] With that, since the Americans did not yet wish to terminate the proceedings, the conference recessed for a week. No decision had been reached on two important subjects: how to end the conference and how to treat Japan. Surely, many delegates sympathized with Hull's admonition to Davis that "there should be no admission of failure in any pronouncement made by the conference."[56] But it would be difficult to base a final resolution on the little tangible evidence of success available.

Meanwhile, additional, futile efforts toward a more forceful response by the Western powers went on behind the scenes. Davis still hoped to change the minds of policymakers in Washington. On 14 November, the chief American delegate strongly urged a commitment to action by his government. Unless some positive steps were taken, "most countries will lose their nerve and fold their hands," and Japan "will soon become firmly convinced that she can pursue her course without any danger of interference." But Hull responded on the fifteenth, "we feel that a strong reaffirmation of the principles which should underlie international relationships . . . would be the best method of off-setting such criticism [of a final resolution]." Hull subsequently reminded Davis that no prospect existed for the modification of the neutrality legislation. If any further proof of American unwillingness to take decisive action were needed, it came with Roosevelt's address to Congress on 15 November. The president did not even mention the Far East or the Brussels Conference, much less raise the issue of the neutrality legislation. On 17 November, Davis conceded defeat and wired Hull, "I bow to your judgment," agreeing to abide by Hull's wishes for a reaffirmation of principles.[57] Clearly, then, emphasis remained on moral diplomacy, rather than on sanctions.

When Delbos left Brussels on the fifteenth, apparently he had no intention of returning unless some clear sign of firm American leadership appeared. This did not mean that he simply sat back to await the results of Davis's exhortations to Washington. On the morning of 16 November, the day following his return to Paris, Delbos met with the Council of Ministers to review the Brussels declaration and to seek their counsel about how best to proceed from that point. Although records of the meeting do not exist, it is likely that Delbos told them what he told Charles Corbin, the French ambassador in London, when he relayed the government's instructions. Davis had consistently avoided all questions linking France and Britain in a common front with the United States in the event that a Japanese reaction to the Brussels action endangered Western interests. As Delbos put it, "We can neither remain in this uncertainty nor return to Brussels without knowing at what point the Washington administration considers itself committed by the common resolutions taken by the conference and whether it is ready to enter in the path of solidarity." Since the declaration had stipulated that the powers would reexamine their "common attitude," it was necessary to begin to do so. Rather than making another direct approach to Washington, the Council of Ministers decided that it would be best to present a common Franco-British démarche to the Americans. Therefore, Corbin was directed to solicit Eden's views about the matter and to see whether Britain would be willing to make a joint démarche, with a "view of leading the American government to define its position."[58]

Delbos's anxiety had been fueled by statements emanating from Japanese officials and by rumors circulating in various capitals. In Brussels, the Japanese ambassador had expressed his purely personal opinion that the adoption of the Brussels text "could have the most serious consequences."[59] Additionally, Delbos worried that if progress were not made soon, the Chinese might in despair turn to Germany and Italy to mediate an end to the conflict. He believed that the Rome-Berlin Axis hoped for such an opportunity, for it would certainly elevate their stature in the Far Eastern negotiating process, from which they had been largely excluded thus far. Such mediation could only damage the position of the French and British in the area. This fear became greater as rumors began floating through the Western capitals that Japan might be willing to accept the good offices of Germany.[60] Painfully, the French must have realized that the democracies could do little to preempt such a German move so long as the Brussels Conference remained in session. A similar offer by Britain or France would undermine the conference, would fly in the face of the moralistic statements of principle that had been issued, and would undoubtedly be unacceptable to Japan in any case. So, as he had maintained throughout, Delbos believed that the situation really rested in the hands of the Americans.

The British response to the French démarche was discouraging. Unable to see Eden, Corbin conveyed the proposal to Robert Vansittart, permanent undersecretary of state at the Foreign Office. The latter indicated that it would not be long before the American attitude was known, for Davis would be receiving new instructions. It would be better to have the Americans "reveal it themselves and spontaneously . . . without having the perhaps unfortunate appearance of having pressed the United States Government."[61] On the following day, 19 November, Eden bleakly elaborated on the British position. The American position, he said, was "unfortunately too well known." Indications received by the British ambassador in Washington left no doubt about the American determination to remain entirely uninvolved in the conflict. The Roosevelt administration believed that sanctions "could only have the effect of inflaming things." Congress simply would not permit any action that violated the neutrality laws. Eden then wondered aloud, "if the United States, as is probable, remains in a negative position, what will the Brussels Conference do?"[62]

What, indeed? By this point, Delbos appears to have given up any hope of prodding the United States into action either at Brussels or Washington. On top of Corbin's bad news from London, Delbos received from Henry in Washington a warning to avoid doing anything that might stimulate American suspicions that "they might become puppets in the hands of Machiavellian intriguers in Europe." He reminded his superiors in Paris of his earlier observation that Roosevelt was far ahead of the American public opinion. Consequently, Henry concluded, "During these touchy times, which perhaps represent a period of transition for the United States, one must remain realistic and not indulge in hopes which later will not be fulfilled."[63]

Delbos signaled his surrender over the issue in a major foreign policy address made before the Chamber of Deputies on 19 November. In his speech, he reviewed the developments related to the Spanish Civil War that had led to the Nyon Conference and the sequence of events in the Far East that had led to the Brussels Conference. The juxtaposition of the success of Nyon and the imminent failure of Brussels could not have been more obvious or effective. The foreign minister declared, "when international law is so disregarded, so badly served by the community, when such an atmosphere of insecurity, uneasiness and menace prevails, it is not the time to appear as a defenseless prey. Peace cannot be obtained through abdications . . . ." He lamented the failure of the League of Nations to deal with the crises but laid the blame on the weakness of the member states rather than upon the strength of the challenges made against the organization. With regard to the Far Eastern crisis, he revealed that three considerations determined French policy and guided the delegation at Brussels: first, France had humanitarian duties as well as responsibilities as a member of the League and a signatory of the Washington Treaty; second, France had special interests in the area requiring that it "look after the preservation in southern China of a situation de jure and de facto on which the security of our Asiatic possessions depends"; and third, France sought to maintain solidarity with the United States and Britain, since they all had similar interests and values. He bemoaned the fact that a lack of unanimity at Brussels had limited the nature of the response agreed upon at the conference, for the lack of a consensus "confirms all the more strongly the collapse of collective security." He took a swipe at American policy by reiterating his conviction that in the "very remote Far East, the prerequisite for success is the certainty of international solidarity, not merely moral but effective." He sought to temper such criticism of American moral diplomacy by gritting his teeth and acknowledging the "close harmonious collaboration" of the American, British and French delegations. But that was strictly for the newspapers. More revealing of his personal feelings was his comment, "What makes it so disheartening is that while all those nations that hold the destiny of mankind in their hands stand idly by and counsel moderation . . . , two wars are going on and military action in the Far East had been increased."[64]

That he now completely anticipated failure at Brussels was revealed on the twentieth, when he advised the disheartened Chinese ambassador in Paris that China could not expect any help from the United States at Brussels. To the British ambassador, Phipps, he complained bitterly about Davis's noncommittal attitude and reiterated that French policy remained clear and simple: France would do anything under a mutual guarantee by Britain and the United States and nothing without it.[65]

The French Foreign Ministry displayed its disdain for the final efforts to wrap up the Brussels Conference by failing to return a delegation there until 22 November, by which time the British and American delegations had hammered out the wording of a final report to be adopted by the conference. De Tessan, who led the French delegation, probably won few friends among the Americans with his offhanded comment that the draft report was purely historical in character—"a synthetic report of what has been done." The French asked to be included among the sponsoring powers but barely summoned up enough interest to read the full text.[66]

Apparently, Delbos had also informed the French news correspondents who had been covering the conference that it would not be worth their time returning to Brussels for the final sessions. In fact, however, many of them had already rendered judgment on the conference by the time it had recessed on 15 November. In a leading editorial on the fifteenth, *Le Temps* expressed the opinion that the state of American opinion would not permit the kind of active cooperation that had been hoped, "an important fact that compels prudence for everyone." Pertinax, in *L'Echo de Paris,* severely criticized the "ridiculous discussions" at Brussels. The reality existed that Japan had the material preponderance in the Far East. The Western powers were ill prepared to restrain her. "Henceforth words are of no value whatsoever and only acts . . . have importance." To Pertinax, the relationship between the Far Eastern and European crises was too important to overlook. Moreover, the Ethiopian crisis had taught the lesson that successful intervention was possible only if several governments "gambled everything and an alliance emerged resolved to throw in the balance a preponderant military force." To do so in this instance would have endangered European peace.[67]

Nothing in the final report and declaration of 24 November changed any minds in Paris, or elsewhere for that matter. Despite considerable British pressure for a more active statement, the final document adhered to Washington's determination not to go beyond a reaffirmation of general principles. No hint of the joint Anglo-American mediation or of the mild sanctions proposed by Britain appeared in the document. After its adoption, the delegates dutifully tried to put on their best faces and eloquently extolled the positive achievements of the conference. Nevertheless, there must have been some uneasy shifting in seats when Wellington Koo, the Chinese delegate, grimly and candidly proclaimed that the mere reaffirmations of principles by the Brussels Conference were simply inadequate to deal with the Far Eastern situation.[68]

Perhaps Geneviève Tabouis, writing in *L'Oeuvre,* was a bit too harsh in her assessment that "in the voluminous history of conferences, after the Treaty of Versailles, that of Brussels will make the most pitiable figure.[69] Yet the fact remains that the conference was a frustrating fiasco. Once again the West had demonstrated its inability to deal effectively with problems in the Far East. Undoubtedly, France must share the responsibility for the failure of the conference. Seeking to take advantage of the munitions question by linking it to the security of Indochina, the French carefully laid the groundwork for obtaining a general guarantee of security for their Far Eastern possessions. But this was exactly the kind of open-ended commitment that the United States government was unwilling to make and which the American public would not tolerate.

Nevertheless, when apportioning the precise blame for the failure of the conference, as futile as that might be, American responsibility remains paramount. The whole series of speeches and actions by American leaders in the fall of 1937, especially Roosevelt's Quarantine Speech, provided hope for those in Europe who eagerly sought some sign—any sign—that Washington would assume a leadership role in international politics. To be sure, in retrospect the Roosevelt administration was mainly interested in educating the public to the dangers confronting international peace and American security. It had no intention of being pushed out front as leader of a stop-Japan movement. But to a European, or, more precisely, to the French, all signs looked favorable. Whether Roosevelt was being adventuresome, cautious, or impetuous made little difference to them. Eager to exploit the tiniest indication of American action, they believed they had received evidence of such an inclination. After all, what people believed to be the case is frequently more important than the reality. In the end, French leaders seriously misinterpreted American intent. Only Jules Henry in Washington remained consistently on target with his warnings to Paris that Roosevelt was ahead of American public opinion, which would not support an adventurous foreign policy. In the end, Roosevelt's reliance upon moralistic diplomacy caused a misinterpretation of the Far Eastern situation and misled the European democracies. As Robert Dallek has argued, in the face of a strongly divided public, in the midst of an economic slowdown, and with the need to gain the support of Congress for proposed domestic legislation, the president was not about to risk a fight over foreign policy. Therefore, he remained without a coherent foreign policy program that could muster broad public support.[70]

Many of the apologists of American foreign policy for the period frequently return to the argument that domestic problems effectively hampered the establishment of a forceful foreign policy. Yet, Europeans are just as frequently criticized by Americans for their willingness to embrace appeasement in dealing with the European dictatorships. In fact, French leaders were confronted with just as many domestic issues in the fall of 1937 as were the Americans. Certainly, French public opinion was probably more divided over major foreign policy, economic, and social issues than that in the United States. The problems confronting the leftist Popular Front government were legion. Yet, Delbos and the Quai d'Orsay (the position of Premier Chautemps remained more problematical) were willing to risk taking an aggressive stance on this issue, and French opinion appeared willing to go along with the government. Had the United States acted, it seems clear that France would have supported its position, and Britain would have fallen in line. The American fear of having to go it alone was unfounded. Without such a strong American lead, however, it would have been unrealistic for the two partially disarmed European powers, already overextended in the Mediterranean and diverted by other European concerns,[71] to have acted on their own.

The linkage between Far Eastern and European affairs surfaced frequently in the minds of French policymakers. It is too much to claim, as some have done, that there was a direct line between the failure at Brussels and the appeasement at Munich, but clearly a strong action at Brussels, coming quickly upon the heels of the success of the Nyon Conference on Spain, would have gone a long way toward establishing a pattern of decisiveness that might have served the democracies in good stead in Europe. As Eden said, however, "The contrast with Nyon could scarcely have been more marked. . . . "[72] This was particularly unfortunate for Delbos, who, shortly after the Brussels Conference, departed for a three-week tour of Eastern European capitals in an attempt to breathe new life into the decaying French security system in that area. But with the mixed record of Nyon and Brussels in mind, Delbos's reception by most Eastern European governments was equally mixed. No small bit of irony must be seen in Delbos's subsequent rationalization that the purpose of the trip had been only a moral one, especially in light of his vehement opposition to the moral diplomacy advocated by the Americans at Brussels.[73]

Herbert Feis might have gone too far when he suggested that the Brussels Conference represented the "last good chance to work out a stable settlement between China and Japan" through strong collective action.[74] But it is safe to say that the conference represented a missed opportunity to reappraise the Washington Treaty system, which, by 1937, had obviously become obsolete. In their mutual suspicion about being pushed out front, none of the Western democracies ever proposed a thorough revision of the Washington system to take into account the changed realities of the Far East. For all of the discussions about mediation, sanctions, mutual guarantees, and other alternatives, nobody seriously thought of initiating negotiations for a comprehensive settlement similar to that which had been negotiated fifteen years earlier. Certainly, there is no evidence to suggest that the French negotiators, in their overriding concern about obtaining a guarantee of security for Indochina, ever contemplated initiating such negotiations. Few, if any, seemed to realize that treaties are not eternal and that the significant changes in the Far East since 1922 warranted another serious study and revision of the existing system. Of course, for the French to recognize the necessity of revising the Washington system would have meant lending credibility to German demands that the Versailles system be revised. But to do so in the latter case remained too bitter a pill to swallow, even though it had already been happening in small doses and would be completed by the time of the Munich Conference ten months later. In the end, then, the fundamental dilemma confronting French policymakers continued to haunt them. The increasingly precarious European situation dictated caution in the Far East. But too much caution in the Far East might only further imperil the situation there and further destabilize the international situation, with inevitable consequences for European affairs. It was a box the French were never able to escape.

six

THE DEEPENING FAR EASTERN DILEMMA AND THE SEARCH FOR ALLIES, 1938–1939

THE Brussels Conference represented the zenith of French efforts to erect a system of Western cooperation in the Far East. The attempt had failed ignobly, and to nobody's surprise the conflict continued to escalate. In the process, it began to pose increasingly difficult dilemmas for French policymakers, both in Europe and in the Far East. During the months that followed the Brussels Conference, the twin issues of Western cooperation and the role and status of Indochina as an element in the Sino-Japanese conflict, especially regarding the transit of arms to China, continued to dominate French Far Eastern concerns. Delbos might confide to British Ambassador Phipps that so long as the United States did not come out into the open against Japan, Great Britain and France must avoid involvement in the Far Eastern conflict, but France was to find out that remaining uninvolved would not be quite that easy. Given the fact that France had long political, economic, and cultural ties with both Japan and China and wished to lose the friendship of neither, and given the fact that Indochina was destined to become an increasingly important strategic area as the conflict dragged on, France would not be afforded the luxury of remaining on the sidelines, whether it wished to or not. Such was the danger inherent in befriending two powers who were enemies to each other.

China's dissatisfaction with the Brussels Conference quickly posed problems for the Western democracies. Barely a week after the end of the conference, Chiang Kai-shek accepted German offers to mediate an end to the dispute. Germany had also been placed in a bind by the hostilities because of her conflicting interests and sympathies in China and Japan. Consequently, in October, Berlin had accepted Tokyo's invitation to act as mediator. The Chinese, hoping for support at Brussels, had delayed responding to Japanese peace terms relayed by the Germans. But on 2 December, with the fall of Nanking imminent and without hope of any dramatic Western aid, Chiang Kai-shek indicated his willingness to consider such negotiations.[1] The German mediation effort, which proved futile after a month of trying, need not detain us here. For France, however, active German participation in the Far Eastern peace process appeared ominous. Thus far, Berlin had been generally excluded from Far Eastern affairs. But if by some strange twist of fate the Nazis were able to negotiate a reconciliation of the two belligerents, their prestige and influence in the area would be increased tremendously, mainly at the expense of France and Britain.

Yet, after the initial concern generated by the German involvement, leading Far Eastern advisers at the Quai d'Orsay, such as Henri Hoppenot, chief of the Far Eastern Department, gradually realized that nothing much would come out of the mediation scheme. As the French had warned the Chinese in advance of the German attempt, the Japanese terms were likely to be so severe that Chiang Kai-shek could not possibly accept them. Alexis Léger, secretary general at the Quai d'Orsay, expressed a concern that the generalissimo's willingness to try mediation may have reflected a certain weakening of China's will to continue to resist. But as long as Chiang's political position held up, he would be able to override defeatist advisers around him.[2]

Information arriving in Paris from French diplomatic posts in the Far East confirmed the likelihood of such a failure of the mediation attempt. French representatives in China concluded that they could not foresee an end to the conflict. As Colonel Gabriel Sabbatier, the French military attaché in Peking, admitted, "Germany has played very adroitly between Japan and China." But Chiang Kai-shek appeared determined to prolong the fight, and Japan had neither the economic wherewithal nor the personnel to force an end to it.[3] When the stiff Japanese terms were relayed to the Chinese, French Ambassador Naggiar reported the Chinese conviction that they would have the effect of an "execution" of China by Japan and that Tokyo did not wish to deal with the Chinese government, hoping instead to find a rationale for setting up their own puppet regime.[4] Other French observers in China believed that the Germans remained eager to mediate a settlement if only to solve their own dilemma as to which side to support. Within German military circles considerable sympathy existed for the Chinese. On the other hand, concern had developed in Berlin that the Japanese army might be prematurely weakened as a result of a prolonged fight in China, and, therefore, would lose its value as a Far Eastern counterweight against the Soviet Union.[5]

From Tokyo, Charles-Arsène Henry argued that France must recognize two principal points: First, Japan was beginning to suffer economically from the hostilities—a fact confirmed by its willingness to accept German good offices. To be sure, its demands remained unacceptable, "but one can hope that the moment draws near where its pretentions will be less leonine." Second, it appeared that Chiang Kai-shek's position continued to gain adherents in China, and he remained convinced that he could continue the struggle. Therefore, Henry concluded that peace was not at hand, and "once more Japan will be dragged along by its adversary in a turn of fortune for which it had not been prepared, and which it had sought to avoid." When it became clear that Tokyo intended to fight on and would cease to recognize the existence of Chiang Kai-shek's government, Henry wired a warning that the decision signaled a victory for the Japanese navy. As a result, France should expect Japan to move south and attack Canton in the very near future. In retrospect, Henry's perception of developments in Tokyo proved to be remarkably clear: "Admiral Suetsugu, in effect, bases his bellicose attitude on the necessity of preventing by all means the supplying of arms to China; but, in spite of all my denials, he is convinced now, rightly or wrongly, that Indochina has, no more than Hong Kong, ceased to furnish war material to the Chinese."[6]

As Henry suggested, Japanese policy had taken a dramatic new twist. Flushed with their success in the capture of Nanking in early December, thereby forcing Chiang Kai-shek's government to retreat into the interior at Chungking, the hard-liners in Tokyo had moved to establish control over China policy. During the month between mid-December and mid-January, this group, led by Prime Minister Konoye and his zealous home minister, Admiral Nobumasa Suetsugu, skillfully outmaneuvered those on the general staff who sought a negotiated settlement of the conflict. The terms extended to the Chinese were calculated to be unacceptable, and at an imperial conference on 11 January their point of view was sanctioned by the emperor. When the Chinese response was predictably deemed inappropriate, Tokyo announced on 16 January that it had broken diplomatic relations with Chiang Kai-shek's government and that it was recognizing the Japanese-sponsored Provisional Government of the Chinese Republic in Peking as the legitimate central government of China.[7] Two days later, Tokyo indicated that it had decided upon a war of annihilation against the Nationalist government.[8]

Understandably, with the breakdown of the German mediation effort following on the heels of the failure of the Brussels Conference, the Chinese quickly turned in other directions to seek help. At the end of January, they initiated one of several attempts to be made over the next few months to persuade the League of Nations to act on their behalf against Japan. Indeed, much of the French effort at Geneva during 1938 was devoted to keeping China from persuading the League to invoke Article Seventeen, which might have brought up the old bogey of sanctions. Delbos warned that if the European powers were to apply sanctions, they would find that the United States would not cooperate, as "the Brussels Conference had shown that there was really no hope." France remained ill-prepared to take overt action without the full cooperation of the United States. The best that France could do would be to help China in whatever way possible, "privately and unofficially."⁹ In the end, the Chinese formally appealed to the League three times during 1938—in January, May, and September—but with a notable lack of success. The most that the League, dominated by France, Britain and the Soviet Union, would do was to pass pious, vague resolutions deploring the intensification of hostilities and expressing moral support for China. In May and again in September, it called upon its members to give sympathetic consideration to China's appeals for aid, but sanctions against Japan clearly remained anathema.¹⁰

Disappointed with their treatment at Geneva and in desperate military straits, the Chinese also made urgent efforts to obtain financial and economic support from the major Western powers by appealing for munitions, loans, and credits. France proved to be no exception. Throughout 1938 and into 1939, as Georges Taboulet put it, "the French government was literally assailed by Chinese solicitations." The Chinese ambassador in Paris, Wellington Koo, as well as Chiang Kai-shek's personal emissaries, repeatedly sought audiences with leading French officials in Paris and Indochina in order to press China's case. The Chinese scramble for funds paid off in Paris, for France became the first Western nation to arrange wartime credits to China. A French banking group in early 1938 advanced about $5 million in credits, which were 80 percent guaranteed by the French government's Credit Insurance Department. The credits were advanced for the purpose of building a railroad from the Indochina border to Nanning in Kwangsi province in southern China. An additional $10 million in credits were arranged in late 1939 after the outbreak of war in Europe. These credits were to be used to finance a railway from Kunming, the terminus of the Indochina Railroad, to the Yangtze River near Chungking. In fact, however, although substantial amounts of credit were apparently advanced by these agreements, neither project was completed, for the Japanese capture of Nanning in December 1939 preempted the usefulness of that route, and France's capitulation to Germany in June 1940 terminated the latter project.[11]

In any case, the credits received by China from France were of relatively little consequence when compared to loans and credits that could be arranged from other sources. Indeed, the United States, Britain, and Russia all eventually became substantial sources of financial aid that provided for currency support, supplies, and services. Of the $513.5 million total foreign credits arranged for China prior to the outbreak of the Pacific war in December 1941, the $15 million provided by France was rather trifling.[12] Neither did France, in the throes of rebuilding its own armed forces, provide much in the way of munitions for Chinese forces. For the beleaguered Chinese, the most valuable service that France could have rendered would have been to facilitate the transshipment of war materiel purchased elsewhere through Indochina into southern and central China. Indeed, the strategic value if Indochina as an entrepôt and supply line during the so-called China incident became the critical issue for France in its relations with China and Japan from early 1938 through mid-1940.

The issue of the Indochina arms connection had been raised, of course, prior to the Brussels Conference, when France had attempted to use its preconference restrictions of October to gain leverage for its position at Brussels. When France took steps to prohibit the flow of munitions through Indochina, every indication had been given that the order would be irrevocable unless concrete guarantees of Indochina's security were obtained. Of course, the guarantees never materialized; yet the issue of Indochina's role in the transit of war materiel to China did not fade. Rather, the issue steadily intensified over the next two years from being a relatively minor irritant in Franco-Japanese relations to being a major source of antagonism that put the two powers on a collision course.

For the hard-pressed Chinese, the question of arms supply was a matter of life or death. Just as it was able to obtain credits from France for the purpose of building railroads from Indochina into southern and central China along which war materiel could flow, so, too, it was ultimately able to secure loans and credits from other nations for the goods that would be sent along the rails. As Arthur N. Young, an American financial adviser to China during the period, subsequently wrote, once the various purchase credits were established with the West by the end of 1938, they "pretty well took care of the supplies China needed, other than strictly military items." The main problem for China proved to be arranging transportation facilities for such goods. The magnitude of the problem can be seen in the demands created by the tremendous increase in the size of the Chinese armies as the fighting escalated. It has been estimated that in nine months of 1938 alone the armies ballooned from two million to eight million men.[13] The supply problems associated with such an increase would have been difficult in the best of times. But these were far from the best of times.

The Chinese used four points of entry to import the materiel needed, but all of them had severe limitations. Despite the establishment of a coastal blockade of China's main ports by 1938, after the Japanese capture of Shanghai, Hong Kong became the most important port of entry into China. An average of 90,000 tons a month, or about 75 percent of the materiel destined for Chiang Kai-shek's forces, went along the Hong Kong–Canton–Hankow route. But this supply line was vulnerable to Japanese attack, and when Japan landed forces to capture Canton in October 1938, the flow of goods was reduced to a trickle. The other route of British transit support was via the Burma Road from Rangoon to Yunnan. But the work on the road, begun in 1938, progressed slowly through the remote jungles and across difficult mountains. By dint of tremendous sacrifice of conscripted Chinese labor, the road was nominally completed by December 1938, although it remained barely passable in good weather and turned into a sea of mud in the rainy season. Consequently, until later in the war the use of the Burma Road remained greatly limited. Initially, the Soviet Union was one of the largest suppliers of war materiel to Chinese forces. But the use of the overland route through central Russia and China's Sinkiang province was made extremely tenuous by the extreme climate and the great distances involved. Consequently, a great deal of Russian aid arrived by sea.[14]

The fourth major route ran through French Indochina, where a French-owned railway ran from the port of Haiphong via Hanoi to Laokai at the Chinese border. From there, a narrow-gauge line climbed 6,500 feet to Kunming in Yunnan province. At the time of its construction early in the century, the costly line had been considered an engineering marvel because of its 3,600 bridges and tunnels, necessitated by some of the most rugged mountainous terrain in China. Because of the difficult nature of the terrain and the narrowness of its gauges, the railroad was not capable of carrying as much traffic as the Hong Kong route; freight shipped along the route in 1937 was estimated at 5,000 tons per month, although at its peak later in the conflict it may have accommodated 15,000 tons a month. Even so, with the fall of Canton, the hard-pressed Chinese found the Indochina link to be a savior and sought to convince the French by whatever means to keep the railroad open to badly needed materiel. As Georges Taboulet put it, China "counted on Haiphong to take the place of Hong Kong as an artificial lung capable of preserving her from total asphyxiation."[15]

For exactly the opposite reasons, Japan became even more determined to cut off this lifeline. Japanese leaders had promised their nation that the China incident would be concluded quickly. But, in fact, the incident had rapidly become a major conflict and threatened to drag on interminably. Chiang Kai-shek's forces, although frequently beaten, could not be routed, and the generalissimo's political position seemed as secure as ever. Meanwhile, Japan was paying grave military, economic, and diplomatic prices. Unable to apply the coup de grace militarily, Japan became more determined to strangle China by cutting off its outside aid. Finding itself caught between two of its traditional friends in the area, France found itself between the proverbial rock and hard place. Whether by acting or by not acting over the critical transit issue, it ran the risk of severely alienating a power that could cause considerable harm to its interests in East and Southeast Asia.

When the Council of Ministers in Paris in October 1937 established the government's policy limiting the transit of goods through Indochina, they had exempted war materiel ordered prior to the outbreak of the conflict in July, as well as materiel already at sea prior to 13 October. But as that decision had been made as much for American consumption as for that of Japan, subsequent revision in November allowed disassembled aircraft to be shipped to Indochina, where they could be reassembled and flown to China.[16] Consequently, just how restrictive the French limitations remained was debatable. But Tokyo, on the verge of a smashing victory at Nanking and anticipating a subsequent mediated settlement, had displayed little concern regarding the arms transit issue through the end of the year. In fact, as a memo to Delbos from the Far Eastern Department reported at the end of February, "The diplomatic and military situation in the Far East has not changed noticeably since the beginning of January."[17]

The issue of arms had caused minor rifts with the Chinese and the Americans, however. Wellington Koo, China's ambassador in Paris and its representative at the League of Nations, sought to gain some practical application to the League's invitation that the powers individually determine the extent to which they might aid China. But the French responded that their own national defense requirements made it impossible for them to send the arms aid requested by China. In any case, they reiterated, such aid could be granted only if the United States agreed to participate and would be willing to provide "binding guarantees"[18] in the event such aid provoked an attack by Japan. Leaked to the press, even discussion of the theoretical involvement of the United States caused a minor flurry of excitement in Washington. Secretary of State Hull hastily announced to the press that the government had no intention of modifying its policy of neutrality, a statement quickly endorsed by Senator Key Pittman, chairman of the Senate Foreign Relations Committee. In the end, the disappointed Chinese were left with but another empty gesture of moral support by the League Council.[19]

The French government clearly demonstrated its disinclination to risk offending the Japanese in the spring, when the governor-general of Indochina, Jules Brévié, who had advocated caution in the fall, now asked for a reconsideration of the French limitations on arms transit through Indochina. In order to help ameliorate the Chinese military situation, he proposed enlarging the categories of goods permitted transit through Indochina, "if not by law, at least in fact." In response to this suggestion, the Far Eastern Department undertook a reevaluation of the policy adopted the previous October. But the Department ultimately decided that the situation did not justify a change in policy. In fact, it feared that an increase in Chinese resistance might actually increase Japan's preoccupation with cutting off the supply of foreign arms and lead her to strike south toward Canton to halt the flow of supplies through Hong Kong. Japan "will be more disposed, under these conditions, to increase its pressure to prevent all development of transit through Indochina." The Department admitted that France's policies would have considerable impact upon existing as well as future Chinese attitudes toward France but urged, nevertheless, that this be weighed against the potential threat to the security of Indochina should Japan move south. The only revision of controls that the Department would contemplate was the possibility that arms contracts might be negotiated with local Chinese security forces in southern China to replace those munitions that had been requisitioned by the Nationalist forces. Such a limited modification of policy would have the virtue of appeasing the potentially troublesome warlords of southern China, providing a display of French goodwill, but at the same time it would allow France to argue to the Japanese that such arms were not directed against them. "Under certain conditions of prudence and discretion, satisfaction could be given in this domain to the desiderata of Chinese authorities."[20]

Before the French could give any serious consideration to modifying the policy regarding arms shipments, however, Japanese pressure began to build concerning the issue. Beginning in the late spring of 1938, the Japanese press launched a virulent campaign against France. Ostensibly, the press campaign was initiated in the aftermath of an agreement by a group of French banks to finance a railroad from Langson, on the Indochina border, to Nanning, in China's Kwangsi province. The prospect that such a link would eventually aid Chiang Kai-shek's forces in gaining access to foreign war materiel opened up the whole issue of arms transit through Indochina.[21] Georges Bonnet, minister for foreign affairs, was incensed by what he considered to be entirely unjustified accusations. He wired Ambassador Henry in Tokyo to protest the accusations as quickly as possible and to reiterate France's rigid adherence to its decision of October. Beyond that, however, he ordered Henry to make certain that Tokyo be warned that "the evolution of any Japanese attitude unfavorable toward us would justify a revision of our policy, notably in the transit of materiel, a revision that would entail for Japan consequences that the Japanese government is in a position to appreciate."[22]

By the time Henry received an audience with the new Japanese foreign minister, General Ugaki Kazushige, the press campaign had temporarily subsided. Nevertheless, Henry took the opportunity to review for him French policy regarding the arms transit issue. Ugaki, whom Konoye had brought into the cabinet to replace the more bellicose Koki Hirota, was a reserve army general who had an interest in improving relations with the Western powers and in initiating peace talks with China.[23] In his long, cordial meeting with Ugaki, Henry was favorably impressed by the general's sincerity and his apparent willingness to smooth over difficulties with the Western powers. Nevertheless, Ugaki introduced a new element into the transit issue. He suggested that if France wished to put a halt to the rumors that arms were being shipped to China through Indochina, perhaps they would permit Japanese "observers" who, "aided in their mission by the governor-general of Indochina, would get a clear idea of the reality of things and would tell it in news from Indochina that the newspapers would publish." Henry quickly discouraged the notion of such a commission of inquiry. The ambassador argued that "it is the current custom that the burden of proof is incumbent upon those who allege a fact and not upon those who deny it." Moreover, in the face of such rumors and charges during the previous months, France had repeatedly asked for specific proof of arms transit, but none had been produced. With that, Ugaki backed off, indicating that he did not personally doubt France's word and that he had only hoped to calm public opinion by his suggestion.[24]

The issue refused to die. French statesmen, both in Paris and Tokyo, were convinced that the press campaign emanated from the government. Such a belief received additional impetus a few days after Henry's meeting with Ugaki. On 19 June, the Japanese foreign minister held a press conference with the foreign press corps in Tokyo. After Ugaki referred vaguely to certain powers who were helping to prolong the conflict by encouraging the Chinese, one correspondent asked if his allusion had been directed at France. Ugaki coyly responded that it was up to France to determine whether it involved them but that one could only believe that "there is no smoke without fire." Ambassador Henry saw the remark as proof that the Japanese government not only tolerated the anti-French campaign but actually orchestrated it. As he saw it, the increasing unpopularity of the war in Japan had placed heavy domestic pressure on the government, which had responded by laying the blame for its failure to defeat China upon aid supplied by foreign powers such as France. The best advice that Henry could offer the Quai d'Orsay was that "we must despite everything not lose our sang-froid before this campaign of lies and I hope that it will come to an end as it ended against England." But he warned, "I know too well that such agitation is dangerous; begun in light of a certain policy, it excites peoples' heads and can greatly exceed the aims of its promoters themselves."[25]

Back in Paris, Foreign Minister Bonnet had learned of Ugaki's remarks through a Havas news agency report even before Henry's despatch arrived. He was outraged at such a statement, because it would further strengthen the impression current in Japanese public opinion that French Far Eastern policy was directed against Japan's interests. Bonnet ordered Henry to demand an immediate meeting with Ugaki and to "tell him with all clarity desirable, the painful impression that his declarations have caused here and to demand from him . . . an official correction without equivocation which ends the persistent press campaign." Miffed that the Japanese should be singling out France for such attacks rather than Britain or Russia, whose assistance to China had been far more substantial, Bonnet warned that if France's policy adopted in October did not merit her better treatment, then the Japanese "must understand that we would henceforth no longer have any reason to maintain a decision which . . . had not been made without affecting at the time the interests of Indochina and our relations with the Chinese government."[26]

When Henry met with Ugaki on 20 June to relay Bonnet's position, the Japanese foreign minister acted embarrassed that such unprepared remarks as he had made would create such a stir. Henry responded by expressing his hope that Ugaki would issue a statement expressing his satisfaction with France's explanations of the transit issue. Henry reminded Ugaki of the danger of exciting the public with such false press campaigns, and he reiterated that if a continuation of the attacks led France to reconsider its policy, Japan's interests would suffer. Ugaki made no promises. Indeed, Henry indicated to Bonnet that such a public retreat probably would not occur: "Such a declaration is not in the Japanese habit and would make him lose face to such an extent that he perhaps would not be able to sustain himself in the government." On the other hand, Henry hoped that such a warning about a revision of French transit policy might have the desired effect of ending the press campaign. "It appears to be certain that the government can stop it overnight."[27]

The press attacks did not stop. Led by the rightist newspapers *Kokumin shimbun, Nichi Nichi,* and *Yomiuri,* the attacks continued through the end of June and into July. *Kokumin* declared that despite French denials nothing altered the fact that war materiel from France was reaching China through Indochina, and it was impossible for this to occur without the knowledge of the authorities in Paris.[28]

In view of the continuing press attacks, following a report by the governor-general of Indochina, again denying some of the more specific Japanese allegations, Bonnet again ordered Henry to protest: "It is your duty to indicate to the General Ugaki personally, that our dignity will not be able to accommodate itself much longer to such treatment . . . ." Once again, Ugaki was to be cautioned that the unjustified Japanese accusations might lead France to change its policy.[29] When Henry received his meeting with the Japanese foreign minister, it proved to be "painfully disagreeable and tense." After Henry delivered the lecture Bonnet had ordered, the Japanese foreign minister retorted that while he was pleased to learn of the French investigation of the transit issue, the fact remained that news of arms shipments never ceased to arrive in Tokyo from certain "reliable sources" (Henry believed them to be the Japanese consuls in Indochina). Ugaki went on to propose once again that the best way to end the rumors that fed the press campaign would be to send Japanese observers to Indochina to verify that arms transit was not occurring. Again, Henry quickly rejected the suggestion. When Ugaki denied that the press attacks had been instigated by the government, Henry retorted that the campaign existed nonetheless and if it did not cease,

"I see matters progressing themselves toward a revision of our policy, . . . which would be deplorable for the interests of Japan." Henry left the meeting believing that Ugaki remained personally convinced that arms shipments were going through Indochina and were being ignored by France. On the other hand, it appeared unlikely to Henry that either Ugaki or his foreign ministry actually promoted the press campaign. More likely, the ambassador believed, the Japanese navy was behind the anti-French campaign, and Ugaki had been a moderating voice. Indeed, the campaign probably reflected the division in the Japanese government between those, especially in the navy, who sought to move south and those like Ugaki who felt they already had enough enemies. For the moment, at least, those who eschewed the road to the south held sway in Tokyo. But Henry warned that the navy was capable of some action that would commit the government to a course that it wished to avoid. "Such individual initiatives, which are unimaginable in a European army, are possible in Japan. That is why I call the attention of the government of the Republic to the special gravity that the raising of the prohibition of transit would assume. Such a measure could provoke the most disastrous reactions, and before taking it, the government of the Republic must consider minutely the possible consequences." If Ambassador Henry had hoped that his protests would have an effect upon Ugaki, there is no evidence of an immediate impact, for the press attacks continued for a couple of additional weeks before they slowly subsided to a halt.[30]

The Japanese motives for the anti-French bullying tactics can only be a matter of speculation. Perhaps the pressures on the economy, politics, and military created by the inconclusive year-long hostilities simply found an outlet through the press attacks. More likely, however, they were tied to the continuing internal political struggle in Tokyo between those who wished to continue to pursue the conflict vigorously and those who wished to end it on the best possible terms as soon as possible. Although Ugaki belonged to the latter group, the press attacks probably suited his purposes well. They allowed his more militant antagonists to divert their attention to whipping verbally a convenient scapegoat. This, in turn, allowed him to undertake secret negotiations with Chinese representatives to end the hostilities far from public gaze. Apparently, he succeeded in preventing word of the ultimately unsuccessful negotiations that occurred during most of the summer from leaking to the press or to the foreign diplomats. Certainly, there is no indication in French sources that France's representatives in either China or Japan knew of the negotiations.

Of course, the issue of munitions transit through Indochina had not been resolved by the exchanges that occurred over the spring and summer of 1938. To be sure, it ultimately became an evermore ticklish issue between the two nations as the Sino-Japanese conflict dragged on. The question remains as to how valid the Japanese protests were in regard to the flow of supplies through Indochina, and also as to how rigidly the French actually did adhere to their policy of October 1937. The evidence is scattered and fragmentary, but a general pattern of behavior can be discerned.

The October decree prohibiting the shipment through Indochina of not-previously-ordered munitions was liberally interpreted by officials in Paris, while local officials in Indochina winked as the goods went through. As Edwin Wilson, the American chargé d'affaires in Paris, reported, the fulfillment of orders "placed before the outbreak of hostilities" was interpreted with some "elasticity." The American ambassador, William Bullitt, who was particularly well connected in French government circles, reported that while Foreign Ministers Delbos and Paul Boncour were at the Quai d'Orsay, "the decree was applied in a manner favorable to the Chinese . . . . " Moreover, observers at the delivery point of the goods in Yannanfu reported seeing tanks, planes, and ammunition as well as gasoline arriving via the railroad.[31] Nevertheless, to the frequent Japanese protests the French profusely continued to deny, perhaps with tongue in cheek, that munitions were being shipped through Indochina. Even in late October 1938, when the Japanese protested in a note "impertinent to the point of insolence," in which Japan warned that "certain steps would have to be taken that would have a regrettable affect upon the amicable relations between France and Japan,"[32] the French blandly responded that Tokyo had failed to produce specific evidence to support their charges. When Japan proposed a joint Franco-Japanese commission to investigate the complaints—a modification of Ugaki's proposal of the summer of 1938—she was flatly turned down by the French. Henri Hoppenot, chief of the Far Eastern Department, indicated that France could not even consider the Japanese proposal. To agree to such a demand would be tantamount to accepting limits on Indochina's sovereignty. It would be perfectly legitimate for the properly accredited Japanese representatives in Indochina to make such inquiries as one would normally expect from the consul general. But to go beyond that to gain access to customs houses and records would not be permitted. Even in the face of a Japanese warning that Japan considered this to be "the last attempt of the imperial government to bring about a friendly settlement of this affair" and Ambassador Henry's nervous appeal stressing that it would be most desirable to "find some accommodation that would allow Konoye to shut the mouths of the extremists," Hoppenot appeared unmoved, chasing the Japanese representative back to bring Japan's terms in writing from the ambassador.[33]

The evidence suggests that when the Japanese exerted heavy pressure, the flow of military hardware was restricted, although nonmilitary items continued forward. For example, for a short time after the Japanese protests of October 1938, the French apparently closed down the transit of war materiel, an act that naturally brought an outcry, noted by Wilson, from the Chinese and led American Secretary of State Hull to inquire pointedly whether the French were "allowing themselves to be unduly impressed with Japanese demands . . . ."[34] When the pressure abated, however, the transit of arms resumed largely unimpeded. When the Japanese, for instance, captured Canton in the fall of 1938 and cut off the flow of materiel entering China through Hong Kong, the Indochina route became even more important, especially since the Burma Road had not yet been completed. Consequently, by early 1939, the French ambassador in China, Emile Naggiar, admitted that "the congestion at Haiphong was quite indescribable" and that French authorities were gravely embarrassed by it. Not only did the railroad fail to keep up with the flow of goods, but the road leading from Indochina into southern China was a "veritable cemetery of motor transport."[35] The American consul in Hong Kong reported that port congestion at Haiphong meant that ships had to wait for days before being allowed to unload their cargoes. Moreover, local French businessmen were beginning to complain because no dock space remained for their exports.[36]

In Paris by February 1939, Premier Edouard Daladier bragged to American Ambassador Bullitt that "daily now he signed personally permits for the export to China of arms and munitions . . . . He was letting China have everything that France could spare and these supplies were being shipped over the French railroad through Indochina." He admitted that there had been delays, but they had not been caused "by an ill-will of the French Government but by the inadequacy of the railroad itself."[37] Georges Mandel, the minister for colonies, subsequently corroborated the government's position when he told Bullitt that there were "no restrictions whatsoever" on shipments through Indochina.[38]

In any case, evidence suggests that even when officials in Paris periodically sought to tighten up the restrictions in response to Japanese pressure, local authorities in Indochina could be "induced to cooperate if approached in the right way . . . . " Additionally, as the French ambassador in London, Charles Corbin, admitted to the British Foreign Office, it was quite likely that a great deal of smuggling was going on through and around Indochina.[39] It is just as likely that much of it had at least the tacit approval of local authorities.

Tokyo, of course, could not tolerate such activity for long. It had been a constant fear of the French that the Japanese would make some overt move to cut this supply route to China by seizing the island of Hainan. From there, Japan could effectively control the Gulf of Tonkin and launch air strikes against that portion of the Haiphong-Yunnanfu Railroad that ran through China. Moreover, it could serve as a convenient base for any adventure that Japan might wish to take against Western interests in Southeast Asia. In fact, the Japanese had cautioned France as early as the fall of 1937 regarding the possibility of such an occupation of Hainan, and it had been ostensibly for this reason that the original decree prohibiting the transit of munitions had been passed prior to the Brussels Conference. But the fact that the Japanese did not act for the next year and a half lends additional credence to the interpretation that France probably did not take too seriously the early Japanese warnings and that the French move was merely a smokescreen behind which France hoped to secure an open commitment of support from the United States. Increasingly, however, as the fighting spread southward, the question of Hainan and other strategic island groups lying in the South China Sea became a chief concern, for it bore directly upon the security of Indochina.

During the troubled year of 1938, both the French and the British governments made several representations to the Japanese, indicating that the occupation of Hainan would be viewed as a matter of grave concern. Short of entirely capitulating to Tokyo's demands that it shut off the flow of all supplies through Indochina, however, France could do little to prevent such a move by Tokyo. The Japanese refused to give categorical assurances that they would not occupy the island, although they indicated that such an act, if in fact it did occur, would be taken strictly for strategic reasons and would not be permanent, for they had no territorial ambitions there. France remained skeptical, suspecting that Tokyo was merely using the Indochina arms transit issue as an excuse for action in the South China Sea. At one point, France tentatively sounded out the British about the possibility of neutralizing Hainan, but London, although concerned that a Japanese takeover would place Japan athwart the British Singapore–Hong Kong communications link, remained unwilling to act. The proposal died a stillbirth.[40]

In mid-June 1938, France took a preemptive initiative to strengthen its strategic position in the South China Sea by establishing an effective occupation of the Paracel Islands. This group of about thirty atolls lying south of Hainan had little economic value, but the fear existed that Japan might try to develop them as a strategic base in the area. Although France had claimed sovereignty over them as part of Annam, China had disputed the claim, and France had refrained from physically occupying the islands until the dispute had been arbitrated, although both nations had generally neglected the islands. But as the shadow of Japanese expansion grew longer, France secretly negotiated with China to resolve their differences. By the summer of 1938, China had tacitly agreed that a French occupation would be far preferable to that of Japan. The fact that Japan had two naval vessels, including a cruiser, in the waters around the islands undoubtedly added to French fears that a Japanese takeover was imminent. Taking care not to provoke the Japanese, the governor-general of Indochina sent mainly civilian technicians to establish weather and communications stations. They were supported by a few Annamese police, ostensibly for protection against pirates that roamed the area. In their notification of occupation to Tokyo on 2 July the French promised to protect the rights of Japanese fishermen and settlers in the area but made it clear that France could not give way on the issue of sovereignty over the islands. By pressing their claims when the Japanese were still on the march in China and not yet willing to foment trouble with France, the French chose a most favorable time. The Japanese responded moderately, although not recognizing the French claim to the islands and reserving their future liberty of action in the area.[41]

By the turn of the year, however, the situation had changed significantly. The Konoye government began to flounder because of its inability to secure a successful end to the China conflict. No new victories had been won since the capture of Canton in October, and although Japan had seized great amounts of territory and killed a great many Chinese, an end to the war seemed as distant as ever. This situation placed additional strain on Japan's fragile domestic front. Consequently, Konoye, undoubtedly tired after eighteen months of navigating through the troubled East Asian waters, resigned as premier on 4 January 1939. Emperor Hirohito appointed Baron Hiranuma Kiichiro, president of the privy council, to succeed Konoye. Under the staunchly reactionary Hiranuma, the "southward advance" strategy favored by the Navy Ministry began to crystalize during the next eight months. Perhaps encouraged by the Western capitulation during the Czechoslovakian crisis the previous

September, movement in the direction of the French and British interests in Southeast Asia must have looked inviting. Rather than launching additional costly military campaigns directly against China, Hiranuma sought to consolidate Japan's grip on the territories already seized and to isolate Chiang Kai-shek's regime by destabilizing its currency and cutting off remaining supply lines to Chungking. This strategy dictated the acquisition of additional bases in the area of the South China Sea for naval and air operations.[42]

Consequently, determined to launch the southward advance and impatient concerning the issue of munitions transit through Indochina, the Japanese seized Hainan Island on 10 February. Largely abandoned by Chiang Kai-shek as indefensible, the island offered the Imperial Marines little organized resistance.[43] The French Foreign Ministry termed the action a "brutal surprise," since France had been given no advance notification. Henri Hoppenot argued that the seizure violated an informal understanding between Tokyo and Paris that had acknowledged the maintenance of the status quo on Hainan as the quid pro quo for French restrictions on the transit of munitions through Indochina. He maintained, rather untruthfully, that France had faithfully honored the agreement regarding the prohibition of munitions, but he declared that in the light of the Japanese stroke France would regard the agreement as terminated.[44]

Ambassador Henry delivered a formal protest to Japanese Foreign Minister Arita Hachiro on 13 February, as did his British and American counterparts shortly thereafter. In response to Henry's demands for an explanation, Arita, in what Henry called a "disagreeable tone," indicated that the occupation had been executed for the purely military purpose of tightening the blockade against southern China, thereby to bring about an early termination of the war. Japan, he declared, had no intention of annexing Hainan or occupying it beyond military necessity.[45] Parisian officials remained skeptical, telling Ambassador Bullitt that they did "not believe for a moment" Japanese assurances. Jean Chauvel, head of the Far Eastern Department, believed that if halting the flow if materiel had been the chief Japanese motive, it would have been more logical and effective to have pushed on along the South China coast to seize Pakhoi and Nanning. He suspected that the occupation was part of a larger plan and that Japan had no intention of abandoning the island.[46] Henri Hoppenot, assistant director for European affairs, felt that Tokyo had taken the initiative in order to rekindle waning domestic enthusiasm for the war and to satisfy extremists in the military. But he speculated that an additional factor may have been rooted in a broader international context. Timid Western reaction to earlier actions made it worth grabbing Hainan as "a pawn of considerable value" should a settlement of the conflict become possible. Or, in the event of a general conflict, it would give Japan a position from which to dominate the Gulf of Tonkin.[47]

While Japanese motives for such an initiative were undoubtedly many, so, too, were the potential consequences, a fact Western capitals quickly appreciated. Strategically, Hainan provided Japan with convenient facilities for air and naval bases from which routes leading into China from Indochina could be much more easily attacked than from existing bases around Canton. Moreover, it placed Japanese forces in position to harass all traffic using the port of Haiphong should their blockade of the Chinese coast be extended to Indochina. Control of the island also placed Japan in a position to dominate the South China Sea and the whole coast of Asia between Hong Kong and the southern tip of Indochina. As the American ambassador in Tokyo, Joseph Grew, fretted, "there emerges the inescapable fact that the Japanese are now in possession of an island which is capable of being developed into a formidable air and naval base and that their radius of operations is thus brought some six hundred miles nearer to American, British, French, and Dutch territories. Hong Kong is cut off, Manila is within easier reach . . . ." Grew concurred with other Western observers in the area that the seizure of Hainan was "in harmony with and constitutes the most logical next step in the development of the so-called 'southward advance policy' of the Japanese." Politically, the feeling persisted among French and British observers that the move reflected a further consolidation of Japanese links with Germany and Italy, since those two powers apparently had been forewarned of the occupation. Moreover, it seemed clear that Japan remained unconcerned and unconvinced about the prospects for a united Western response.[48]

French security fears were heightened a month and a half later, on 31 March, when the Japanese announced the annexation of the Spratly Islands, lying in the south China Sea between Indochina and the Philippines and situated midway between Saigon and British Borneo. These islands had been the subject of conflicting French and Japanese claims ever since France had claimed them in 1933. Considering themselves heirs to the emperors of Annam, the French regarded themselves as sovereign over the Spratlys, even though Japan had occupied them after World War I. But France had done little to develop the tiny islets until 1937, when Japanese settlers were discovered exploiting the guano deposits there. This had spurred the French in April 1938 to dispatch gunboats and work crews to establish communications stations on the islands. At this point, the issue was joined. Neither side was willing to surrender its jurisdiction over the area. The French navy believed that the islands were too far away from Indochina's facilities at Cam Ranh Bay to be adequately protected. Certainly, the navy argued, the value of the islands was not worth antagonizing the Japanese, and it recommended cautious prudence. Nervous about Singapore's defense, Britain proposed the possibility of a joint base in the islands, but France poured cold water over the idea. So the situation had resulted in a standoff until Japan ultimately let the matter drop in the fall of 1938. Clearly, however, the issue was not forgotten in Tokyo, as Japanese action proved six months later.[49]

In a statement of March 1939, the Japanese placed the Spratlys under the jurisdiction of the Government General of Formosa, and indicated that the step had been motivated by a "desire to avoid the possibility of further complications with the French Government . . . ." They repeated earlier arguments that the islands had been ownerless until Japan had established economic enterprises in 1917. Although France had given notice of annexation of the islands in 1933, Tokyo noted, she had never taken necessary steps to make the occupation effective.[50]

The cabinet of Edouard Daladier, preoccupied with grave financial crisis and beset by domestic political division, met on the morning of 1 April to develop a response to the Japanese move. Although a response to a Japanese retaliatory action in the aftermath of a French occupation had been contemplated during the previous spring, there is no evidence that France seriously anticipated that Japan would make the first move. Serious concern existed at the Foreign Ministry, where the Japanese action was regarded as the first occupation of French territory. The suspicion existed that Tokyo's action had been undertaken for several reasons: first, to place Japan's claims to the area on a juridical parity with those of France; second, to acquire additional territory for potential naval and seaplane bases; and, last, to shore up the government's weakening position at home by taking another military–diplomatic initiative.[51]

Tokyo's timing was opportune. Europe was in crisis as a result of Hitler's mid-March rape of the truncated Czechoslovakian state that had been left after the Munich Conference. In the flurry of activity in Western capitals, designed finally to resist Hitler's advances, little attention was focused upon the Far East. The French responded to the Japanese initiative only on 3 April. The French note formally protested the Japanese occupation and refused to recognize the Japanese action which "can in no degree and in no case affect the sovereign rights of France in the Spratly Archipelago." Additionally, France concluded that the Japanese move violated the Franco-Japanese Treaty of 1907 and that it would force France to "reexamine the position which it has believed it desirable to take or maintain with regard to the various existing problems in the Far East."[52] The Japanese response was blunt: "There is no room for consideration regarding the issue." The French protest, they indicated, would be used only as a matter of reference.[53] Clearly, Japan would not be deterred by diplomatic protest from France alone.

Little support could be found elsewhere. Britain had also laid claim to the Spratlys because of their potential use as an advance-warning base for the defense of Singapore. But London had ultimately withdrawn its claim in favor of the French after France had refused to abandon her sovereignty, and it had been determined that insufficient legal basis existed for the British claim.[54] At the same time, however, Britain had impressed upon the French the necessity of moving quickly to establish effective occupation in order to preempt a Japanese move. When Japan announced its annexation in March, some British officials displayed an obvious irritation over France's dilatory tactics in establishing control over the islands and thereby allowing Japan to steal the march on them. London regarded the Japanese seizure with great concern because of the islands' potential as a post for air and naval surveillance of Singapore's activities.[55] While Britain had been willing to support a vigorous French response to such a Japanese initiative a year earlier, by the spring of 1939 differences of opinion within the Chamberlain government concerning the nature of Japanese retaliation to British economic pressure led to Britain's failure to do anything more than issue a formal protest and refuse to accept that the Japanese claim had any legal foundation.[56]

In Washington, a French inquiry regarding possible American action met with the response that the Japanese action would be studied. When Ambassador René Saint-Quentin attempted to equate the Spratlys with Hong Kong or Indochina as a violation of a power's sovereignty, Maxwell Hamilton, chief of the Far Eastern Division of the Department of State, quickly pointed out the distinction that claims of ownership over the Spratlys had been disputed, while those of Hong Kong and Indochina had not, although he admitted that Japan had acted in an unfortunate manner. In the end, the United States simply issued its own protest to Tokyo, regretting that negotiation had not been allowed to settle the Franco-Japanese dispute concerning the Spratlys and denying that Washington would recognize the validity of the Japanese claim to the islands. As French Foreign Minister Georges Bonnet later lamented, although the Americans "understood the situation perfectly, they made it clear that the state of their armaments made it necessary to avoid a conflict."[57]

Only China displayed a willingness to side with France against Japan. Indeed, the Western powers considered the Chinese far too willing to act. Consequently, when Chungking offered to collaborate in the defense of Indochina in the event of a Japanese attack, the response in Paris and London, where the French quickly touched base, was decidedly cool. Besides the fact that Chinese forces were too weak to be of serious assistance, such an arrangement might actually provoke the Japanese blow that France sought to dodge.[58]

If Japan though its occupation of Hainan and the Spratlys would intimidate France and completely end the transit of supplies through Indochina, she was to be disappointed. In his note of 10 February protesting the Japanese seizure of Hainan, Bonnet warned that the move would force France to reconsider its obligations in the Far East, a warning that was reiterated in the aftermath of the Spratly operation. Within ten days of Tokyo's coup in Hainan, the French government decided that henceforth the regulation of the transit of supplies through Indochina would be less rigorously interpreted and would be determined on the basis of the Geneva Convention of 1925. This had the effect of broadening the variety of materiel shipped into China. As Chauvel subsequently confirmed, "certain materiel which had hitherto been held up was now going forward."[59]

Additionally, the French placed their own semi-embargo on strategic raw materials being exported from Indochina to Japan. By a decree issued in September 1938, the export of iron ore had been prohibited, although contracts previously negotiated would be honored. After the Hainan occupation, all deliveries of iron ore to Japan were suspended, and other ores, such as tungsten, lead, and coal, were halted. To Tokyo's inquiries about the prolonged "delays" that began to confound shipments, the French merely indicated the need for France to rebuild its own stockpiles of such resources and the need to marshal such materiel for munitions production in Indochina. There was no intention, it was claimed, to discriminate against Japan, but Bonnet suggested to the Japanese chargé d'affaires in Paris that earlier French assurances about taking into account Japan's interests "would conserve their full value only if the goodwill were reciprocated." Undoubtedly, the message was clearly interpreted in Tokyo.

In fact, on 27 April, the French went a step further by decreeing a prohibition of Japanese imports into France and Indochina.[60]

Unfortunately for France and for Indochina, perhaps as much as 80 to 90 percent of Indochina's mineral ores had been exported to Japan. Barely a month after imposing its quasi-embargo, French officials began to realize the serious financial and economic implications that the move meant for the colony. Laborers in the mines and on the docks had been thrown out of work, thereby causing strong protests from them. Local revenues began to dry up. Most disconcerting to the French, however, was the belief that their action had been undermined by Japan's ability to purchase such ores from British Malaya and the American Philippines. Bonnet lamented that "as long as this possibility exists, our measures will remain without real effect on the Japanese conflict, while exposing Indochina to economic and social difficulties at the same time as Japanese reprisals."[61] When the French complained to London, the British indicated that it was senseless for them to terminate exports of iron ore to Japan so long as Tokyo could obtain all that it needed from the United States. The British were reluctant to limit ore exported from Malaya except as "part of a general scheme for bringing pressure to bear on the Japanese." Such general pressure necessarily required the participation of the United States, but French and British feelers concerning the matter met with a chilly reception in Washington.[62]

The available documentation leaves unclear the final disposition of the French embargo, but in June, when Britain raised the issue of possible retaliation against Japan, France's response was clearly that of a nation that had been previously burned: "France will definitely not get out in front and appear to take the initiative in the matter. . . . On the other hand, if several governments adopt a common policy in this regard so that the risks of Japanese retaliation are spread, France will be willing to take part in such policy. . . . Cooperation in this matter of France, Great Britain and the United States is essential." Moreover, the French position stipulated that "if measures of reprisal, such as an embargo upon Japanese exports and upon the import into Japan of raw materials and raw materials from other powers, are to be placed in effect, France would require not only that such measures be undertaken by common accord . . . between France, Great Britain and the United States, but would likewise require guarantees of assistance in the event that such a policy should result in an attack by Japan upon French colonial possessions."[63]

Yet the prospects for obtaining significant Western cooperation in Far Eastern affairs remained as elusive as ever. For months of 1938 and 1939, as Japanese attacks in China destroyed American ships, property, commerce, and lives, the United States had basically sought to remain on the sidelines of the contest. Indeed, the larger part of the American people initially would have preferred to stay away from the ballpark altogether. Nevertheless, the brutality of the Japanese campaign and their disregard for American interests increasingly generated an anti-Japanese mood in the United States, perhaps best displayed in a Gallup poll in May 1939, which indicated that 72 percent of those questioned favored an embargo on war materiel exported to Japan.[64] This shift in the public mood corresponded in the government with the views of a small but vigorous cadre of officials like Stanley Hornbeck who believed that only a more determined stand by the United States would restrain Japan. Already, by the fall of 1938, a series of Japanese actions and American statements had led some foreign observers to believe that the United States might finally be ready to participate in a coordinated Western response to Japan's aggression.

On 2 November 1938, intoxicated by their victories at Canton and Hankow, thereby establishing control over a large stretch of the Yangtze River and over all of the major cities of China, undoubtedly emboldened by the Munich humiliation of the democratic powers at the end of September, the Japanese Foreign Ministry issued a statement, boldly announcing its determination to create a "new order in East Asia." The basis of the new order was to be "a tripartite relationship of mutual aid and coordination between Japan, Manchukuo, and China in political, economic, cultural, and other fields." The Western powers were urged to "adapt their attitude to the new conditions prevailing in East Asia." Here, it appeared, was a direct challenge to Western interests and influence in East Asia and proof of a Japanese design to monopolize the economic, political, and cultural life of China.[65]

This statement, coming at a time of increased Japanese harassment of American shipping along the Yangtze River, produced a lively response by the United States. The State Department refused to recognize the "new order" and reiterated its commitment to the Open Door. Any change in the status quo and existing agreements governing relations in East Asia could be brought about only through negotiations, not by a unilateral announcement. Washington invited the other interested Western powers to deliver parallel protests, and Paris and London quickly did so. Additionally,

Roosevelt announced in December that a financial loan had been negotiated for the beleaguered Chinese.[66]

Overseas, such steps were watched with considerable anticipation, tempered by a suspicion that the American propensity to return to its familiar posture of sitting back happily with hands folded could occur at any time. Nevertheless, French observers, among others, hoped for the best. From Washington, Ambassador René de Saint-Quentin cautiously reported that Undersecretary of State Sumner Welles believed that Japan would retreat in the face of concerted Western financial pressure.[67] Although Saint-Quentin admitted that other officials, such as Hornbeck, were not thinking along the same lines, Bonnet quickly urged the French ambassador to pursue the possibility of promoting a unified Western response to Japan's actions. Bonnet found hope in the fact that in dealing with the Yangtze navigation issue, the United States for the first time had taken the initiative of proposing a concerted Western action. Bonnet admonished Saint-Quentin to warn Washington that the nature of the problem had changed during the course of the year since the Brussels Conference. Earlier, the concern had been to maintain adherence to the Nine Power Treaty guaranteeing the territorial integrity of China. But events over the past year, culminating with Konoye's statement establishing a new order in Asia, showed that Japan intended to repudiate the Open Door and equality of opportunity in China. The original Japanese threat to China's territorial integrity now had become a challenge to the interests in China of all major powers. On the grounds of defending their economic, financial, and territorial treaty rights, France, the United States, and Britain must present a common front in the Far East. "The solidarity thus affirmed between the three countries would defend, in fact, morally, in the eyes of Japan, the harmony of their positions in the Far East." Bonnet reminded the French ambassador, as if he needed reminding, that "the establishment of a common front in the Far East by the three democratic powers would have, for our own interest, most desirable consequences." As the foreign minister warned the American chargé d'affaires in Paris, Edwin Wilson, on 10 November, the day after wiring his charge to Saint-Quentin, he was pessimistic about the Far Eastern situation. He did not believe that Japan would simply bog down the deeper it got drawn into China.[68]

Henri Hoppenot, chief of the Far Eastern Department of the Quai d'Orsay, outlined the course of action contemplated by the French policymakers. The three Western powers should, at approximately the same time (thus avoiding Washington's opposition to strictly joint action), secretly tell the Japanese (in order to avoid Tokyo's concern about losing face) that they recognized that changes had occurred in China. This would necessarily be taken into account in any new treaty. But these changes could not be imposed unilaterally by Japan. Rather, change could only be effected by the participants of the Nine Power Treaty, including a government representing China. Meanwhile, the status quo regarding Western rights in China must be defended.[69]

In London, Ambassador Corbin sounded out the British as to their response to the Japanese action and the potential for an American initiative with which Britain and France might associate themselves. Alexander Cadogan, permanent undersecretary at the Foreign Office, was not optimistic. Britain, he pointed out, had studied the issue and believed that it would join an American initiative. But he remained skeptical about the American tendency to change course after deciding to act. He agreed, however, that only an American action would have enough impact to alter Japan's course. Britain, he indicated, was too preoccupied with more immediate security issues to organize a common front and bear the associated risks. In fact, a consensus concerning British policy did not exist in London. The developments of the period in the Far East and the apparent American willingness to cooperate with the other Western powers had stimulated a general review of British policy. But as the process dragged on through the end of the year, the divisions in policy-making circles became increasingly apparent. Prime Minister Chamberlain particularly opposed undertaking joint economic action against Japan. As Bradford Lee concluded, "the British . . . wanted [to appear] to be willing to join the United States in retaliatory measures, but gently trying to dissuade her from them." The fear that overt economic retaliation against Japan might provoke an attack against Hong Kong at a time when Britain's attention necessarily focused upon the volatile European situation led London to prefer financial aid for China rather than sanctions against Japan.[70]

The French received a firsthand account of Britain's attitude at the Anglo-French conversations held in Paris on 24 November, attended by the leading officials of both governments. While the major items of business concerned the European situation, toward the very end of the second session of the day Bonnet raised the issue of the Far East and reiterated French hopes for a united action that included the United States. Neville Chamberlain's limp response could not have encouraged the French to believe that Britain would be of much help in prodding the Americans to action. The fact that Washington had not made any specific proposals, he suggested, indicated that they had none to make. Chamberlain preferred to emphasize the value of financial aid to China in the hope that Japan "would eventually be exhausted." This, of course, was a hope in which Bonnet had little faith. He might have taken some solace from a Foreign Office study completed during the same period, which concluded, "we should aim at giving Japan enough rope to hang herself with and advancing by all the means in our power the moment of actual suffocation." But the position of the United States remained an unknown factor. As the author of the report sarcastically noted, so far the United States had been "disposed to take a high moral tone well suited to their principal interest in China, missionary enterprise"![71]

In the end, the Western responses to the Japanese statements came dribbling into Tokyo in such a manner as to be of very little concern to Japan's leaders. The American protest of 30 December denied Japan's right unilaterally to abrogate established treaties, although expressing a willingness to negotiate proposals designed to resolve the problems of the area. But the United States would not, meanwhile, relinquish her treaty rights. A fortnight later, on 14 January, the British responded in a similar vein.[72]

The French now were confronted with the nature of their response. Once again, external considerations dictated the options available. From Washington, Saint-Quentin warned the Quai d'Orsay that although the United States had reserved its freedom of action it seemed obvious that no action was contemplated—certainly not of the cooperative nature that had seemed in the offing a few short weeks earlier. Even Sumner Welles could not hide the fact that public opinion was evolving more slowly than anticipated.[73] This caveat dovetailed neatly with an assessment rendered by Hoppenot on 9 January. After reviewing the range of options available to France—from direct economic action against Japan to financial aid to China—the chief of the Far Eastern Department returned once again to the same bottom line. Any decisive action could be taken only if American and British guarantees were to be made to offset the risks to French interests in the Far East.[74] From Tokyo, Ambassador Charles-Arsène Henry urged that France keep in line with Britain and the United States if for no other reason than to keep encouraging the latter to remain involved in the affairs of the area. Moreover, France must continuously defend its position and interests. Henry suggested, however, that with a new Japanese cabinet in place as a result of Konoye's resignation on 4 January, it would be useful "to raise the tone a little in speaking to the Japanese." This tactic might encourage the moderates, the only group with which the Western powers could hope to deal. In view of the consensus that emerged, then, in the aftermath of the American protest, it should have been no surprise when the French démarche sent by Bonnet on 14 January paralleled very closely those submitted by the United States and Britain. It upheld the sanctity of the Nine Power Treaty but indicated a willingness to negotiate modifications of the treaty properly submitted to the signatories.[75]

In another of his moves that appeared promising, however, President Roosevelt stimulated new hope abroad for American action when he gave his annual State of the Union message to Congress on 4 January 1939. During a lengthy comment upon the state of the international situation, he warned of the dangers to the democracies should they fail to react effectively against acts of aggression. He went on to explain: "There are many methods short of war, but stronger and more effective than words, of bringing home to aggesssor governments the aggregate sentiments of our peoples. At the very least, we can and should avoid any action, or any lack of action, which will encourage, assist or build up an aggressor." Roosevelt then revealed that he would soon propose new measures for defense, and he obliquely criticized the existing neutrality laws. "We have learned that when we deliberately try to legislate neutrality, our neutrality laws may operate unevenly and unfairly—many actually give aid to an aggressor and deny it to the victim. The instinct of self-preservation should warn us that we ought not to let that happen any more." The speech was widely interpreted as a call for revision of the existing neutrality laws that would be due for renewal in May.[76]

Naturally, the address caught the attention of many foreign observers. It was exactly the kind of statement that many would seize upon as a harbinger of change in American policy. For France, revisions of the neutrality laws would have ramifications for the European situation as well as the Far East. French Ambassador Saint-Quentin had caught wind of possible revision of the neutrality laws several weeks earlier. The dawning conviction among many Americans that the laws had actually helped the aggesssors in the Ethiopian crisis and the Spanish Civil War had stimulated interest in revision. The Czech crisis of September 1938 had increased such interest, but in the post-Munich lull the interest in change had waned. The State Department still favored revision, but public opinion and its consequent effect on Congress had remained the great unknown element. But with the president apparently ready to run with the ball, perhaps the momentum could be changed. To be sure, Saint-Quentin's analysis of the prospects remained guardedly optimistic. Although the president had moved very carefully with Congress—emphasizing the reduction of isolation rather than intervention—the press reaction had been quite divided, leading the French ambassador to conclude that "the discussion in Congress will not go without difficulties."[77]

Indeed, the revisionist legislation limped forward through the Senate under the desultory guidance of Senator Key Pittman, chairman of the Foreign Relations Committee. Roosevelt's political position had itself become so weakened that he believed that it would be counterproductive to take a leading role in the discussions.[78]

French observers kept close watch on the debate, but, amidst a series of proposals put forth by both sides, they developed little sense of the direction to which Congress might jump. Indeed, near the end of January, France inadvertently strengthened the isolationist opponents of revision when the American press learned that a French military officer had been injured in the crash of an American test bomber in California. The resulting furor concerning the role of a French mission in the United States led by Jean Monnet and the purchase by France of American planes led Roosevelt to intervene to limit the damage. But in the course of a discussion with leading congressmen, intended to explain the need to sell warplanes to France, the president compounded the problem by referring to the defense of the Rhine River as America's concern. Despite a pledge of secrecy, the statement hit the press, resulting in distortions of his meaning and a clamorous reaction from the isolationists. All of this forced the president into the open. In a press conference on 3 February, Roosevelt condemned as deliberate lies the stories that had been leaked to the press, and he attempted to reassure the public that American foreign policy had not changed. The damage had been done, however, and, as Saint-Quentin observed, Roosevelt's assurances had scarcely the result intended, and there continued to prevail "a feeling of confusion and even a certain discontent."[79]

The hearings and debate concerning the revisionist legislation continued for the next month, but Roosevelt now kept his silence as various proposals and amendments came and went. To the French observers, this state of affairs hardly augured well for favorable revision. Indeed, with considerable prescience, as it turned out, Saint-Quentin cautioned Paris, "It is necessary to deal with the possibility that with opposing opinions neutralizing each other, Congress [might] extend purely and simply at the last moment the neutrality law in its present text," even if it meant "not strictly enforcing it against regimes that it recognizes as being at fault."[80]

In the end, it was Hitler who helped break the deadlocked debate. The Nazi seizure of the rump of Czechoslovakia on 15 March, in violation of the Munich accords, outraged the public and shook the Congress into acting. Within a few days, Pittman introduced the Peace Act of 1939, draft legislation that provided for a repeal of the arms embargo and put all trade with belligerents on a cash-and-carry basis. At first glance, the proposal looked favorable to France and Britain because of their potential for controlling the sea lanes of the Atlantic. But upon further analysis, as Roosevelt lamented to Secretary of State Hull, while the plan "works all right in the Atlantic, it works all wrong in the Pacific."[81] Indeed, France and Britain stood to benefit in the Atlantic for exactly the same reasons that would cause Japan profit in the Pacific, at the expense of China. Roosevelt now believed that the neutrality legislation must be repealed in toto. This proved to be more than Congress would accept. During the next several weeks, while amendments were added, the momentum for repeal established in mid-March dissipated. Even though opinion polls consistently showed the public to favor repeal of the arms embargo, divisions between isolationists and revisionists and ineffective leadership in Congress culminated in a defeat for the administration's efforts at repealing the arms embargo provision of the neutrality laws. At a meeting with Senate leaders on 18 July, the president was finally forced to admit defeat, and it was agreed that the neutrality legislation would be considered at the next session of the Senate.[82]

During the imbroglio, the French found themselves on the horns of another dilemma. They ardently hoped for a revision of the neutrality laws, for it would surely strengthen their position vis-à-vis Germany, and, in fact, might deter the Germans from risking additional aggression. On the other hand, they feared that any overt promotion of revision on the part of France might well backfire by producing an adverse reaction among the American public and in Congress. Saint-Quentin initially concurred with the British ambassador, Sir Ronald Lindsay, that, if worse came to worst, at the last minute Roosevelt's administration would get its way with Congress. The Frenchman, however, recognized that the slightest misstep could tip the scales in favor of the isolationists. For that reason, he warned the Quai d'Orsay of the need to restrain the French press, because "except in moments where it is swept away by indignation, average American opinion feels an instinctive mistrust for foreign nations which appear to solicit the cooperation or even aid from the United States." Saint-Quentin's emphasis upon prudence in dealing with the situation was revealed in early April, when Bonnet, during the Albanian crisis, urged him to see Hull and Welles and to urge upon them the importance of neutrality revision as soon as possible because of its potential effect upon the totalitarian states. The position taken by Congress "could still have in good time a capital effect on the evolution of events." When the ambassador carried out his instructions, however, he carefully avoided giving the impression that he was doing so in an official capacity. He warned Bonnet that if "such a démarche had been made and were made known, the reactions of Congress and of general opinion would risk being the most troublesome. For the most convinced partisans of the assistance to the democratic powers want the American government to seem to act on its own initiative and in consideration of its own interests without ceding to the solicitations of France or England."[83]

In fact, there is no evidence that France attempted to influence the debate in Washington. There was undoubtedly little that the French could usefully do that might not have the adverse effects that Saint-Quentin feared, and, in any case, French negotiations led by Jean Monnet during the winter and spring of 1939 to buy large quantities of aircraft and aircraft engines was meeting with limited success. Any detailed analysis the efforts of the Monnet mission are beyond the scope of this study, but it is clear that the urgent French need for advanced models of American military aircraft necessarily took precedence and made them wary of committing a misstep that might call any additional attention to the bold negotiations that Roosevelt and Secretary of the Treasury Henry Morgenthau were trying to keep out of the spotlight. It will be recalled that the aircraft accident involving a French observer had raised a howl in isolationist circles in January. The last thing that negotiators on both sides wanted was another incident that would increase the obstacles in the United States as well as in France.

As for French cooperation with Britain in creating a united front in the Far East, little seemed possible during the winter of 1938–39, as London also focused primarily on American cooperation. In London, division continued between the Foreign Office, which was on the whole more inclined to react more aggressively toward Japan, and other departments such as Treasury, which clearly opposed such steps as economic embargoes. Prime Minister Neville Chamberlain vacillated, finally assenting to provide financial aid to China in March 1939.[84] By the spring, however, their attention began to shift increasingly to the European situation. When the Far East received top-level consideration, it did so in the context of the European circumstances.

This became particularly the case during consideration of defense measures for the Far East in the event of a war in Europe. Under the pressure of events during the spring of 1939, the Admiralty had become increasingly alarmed at the prospect of having to withdraw the Royal Navy from the troubled Mediterranean waters to send it to the Far East to confront Japan. By May, policymakers finally admitted that the European scene was so dangerous that Britain could not foresee when and in what force a fleet might be sent to the Far East. This admission, of course, was extremely embarrassing in view of previous assurances to the dominions, such as Australia, that the fleet would be dispatched. Now it had become apparent that the main fleet might not go to Singapore at all.[85]

A major factor in the British decision was the attitude of France. For most of the interwar period, there had been little military cooperation between the two powers, although London had assumed that the French fleet would be available in the Mediterranean should the British fleet be sent to the Far East. But only after the German invasion of Czechoslovakia in March 1939 did Franco-British military staff talks begin, with an eye toward taking steps to protect their common interests, not only in Europe but in the Far East as well. Previously, the British had relegated such staff talks to a relatively low level, but the events of the spring had led the French to press hard for higher-level army and naval talks. The Franco-British staff talks that resulted were held in several stages. The first conversations, held in London from 29 March to 4 April, established a common strategic policy for the conduct of a war. The second, also held in London, from 24 April to 3 May, dealt with operational plans for the implementation of the policy. These sessions were followed by local commanders in the principal theaters of war working out theater-level plans. In London, the talks focused primarily on the European theater and the Mediterranean area, which consumed ever-increasing British attention. These talks were of no concern in the present discussion except in their capacity to affect allocations for the Far Eastern theater. The European theater necessarily received considerable attention as well as money, materiel, and personnel.

The staff conversations concerning the Far East focused upon three issues.[86] First, the conferees agreed upon the importance of American support, or, at the very least, benevolent neutrality in the event that Japan took advantage of a war in Europe by attacking Western interests. If the United States were unwilling to enter the fight, it should be at least encouraged to send its fleet to the Pacific to deter the Japanese. Second, they reconciled differences about whether a British fleet should be dispatched to the Far East. While the British, in accordance with discussions within the government, recognized that circumstances would determine the size and timing of such a fleet transfer, they had not, because of their extensive interests and fears of Dominion reaction, completely discarded the notion of sending such a fleet. For the French, however, the focus of attention remained on Europe, and they feared a premature departure of a British fleet from the Mediterranean. Even before the staff conversations began, Daladier and Bonnet had made their strongest feelings known about the relative importance of the Mediterranean and Far Eastern theaters. In the aftermath of the Italian coup in Albania in early April, Daladier told Phipps, "If [the Mediterranean] is lost, all is lost, whereas if we are victorious in Europe we can make good later on any temporary defeat we may suffer in the Far East." Bonnet subsequently reiterated that France would regard as "catastrophic" a British decision to send a fleet to the Far East. A French naval staff position paper of 25 April reflected this thinking and clearly delineated the French position: "It is better to adopt a defensive posture provisionally in the Far East than to lose mastery of the eastern Mediterranean." Putting it more succinctly, Vice-Admiral Jean Odend'hal, head of the French delegation, warned, "Although the loss of Singapore would be a severe blow, the loss of the war in Europe would be disastrous." During the staff conversations, then, it was not surprising to find the French doing, as William Gregory Perett put it, "everything possible to dissuade the British from contemplating any serious naval effort in the Far East." France preferred to assume a strictly defensive stance in the Far East, hoping that an American and Soviet deterrence would hold Japan in check until a European conflict had been resolved, or at least until Italy had been defeated. In the end, the staffs sidestepped the issue, leaving the decision about fleet movement to be determined jointly when the need arose. The third issue discussed by the staffs was that of land defenses for their scattered territorial holdings. They quickly appreciated that the limited naval and air support would determine more than manpower whether or not key positions such as Hong Kong could be defended. The French sought to deemphasize the naval and air deficiencies by proposing a highly dubious scheme of having Chiang Kai-shek's army launch a counterattack toward Hong Kong to divert the Japanese. The British rightly remained skeptical.[87]

The Far Eastern theater talks followed in Singapore on 22–27 June, after a delay caused by the Anglophobic Admiral Jean Decoux, who was in charge of French naval forces in the Far East. But under the pressure of the Tientsin crisis in China[88] and Danzig debate in Europe, once the conferees got down to business, they established a working relationship and consensus with a quickness that astonished everyone. Within five days, they produced a plan for the coordinated defense of their interests in the Far East. In the event of war in the Far East, the basic policy provided for remaining on the defensive until reinforced, retreating to Indochina and Singapore, with a unified command centered at Singapore. The major concern of the French delegation, led by General Maurice Martin, commander-in-chief of the French army in Indochina, aided by Decoux, was the defense of Indochina. The British were no less interested in the colony, for they saw it as a vital advance base in the defense of Singapore and other Allied possessions in the area. Therefore, they agreed that "all necessary measures should be taken to secure the integrity of the coast of Indo-China . . . and also of the land frontiers from which the coast may be threatened." In this regard, the French insisted on helping the Chinese defend western Kwantung in case operations should be undertaken toward Canton. Moreover, to accomplish these goals the participants recommended an increase in military, naval, and air forces in Indochina as soon as possible, with an accelerated development of the naval facilities at Cam Ranh Bay.[89]

Analysis of the record of the conference reveals the striking ironies of the situation. The British naturally tended to emphasize the role of naval defense in stopping Japan, but Admiral Sir Percy Noble had no fleet. The French stressed military operations to check Japan, but they had no army. In their summary of the conference's proceedings, the commanders acknowledged their tenuous situation: "The Conference wishes to place on record its grave concern at the present inadequacy of the Allied Naval and Air Forces in the Far East. This weakness places the Japanese in a position of such superiority that we can neither assure our essential communications nor prevent enemy occupation of advanced bases that directly threaten our vital interests. The Japanese can be expected to exploit this position in full during the period in which they are likely to hold such an advantage." Since the European situation made it unlikely that naval and military reinforcements could be expected soon, the conference placed "paramount importance" on provision of "appreciably larger" Allied air forces, to be permanently stationed in the area. Such air power would "form the only mobile, effective, and practical solution to the problem of preventing important Japanese successes at the beginning of the war." All of this was only two-thirds correct. True enough, such an air force would have been mobile and effective. But at a time when Jean

Monnet was scrounging aircraft in the United States, it was hardly practical to assume that the Far Eastern theater would receive modern planes desperately needed in Europe. Again, the final irony was that both staffs agreed on the importance of air power to offset other deficiencies—but neither had such an air force available.[90]

This did not matter, however. For France, the staff talks of the spring and early summer of 1939 represented a great leap forward out of the military-diplomatic isolation it had endured since the end of World War I. Clearly, the decisions made represented a far greater commitment for both nations toward each other than either could have contemplated a few short months earlier. In many French minds, this must have relieved the considerable anxiety at not being able to secure a united front with the United States. Even so, Bonnet remained pessimistic. On 17 June, he had revealed his fear to Phipps that France would be unable to defend Indochina and that "without the whole-hearted collaboration of the United States in the Far East there is little that we can do to bring Japan to reason." Moreover, he believed that, in the event of any serious trouble in the Far East, Germany would quickly take the opportunity to move against Danzig. Therefore, Bonnet continued to urge Britain to avoid economic sanctions or any other pinpricks against Japan unless they could be effective. Indeed, concern about Danzig even led General Jules Bührer, chief of staff for the colonies, to advise General Maurice Gamelin on 26 July, "It seems certain to me that the European situation requires us for the time being not to disperse our military and naval efforts."[91]

By the spring and summer of 1939, however, the mounting European crisis had the effect of clouding the Far Eastern situation in the minds of most officials at the Quai d'Orsay. At the top, Bonnet appeared so concerned with the European situation that he left the impression to observers such as Wellington Koo that "he paid but slight attention to Far Eastern questions and left them to others in the Foreign Office."[92] But Jean Chauvel, head of the Far Eastern Department, later recalled that he could devote only part of his attention to Far Eastern affairs. In fact, he found that even Secretary General Léger was only vaguely aware of the situation in the Far East. In effect, the French, forced to "concentrate their efforts on [a] Europe menaced by German expansion, could not effectually watch over this other front."[93]

Indeed, throughout the entire period the European situation was the most constant and important factor in the minds of the French decision makers. At virtually every point and with nearly every decision, European considerations dominated French policy toward the Far East. From the very beginning of the Sino-Japanese conflict, the Quai d'Orsay had warned that "French policy must, in the present circumstances, concentrate its action in Europe."[94] For this reason, it had been of the utmost importance to avoid involving the League in any far-off enterprise that would only weaken still further its waning influence and thus make it unable to affect the European crisis. As a result of this fear, American support in the Far East had assumed even greater importance. This had been one of the principal motivations for France's support of the idea of a Nine Power Conference, for the conference would directly involve the United States in the issue. But before the Brussels Conference met, of course, the French had made it manifest that the two crises—in Europe and in the Far East—were related. Léger had indicated that "it was clear that as long as the present tension existed in Europe it would be impossible for France, or for that matter for England, to take part in any common action in the Far East which might involve or imply at some later stages the furnishing of armed forces." Regrettably, Léger conceded, this situation facilitated aggression in the Far East, but it was "a fact and had to be faced." Yet, there is another European-related dimension to the French desire to gain the support of the United States. The impression that Delbos had given Davis at the Brussels Conference was that if a strong Franco-Anglo-American stance could be established with regard to the Far East, it might well have a deterring effect on the fascist states of Europe.[95] In fact, Delbos had revealed to the British ambassador in Paris that he was thinking in more ambitious terms: "So long as the United States did not come out into the open against Japan, Great Britain and France must decline to be drawn into the conflict. If, on the other hand, the United States did decide to fight Japan, we could do anything we liked, for in that case the United States would be with us, not only in the Far East, but in Europe." Undoubtedly, the United States occupied a key position in French thinking in other ways as well. The unstated belief that lurked in the minds of many French policymakers was that effective United States action in the Far East on behalf of peace and stability would create a forceful impetus toward the maintenance of peace and stability in Europe. If the United States had been willing to restrain Japan effectively, so the argument went, the French and British would have been able to restrain Germany in Czechoslovakia. But American's inactivity in the Far Eastern crisis paralyzed French and British action in both Europe and the Far East. As late as 31 July 1939, when Léger glumly apprised Ambassador Bullitt of the

Franco-British decision to withdraw from its positions in the Far East, if necessary, to avoid war with Japan, the Frenchman reiterated that the European situation made the decision necessary and that only the active support of the United States in the Far East could alter the plan.[96]

The French also feared that Britain might become involved in the conflict in the Far East and thus be unable to act in Europe. France would be left alone to face Germany and Italy, who would then be encouraged to strike. In fact, the French wanted the United States to take the lead in the Far East so that Britain would not be forced to take prolonged action that would divert its attention from more pressing matters closer to home.[97] Consequently, there is no evidence that the French ever seriously suggested a combined Franco-British initiative in the Far East without American support. Moreover, while Franco-Soviet relations had cooled considerably by the time hostilities broke out in the Far East, the French feared that Russia might ultimately become too involved in aiding China. Many French statesmen worried that Russia's involvement there would divert her from playing her role as a counterweight against Nazi expansion in eastern Europe. Therefore, while the French were unwilling to put teeth into the Franco-Soviet Pact of 1935 by negotiating a military convention, it was widely rumored that they did everything possible to deter the Soviets from extending direct military aid to China.[98]

As the succession of European crises developed during 1938, many suspected that the Japanese were taking advantage of European tension to push ahead more rapidly with their southward advance.[99] The Japanese invasion of South China shortly after the Czechoslovakian crisis and Tokyo's subsequent declarations of the establishment of a New Order in East Asia were hardly calculated to assuage French sensitivities.[100] Chauvel reflected this belief as late as the middle of August 1939, telling the British chargé d'affaires, Ronald Campbell, that the Japanese attitude depended on the situation in Europe. If the situation improved in Europe, "this was likely to be reflected by a pause in Tokyo. If, on the other hand, the situation in Europe deteriorated, the Japanese were likely to become more aggressive, If there were a war in Europe, he thought that the Japanese would proceed actively against foreign concessions."[101]

During the winter and spring of 1939, considerable fear also developed that the Anti-Comintern Pact might be transformed into a firm military alliance among Tokyo, Rome, and Berlin. Paris and London received a steady stream of confusing and often contradictory speculation from the Far East about the status of Japanese negotiations with Germany and Italy. When France and Britain undertook negotiations with the Soviet Union during the late spring and summer of 1939, they feared that Japan's virulent hatred of the Soviets would throw Tokyo into Germany's arms.[102] Both the French and the British sought to keep Japan "in play" by assuring her that any agreement negotiated with the Soviets would apply only to the West. No commitments would be undertaken with regard to the Far East. If, however, Japan should conclude a general military alliance with the totalitarian states of Europe, the democracies would be forced to reconsider their position.[103] Certainly, some in the Quai d'Orsay held no illusions about the situation. Even if pressure by the military party in Japan did not become great enough to force the government to sign an alliance, the existing regime would still pursue what Chauvel labeled a policy of "squeezing us out rather than of chucking us out." By August, as negotiations reached a critical stage in Moscow and tensions mounted in China, the distinct possibility arose that a Nazi-Japanese alliance would put the European powers in an extremely tenuous position in the Far East.[104]

Ironically, the democracies were temporarily rescued by assistance from an unexpected quarter. The signing of the Nazi-Soviet Pact on 23 August caught Tokyo as much by surprise as it did Paris and London. The reports from Tokyo that reached the Quai d'Orsay for the next few days indicated that the Nazi-Soviet Pact had created a profound reaction in Japan. Some Frenchmen thought that it might be possible to exploit the sudden turn of events. Foreign Minister Bonnet suggested that Japanese policymakers "hesitated between a policy of complete independence and a rapprochement with the Western powers." Consequently, a window of opportunity existed for a Franco-British mediation of the Sino-Japanese conflict. Bonnet stated that "the goal of such action would be the appeasement and neutralization of the Far East."[105] Chauvel, with Bonnet's approval, proposed such a step to the British. He argued that without appearing to abandon the Chinese, it might be possible to move closer to Japan in an effort to bring the two belligerents to some agreement, even if only temporarily. The chances of reaching such an accord would be facilitated if the United States could be discreetly persuaded to take some early action. Chauvel thought that the situation might be stabilized to such a degree that French and British interests in the Far East would enjoy a measure of security if war broke out in Europe.[106]

The British Foreign Office reacted unfavorably to the idea, arguing that Japan would probably play a lone hand in the Far East, while looking about for more "trustworthy friends."[107] In any event, within a week Europe was plunging headlong into another catastrophe. The outbreak of war in Europe placed the whole Far Eastern question in a radically different light, and the French response to the new situation, the ensuing debacle of 1940, and the wartime role and position of Indochina belong to another chapter in the story of the decline of the French position in the Far East.

The outbreak of the Sino-Japanese conflict placed France on the horns of a difficult dilemma. Her large political, economic, and strategic interests in the Far East meant that she could hardly ignore the possible consequences of a Japanese conquest of China. On the other hand, France did not have sufficient strength to take effective unilateral action in defense of these interests and at the same time protect her more vital interest of security in Europe. Consequently, the French vigorously pressed for great-power cooperation to bring an end to the hostilities. But when the United States refused to play its allotted role, one senior diplomat compared this to the croquet game in the story of Alice in Wonderland. When one of the hedgehogs uncurled itself and crawled off the field, for all intents and purposes the game was over. Yet the problem would not just go away. The French wished neither to appease Japan nor to oppose her openly. Consequently, they adopted a policy that Sir John Pratt of the British Foreign Office characterized as "running with the hare and hunting with the hounds."[108] They tried to give whatever aid possible to the Chinese to keep them fighting, while at the same time trying to keep on good terms with Japan. The French behavior with regard to the shipment of munitions through Indochina illustrates the policy in bold relief. While publicly forbidding such shipments and privately reassuring Japan of their good intentions, they continued to permit considerable quantities to be shipped to China. Ultimately, however, the European situation so preoccupied France that it became doubly difficult for her to focus on the Far Eastern conflict, much less take necessary action to protect her interests there. Too weak and overextended to protect her vital interests in Europe and her material interests in the Far East, France was forced to learn a bitter lesson: no matter how adroit her diplomatic gymnastics, to borrow the title from Christopher Thorne's study of the Manchurian crisis, there are indeed limits of foreign policy. By attempting to maintain interests and ties with both of its traditional Far Eastern friends, France merely succeeded in antagonizing both. Certainly, by the time of the outbreak of war in 1939 French stock in Japan and China had deteriorated to its lowest point in twenty years—a natural result of trying to befriend two powers who are enemies.

seven

POLICY ADRIFT: SEPTEMBER
1939–JUNE 1940

THE Nazi-Soviet Pact of 23 August, and the consequent outbreak of war in Europe a week later, proved to be both a boon and a blight for Western interests in the Far East. On the one hand, the Western powers were given a short breathing space. Humiliated by the Nazi actions, the government of Baron Hiranauma collapsed and was succeeded by a cabinet formed by the politically inexperienced General Nobayuki Abe, who, in retrospect, merely presided over a caretaker government while Japan sorted out its situation and adjusted to the new diplomatic alignment. Some Western diplomats argued that it would be an opportune time to negotiate a settlement with Japan.[1] But, in fact, although the much-dreaded possibility of a Tokyo-Berlin-Rome partnership had vanished for the moment, Abe, while reiterating Japan's determination to build the new Asian order, also indicated that his government would adopt a policy of "strict neutrality" toward European affairs.[2]

On the other hand, freed somewhat from its fears regarding Germany in the West, the Soviet Union could now afford to devote more attention to and expend more energy in the East. "Unofficial" fighting between Japan and Russia had already occurred along the border of Outer Mongolia, and Japan's Kwantung Army had incurred heavy casualties. Such a situation strengthened the hand of those factions in Tokyo who believed that Japan's real interests lay to the south. Certainly, if Japan sought to expand in the direction of least resistance, the southward advance seemed most logical. Moreover, as military expenditures for the war in China placed ever-increasing demands on Japan's economy, the government sought ways to divert domestic opposition, justify new taxes, and rationalize its acts in China and Manchuria. Japan's economic prospects had suffered an additional jolt in July when the United States notified Tokyo that it had decided to terminate its Commercial Agreement of 1911 and that, henceforth, Japanese-American trade would be based on "circumstances and . . . future developments."[3]

All of this meant that Japan increasingly turned its attention southward. Indeed, as Akira Iriye has noted, the southern advance had been a basic Japanese policy since 1938. The economic bloc set up by Japan in Manchukuo and North China had proved to be far less lucrative than anticipated, and it seemed logical to include the mineral-rich Southeast Asian area under the Japanese umbrella, thus making Japan much less dependent upon American resources. The Japanese navy, never happy with the North China orientation of Japan's army leaders, was particularly enthusiastic about a southern advance. It would focus more attention upon the navy's budget requests, and it would provide a convenient supply of oil for the Japanese fleet.[4] Obviously, however, such a policy would directly threaten Western interests that predominated in Southeast Asia, and a key to the success for any such Japanese thrust—and this was fully recognized in Western capitals as well as in Tokyo—was the French possession of Indochina. Yet, a move toward the south could hardly be contemplated so long as the China incident remained unresolved. For all of these reasons, then, it was inevitable that increased Japanese pressure would be exerted upon the Western powers and especially upon the French.

The respite enjoyed by the Western powers in the Far East proved, therefore, to be short-lived. Even the cautious Abe government could not long resist the temptation—made well-nigh irresistible by pressure from public opinion and the army—to seize upon the golden opportunity presented by the obvious Western preoccupation with the European war to force an end to the West's support of Chiang Kai-shek and thus expedite a termination of the Chinese conflict. Japanese hesitation ended on 5 September, when Japanese vice-minister for foreign affairs, Shigero Sawada, handed a note to the French, British, German, and Polish representatives in Tokyo, indicating that Japan wished to avoid becoming involved in the European war and sought instead "to devote its energies to settling the China incident." The note went on to offer the belligerent powers the "friendly advice" that they voluntarily withdraw their military and naval forces from those parts of China occupied by Japan, ostensibly to prevent the spread of Western hostilities to the Far East that might result in "unfortunate incidents and in a condition of affairs ill adapted to Japan's non-involvement policy."[5]

The Western response to such a blatantly transparent attempt to force the withdrawal of the European presence in China was

predictable. Since neither Germany nor Poland had military personnel in China, the note was obviously directed at Britain and France,
both of whom had small land forces in Tientsin and Shanghai. Japan's
"advice" sparked considerable debate in British government circles.
The British ambassador in Tokyo, Robert Craigie, suggested that
Britain should respond that it was unable to see why the outbreak of
war in Europe should present any difficulties with Japan, and it therefore saw no reason for withdrawing its forces. London should indicate that it intended to keep its forces in the Far East as long as
necessary for the defense of British interests. Actually, with the outbreak of the war in Europe, the British had planned to reduce their
garrisons anyway, but now they became most reluctant to carry out
such a withdrawal lest it appear that they were surrendering too easily
to Japanese pressure. As M. E. Dening of the Foreign Office put it,
"We can . . . remove sources of friction and if our garrisons are withdrawn the tension is likely to relax. This will mean that the Japanese
will be largely free to do as they like, and we shall have to put up with
the results at least for as long as we are involved in war in Europe.
But we need not and should not acquiesce in what Japan does [except]
to force majeure." But Sir John Brenan argued, "It is of course by no
means certain that the withdrawal of the garrison and the abandonment of the Concession to Japanese control will produce a more
friendly feeling on the part of the Japanese, but at all events it cannot
fail to remove the main cause of friction between the two countries so
far as North China is concerned, and our consolation for the loss of
our position must be that it is in any case untenable whilst we are at
war in Europe and would have to go sooner or later. If the Chinese
Government can do nothing to save this part of their territory we certainly cannot do it for them." In the end, the War Cabinet decided to
ignore the Japanese "advice" until the attitudes of France and the
United States could be ascertained.[6]

Although Tokyo had merely told Washington for "its information" about the Japanese "advice" to France and Britain, the
State Department had reacted vigorously. On 7 September, Secretary
of State Cordell Hull called in Japanese Ambassador Kensuke
Horinouchi and bluntly informed him that the Japanese action "directly affects rights and interests of the United States" and that
"withdrawal of the British and French forces would create a situation
fraught with extreme difficulties both for Japan and for the United
States." The United States must conclude, Hull asserted, that the
purpose behind the Japanese move "is not a mere innocent, friendly
purpose," but rather one designed to exclude all foreign interests

from China. Tokyo could respond only with the weakest assurances of goodwill when confronted with the apparent American determination to prevent the expulsion of Western forces from China.[7]

For her part, France fell somewhere between the British inclination to pull out and the American determination to stay. News of Hull's conversation with Horinouchi soon made its way to the Quai d'Orsay, where it undoubtedly made a considerable impression. Both Léger and the chief of the Far Eastern Department, Jean Chauvel, believed that Hull's statements had been of the utmost importance, for if the Western powers, led by a determined United States, displayed sufficient firmness, it might be possible to reach a settlement in the Sino-Japanese war. Should the West withdraw its troops, the Japanese would merely be "encouraged to make further demands." Therefore, when the British submitted a note to the French on 10 September, suggesting that Britain and France withdraw their troops on the grounds that they were needed for use in Europe, Paris demurred, preferring to take no action without consulting with the American government.[8] After all, it had been the cardinal tenet of French strategy and policy that French, British, and American security were interdependent in the Far East. It would have been out of character for the French to fail to grasp at any sign that the Americans were about to play a larger role in that area. Certainly, the officials at the Quai d'Orsay believed that they would be inviting reproach if they did not at least go through the process of asking the Americans about their intentions. In any event, the French Foreign Ministry thought it "desirable to make the United States Government face their responsibilities: if they accept them, the French and British Governments might think it worthwhile and safe not to abdicate their position in China; if they do not accept them, then as far as the United States Government are concerned, French and British Governments are free to pursue a policy of withdrawal with best grace possible."[9] In other words, the French position hinged upon the extent to which the United States could be counted upon to cooperate should France choose to disregard the Japanese "advice."

The French official response on 12 September to the British démarche basically adhered to the Quai d'Orsay's attitude. France had "serious objections" to withdrawing upon Japanese demand. The Japanese objective appeared to be to test British and French response to pressure in the Far East while engaged in a European war. If the Western powers capitulated to such pressure, "the Japanese Government might push the experiment to the point of imperilling the whole British and French position in occupied China." The

French pointed out that Hull's representations to the Japanese seemed to indicate renewed American interest in the whole matter. Therefore, it would be "advisable not to give an America which is ready to come to their aid an impression that the British and French Governments wish to commit suicide." For these reasons, an approach should be made to Washington before replying to Tokyo. Should the American response indicate a lack of determination to cooperate in resisting Japanese demands, the French and British governments should make it clear that they would resume their freedom of action.[10] In the latter event, one must assume that the French would be willing to strike whatever deal might be necessary to produce a relaxation of tensions with Japan.

How much the British were influenced by the French stance is uncertain, but London, although differing with Paris as to the manner of approach to be made to Washington, agreed to cooperate in pressing the Americans to clarify their position and to have their ambassadors in Washington deliver similar notes to the State Department.[11] The French aide-mémoire was delivered on 20 September. It spelled out the French position quite clearly. They pointed out that because of the European situation, the French inclination, if it were to consider its interests alone, was to inform Japan that the reduction of the French garrisons had been under examination for some time, and they would probably be withdrawn in the near future. France would reiterate the responsibility of the Japanese to undertake the protection of French citizens and property left behind. The French note went on to say that if the United States would adopt a stiff policy of safeguarding its interests in the Far East and "would likewise take into consideration the common interest, and if the United States Government thought that the withdrawal of the French garrisons would weaken the position which it wishes to take, the Government of the Republic would be happy to consider the question from that angle." It could not do so, however, without knowing the views of Washington and without evidence of "concrete suggestions" that the Americans held concerning the maintenance of such a firm attitude. In any case, the French reiterated that it did not have the resources available with which to resist any prolonged Japanese pressure. "Accordingly, if it were not assured of finding some support from the United States, it would deem it preferable to withdraw without sacrificing principles. It would in that case have the intention of withdrawing its armed forces from North China within a short time."[12] Clearly, the French had once again punted to the Americans and hoped that Washington would make a good run with the ball.

The French ambassador in Washington, René de Saint-Quentin, was mildly pessimistic about the anticipated American response. Undoubtedly, the United States wanted to remain in China and was anxious to have France and Britain do the same. But the deciding factor would be American public opinion, and Saint-Quentin was uncertain that it would support a firm United States stand. Perhaps, however, if France abandoned Tientsin in the face of Japanese force majeur, the action might produce a strong enough public reaction in America to allow Washington to stand with the French and British against further retreat from their other holdings in China.[13]

Saint-Quentin's estimate of the role of the American public opinion proved to be quite correct. In the face of vigorous public opposition and the certainty of a congressional storm, Hull obviously could not commit the United States to the kind of specific aid that the French and British sought. But he still sought to bolster them in other ways. He reminded them of the earnest representations that Washington had made to Japan, including another tête-à-tête with Horinouchi on 15 September. He assured them that the United States had no intention of withdrawing its forces from China. On 27 September, Stanley Hornbeck, adviser on political relations in the State Department, handed the French ambassador an aide-mémoire responding to the French note of the twentieth. In it, the State Department reiterated America's intention of maintaining its armed forces in China.[14] Although Saint-Quentin expressed his pleasure with the American statement—indeed, a day earlier Chauvel had indicated that his government believed that a mere statement that the United States did not desire that the French troops leave Shanghai would be considered as a sufficiently affirmative reply—it seems clear that the Quai d'Orsay was less than optimistic about the prospects of active American support on behalf of Western influence in North China. In fact, it did not consider the American response to be "sufficiently affirmative to enable the French and British Governments to base their policy upon it." Therefore, on 30 September, Léger informed Ambassador Bullitt of the French decision to withdraw all of its gunboats and troops from all areas of China. Léger justified the move by arguing that Japan was merely waiting for the German attack in the West before attempting to drive France and Britain out of the Far East.[15]

For a variety of reasons, the French decision to withdraw its forces remained unenforced for the moment. Probably most important was the fact that, after giving its initial "advice," Tokyo had let the matter drop. Although this allowed the Quai d'Orsay to reevaluate its position, the reexamination revealed a split in the ranks. Léger, apparently afraid that the Soviet Union might join Germany in the war against France, wanted to placate Japan and perhaps eventually induce her to attack the Soviets from the East and thus divert Soviet attention. Chauvel, on the other hand, who had opposed the decision to withdraw, believed that the American statements had deterred Japan from acting and that so long as Japan did not press for an answer, the French need not act. Ironically, however, he advocated making some official reply to the Japanese, which would have had the effect of reopening the issue.[16] Surely, it would have been to France's advantage to allow the issue to die if the Japanese were not inclined to force it.

Indeed, the whole problem remained in a curious limbo for the next three weeks. But on 20 October, the British, taking advantage of severe flooding in China that would have necessitated additional expenditures to repair their installations in the area around Tientsin, indicated to the State Department that they were planning to withdraw their forces from Tientsin and Peking as early as possible, although not from Shanghai. They insisted that the withdrawal had not been induced by the Japanese. A few days later, the French revealed that they, too, had prepared a plan for the reduction of the French garrisons in China. Finally, on 13 November, while reiterating that they were not surrendering their extraterritorial rights in China, the French announced that they would reduce their garrisons to a "skeleton force." Only at Shanghai would they retain a substantial force of five hundred French and eight hundred Asian troops. Elsewhere, their forces would be reduced to symbolic detachments of only a few men.[17]

It is undoubtedly true that France would have eventually withdrawn the bulk of its troops from China, for they were urgently needed elsewhere, but the Japanese decision to apply pressure put the question in a new light. Preoccupied with the European war, the French undoubtedly felt terribly exposed in North China, especially in those concessions like Tientsin where the Americans had no military presence. But after receiving the Japanese "advice," the problem of how to withdraw gracefully without giving the impression of knuckling under to Japanese pressure became a ticklish one. Fortunately, Japan's domestic political problems probably prevented her from vigorously pursuing the matter, and the French, along with the British, were given a decent interval to reduce their presence. They still hoped, however, that by avoiding an obvious and precipitous withdrawal under pressure and by retaining token forces in the area, their loss of prestige would not be too great. By keeping the flag flying, they would retain a foot in the door for their return later. In the final analysis, however, as Champtier de Ribes, French undersecretary of state for foreign affairs, argued, France simply could not run the risk of precipitating a conflict with Japan. France would henceforth try to base its policy upon remaining on the best possible terms with both Japan and China.[18]

The French desire to remain on good terms with both belligerents in the Far East was still complicated by the old, reoccurring nemesis of supplying munitions to China through Indochina. The French had been playing a very delicate game, publicly maintaining that arms were not being imported into China through Indochina but giving their local authorities such liberal instructions that fairly large quantities undoubtedly went through. Certainly, the Japanese held no illusions regarding the situation. But with the Japanese militarists temporarily eclipsed in the aftermath of the Nazi-Soviet Pact, Tokyo drifted along, unable to decide how to deal with the problem. For their part, the French, anxiously uncertain at first about what the Japanese might do upon the outbreak of the European war, had more strictly interpreted the restrictions regarding the transit of materiel across Indochina. On 6 September, automobiles, trucks, and petroleum were added to the list of commodities prohibited, although implementation was subsequently delayed until 30 October. Undoubtedly, the French sought to persuade Tokyo that they were not assisting the Chinese. But it seems likely that the French also sought to prod the Chinese into expediting the shipment of supplies consigned to the Chinese government that had accumulated at Haiphong. In fact, the congestion of cargo had reached embarrassing proportions. The Chinese blamed the French for delays and lack of cooperation, and the French criticized the various Chinese agencies for blundering and inefficient organization. Further complicating the incredible confusion in Haiphong was the fact that extraordinarily heavy September rains had caused serious landslides along the Haiphong-Yunnanfu Railroad, at times forcing a complete halt to the flow of goods along that route. By the beginning of October, it was estimated that perhaps as much as 220,000 tons of freight awaited transit into China. Since the railway could convey only about 12,000 tons per month, much materiel spent long months rotting on the docks before being shipped.

If the French intended to force the Chinese to action, they met with limited success. While the backlog of cargo did not shrink appreciably, there was an acceleration in the transshipment of goods, and the congestion was made less conspicuous by the dispersal of part of the surplus to areas less noticeable to prying eyes. By 16 October, word had leaked out that the ban scheduled for the thirtieth would not be enforced, at least for the time being. By early November, certain "tolerances" were quietly being allowed. As Léger put it, the exigencies of the situation confronting the Allies made it prudent that France humor Japan. Yet France also wished to reassure China of its sympathy.[19] Furthermore, the French undoubtedly wished to avoid alienating Washington by detaining arms destined for China from the United States. Although some in the State Department, like Stanley Hornbeck, "doubted whether the French Government's 'bite' would be as bad as its 'bark,' " the Americans sought assurances that the transit of their shipments would be maintained by the French.[20] In order to avoid undue embarrassment for the French, who maintained that they were abiding by the Geneva Convention of 1925, even though that document had never been ratified by enough countries to bring it into effect, Ambassador Bullitt suggested that arms being shipped be falsely labeled, "under the principle that a rose by any other name would smell as sweet."[21]

Japan was not humored by the situation. Frustrated once again by the French policy of political expediency, the shaky Abe government, which had earlier proclaimed that Japan would "inflexibly oppose all who would obstruct her mission" of creating a new Asian order,[22] had to do something. Correspondingly, on 30 November Japanese foreign minister Admiral Kichisaburo Nomura called in French Ambassador Henry and rapidly read to him a lengthy and extraordinary document in which he vented Tokyo's displeasure. Nomura expressed Japan's desire to readjust the relations between the two countries, but he pointed to several obstacles that stood in the way. First, he criticized the continued French permission of arms shipments to China via the French railroad. If France really wished to reestablish good relations with Japan, not only should she break relations with Chiang Kai-shek's regime, but she should adopt a more benevolent attitude toward Japan. "French Indochina thus presents the appearance of a lobby of pro–Chiang Kai-shek and anti-Japanese activity." The Japanese note argued that it was not only a matter of the supposedly forbidden transit of armaments that was nettlesome. There also existed the question of other commodities such as food, automobiles and trucks, gasoline, and various machinery, which, while not categorized as munitions, served to strengthen China's resistance to Japan. The note pointed out that such materiel had been listed as contraband in connection with the war in Europe, but that France had refused to consider it as such in the Sino-Japanese conflict. "This logic is irrefutable in practice, whether war is declared or not. The Japanese Government hopes that the French Government will refrain from clinging to abstract juridical arguments and, basing its point of view on a policy attached to the realities, will resolve to forbid the transportation of all articles destined to the Chiang Kai-shek regime." Nomura declared that because of such a flow of goods, despite Tokyo's repeated protests, Japan felt obligated to cut this route by force. For this reason, she had initiated military operations in Kwangsi province adjacent to Indochina. Regrettably, aerial bombardment of the railroad had led to Japanese accidental overflights of French territory. If French actions in favor of China ended, Japan could ensure that incidents would cease.

Second, Nomura complained about economic barriers that had been set up against Japan by France's Far Eastern possessions. High duties and quotas levied against Japanese goods, he argued, violated the spirit of commercial treaties between France and Japan. Moreover, the restrictions of exports of raw materials, especially iron ore, from Indochina and New Caledonia, which had only been recently terminated, must not be reinstituted. Furthermore, the French "should spontaneously accord Japan facilities and active support in these territories."

Finally, Nomura concluded, "In view of the fact that the essential part of the problem concerns French Indochina, I believe it both useful and necessary to send at this moment to the Japanese Consul General at Hanoi an official of this Ministry whose duty it will be to inform the latter on the general situation, in order to facilitate him in his contacts with the French Indo-China authorities." Additionally, for the purpose of explaining to Indochina's authorities the nature of the Japanese military operations being undertaken increasingly close to the Indochina frontier, a high-ranking Japanese military officer should accompany Nomura's diplomat.[23] Simply put, under the guise of clarifying Japanese actions, Japan wanted to send two observers to monitor the shipments going to China over the French railroad.

When Nomura had finished, Henry protested the Japanese charges regarding Indochina, but he refused to comment on the remainder of Nomura's highly critical statement. Little is known about how the Japanese note was received in Paris, but on 7 December Premier Daladier instructed Henry to express his "painful surprise" at the Japanese complaints and to deny once again that military supplies were going through Indochina to China. In any case, if the Japanese wished to take up complaints against the French government, the latter could also raise a host of complaints against Japan—the occupation of Hainan, the annexation of the Spratly Islands, the restrictions of freedom of navigation on the Yangtze River, the restrictions on the freedom of commerce in territory occupied by Japan in China, "and in general all other discriminations suffered by French interests in China since the outbreak of the 'incident.' " He stipulated that the French government would not receive in any official capacity in Indochina the Japanese representatives that Tokyo proposed to send there. It was difficult, the French argued, "to see that any practical purpose would be served thereby." Finally, the French took the Japanese to task for their military initiatives in the provinces adjacent to Indochina. They reminded Tokyo that "the abstention of the Japanese from the Gulf of Tonking constituted in the mind of the French Government a counterbalance for the measures which it took to prevent the transit of war materiels across Indochina. Such transit, even if it had taken place, could not furthermore, have evoked any objection from the point of view of international law." After all, a state of war had not been officially declared.[24]

Undaunted, the Japanese at this point launched another ill-conceived attempt to place an observer in Indochina, thus precipitating the curious, so-called Catroux-Tsuchihashi encounter. Major General Yuitsu Tsuchihashi, who had formerly served in Paris as Japan's military attaché and had recently been appointed chief of the Second Bureau of the General Staff at the War Office in Tokyo, applied for and received permission to visit Indochina in a private capacity. On 20 December, he met with Governor General Georges Catroux and stated that as a "friend of France" he wished to set Japanese minds at ease by seeing for himself that French claims regarding munitions traffic were true. Catroux again denied that arms were crossing the Indochinese frontier into China, and he refused permission for Tsuchihashi to visit the frontier. The Japanese officer then became highly excited and stormed out, threatening that "complications might occur." The following day, he apologized to Catroux, but upon again being denied the necessary permission Tsuchihashi flew into a rage, warning that it would be a simple matter for Japanese forces to invade Indochina. Catroux calmly replied that precisely the opposite would be true. When Tsuchihashi indicated that Japan would guarantee the independence of Indochina if French authorities halted the flow of trucks and gasoline through the colony, Catroux demurred, indicating that such questions were up to the diplomats to handle. Before leaving Hanoi, the Japanese general met with the local press and issued some "sibylline" statements about the Sino-Japanese war and Franco-Japanese relations. Catroux promptly squelched publication of the statements and warned the general that his statements were "inopportune." Thus ended one of the more curious, hastily conceived, and poorly executed exercises in Japanese "diplomacy."

Tokyo's motivation for again bringing the issue of Indochina to the fore at this particular point is unclear. Certainly, the matter had been raised before and would be again, but it is uncertain why the Japanese had raised the stakes at this point by enlarging the question to include economic relations with French Oceania and, more importantly, to request permission to send what amounted to Japanese observers to Indochina. Undoubtedly, the economic pinch created by the war with China was beginning to be felt. But French trade restrictions had made little impact and, therefore, seem to have been merely a subsidiary concern. The real objective lay in ending the Indochina connection with Chungking. As one of the only two viable routes of supply remaining for Chiang Kai-shek's forces—the other being Britain's Burma Road—its closure would put a serious strain on China's capacity to continue the fight. The subject of Japanese "controllers" had been raised rather obliquely earlier and had been rejected by France,[25] and it was extremely unlikely that the French would permit such a plan now. Clearly, such requests could be construed as violating French sovereignty, and once the Japanese had their foot in the door, who could foretell subsequent developments? Certainly, Tokyo wished to test the waters again in view of the new situation created by the European war. But in the final analysis, as Ambassador Henry correctly speculated, the Japanese note probably reflected the increasingly tenuous position of the already shaky Abe government. Unable to achieve a breakthrough in the Chinese war and confronted with the necessity of submitting to the Japanese Diet an unprecedented budget (and taxes), Tokyo, Henry believed, sought to divert attention from these failures by initiating a controversy with France. Surely, Tokyo did not need another controversy at the moment, but by fishing in the troubled waters of the European war, it might find a catch that could help to ameliorate the domestic situation. Henry found further evidence of the government's distraction when he delivered the French rebuff to Nomura. He found the Japanese foreign minister cordial—even intimate—but also quite uncertain about the future.[26] Indeed, about a month later Abe's government collapsed.

Within that time, Japan had initiated a military drive into Kwangsi province of South China, hoping to achieve through military force what they had not accomplished by diplomatic negotiation. By the end of November, Japanese forces had captured Nanning. This move had the effect of cutting off the shipment of supplies that had been flowing by truck from Indochina to Nanning over an important auxiliary route that utilized a new railroad bed that had not yet been completed. But, more importantly, it now gave the Japanese a base from which they could threaten all Chinese internal road and rail communications as far away as the Burma Road. From the French perspective, the position of Japanese-controlled Nanning within easy striking distance of the Haiphong–Yunnanfu Railroad and the Indochina frontiers now meant that Japan might be in a better position to intimidate French authorities and force the closing of the remaining rail route into China from Indochina. Barring that, the Japanese were still in a good position to close the Chinese end of the railway by bombing it into uselessness for long periods.[27]

French officials were disturbed by the Japanese advance. Georges Mandel, minister for colonies, who had been a leading advocate of supporting China's resistance, believed that the loss of Nanning drove another nail in the Chinese coffin. Certainly, it reflected a greater Chinese military feebleness than had been supposed. Others, like Chauvel, clung to the hope that Chiang Kai-shek's forces would be able to launch a successful counterattack.[28]

Regardless, given the disinclination of the French to halt the transit of supplies to China, as made clear in their rebuff of the Japanese note of 30 November,[29] the Japanese moved quickly to take advantage of their newly won strategic position. Beginning on 30 December and continuing through January and into the early part of February, Japan opened a systematic bombing campaign against the French-owned and -operated Chinese end of the Haiphong-Yunnanfu Railroad. There ensued a recurring pattern of Japanese violations of French commercial and territorial rights, followed by vigorous French protests about the loss of property and lives, that led to a steady deterioration of Franco-Japanese relations during the winter and spring of 1940.[30] Initially, the Japanese scrupulously avoided French territory, but before long it became routine for Japanese aircraft to short-cut across Indochinese territory on their way to their targets. Even after the railroad traffic had been brought to a standstill, reconnaissance planes continued to violate Indochina's airspace. Paris forbade any form of military action against the Japanese aircraft, sending instead "lots of paper to Tokyo about it." The standard Japanese response was usually one of expressed regrets, while blaming the military officers on the spot for such violations.[31]

On 12 January, Ambassador Henry made a particularly vigorous protest about the bombardment of the railroad, which by this time, the French complained, had been so severely damaged that it would be unusable for several weeks. Admiral Nomura, the foreign minister, responded by handing the French ambassador a stiff note indicating that Japan would continue bombing the railroad as long as war materiel and supplies were being shipped along it to Chinese forces. When Henry protested that arms were not being transshipped, Nomura made it clear that it was not merely a matter of munitions but also of trucks, fuel, and other supplies that might help Chiang Kai-shek continue the war. He even intimated that the Japanese navy might begin to intercept ships bound for Indochina to remove such goods which appeared destined for China. Henry retorted that since Japan was not officially at war, it did not have belligerent rights, and, therefore, such actions as it had taken to interfere with international trade were completely illegal.[32]

The French government was clearly upset by this new Japanese communication, but it was divided as to the proper response. Chauvel confessed to Bullitt that if he had his way he would like to send a few pursuit planes to shoot down any Japanese bombers sent against the French railroad. Mandel leaned in the direction of getting the United States to apply pressure on Japan during the course of trade negotiations between the two countries. After all, American trade with China as well as that of other nations was being restricted by Japan's illegal action. Chauvel ultimately decided to recommend to Daladier and Léger that the new Japanese ambassador in Paris, Renzo Sawada, should be told that as long as the bombing of the railroad continued the French government "would be unable to have any conversations of any importance with him in Paris on any subject."[33]

The official French protest to Tokyo was strong and uncompromising. Since Japan refused to admit that a state of war existed with China, it had no right to claim what amounted to belligerent rights. Therefore, France had no legal obligation to Japan regarding international trade with China through Indochina. Furthermore, should the frontier with China be closed, the French government would be compelled to stop exportation of certain products to Japan.[34]

The prospect of restricting exports of raw materials from French colonies was again raised by Daladier to Sawada in early February. While the Japanese ambassador replied that he did not think that his government would be seriously perturbed by such a development, Daladier received the clear impression that Sawada really thought otherwise.[35] In fact, by the spring of 1940 the economic argument probably had considerable impact on Tokyo. Indeed, Japan had come under increased economic pressure from the United States, where in January the influence of public opinion had led President Roosevelt to abrogate America's 1911 Treaty of Commerce and Navigation with Japan. Despite various Japanese attempts to initiate new treaty negotiations prior to its expiration, the Americans had made it clear by December that trade would continue without restriction only on a day-to-day basis. In the meantime, the United States would have a free hand to terminate exports to Japan or to impose sanctions should Japanese behavior warrant such steps. Japan's commercial relations with Britain limped along on a similar short-term basis.[36] Undoubtedly, Japan did not want to risk unnecessarily the flow of raw materials from other potential suppliers. The iron ore, rubber, nickel, and other commodities that could be obtained from the French colonies might be used to offset the possible loss of raw materials from the British Commonwealth and the United States. To retain access to such French raw materials, Tokyo could either reconcile its differences with the French concerning Indochina to assure a flow of needed goods, or it could take steps to seize such supplies and thus guarantee access to them. In the long run, the latter course proved to be the more attractive, but already Japan was feeling the pinch, and the French allusion to restrictions did not assuage the concerns of a government still unsure of the direction to take.

Still, at this point the Japanese gave little indication that they were ready to back off. On 5 February, when Henry delivered another protest about the Japanese bombing of a train on which a number of civilians were killed, the Foreign Ministry greeted him with a list of articles and commodities—including trucks, fuel, machines, and medical supplies—that Japan wanted the French to prohibit from traveling on the Yunnan Railway. The Japanese suggested that France merely refrain from repairing the railroad on which traffic had by now come to nearly a complete standstill. If France would be willing to do this, Japan would help obtain favorable commercial conditions for her in the new China that would be established under Japan's puppet, Wang Ching-wei. As Masayuki Tani, vice-minister for foreign affairs, put it, Japan "asked no more of the French than that they should prevent certain specified goods from reaching Japan's enemy." Japan regretted the loss of life and was ready in principle to pay compensation, but it remained determined to stop the flow of supplies to China.[37]

The French response noted that the Japanese communication appeared to leave France only two choices: either it could allow the railroad to continue to be bombarded, or else it could join in "clandestine complicity" with Japan against China. France therefore rejected Tokyo's démarche as "unacceptable in form and substance." The

Japanese ambassador in Paris was told that, given the series of actions regarding Hainan, the Spratly Islands, and the Paracels, the confidence necessary to arrive at an agreement was lacking, and "the only way out of the impasse was for the Japanese Government to reconsider her position."[38]

If the Japanese policy were designed to browbeat the French into weakening, while simultaneously dangling the bait of favorable treatment in the new China, it proved to be singularly unsuccessful. In fact, the British representative in Paris reported that the French were determined to resist, and, where possible, push back if they could do so without unduly aggravating the situation. France refused to enter into commercial negotiations for the renewal of the Franco-Japanese Commercial Treaty, due to expire on 15 March. Moreover, the government indicated its inclination to be obstructive in other ways.[39] For example, the French delayed the inauguration of the new Formosa-Bangkok air route by refusing to authorize the flight of Japanese passenger aircraft over Indochina. Under the pretext of war measures, the export of nickel to Japan from French New Caledonia was curtailed.[40] Despite Japanese protests and repeated excuses by the French authorities, it became quite clear that the French would continue such behavior so long as the bombings of the Yunnan railroad continued.

Having succeeded in effectively limiting, even temporarily ending, traffic along the Yunnan Railway through their bombing campaign, but somewhat stymied by the French obstructionism, the Japanese appeared to back off slightly toward the end of February. On the twentieth, much to the surprise of the French government, Henry was called to the Japanese Foreign Ministry and handed a note in which the Japanese government expressed its formal regrets for bombing of the railway on 1 February that had resulted in a large loss of life. Tani, the Japanese vice-minister, even declared Japan's willingness to compensate the victims. Tani then took the opportunity to indicate that Japan wished to enter "far-reaching" conversations with the French government that would cover not only the Far East but matters of world policy as well. He suggested that such negotiations be opened in Paris.

The French government, although cautious, was quite pleased by the turn of events. The opening of such conversations might ultimately lead to a better understanding with Japan and perhaps eventually lead to Japan's collaboration in the European war. Correspondingly, the official French reply indicated that they would be glad to listen to the Japanese proposals, but they reminded Tokyo that it would be Japan's responsibility to ensure that no further incidents occurred against the Yunnan Railway while the talks were in progress. Since the Japanese démarche did not include mention of Tani's earlier unacceptable proposal that France refrain from repairing the railway in return for favorable commercial considerations once the Wang Ching-wei government was established, and since the Japanese obviously sought a settlement of the China incident, Paris held some hope that Japan might be ready to launch a new policy direction. Certainly, it behooved France to find out. Some concern existed, however, about the durability of the apparently irresolute government of Mitsumasa Yonai—the fear being that it might be overthrown and replaced by a more extremist regime. What such an occurrence would mean for any negotiations could only be guessed, but at least the talks could be initiated even if the fruits might prove to be far down the road. Meanwhile, anxious to keep in step with the British and Americans, France sought to ascertain their views concerning the possibilities for the proposed Franco-Japanese conversations.[41]

When Japanese Ambassador Sawada presented Tokyo's proposals to Léger at the Quai d'Orsay on 29 February, French skepticism proved well founded. Clearly, the Japanese position remained unchanged. They suggested that France sign a formula agreed to by Britain the previous July regarding the Tientsin issue. Additionally, France should close the Indochina frontier to prevent arms, fuel, and trucks from reaching China. In return, Japan would respect French rights and interests in the Far East. When asked if French interests in Hainan, the Spratlys, and the Paracels would be included, Sawada said no.[42]

It is unclear why Japan made its démarche. Perhaps it sought to make some small concessions on various issues in the hopes of dragging large concessions out of France, which could be used as an opening wedge to obtain an end to support of China by other Western governments. More likely, however, in the face of rabid public opinion at home the weak government in Tokyo could not make concessions large enough to produce a breakthrough and so merely attempted to get a hearing for its standard proposals at as high an echelon as possible. Still diplomatically isolated and uncertain about the direction of the war in Europe as the "phony war" dragged on, Japan simply could not make large enough concessions either to satisfy the democracies or to achieve peace with China. Consequently, relations with France returned nearly to square one.

In early March, after being closed for most of February because of the need for extensive repairs caused by the Japanese bombardment, the Yunnan railroad reopened. The Japanese warned that they would not hesitate to bomb it again if oil and trucks should be shipped to China. Chauvel, at the Quai d'Orsay, replied that in fact oil and trucks were being transported over the railway, but that it would seem "extraordinary that the Japanese Government should consider bombarding the French railroad at a time when the Japanese Government was engaged in commercial negotiations with the French Government." Apparently, the argument held considerable weight in Tokyo, because for nearly two months traffic along the railway went unhampered by Japanese attacks. Finally, by the end of April, the Japanese government could no longer restrain the military leaders, and the bombing resumed.[43]

Meanwhile, commercial negotiations had limped along since the expiration of the Franco-Japanese trade treaty on 15 March. A temporary, one-month agreement was concluded and went into effect on 15 April. But the French, realizing that Japan's desire for a long-term agreement gave them some leverage, displayed no hurry to arrive at a final accord. Paris sought to attach a quid pro quo: a permanent end to the bombing of the railway and an assurance that Japan would prevent the reexport of French colonial raw materials and other commodities to the Soviet Union—and from there, it was assumed, to Germany.[44] The negotiations were further complicated by the apparent French determination to link immunity for the Yunnan railroad with the Tientsin silver question, which had been dragging on for months. But the Tientsin issue involved the British, whose concession there had remained blockaded along with the French. The Japanese, for their part, sought to divide the Western powers by reaching a settlement with Britain and then using the latter to bring pressure to bear on France.[45] In any event, little tangible progress had been made regarding either the commercial treaty or the Tientsin issue by the time of the climactic events that shook Europe during May and June 1940.

As the southward intentions of the Japanese became increasingly a matter for French concern and the threat to Indochina became ever more obvious, the French took steps to improve the defense capability of their colony. Yet, of the French colonial holdings, Indochina found itself in a unique situation with the outbreak of the war in Europe. Along with other parts of the Empire, demands were placed on it to supply large numbers of troops (during World War I the 46,000 combatants Indochina furnished had placed it second behind those supplied by French Equatorial Africa) and materiel for metropolitan France. But with the increasing threat of Japan and the unlikelihood that France could do much to aid in its defense, many in Indochina felt that the colony should utilize its resources for its own defense.

Georges Mandel, minister for the colonies, probably reflecting the belief of many Frenchmen that part of the raison d'etre of the Empire was to support Mother France, quickly decided that Indochina, like the other colonies, should place the bulk of its resources at the disposition of France. Mandel judged that although the Japanese expansionism constituted a real threat to Indochina and other French Far Eastern interests, at the moment they were too absorbed in China and concerned about the Soviet Union to move against French possessions. Japan's preoccupation with China, though, made it imperative that Chiang Kai-shek's forces be sustained.[46]

Ever since taking over the Colonial Ministry in 1938, Mandel had worked vigorously and had taken several steps to improve the effectiveness of the colonial contribution to their own defense and to integrate them better into the plans for the defense of France: a General Staff for colonial troops had been created and placed under the command of General Jules Bührer; the minister for the colonies finally had been admitted to the Supreme Council of National Defense; and the size of the French colonial army had been doubled to 120,000 men (not including Tunisian, Algerian, and Moroccan troops, who did not come under the control of the colonial minister), with plans to increase it to 2 million in the event of war.[47] Certainly, the armed forces to be used in defense of the individual colonies had not been entirely neglected. Even before the war erupted in Europe, Mandel had been moving against tremendous obstacles to improve defense capabilities of the various colonies. In Indochina, 20,000 new recruits had been ordered, and, upon the outbreak of war, provision was made to increase the army to 100,000 men. Since metropolitan France utilized most of its funds at home, new taxes were raised in the colonies to pay for their own defense. Funds were urgently raised to recruit, train, and equip additional troops, improve port facilities, and build new roads. If local authorities refused, heads rolled.[48] In Indochina, enlistment bonuses and family allowances were instituted, and officer training for Indochinese was increased. The 1940 budget of 1,380 million francs for military expenditures represented an increase of 270 million francs over that of 1939, and constituted 31 percent of the total budget. That sixty-two-year-old General Georges Catroux was brought out of retirement to become governor-general—the first military officer to hold that position in over half a century—indicated the seriousness with which the French took the situation. In return for these sacrifices on the part of the local populations, Mandel anticipated that the efforts on behalf of national defense granted by the colonies must be rewarded by the grant of ever-increasing rights to the indigenous populations.[49]

The long-neglected French naval forces in the Far East also needed strengthening. In Cam Ranh Bay, the French had one of the best natural harbors in the Far East, and they busily began building a naval base there. But no fleet to speak of existed to utilize such facilities. French strategic planners had long realized that no sizable fleet could be sent to the Far East. Confronted with a powerful German fleet in the North Sea and a potential Italian threat in the Mediterranean, the French would have to keep their fleet in European waters and would be hard-pressed to protect the sea lanes to North Africa and to assist British vessels straining to protect the lifeline to the Near East and beyond. Thus, there could be no question of sending additional naval forces to the Far East. Consequently, to defend the long and vulnerable Indochinese coast the French had one cruiser, the *Lamotte-Picquet,* four sloops, and an assortment of smaller vessels, all under the command of Admiral Jean Decoux, headquartered in Saigon. Such a force, even when united with a similarly weak British Far Eastern force, surely could not hope to hold its own against the entire Japanese fleet. Winston Churchill might declare to his fellow M.P.s in the House of Commons on 8 November that the French navy had "never been, for many generations, as powerful and as effective as it is now,"[50] but, strained to the limit in European waters, it could not help being outclassed in the Far East. So long as Japan did not move against French possessions, there was little likelihood that additional naval forces would be sent. But even if fighting broke out in the Far East, it was clear that virtually no reinforcements could be sent.

With these limited resources at his command, General Catroux estimated, perhaps somewhat optimistically, that in the event of a war in the Far East, French forces in Indochina would be capable of holding out for only about a month. General Maurice Martin, commander of the army in Indochina, judged that two to three months would be the limit. Given these circumstances, it was logical that increased efforts be made to coordinate combined Franco-British defense efforts in the Far East. While such inter-Allied planning did not take place at the general-staff level, there were attempts by the local French and British commanders to continue with the efforts, begun at the Singapore Conference in June 1939, to promote effective Allied cooperation in the Far East. Indeed, during December 1940, General Sir Lionel Bond, commanding British troops in Malaya, visited

General Martin, and Admiral Sir Percy Noble, commander of the British Far Eastern fleet, called upon Admiral Decoux to discuss matters of common concern. In mid-March, Mandel invited the British secretary of state for colonies to Paris in order to discuss means of promoting cooperation between the British and French empires. Unfortunately, they generally dealt with matters of trade, transport, and communications rather than with the more pressing issues of a common defense posture. For the most part, few concrete results came from these meetings. Undoubtedly, General Bührer, chief of staff of the Colonial Army, was partly correct when he attributed to Mandel the fact that "the Empire . . . was brought to its apogee during the war by the persistent, forceful, unremitting efforts of a Minister of Colonies endowed with all the qualities of a great statesman."[51] But one should add that, for the Far Eastern Empire at least, it was a classic case of too little too late.

The period from September 1939 to June 1940 saw a curious interlude in Franco-Japanese relations. The outbreak of war in Europe naturally altered the situation in the Far East, but it put Japanese strategists in a dilemma. On the one hand, with the attention of the democracies necessarily riveted upon the European situation, it seemed a most propitious moment to put increased pressure on them to make concessions to Japan's new order. Yet, circumstances surrounding the outbreak of the war—namely, the Nazi-Soviet Pact—had left Tokyo feeling jilted and had temporarily discredited those in the Japanese military who had so ardently pressed for an aggressive anti-Western policy.[52] The weak Abe and Yonai governments that held power during the period vacillated and generally pursued a cautious policy vis-à-vis Western interests.

Such a course was dictate by several considerations. First, during the course of the "phony war," when little fighting went on in Europe after the defeat of Poland, it was difficult to determine the outcome of events in Europe. A premature false step might find Japan on the wrong side and could be fatal for her prospects for expansion in East Asia. Certainly, if France and Britain emerged victorious, they would be in no mood to humor Japan after the humiliations of the 1930s. But even if Germany won, there was some suspicion that Berlin might lay claim to her former possessions in the Far East and thus run across Japan's interests. Perhaps even worse, should the war result in an exhausting stalemate, Japan's old antagonist, Russia, might emerge as the strongest Western state, with obvious repercussions for already-strained Russo-Japanese relations.[53] Confronted by such an array of possibilities, wisdom dictated that Japan pursue its course of noninvolvement and remain on the sidelines until its opportunity arrived.

Second, the tug of war among Japan's civil and military leaders concerning the direction that should be taken to expand her interests and influence meant that no group or policy could establish dominance. Some wanted to focus attention upon successfully terminating the Chinese war while Europe's attentions were diverted. Others sought to take advantage of the situation to undertake new initiatives either against the Soviet Union or toward Western European–dominated Southeast Asia. Given such factious discord, Japanese policy sometimes jerked in fits and starts, but generally drifted languidly.

Third, as early as August 1936, Japan had begun thinking about expanding into Southeast Asia for the purpose of exploiting the raw materials of the area to support its new and growing empire.[54] The financial and economic strain created by the Chinese war had exacerbated the need for strategic materials such as rubber, oil, tin, iron ore, and nickel, among others. For most of the period up to 1940, however, Japan wished to avoid unnecessarily alienating those powers that controlled access to such supplies—the United States, Britain, the Netherlands, and France. When the United States abrogated its commercial treaty with Japan, a new policy became attractive. Undoubtedly, in the long run, uncertainty about access to American resources had significant repercussions and helped to push Tokyo into a more aggressive and acquisitive stance with regard to other potential suppliers, a fact apparently little appreciated in Washington or Paris. But for the moment, as Japan groped for a suitable policy, it attempted to remain at least on tolerable terms with the European powers that controlled access to needed raw materials from their Far Eastern possessions.

For all of these reasons, plus the crucial uncertainty about the attitude of the United States, which was giving sporadic but ever-increasing signs that it would resist any Japanese invasion of Western possessions, Japan's policy toward the nations involved in the European war remained cautious and ambivalent. Born out of uncertainty and perpetuated by division,[55] Tokyo's policy remained surprisingly moderate given the unbridled opportunities in the Far East provided by the European war.

For France, the situation provided a much-needed breathing space. Unfortunately, the time was poorly used, and little change occurred in French policy. Despite its uncertainty about how best to take advantage of the European situation, Tokyo by no means gave up on its

attempts to pressure France into closing it Indochinese-Chinese frontier and thus to hasten the end of the Chinese war. The French met
the Japanese demands with stalling tactics and minor concessions only
when the pressure became too great to resist—hardly the stuff of appeasement that had characterized France's policy in Europe. Surprisingly, too, when France periodically retaliated, she found Japan was
unwilling to go to the limit in a full-fledged confrontation.

The fact that British and American presence in the Far East, militarily and economically, overshadowed that of France, combined
with Tokyo's concern about its relations with Germany and Russia,
probably meant that at times Franco-Japanese problems may have
gotten lost in the shuffle. But such respites were only temporary, for
the Chinese war and the question of the transit of supplies through
Indochina were constant irritants to the Japanese.

France remained in the ticklish position of continuing to be one of
the chief supporters of Chiang Kai-shek, while at the same time trying to avoid driving Japan back into Germany's arms and preventing
a rapproachement between Japan and the Soviet Union. Both possibilities loomed large in the thinking of the Quai d'Orsay.[56] Consequently, the government was unwilling to risk a complete rupture
with Tokyo, and for that matter, carefully avoided pushing back too
hard. At various times, the government publicly took steps to assuage Japanese sensitivities and to relieve tension. On 7 February, for
example, the semiofficial daily newspaper, *Le Temps,* argued that it
was most difficult to reconcile the Japanese bombing of the Yunnan
railroad with Tokyo's public statements that it in no way sought to
eliminate the legitimate rights and interests of third powers. But, the
article stated, "until there is evidence to the contrary the good faith
of the Japanese Government should not be called into question." It
seems probable that such a statement was inspired by the Quai
d'Orsay. At the end of February, Daladier granted a rare interview to
the foreign editor of the Tokyo *Nichi Nichi,* during which he was reported to have been most conciliatory. He denied again that arms
traveled over the Yunnan railroad. He stated that he had always favored a policy of cordial relations with Japan, and he was widely reported to have indicated that conversations regarding the possibility
of French recognition of Manchukuo were in the offing. Subsequently, Daladier denied having made such a statement about
Manchukuo or that France planned to jettison China, but it is clear
that he sought to keep open French lines of communication with
Tokyo.[57]

In the end, French policy generally drifted as did Japan's. The Japanese were entirely correct in assuming the French attentions would be preoccupied with the European war. Daladier even admitted to Japanese journalists that he was "thinking a great deal more of Hitler and Germany" than he was about China. Chauvel, who had always been dismayed at the pitifully little sustained attention paid to Far Eastern matters by the upper echelons of Quai d'Orsay (most notably by Léger), found it necessary, as head of the Far Eastern Department, to request that information from other governments concerning Far Eastern matters come directly through him. Only in this way, apparently, could his department keep abreast of changes in their policies and be able to keep French policies in step with those of the other Western nations.[58] As a result, French policy-making was most often left to the middle-ranking officials in the Far Eastern Department, with cabinet-level leadership remaining fitful. Only in isolated instances would the cabinet, the premier, the foreign minister, or the secretary general of the Quai d'Orsay actively lend direction to French policy. The policy, therefore, tended to reflect the ideas and attitudes of Chauvel, who often expressed his opinion that France should present a hard line to Japan. But on various isolated occasions, cabinet-level leadership was asserted that resulted in moderations of the French position. Consequently, if Japanese policy were prone to fits and starts as Tokyo attempted to sort out its situation and opportunities, French policy drifted along in erratic fashion as well. France's own commitments in Europe were so great as to dictate the avoidance of an open clash with Japan. Even if piecemeal concessions, grudgingly given, alleviated the tensions only periodically and temporarily, to be followed by additional Japanese demands, the French situation meant that they had to make a virtue out of military necessity. The question, of course, was how to do so as gracefully as possible. Additionally, it was fully realized that in the long run the only real deterrent to Japanese expansion southward lay with the United States; so every effort would have to be made to keep in step with Washington and to seize any opportunity to prod the Americans into restraining Tokyo. The danger, of course, lay in the possibility that strong American pressure—especially economic—might force Japan into fresh ventures to secure those resources unobtainable from the United States. So France found itself in a delicate position; it sought to aid China and thus keep Japan's attentions diverted from other potential expansionist moves. Yet, at the same time Paris realized that if France went too far down this road, Japan would be tempted to act anyway. So the French sought, because of the European situation, to avoid or remove as many sources of friction with Japan as possible. As Ambassador Henry put it, they "could not afford to do anything else."[59]

If France's attention remained glued primarily on Europe, the course of the war there justified such anxieties. Indeed, events in the Far East quickly paled in comparison to the drama unfolding in the West. Successively, French attentions were caught by the quick defeat of Poland, the winter war between Russia and Finland, which brought about a governmental crisis in Paris and the replacement of Daladier by Paul Reynaud, and the swift German victory in Norway. But all of this was a mere prelude to the main event—the momentous sixty days that shook the West in May and June 1940, culminating with the shocking debacle that France incurred. The ramifications of the defeat of France, as well as the Dutch, had immediate and far-reaching effects in the Far East. France's increasingly tenuous position in the Far East went up in the flames of defeat in Europe.

eight

BOWING TO THE FORCE MAJEURE:
JAPAN'S ADVANCE INTO INDOCHINA

THE sudden collapse of France in June 1940 presented Japan with a golden opportunity to exploit French discomfiture and remove several obstacles to its new order in East Asia. Japanese military extremists, who had been temporarily held in check since the humiliation caused by the Nazi-Soviet Pact of August 1939, could no longer be restrained.[1] By seizing Indochina, Japan would be in a strong position to force an end to its interminable struggle with China on its own terms. The large quantity of supplies that had flowed through Indochina to Chinese forces—a situation that had greatly embittered the Japanese and had slowly poisoned Franco-Japanese relations during the past three years—could be brought to a halt.[2] Chiang Kai-shek, further isolated and confronted with the loss of one of his few remaining supply channels, might be finally forced to give up the fight. Moreover, Indochina could provide Japan with significant supplies of rubber, tin, coal, and rice and thus go a long way toward ending its dependence upon foreign sources for these strategic raw materials. Finally, the strategic location of Indochina meant that it could serve admirably as an advanced base from which the Japanese could strike out against the Far Eastern possessions of the other Western colonial powers—the East Indies, Malaya, Burma, and the Philippines. For French and Indochinese officials, finding themselves in the path of an aggressively expansionistic Japan, the problem was how to maintain their control in Indochina in the aftermath of the debacle in Europe and the concomitant loss of power and prestige around the world. In fact, as the events of the next months were to prove, the ability of France to determine the destiny of the pearl of its Far Eastern empire was little more than a myopic illusion.

Japan launched its anticipated diplomatic offensive even as the bewildered French government was retreating to Bordeaux. On 17 June, as German columns knifed deep into France and the new government of Marshal Philippe Pétain asked the Germans to state their terms for an armistice, in Tokyo the vice-minister for foreign affairs, Masayuki Tani, declared at a press conference that all arms traffic across Indochina to China must cease.[3] The next step was obvious. Two days later, on 19 June, Charles-Arsène Henry, the French ambassador in Tokyo, was handed the expected ultimatum. The Japanese "requests" included two provisions: first, the frontier between China and Indochina must be closed; second, a Japanese control commission should be established in Indochina to supervise the implementation of the agreement.[4] Familiar Japanese requests had suddenly become demands. Henry quickly relayed the Japanese demands to the governor-general of Indochina, General Georges Catroux, advising him that under the circumstances it would be best to accede to the Japanese dictates and temporarily close the frontier, even though no assurance existed that these would be Japan's last demands on Indochina. At least the pretext for a Japanese attack would be removed for the moment, and control over the military extremists by the moderate government of Mitsumasa Yonai might be enhanced.[5]

Actually, on 16 June, in anticipation of such a Japanese move, Catroux had already stopped the shipment of gasoline into China. More than that, responding to instructions from the Quai d'Orsay, he had appealed directly to Washington and London for aid. Besides soliciting 120 aircraft and anti-aircraft guns, René de Saint-Quentin, the French ambassador in Washington, was ordered to urge the Americans to make it clear to the Japanese that they would not tolerate a shift in the status quo in the Pacific. In the absence of such American intervention, he was directed to warn Washington, Indochina would have to bow to Japan's demands. The American response was disappointing but predictable. Assistant Secretary of State Sumner Welles met with Saint-Quentin on 19 June and indicated that the United States could not risk provoking an attack by Japan and therefore could do nothing to thwart an attack on Indochina. When Saint-Quentin observed that France had no choice but to close the Indochinese frontier, Welles is reputed to have said, "that is what I would do in your place."[6] Shortly thereafter, the French ambassador received a telegram from Catroux telling him of the Japanese ultimatum. Therefore, on the following day Saint-Quentin returned to the State Department to meet with Stanley Hornbeck, the State Department's chief adviser on Far Eastern affairs. When that conversation proved equally disappointing,[7] the French ambassador hastily informed Catroux that no aid could be expected from the United States.

The British, now alone and desperately fighting Germany and Italy and on the verge of capitulating to Japanese pressure to close the Burma Road, even if only temporarily, were obviously in no position to antagonize Japan. London's reply to French appeals, received only after Catroux made his decision, merely confirmed the obvious: the "fate of Indo-China and of the British Empire was bound up with the defeat of Germany and that all British military resources should be devoted to this end." It was in the best interests of the British Empire and Indochina to avoid becoming involved in hostilities in the Far East. The British hoped that Japan limited its aims merely to ending the war with China.[8] Britain reiterated her position on 29 June, when, in reply to a request by Catroux for economic, political, and military aid, the governor-general was informed by Britain's consul general in Hanoi that he could rely on London's full diplomatic and political support and certain types of economic aid, but he was warned not to expect military support.[9]

Meanwhile, Catroux had conferred with various local French and Indochinese officials. Perhaps he was impressed with the argument of one of Indochina's prominent personalities, the Francophile Hoang Trong Phu, who declared, "It would be better for Indochina that the French administration continue to function, even under the control of Japan, . . . [for] as long as the French administration, as long as the French Army maintains itself on Indochinese soil even in the most precarious conditions, nothing will be lost for France."[10]

Finally, on the evening of 20 June, with time running out as Japanese troops moved up to the Indochinese border and units of the Japanese navy maneuvered in the Gulf of Tonkin, Catroux had to decide. Isolated from France, denied diplomatic and military assistance from the United States and Great Britain, and with only the feeblest forces at his own command, Catroux did the only thing possible—he bowed to Japan's terms.[11] In the *New York Times,* he defended his decision this way: "We would have had to face at once an attack by sea and an attack by land. The result of the struggle, if joined, was therefore not in doubt. It was bound to lead us to the occupation of Indo-China by the right of conquest and as a result to destroy French sovereignty." In a note to his government of 26 June, Catroux defended his action:

This event will permit you to understand better the downfall which France's capitulation has caused her in the Far East and to understand that it is no longer the moment for us to talk firmly to Japan.

When one is beaten, when one has few planes and little anti-aircraft defense, no submarines, one tries to keep one's property without having to fight and one negotiates. That is what I have done.[12]

When the news of Catroux's decision finally arrived in France, Pétain's government, scarcely installed at Vichy amidst incredible confusion, reacted vigorously and thus precipitated one of the most bizarre affairs to occur in wartime Franco-Indochinese relations. On 25 June, Pétain's Council of Ministers met and for the first time learned about the situation in Indochina. Catroux's superior, Albert Rivière, the minister for colonies, fumed that Catroux had not even consulted with the French government before caving in to Japanese demands that gave them a partial grip on Indochina. The governor-general's predilection for independent action could not be tolerated, and Rivière pressed for his immediate removal. Admiral François Darlan suggested that Catroux be replaced by Admiral Jean Decoux, commander in chief of French naval forces in the Far East, whose obedience Darlan guaranteed. The Council agreed, some members undoubtedly feeling that such a change might temporarily restrain the Japanese.[13]

But Catroux apparently was determined not to give in easily. He simply refused to acknowledge receipt of the order and continued governing and negotiating with the Japanese as if nothing had happened. For nearly a month, a confused, almost comical situation existed, with Catroux refusing to step down, Decoux, unwilling to assert himself, asking for confirmation of his appointment, and the infuriated Vichy government issuing repeated orders to Catroux to resign. Only on 20 July did Catroux officially relinquish his office.[14]

What were the real reasons for Catroux's dismissal? While there was some merit in Rivière's irritation at not being informed by Catroux at every step regarding his decision, common sense would have indicated that such communication was impossible, given the chaotic condition of the French government as it fled south from Paris. In any event, by prior arrangement, Catroux had in fact directly consulted French representatives in Tokyo, London, Washington, and Chungking. The information and advice coming from those capitals supported his decision. Certainly, Ambassador Henry in Tokyo was as eager as Catroux, if not more so, to give in to Japan's demands. But the government in Vichy did not replace him.

Furthermore, while Catroux's inclination to independent action might be worrisome, the French Foreign Ministry had actually recommended on the twentieth that in the eventuality of a disruption of communications between France and its overseas territories colonial officials should be given the broadest possible powers to deal with important policy matters that would normally be handled in Paris. Colonial officials should be encouraged to consult with each other and with other governments in order to assure the defense of French interests and possessions. A decree to this effect was drawn up by Jean Chauvel, head of the Far Eastern Department, and approved by the new secretary general of the Foreign Ministry, François Charles-Roux, and the minister for foreign affairs, Paul Baudouin. Albert Rivière, who headed the Colonial Ministry for less than a month in Pétain's first government, had rejected the plan.[15] The fact remains, however, that Catroux had proceeded in a manner that a number of responsible officials would have approved.

One of the criticisms of Catroux made during the 25 June meeting centered on the belief that he had opened the door to eventual Japanese control of Indochina. When rationalizing his own subsequent agreements with Japan, Decoux would later charge that Catroux's concessions compromised whatever chance there may have been of resisting future Japanese demands. Yet, nowhere in the Council or in Indochina did anyone suggest a rational alternative. Certainly, the Council, absorbed and confused by the shattering events occurring in France, had no basis of information upon which to formulate a different policy, even if they had the luxury of time to devote to it. To the discredit of the French Foreign and Colonial ministries, the tendency to follow a policy of wait-and-see—hardly a policy at all—meant that apparently no contingency plan for the Council's consideration had been developed to deal with such a situation.

Even though Catroux's rather high-minded treatment of the French government was distasteful to it and his policy smacked a bit too much of appeasement, his actions were explainable and do not satisfactorily account for his removal. Perhaps the real reason, then, for his dismissal related not what Catroux did or how he did it, but rather the direction in which he seemed to be heading in the ticklish Vichy-London-Berlin relationship. There is no doubt that there was no love lost for the Albion *perfide* among Pétain's ministers. The defeat of Britain seemed just over the horizon, and many Anglophobes in Vichy gleefully rubbed their hands in anticipation.[16] Yet, Catroux showed dangerous signs of heading toward the British camp. Not only had he solicited British military and diplomatic support, but he had actively taken steps to align Indochina with a Britain that harbored Charles de Gaulle, who, on 18 June, had made his impassioned plea for French officers and men to join him in London to carry on the struggle.[17] Catroux and Indochina did not hear the broadcast—few did—but the situation had to be of concern to the Vichy regime as it began to compete with the Free French movement for the allegiance of the Empire. Catroux's loyalty was questionable, while Decoux's posed no danger.

As early as 19 June, in reply to a British inquiry, Catroux expressed his support for Britain and its determination to fight on:

> Whatever may happen regarding events in Europe I consider that Anglo-French alliance continues and must continue with regard to Indo-China and I hold as always valid the agreements or cooperation and military assistance resulting from [the] alliance and Singapore Conference. . . . It is not necessary for me to tell you that the British decision to continue war until victory receives my entire approbation. Your Government is assured of my entire assistance.[18]

Admittedly, Catroux made this statement while awaiting a reply to his appeal to London for aid. Yet, on 27 June, the day he received notice of his recall, and after his request to London had been denied, he repeated his position: "I have already declared, and I confirm, that no matter what happens I remain faithful to [the] Franco-British alliance, and I stand entirely with Great Britain until victory which will restore France." He also expressed his determination to defend Indochina against all aggression. François Charles-Roux guessed that the Vichy government "viewed in the resolution to safeguard bonds between Indochina and the British Empire, a tendency for Colonial 'dissidence.' " Catroux's recall clearly indicated their lack of confidence in him to carry out their policy of collaboration with the Axis powers.[19]

It seems clear that Catroux was not far off the mark when he charged after the war that "my behavior in the Japanese affair was not disavowed, but my rude sincerity and my independence and, without doubt also, my faithfulness to the British alliance had displeased and were penalized."[20]

Initially, the British did everything in their power to persuade Catroux to remain in office, for the allegiance of the French Empire— Indochina and France's other Far Eastern possessions as well as those in Africa—was of great concern to London. Indeed, during the summer and fall of 1940 Britain did everything possible to gain colonial adherence to Charles de Gaulle's movement. In its reply to another plea by Catroux made on 27 June, the British government was unable to offer military aid, but it promised to provide economic and financial aid requested by Catroux, and it agreed to work for similar assurances from the United States. It undertook to support the currency of Indochina with sterling deposits and credits for the Bank of Indochina. It pledged to facilitate exports from Indochina and to do all it could to provide supplies from British Dominions and possessions. Finally, it promised to give sympathetic consideration to Catroux's request for credits for the purchase of armaments for Indochina. As the Foreign Office told Catroux, it hoped that his fidelity to the Franco-British alliance "will prove an inspiration to all Frenchmen holding positions of authority in French overseas territory."[21]

The question that arises about Catroux's behavior until his departure from Indochina on 20 July is why he failed to try to rally Indochina to the side of Britain and the Free French. At least two factors influenced his decision. First was the confused internal situation in Indochina. The initial reaction of the colony's European population to the defeat of France was one of incredulity and indignation. A large section of the local community, especially the troops under the command of General Martin, commander in chief of the Indochinese army, seemed determined not to surrender. Many officers called at the British consulate offering their services in the event that the local administration decided not to defend Indochina. Numerous representations were made to Catroux, urging him to continue the war. The local press expressed resentment at peace overtures. But upon deeper analysis of the situation, Catroux could not have been so sanguine as to expect that such enthusiasm would continue. Although many of the merchants and plantation owners of the south tended to sympathize with the Gaullists, the French in the capital of Hanoi were more directly linked either politically or economically with metropolitan France, regardless of who was running the government.[22] The long-term support for continued resistance from this group was dubious—its complaisance regarding subsequent Japanese demands is further proof—and Catroux must have realized it.

A second, and more important, reason for not rallying Indochina to Free France was that Catroux feared that such an open commitment to the British cause would merely provide the Japanese with a pretext to upset further the status quo of the area by seizing the colony. Catroux concluded, "It would therefore be playing the game of the Japanese . . . to cause an insurrection."[23] Indochina could not defend itself without British naval and air support, and while the British had offered to do everything in their power to assist Indochina, they clearly could not provide the necessary military aid.

The British, concerned lest Japan find an excuse to seize Indochina and thus place themselves closer to British territory, eventually agreed with Catroux's analysis. One leading Foreign Office official put it in the following terms:

> If Indochina goes over to General de Gaulle openly, then the Japanese will believe, or affect to believe, that this is merely a cunning British way of putting the colony under British protection. In such circumstances they might think it advisable to walk in before we could do anything. . . . In these circumstances we feel that nominal subservience to Vichy may suit the General's purposes as well as our own for the time being, and that no attempt should be made on our part to force the situation.[24]

For most of the remainder of the period up to the Japanese attack in December 1941, the British position remained the same—discouraging whenever and however possible any efforts by the Gaullists to precipitate an anti-Vichy revolt in Indochina, even going so far as to halt pro-Allied propaganda broadcasts to Indochina from Singapore.[25]

In any event, on 20 July, three days after the British temporarily closed the Burma Road, Catroux finally turned over his office to Decoux, proclaiming before he left for de Gaulle's headquarters, "I have shouldered my responsibilities and saved you your land, your money, your foreign currency, your possessions, and what are more precious to you, your honor and your flag."[26]

During the summer of 1940, Japanese demands continued to mount. Catroux, who later argued that his policy was "to temporize and hold on, waiting for a more favorable turn in the war," sought to avoid giving the Japanese any pretext for intervention by slowly conceding when necessary and resisting when possible. He hoped ultimately to create a more relaxed atmosphere with the Japanese and to secure their recognition of France's sovereign rights in Indochina.[27] Undoubtedly, any limited success that he had in staving off the Japanese was due mostly to the drift in Japanese policy caused by a political crisis in Tokyo. The lackluster performance of the Yonai government and its failure to exploit more fully the dramatic events in Europe finally led the disgruntled army to force it from office on 16 July. The composition of the new cabinet headed by Prince Konoye did little to reassure Catroux's successor, Decoux, who took office just a few days later.

If it can be said that there was a lull before the storm, it did not last long, for on 1 August Henry was invited to the Japanese Foreign

Ministry, where Yosuke Matsuoka, the new foreign minister, greeted him with additional Japanese requirements. In what amounted to an ultimatum, Matsuoka demanded that France make available transit facilities and airfields in Indochina for Japanese troops fighting against China. Henry protested that the Japanese request amounted to compelling France to declare war against China, even though Japan had not yet done so itself. Matsuoka denied that the step would violate French neutrality, and he clearly intimated that Japan would use force unless France complied immediately. Henry, having first expressed his concern over Japan's greater and greater demands, agreed to transmit the demands to Vichy.[28]

When Baudouin revealed the new Japanese demands to the Council of Ministers on 3 August, the government overwhelmingly rejected them. But the Council agreed that it would be willing to enter into broader negotiations involving the possibility of granting "exceptional facilities to Japan temporarily in return for a formal assurance that she has no territorial designs on Indochina." When Baudouin informed the Japanese ambassador in Paris, Renzo Sawada, of the French position, the French foreign minister suggested that they had "left the door open to an agreement freely and rapidly discussed."[29]

As the negotiations with Japan lurched ahead during August, disagreement began to tear at the French government's initial unity. As Japanese pressure increased, attitudes crystallized, and stormy debate raged between those who wished to stand firm against further Japanese encroachments and those who favored negotiations. Among the permanent Foreign Ministry officials, Chauvel best argued the case for resistance, and as usual, he pinned his hopes on the United States. Washington, he argued, had been "surprised and mortified" by the French collapse in Europe. There was nothing now that it could or would do in that area beyond issuing moralistic statements. But in the Far East American interests would be more directly threatened and might arouse American public opinion more easily. French resistance might hasten the evolution of the American position. In any case, Chauvel argued, "because of the ties established between Berlin and Tokyo, the Asian war and the European war were essentially the same war, which would be recognized one day." The United States would eventually enter that war, but through the Pacific. Therefore, France "must avoid at all costs playing the Japanese game in the Pacific." If it became absolutely necessary to make accommodations with Japan, "we must on each occasion drive the United States into a corner, to lead them to recognize their impotence to help us, to make them admit that the maintenance of a French presence . . . was preferable to an eviction which had left all freedom to their adversary."[30]

Chauvel's arguments convinced few, for the Foreign Ministry and its permanent officials were largely excluded from the decision-making process in this matter. Much of the correspondence regarding Indochina went through the Colonial Ministry, now headed by Henry Lémery, senator from Martinique. Information that went through the Foreign Ministry was handled personally by the foreign minister, Paul Baudouin, or by his personal secretary, Jacques Guérard. Consequently, the major battle over policy and the French reaction to the Japanese demands was fought out within the cabinet over a period of several days. Lémery was vehemently opposed to making concessions and favored resistance even if the outcome were uncertain. He argued that the slightest concession would have "catastrophic results" in Indochina and throughout the rest of the Empire. "It would be better to be beaten than not to fight at all," he implored. Lémery was supported by General Maxime Weygand, who thought it would be better to resist and fight than to accept Japanese interference and thus weaken French sovereignty over Indochina, in essence, throwing out the baby with the bath water. Adrien Marquet, one of Laval's henchmen and minister of the interior, who had been eager to surrender to the Germans in June, now opposed giving in to the Japanese in August, insisting that China would come to Indochina's defense.[31] But the most ardent proponent of a strong stance was General Jules Bührer, chief of the Colonial General Staff. He argued that Indochina was admirably prepared and situated to resist. With 100,000 troops, 100 aircraft, and munitions sufficient for three months of fighting, the French could resist a Japanese attack for a considerable period. He optimistically argued that morale was high and that Indochina had all of the physical capability to resist. "Indochina," the general declared, "can and should reply to force with force." In any case, France must make the effort, or else it would "lose face" with the Indochinese population: "To abandon Indochina is to erase a glorious past, more than half a century of effort and sacrifice, to accept without a fight the retreat of the French and the white man from the Far East." From afar, Decoux urged a similar response. Once the passage of troops was accepted, it would be impossible to prevent new encroachments that "could quickly lead to total eviction of our authority. . . ." Japanese demands must be refused "courteously but firmly," for there was "no other chance of salvation for French Indochina."[32]

The burden of challenging those who favored resistance fell to the foreign minister, Baudouin, who eagerly asserted himself. Baudouin, who had been general manager of the Bank of Indochina and who was married to an Indochinese woman, considered himself to be an expert on Far Eastern matters. Indeed, he received high marks from the American chargé d'affaires in Vichy, Robert Murphy, who credited Baudouin with a full grasp of the importance of the events in Indochina.[33] Baudouin believed that Vichy could do little to check the Japanese should they decide to move in. France was at a crossroads; the only way to retain Indochina would be by agreement with Japan.

> The position is unhappily very simple; if we refuse Japan she will attack Indo-China which is incapable of being defended. Indo-China will be a hundred per cent lost. If we negotiate with Japan, if we avoid the worst, that is to say the total loss of the colony, we preserve the chances that the future may perhaps bring us.

He refuted Bührer's claims that Indochina had the military capability to defend itself. The materiel was largely obsolete, the ability of the troops, about two-thirds of whom were native levies, was questionable, and munitions were in short supply. Moreover, no possibility existed that either men or materiel could be replaced. "To fight," he argued, "would be to court disaster." Baudouin dismissed the possibility of receiving aid from the United States, Britain, or China. The United States would confine itself to expressions of disapproval—an attitude confirmed by American Chargé Murphy—and Britain, fighting for its existence in Europe, was in no position to lend assistance to the Far East. As Baudouin saw it, "Anglo-Saxon power, in the shade of which we lived, if not diminished was very much in question, and at the moment Japan was the preponderant force in the Far East."[34]

Certainly, the American response could not have been encouraging. As early as 6 August, Saint-Quentin had conferred with James C. Dunn, a senior official of the State Department. The latter, after conferring with President Roosevelt, had stated, "We have done and will do everything possible to stabilize the situation in the Far East." But he made no commitment of American action and could only hope that the negotiations "will be slowed as much as possible." Dunn added that the British ambassador in Washington, Philip Kerr, Lord Lothian, when informed of the French démarche, had expressed the hope that France could prolong the negotiations because "the Japanese government is not in the habit of hurrying things." As Charles-Roux later contended, "The response from Washington did not furnish us with any reason for counting on either American or English aid in the defense of Indochina." Saint-Quentin drew a similar conclusion: "The United States government will not take any decisive measure against Japan, as long as there is not dispelled the menace of a final German victory over England."[35]

The bleak prospects for aid from the United States and Britain naturally inclined Pétain's government toward negotiation and concession. It was Baudouin who drafted and steered through the Council of Ministers on 15 August a French plan for meeting the crisis. The Japanese ultimatum as presented was unacceptable, Baudouin argued, but France would be willing to enter into broad political negotiations.[36] When Henry relayed the Vichy position, he reminded the Japanese of earlier French concessions and indicated that France was disposed to recognize Japan's special interests in the Far East and would search for a basis of economic cooperation between France and Japan in Indochina. In return, Japan must undertake to respect the territorial integrity of Indochina. These negotiations would provide the framework for later military discussions. When presented with the French response, Matsuoka made no effort to mask his displeasure, for it did not even address Japan's military demands. He made it quite clear that Japan would not hesitate to utilize its army to gain satisfaction. Henry left the encounter convinced that if Vichy did not agree to the presence of Japanese troops in Indochina, they would force their way in.[37]

Baudouin, who had already arrived at the same conclusion, now became determined to meet the Japanese demands:

> We must choose. If we refuse to let the Japanese through they will launch an attack . . . and we shall lose the whole of Indo-China. On the other hand if we try to come to an agreement with Japan, this will begin by recognizing our complete sovereignty over Indo-China and we shall only partly lose the colony. . . . Between the two evils one must choose the lesser, and I choose an understanding with Japan.[38]

After convincing the Council to adopt his reasoning, Baudouin instructed Henry to maintain the French requirements that Japan respect the sovereignty of Indochina and that the Japanese occupation be temporary. But he should indicate that France would yield on the matter of military conversations with General Nishihara in Saigon regarding the military facilities to be accorded Japanese forces in Indochina.[39]

For several days after the French response of 17 August, intense diplomatic activity occurred on several fronts. Besides the negotiations in Tokyo between Henry and the Japanese Foreign Ministry, both the French and Japanese sought diplomatic support from abroad for their positions. While not deceiving themselves that forceful American military aid would be forthcoming, the French still recognized that considerable American diplomatic pressure might be exerted in Tokyo on their behalf. Moreover, it seems clear that Vichy sought to keep Washington informed of its actions.[40] In fact, the American ambassador in Tokyo, Joseph C. Grew, had already become aware of the situation and had, apparently without instruction, emphasized to the Japanese that United States concern about the fate of the Dutch East Indies applied equally to Indochina. Back in Vichy, however, Murphy warned the French not to expect strong support from Washington. "France's situation was regrettable, but his government was not in a position to support [France] other than by a condemnation of Japanese initiatives."[41] Further confirmation of the American attitude came on 21 August. Upon being informed of Murphy's statement, Saint-Quentin solicited the views of the State Department. Sumner Welles laid out the American position in the following terms:

> We understand the situation of the French Government and, since we are not in a position to come to its assistance, we do not feel that we have the right to reproach it for according military facilities to Japan. But, if we were to recommend to Tokyo that its occupation be temporary, we would be accepting the principle of it. But this would be a violation of the status quo, the maintenance of which we shall continue to insist upon.

Given the apparent American commitment to the status quo, Saint-Quentin quickly let the matter drop, preferring not to indicate the extent of the concessions that France might be forced to accept.[42] In any event, it was quite certain that no substantive aid could be expected from the United States.

In Tokyo, the negotiations between Henry and the Gaimusho continued. The French ambassador, who daily urged Vichy and Decoux to appease the Japanese at once, did an admirable job of stalling, while Baudouin orchestrated the French position from Vichy. Rarely did the latter consult with the French Foreign Ministry, probably knowing full well Chauvel's opposition to granting concessions and preferring instead to consult directly with Japanese Ambassador Sawada and to seek his help in dealing with Tokyo.[43]

French persistence paid off. The Japanese, confronted with the vehement objections of the United States and Britain, and with only lukewarm support from Berlin,[44] decided to extend to Vichy the political guarantee it sought. On 26 August, Baudouin received the news from Henry, and late that afternoon the Council of Ministers met to give their final approval. Despite Decoux's continued calls for resistance to the Japanese demands and some feeble second thoughts by Lémery, the Council unanimously agreed to negotiate an agreement with Tokyo. Meanwhile, fearing the possibility of a preemptive Chinese invasion, Decoux was ordered to resist any such move, by either the Chinese or Japanese.[45]

On 30 August, Henry and Matsuoka concluded a preliminary agreement in Tokyo. Japan guaranteed that it would respect French rights and interests in the Far East, and in particular it recognized the "permanent French interests in Indochina." In return, France recognized the economic and political predominance of Japan in the Far East and agreed to grant her special economic privileges in Indochina, thus making the agreement more appealing to Tokyo. With the stipulations that the military privileges sought by Tokyo would be utilized solely for the purpose of bringing to an end the Sino-Japanese war and that they would be limited and temporary, France indicated that it would order Decoux to negotiate a military settlement with the Japanese commander in Hanoi. France would not assume any expenditure for the maintenance of such Japanese forces, and should the Sino-Japanese conflict spread to Indochina as a result of the facilities granted to Japanese forces, as the Chinese threatened, France would receive compensation.[46]

The way now seemed open for the military negotiations that Japan so eagerly sought to have initiated in Hanoi. But once again Japanese behavior provided France with another excuse for delay. On 30 August, even before Decoux had been notified of the agreement in Tokyo, General Nishihara, possibly in consultation with Tokyo, but more likely on his own initiative, presented the French governor-general with a list of demands and ordered compliance by midnight of 2 September. When Decoux replied that he needed instructions from Vichy, Nishihara arrogantly warned him "to stop sleeping, to get busy, or take the consequences."[47]

Decoux, not in favor of an agreement with Japan anyway, rejected such an ultimatum and responded with a general mobilization of Indochinese forces. Vichy quickly appealed to Tokyo, where the Japanese government disavowed Nishihara's action. On 4 September, tensions eased somewhat when General Martin and Nashihara signed a preliminary military agreement. It stipulated that the number of Japanese personnel, including noncombatants, at the bases to be granted to Japan would never exceed two-thirds of the 25,000 troops for which Japan sought passage through Indochina. But pending a final settlement, no Japanese troops were to be permitted to enter Indochina. Any violation of this preliminary agreement would constitute a breach of faith and would entitle the French to regain their freedom of action. As luck would have it, on 6 September, the very day that Nishihara expected a final agreement to be reached, elements of Japan's rambunctious Canton Army crossed into Indochinese territory. Decoux, eager to seize upon any pretext for delay, declared the Japanese action to be a violation of the preliminary agreement and broke off the negotiations. At Vichy, Baudouin could not have been too disappointed by this turn of events, for Tokyo had been disinclined to make public the Henry-Matsuoka agreement of 30 August, perhaps a sign that they had no intention of abiding by its provisions. Here might be a way of exerting pressure on the Japanese government to give way.[48] In any event, the military negotiations remained at a standstill for the time being.

Meanwhile, the United States, aware of the Japanese pressure on France, took some belated steps after the agreement of 30 August to buttress the French position. Ambassador Grew was told by Secretary Hull on 3 September to caution the Japanese that an agreement allowing Japanese forces to use Indochinese military bases would have "an unfortunate effect on American public opinion." Such an agreement, of course, was in the offing, and only the details remained to be worked out. Indeed, only two days later, on 5 September, did the Vichy Foreign Ministry notify the State Department of the agreement of 30 August. Secretary of State Hull was visibly irritated with the French action, instructing H. Freeman Matthews, the American chargé d'affaires in Vichy to complain about Vichy's failure to keep the United States informed and to express the dismay felt in Washington at the French capitulation. Two days later, on 11 September, when the new French ambassador in Washington, Gaston Henry-Haye, visited Hull, the secretary of state declared that "the French Government cannot imagine our surprise and disappointment when it took this step without any notice whatever to us." There existed little reason, Hull emphasized, for entering into such agreements that derogated basic principles. Besides, he queried, what value could one give to Japanese assurances?[49]

The American reaction was not unexpected in Vichy, but the French were not about to concede to the United States position. On the following day, the Foreign Ministry issued its rejoinder. It recounted the unfavorable conditions under which the negotiations had occurred. It recognized Washington's concern regarding the status quo in the Far East, but France had found itself confronted with the option either "of waging alone an unequal battle with Japan, or making concessions. The absence of material aid from the United States compelled us to negotiate." If the United States wished France to behave differently, which was still possible, Washington would have to realize that France would lose any war that resulted and the effect would be a modification of the status quo anyhow, only by force. Of course, the Americans never openly counseled breaking off negotiations with Japan, although Washington continued to chafe about the extent to which France would make concessions to Japan. For its part, Vichy sought to allay Washington's fears by pledging to resist the use of force by Japan.[50] Baudouin clearly stated his position in a long note handed to the American chargé d'affaires in Vichy on 19 September:

> The positions of principle recently [publicly] taken on different occasions by foreign powers have not prevented Japan from occupying and organizing Manchukuo; more recently they had not prevented the development of the Sino-Japanese war . . . .
> In the light of these precedents it is permissible to feel that similar declarations would not have sufficed to halt a Japanese attack on Indochina nor once this was carried out to persuade Japan to evacuate conquered territory. Since the only power in a position to intervene effectively in the Far East made it known to the French Government that it was not in a position to do so, either by affording naval support or supplying war materiel immediately necessary or in any other way, the latter could not but consider itself justified in defending its position by adopting the only line of conduct which took into consideration the factual situation with which it was faced.[51]

Vichy remained concerned about repeated Chinese threats to move into Indochina to forestall a Japanese occupation of that colony. Such a move might well have turned the French possession into another battleground in the ever-widening Sino-Japanese conflict. On 3 September, after learning of the Franco-Japanese agreement of 30 August, Wellington Koo, the Chinese ambassador in Paris, visited Charles-Roux and warned of the grave nature of the French act and offered Chinese troops to aid in the defense of Indochina. The offer was reviewed by the Council of Ministers on 14 September. But as they had done in June, the French rejected such offers, probably fearing that such a move would merely incite a Japanese attack. Moreover, since Vichy considered Japan to be virtually an ally of Germany, it hoped that Berlin might be persuaded to intervene to moderate Japan's demands. Consequently, it would be inopportune to side too closely with Japan's arch enemy, China.[52] So Vichy consistently rejected Chungking's offers. In any event, it was doubtful that Chinese forces could accomplish in Indochina what they had not been able to achieve in China itself.

Given these circumstances, and following a suitable delay and a proper Japanese apology for the incident of 6 September, Baudouin ordered Decoux on 13 September to reopen the negotiations with Nishihara in Hanoi. Without going into details of the negotiations, which were marked by considerable tension, abrupt changes of position, and irritating provocations, it is sufficient to indicate that Decoux dragged his feet every step of the way, hoping, he said later, that American intervention might still be forthcoming. Generally, the Japanese sought rights for the passage and stationing of an unlimited number of troops in Tonkin, while Decoux sought to place definite limitations upon the number and location of Japanese troops. On the seventeenth, Nishihara demanded the use of six airfields and the admission of 25,000 Japanese troops into Tonkin. When Vichy ordered Decoux to reject these new demands, the Japanese indicated that Decoux had stalled long enough. In an ultimatum, given simultaneously to Henry in Tokyo and to Decoux in Hanoi on 19 September, the Japanese stipulated that if an agreement had not been concluded by midnight of the twenty-second, Japanese troops would invade Indochina.[53] Clearly, the French tactics had carried them as far as possible. For the next three days, tensions increased dramatically as Japanese pressure grew. Japanese warships and transports steamed back and forth in the Gulf of Tonkin, Japanese residents in Indochina were advised to leave the country, and a large part of the Japanese military mission cockily left Hanoi for Haiphong.[54]

The United States made yet another protest to Tokyo, but Hull had already admitted to the British ambassador, Lord Lothian, four days earlier that it would be difficult to lend military aid to Indochina when France was not in any position to aid its own colony. All that could be done, Hull said, was what the United States had already done, to encourage France "to delay, and parley and hold out until the last minute against Japanese demands." The question, of course, was whether the French had delayed as long as possible. Vichy obviously thought they had, but Hull apparently believed they had not, arguing that Japan would not attack at this time. Lest the British might be having second thoughts about aiding Indochina, Hull reminded them that should aid to Indochina result in a major Far Eastern war involving the United States, it would necessarily result in the reduction of supplies to Britain for its war in Europe and "the fate of both eastern and western worlds will be tremendously affected."[55] Obviously, the United States would continue to restrict itself to diplomatic protests and economic pressure against Japan. On the twenty-first, Baudouin wired Decoux that the United States could not be expected to go beyond a diplomatic effort.

For Vichy, the scenario had been determined. Exposed, isolated, and confronted with a genuine Japanese threat (it is doubtful that Tokyo was bluffing—the military would not permit another climbdown), the French capitulated, and Decoux signed a military accord just a few hours before the Japanese deadline expired on 22 September. Considering the circumstances, the French emerged in relatively good condition. The agreement restricted the Japanese to comparatively acceptable limits. It provided for Japanese use of three airfields in Tonkin, where they had the right to station 6,000 troops. They were permitted to send not more than 25,000 men through Tonkin to attack China. The Japanese division massed at the Indochina border near Langson could be evacuated through Indochina, but this would be the subject of a separate agreement still to be negotiated.[56]

Unfortunately, this last part of the agreement proved to be the basis for a sordid sequel, called the Langson incident, which provided confirmation of French weakness in Indochina for those who doubted it. Japan's South China, or Canton, Army, which had been massed along the Indochinese frontier in anticipation of either invasion or immediate evacuation, had barely been held in check during the weeks of prolonged negotiations. Now, with the prospect of more negotiations, it could no longer be restrained. Despite apparent efforts by Nishihara to forestall such an act, shortly before midnight, 22 September, detachments of the army attacked the French garrison at Langson. Fighting continued for the next several days, with the key French position of Langson falling on the twenty-fifth, thus leaving open the road to Hanoi. It was clear that the ill-prepared, poorly equipped, and demoralized French forces had suffered a major defeat. Only when Baudouin and Decoux appealed directly to Tokyo and the emperor issued a personal order to his troops to stop their advance did the fighting end. General Hideki Tojo, the war minister, removed Nishihara and General Rikichi Ando, the commander responsible for the outbreak. The Japanese government apologized for the attack and evacuated Langson, and as rapidly as possible the belligerent Japanese division was evacuated through Haiphong.[57] Although the Japanese had originally described the incident as a "peaceful and friendly entry," the French clearly breathed a sigh of relief when it was over. Moreover, Baudouin's doubts about the capability of the Indochinese forces were justified, while the optimism of Generals Bührer and Martin was found wanting. As Baudouin noted in his diary when it was all over, "How right I was not to follow the advice of the military."[58]

In February 1941, one foreign observer, commenting on the Far Eastern situation, lamented that "Indochina is virtually lost to the Japanese." In reality, the crisis of September 1940 had already proved that France had lost Indochina and could do little to influence the march of events in the Far East. If France's fumbling, diplomatic isolation, and military weakness had placed her in a precarious position earlier, the stationing of Japanese troops in Tonkin had made the situation nearly impossible. During the next few months, Japan solemnly adhered to its pledge of August to respect the sovereignty of Indochina and were "punctilious in getting permission to do anything out of the ordinary." But while outwardly continuing to preserve the status quo, Japan continued to penetrate slowly but surely into Indochina. Anxious to incorporate the colony into its East Asian economic bloc, within weeks Japan had pressed the French into opening economic negotiations in Tokyo.[59] In normal times, the French might have successfully resisted, but the Indochinese economy, ordinarily tied closely to that of France, had become badly *desorienté* because of the war. The logical place to turn was Japan.

Given their extremely tenuous situation, French authorities in Vichy and in Indochina could only continue to play for time and hope for a more favorable turn of events before adopting a very active policy. If their economic situation seemed to indicate a closer relationship with Japan, so too did they realize that their continued independent political existence depended upon cooperating with the Japanese. On the other hand, while closer ties with Japan might be unavoidable, the French were not yet willing to abandon equally important political and economic links with the United States, Britain, and the Dutch East Indies. Consequently, France's policy during the next ten months was dominated by several objectives: (1) to avoid provoking a Japanese attack; (2) to preserve territorial integrity in Indochina and to relinquish its authority as slowly as possible; and (3) to remain, as far as relations with Japan would permit, friendly with the United States, the Netherlands, and Britain, despite bitter memories of the sinking of the French fleet Mers-el-Kebir, by the Royal Navy. More specifically, France sought in the short run to resist Japan's worst economic demands by binding themselves in agreements with the

United States, the Dutch East Indies, and other countries, while they prolonged the economic negotiations in Tokyo. In this way, they could argue that these commitments would not permit them to accede to many of Japan's most undesirable demands.[60]

The French achieved only minimal success in pursuing their goals. They were able to arrive at a local modus vivendi with the British, resuming trade between Indochina and the neighboring British possessions that had been suspended since the German defeat of France. Decoux also managed to negotiate an understanding with the British to halt the bothersome flow of Free French propaganda directed at Indochina from British facilities. Decoux argued that such propaganda might stimulate internal disruption in Indochina and provide the Japanese with a "heaven-sent opportunity for further penetration." The British, fearing the implications of such a Japanese move for its own exposed southeast Asian colonies, agreed and persuaded General de Gaulle that it was in the best interests of the Allied cause to help the local French authorities preserve the unity of Indochina and to refrain from any action that might weaken their ability to do so. As one British official rationalized it, the preservation of the French Empire "may require different methods in different places."[61]

Preliminary negotiations were initiated with the Dutch East Indies, but as for the Americans, whom Chester L. Cooper aptly described as merely indulging in "vigorous handwringing," the French were noticeably unsuccessful. After urging the French to delay and parley while holding out until the last minute against additional Japanese demands, Washington confined itself to verbal and moral condemnations of Japan.[62] As Sir Robert Craigie observed from Tokyo, it was as if the United States regarded the Japanese absorption of Indochina as inevitable, and aside from applying some economic pressure on Japan it did not appear ready to take effective action to prevent a Japanese takeover.[63] To a series of requests for military and economic aid, the Americans responded evasively or negatively. Only very late in July 1941 did they consider the possibility of granting a loan to France to help it resist Japan, but by then it was too late.[64]

Unfortunately for the French, their efforts to resist the Japanese were further undermined by the actions of neighboring Thailand. With Japan's encouragement, Thailand sought to take advantage of France's obvious preoccupations to press claims for the return of territory that it had been forced to surrender during the previous half-century. As Samuel Eliot Morison has so perceptively put it, "The Thai Government was trying to pluck a few feathers from the beaten

Gallic cock."[65] The French stood firm, naturally reluctant to pander to a country that they had successfully bullied in the past, and also fearful that surrender to the Thais might ruin their prestige among the Indochinese population. As a result, in the fall of 1940 sporadic hostilities erupted, and by the beginning of 1941 a state of undeclared war existed between the two sides. The French, convinced that the Thai action was being orchestrated and supplied from Tokyo, sought to have the British or Americans mediate the conflict. But since the former were unable and the latter unwilling, the Japanese were delighted to seize the opportunity to establish a special position in Thailand and further weaken Indochina. When the Thais suffered a major military reversal at the naval battle of Koh Chang in January 1941, Japan stepped in and "brutally imposed an ultimatum for mediation." During the spring, arduous negotiations in Tokyo produced an agreement, signed on 9 May, that was highly unfavorable to Indochina and granted Thailand substantial territory along the Mekong River. Vichy and Indochinese officials, especially in military circles, greeted the agreement with resentment and indignation. Vichy, contending that Thailand had not been victorious, signed under protest and made it clear that the government was conceding to force and did not recognize the settlement as juridically valid. As one Frenchman bitterly complained, "The Siamese, as brilliant seconds, completely played the Japanese game."[66]

By fishing in the troubled Thai-Indochinese waters as mediator, Japan greatly enhanced her prestige and claim to leadership in the Far East. Moreover, as guarantor of the settlement she now had ample reason for keeping naval and military forces hovering near south Indochina. Additionally, the Japanese now found themselves in a strong position to pressure the French into concluding the economic negotiations that had been dragging on in Tokyo since November. It was no accident that a commercial agreement granting large concessions to Japan was reached just three days before the final signing of the Thai-Indochina settlement. As a price for Japanese mediation, the French were forced to agree that they would "conclude no agreement concerning Indo-China with a third power which might imply political, economic and military collaboration involving direct or indirect opposition to Japanese interests."[67] It clearly demonstrated the extension of Japanese influence and sense of direction by the late spring of 1941.

Japan made no other demands for the moment, and there followed a slight breathing spell for the French as Tokyo sorted out its plans and marked time while dramatic events in Europe reached a climax with Hitler's invasion of the Soviet Union. But as one diplomat noted, "The cat usually allows the mouse a little latitude before the final pounce."[68] Indeed, the final pounce was not long in coming. Freed from the fear of a Soviet threat in the north, Tokyo decided to proceed with its southward advance.[69] On 14 July, the Japanese presented Vichy with an ultimatum that would allow the establishment of Japanese bases and troops in southern Indochina. They warned Vichy that "if the French accept . . . it will be a peaceful advancement; if not, an armed advance." Admiral Darlan, who now headed the government in Vichy, gave fleeting thought to putting up a "symbolic defense" should the Japanese resort to force. But he quickly concluded that such resistance would merely result in the internment of all of Indochina's military forces and the assumption of full sovereignty over the colony by Japan. As Darlan bitterly told Admiral William Leahy, the American representative in Vichy, "At least there is a possibility of saving something for France in Indochina, whereas to fight, without outside help, would have meant the certain loss of the colony."[70] Consequently, Vichy again bowed to the force majeure in an effort to maintain whatever shadow of authority Japan might be willing to bestow, however humiliating it might be. Vichy could merely console itself with a personal message to Marshal Pétain from Prince Konoye promising to respect Vichy's sovereignty over Indochina. On 21 July, Admiral Darlan agreed to Tokyo's demands, and by the twenty-fourth Japanese troops began pouring into southern Indochina.[71]

This act, followed closely by the American decision to freeze Japanese assets in the United States, undoubtedly launched a series of actions and reactions that put the two Pacific powers on a collision course culminating in the outbreak of war less than five months later. But for France, the time had long passed when it could play a significant role in determining the march of events in the Far East.

Following its debacle in Europe, France's only hope for keeping Indochina out of the Japanese orbit was for Britain or the United States to take some dramatic action that would forestall any overt Japanese move. As one Far Eastern observer put it, "Indochina is now to all intents but a pawn in the game of power politics."[72] In fact, it was doubtful that any Western power could act to save Indochina from Japan's grasp. Britain stood helpless in the Far East as she marshaled her resources for the Battle of Britain. The United States remained uncertain, unwilling, and unprepared to offer any effective assistance. Besides, Washington feared doing anything that might precipitate a Japanese attack against the beleaguered British. As

Herbert Feis later wrote, the Americans "would make no gesture that would have to be supported by action."[73]

Never was the interdependence of events in Europe and East Asia more apparent than after June 1940. With its own weakness laid bare, compounded by Britain's frailty and America's passivity, France, confronted with Japan's peremptory demands, could only stall and make minor, grudging concessions in an effort to take some steam out of Japan's expansionism. But if the French sought to moderate Tokyo's behavior by making timely concessions (it was called "appeasement" in Europe), they went about it in an ineffective manner. Rather than advancing concrete, comprehensive suggestions that might have assuaged Japan's aspirations, French officials consistently found themselves on the defensive, reacting to Japanese demands. But this was in large part the result of events and circumstances in Europe that diverted French attention and made comprehensive planning in the Far East most improbable. Even so, in the short term the French tactics worked surprisingly well, although this was at least as much due to Japanese division as it was to French policy. In the long run, however, given the strength of its position, Japan's moderation could not continue, and the dribble of French concessions begun under Catroux eventually became a deluge. In the final analysis, the French predicament was insoluble given the situation in which they found themselves, and, realistically, the policy that France adopted was the best she could pursue under the circumstances.

nine

THE QUEST FOR SYMBOLS OF POWER AND GLORY: FRANCE AND THE ALLIED FAR EASTERN WAR

In his memoirs of World War II, Charles de Gaulle recalled his feelings during the bleak days of 1940, as he sat in London and helplessly watched the deterioration of the French position in the Far East:

> To me, steering a very small boat on the ocean of war, Indochina seemed like a great ship out of control, to which I could give no aid until I had slowly got together the means of rescue. As I saw her move away into the mist, I swore to myself that I would one day bring her in.[1]

It is doubtful, however, that even the haughty de Gaulle could have guessed at the difficulties that would be encountered in returning Indochina to the fold of the once-mighty French Empire.

Not only did de Gaulle have to contend with the desperately weak political and military position of his Free French government, the division of French allegiance between his government and the Vichy regime, and the apparently overwhelming strength of Japan in the Far East, but he also found himself frustrated by an American ally strongly determined to prevent the return of Indochina to postwar French control. Indeed, President Roosevelt's plans provided for replacing French rule in Indochina with a United Nations trusteeship that would be dominated by the United States. Since Indochina had been a crucial factor in the United States' involvement in World War II, the Americans clearly believed that they had a considerable stake in its future, and Roosevelt would not be easily deflected from his course.[2] Yet it was France's colony, and de Gaulle's vigorous determination to influence the course of events there and to reclaim it led to stormy debate between the French and the Americans concerning its future. But the struggle was more than a mere pas de deux. The British found themselves in a ticklish position concerning the question. They could hardly afford to alienate the Americans, upon whom so much of their war effort depended; yet they feared that Roosevelt's attitude about the French Empire might be a harbinger of the liquidation of their own Far Eastern Empire. Moreover, the British sought to avoid estranging France for fear of undermining the prospects for postwar cooperation with her in Europe. Consequently, the British found themselves cast in a significant role in the diplomacy regarding France's Far Eastern possessions in general and Indochina in particular.

From the very beginning of the Free French movement, the French Empire played an indispensable role in de Gaulle's thinking. In his dramatic radio appeal to the French people from London on 18 June 1940, the general proclaimed, "France is not alone! She has a great Empire behind her. Together with the British Empire, she can form a bloc that controls the seas and continue the struggle."[3] For de Gaulle, the Empire was important for both strategic and political reasons. Not only would it supply men and materiel for the continuing struggle against Germany; it would also provide de Gaulle a political and territorial base and, therefore, lend his Free French movement legitimacy as the authentic representative of the nation. But most importantly, the Empire would serve as the basis for the ultimate return of France to the ranks of the great powers of the world, for as he declared, "France cannot be France without greatness."[4] Maintenance of the ties between the colonies and metropolitan France would be the quickest and surest way of reestablishing such stature.

Indochina was an important element in de Gaulle's scheme, for next to Algeria it was considered the most valuable French overseas possession, and de Gaulle never seriously considered any status for it short of complete restoration to the control of Paris. Influenced by its exposed position vis-à-vis Japan, as seen above, the colony remained attached to Vichy, and during 1940 and 1941 it signed a series of agreements with Tokyo that permitted Japanese occupation in return for nominal recognition of French sovereignty over the area. For the first couple of years of the war, there was little that de Gaulle could do to influence the course of events in Indochina. Involved in attempting to establish his movement closer to home, he had neither the resources nor the means to penetrate that colony. Moreover, the British, fearing that a close association between Indochina and Free France might provoke a complete Japanese takeover and thus endanger Malaya and Singapore, pressured de Gaulle to refrain from actively encouraging a Gaullist movement in Indochina.[5] Handcuffed regarding Indochina, de Gaulle was reduced to issuing statements and broadcasting appeals to the rest of the Empire,[6] biding his time until he could assert himself.

In the meantime, de Gaulle moved to obtain assurances regarding the future of the French Empire from Britain and the United States. A pledge from Churchill came quickly. On 25 June 1940, the prime minister promised that "the aim of Great Britain is the complete restoration of French territory, colonial and metropolitan."[7] In August, Churchill reiterated his pledge: "It is the determination of H. M. Government . . . to secure the full restoration of the independence and greatness of France." Rather ominously, however, Churchill had already hedged. In a secret letter to de Gaulle, he stated, "I think it is necessary to put on record that the expression 'full restoration of the independence and greatness of France' has no precise relation to territorial frontiers of any nation acting with us, but, of course, we shall do our best." Moreover, Foreign Secretary Anthony Eden subsequently revealed Britain's caution when he wrote to the American ambassador in London that Britain had "taken great care to avoid guaranteeing the integrity of the French Empire and . . . concentrated upon asserting our intention to restore 'the independence and greatness of France.' "[8] De Gaulle, of course, could not conceive of separating greatness from empire.

De Gaulle had far less success with the Americans. While maintaining diplomatic relations with Vichy, Washington virtually ignored every démarche made by the Free French. When René Pleven was sent to Washington in July 1941 to establish permanent and direct relations with the State Department and to obtain a clear expression of support for the preservation of the French Empire, he received a decidedly cool reception. Indeed, Pleven had to report that he had been invited to sit on some Anglo-American meetings only as an "expert" rather than as a "representative" of Free France. De Gaulle shot back his reply: "You will attend with rights equal to the other participants or you will not attend."[9] Only in October did Ray Atherton, acting chief of the Division of European Affairs, address a semiofficial letter to Pleven, in which he stated that United States policy was "based upon the maintenance of the integrity of France and on the eventual restoration of the complete independence of all French territories."[10] It was an encouraging sign, but in the weeks that followed there was little to suggest that Washington would officially support the Free French position.

With the entry of the United States into the war, the Free French quickly offered to support by all possible means the Allied cause in the Pacific, but de Gaulle also took the opportunity to declare,

"French Indochina must be reintegrated in the French community."[11] Still, the United States hesitated to give any expression of support for the preservation of the French Empire. Only on 26 February 1942 did Undersecretary of State Sumner Welles appear to make such a commitment, when he communicated to Thierry d'Argenlieu, a member of the French Committee of National Liberation, a statement that American policy was "based upon the maintenance of the integrity of France and of the French Empire and of the eventual restoration of complete independence of all French territories." But Welles qualified his statement by warning that American policy would "be governed by the manifest effectiveness with which [French] authorities endeavor to protect their territories from domination and control by the enemy."[12] Despite Free French persistence, this was the closest the movement could come to obtaining a more general recognition of the authority of the French National Committee over French territory.[13]

Nevertheless, de Gaulle enthusiastically professed to believe that Welles's statement was of "capital importance as regards the future of France," for it was the first public commitment made by the United States, and it was "tantamount to a promise to restore the complete independence of all French territories, whether at home or in the Empire." De Gaulle realized the implications of Welles's qualifying phrases, but he welcomed such a principle, because it might well lead to American and Free French forces fighting together around the world, drawing them closer together militarily, politically, and diplomatically.[14]

As a matter of fact, by the end of 1942, high-ranking American officials had made a series of reassuring statements, public and private about the future of French territories. Perhaps the most important of these was issued by Robert Murphy, Roosevelt's personal emissary, to General Henri Giraud in November 1942, shortly before the American invasion of North Africa. "It is thoroughly understood," Murphy pledged, "that French sovereignty will be reestablished as soon as possible throughout all the territory, metropolitan and colonial, over which flew the French flag in 1939."[15] Despite such promises, the climate of opinion in the United States regarding the restoration of French colonies remained decidedly hostile. Roosevelt set a clearly anticolonialist tone that reflected the attitude of many Americans and U.S. press editors. On the other hand, he failed to develop his anticolonialist statements into a coherent and practical policy because of what Christopher Thorne has called "the highly personal and shambolic manner in which Roosevelt conducted most of his wartime relations."[16] Since no clear, consistent policy statement emanated from the president, the State Department's European and Far Eastern Divisions continued to bicker over the proper approach to take concerning the issue.[17]

As he apparently worked it out in his own mind, Roosevelt conceived the notion that there should be established a postwar system of trusteeships for colonies and mandates severed from their ruling countries by the war. Three or four members of the United Nations would assume responsibility for preparing the former subject peoples for independence, and this would be buttressed by a system of international inspection of territories remaining under colonial control. Hypocritically, thought foreign observers, Roosevelt sought to bend the trusteeship concept to allow the United States to retain certain areas in the Pacific for development as strategic bases for postwar security.[18]

French Indochina was targeted early by Roosevelt as one of those colonial territories that should be brought under a United Nations trusteeship until it was ready for self-rule. As ill-defined in policy terms as his plans may have been, his frequent utterances about Indochina left little doubt as to his basic inclination. Indeed, in January 1944, when Secretary of State Hull sent the president a reminder about the pledges that had been made regarding French territory, Roosevelt fired back a memo declaring, "The case of Indo-China is perfectly clear. France has milked it for one hundred years. The people of Indo-China are entitled to something better than that." He revealed that he had recently told Lord Halifax, the British ambassador in Washington, that "Indo-China should not go back to France but that it should be administered by an international trusteeship." Clearly, earlier statements such as that made by Murphy went further than the president wished to go in regard to France's return to control in postwar Indochina, and he did not particularly care who heard him say so.[19] Obviously, his anticolonial attitude in general and his position about Indochina specifically clashed head-on with de Gaulle's objectives and plans for the revitalization of postwar France, and the Frenchman quickly resolved to counteract Roosevelt's plans.

Shortly after the American entry into the war, de Gaulle sought to be included in the planning deliberations for the Far Eastern war, repeatedly asking in early 1942 to be accorded a permanent seat on the Pacific War Council.[20] The British opposed the inclusion of the French on several counts: first, rapid action would be more difficult if the scope of the council were expanded. As General Sir Hastings Ismay observed, "The gallant General is not an easy person to deal with"; second, the Free French material contribution to the Pacific war would necessarily be very small; and, third, their inclusion would increase the danger of leakage. Foreign Secretary Eden cautioned, "I am very nervous of this. The French leak so badly." Undoubtedly, de Gaulle's movement controlled strategically important territories in the Pacific, but the British argued that they were in the American area of responsibility, and planning would therefore be undertaken in the Washington counterpart of the Pacific War Council. Ultimately, it was decided that "should matters directly affecting French possessions in the Pacific under the authority of the Free French National Committee come before the Council the National Committee will be informed, and, if necessary, invited to be represented at the meeting." But the key to the statement came in the last sentence of Eden's 4 March letter to de Gaulle: "due consideration is given to the Committee's point of view insofar as such matters are discussed in London."[21] The London Council rarely met. The Pacific Council meetings held in Washington were far more numerous and important since the Pacific area was in the American sphere of operations. But the Americans showed no disposition to include the Free French in the Washington deliberations. By the fall of 1943, however, when confronted by another determined effort by de Gaulle to gain admission, the Foreign Office became inclined to admit the French, if only to afford them a safety valve to "let off steam." Nevertheless, Churchill preferred not to broach the issue with Roosevelt, instructing the Foreign Office, "Better leave this quiet for a bit."[22]

Meanwhile, in October 1943, the French had brought the issue directly before the Americans. While some officials in the State Department were inclined to recommend participation by the French in the Pacific War Council, other influential members of the government had their doubts. Stanley Hornbeck, the State Department's legal adviser on political relations, objected strongly to any suggestion that the admission of the French to the Pacific War Council might imply a right to their return to Indochina at the end of the war. "The United States," he said, "were not fighting for the restoration of any colonies to any colonial powers."[23]

In fact, countering American anticolonialism was the very basis for the French eagerness to participate in the Council meetings. Apparently, President Roosevelt frequently used the meetings to float trial balloons concerning his plans for former colonial possessions in the postwar world. One high British official described the Council and Roosevelt's ideas in the following manner:

The Pacific Council in Washington is for practical purposes a futile and grotesque body. In fact it is rather dangerous, as President Roosevelt tends there to voice ill-conceived and typically American-woolly views on the future of other people's possessions in the Far East, which are nonsense to some but nectar to the Chinese and Filipinos who grace the Washington Pacific Council.[24]

As for the preservation of the French Empire, at a meeting of the Pacific Council in May 1942, Roosevelt trotted out his pet project. He "casually observed" that he did not feel at all certain that it would be a good plan to return all the French Far Eastern possessions after the war. He remarked that the French did not seem to be very good colonizers, especially in Indochina, and he hinted that the colony might be placed under an international trusteeship. He hoped that none of the states represented on the council would give any additional pledges to France about the restoration of all French territory.[25] In December 1942, Roosevelt again brought up the question of the future of Indochina, indicating that the French had been in that area since 1832 but had done little to improve the lot of the natives. When New Zealand's representative asked what commitments had been made to the French concerning its empire, Roosevelt spuriously replied, "No firm commitment had been made."[26]

Roosevelt's statements aroused considerable reaction in British governing circles. Eden wrote to Churchill, "The American position is becoming highly absurd." Sir David Scott, assistant undersecretary of state at the Foreign Office, was prompted to warn, "I am afraid that the American substitute for a colonial empire is American big business, and it is significant that [in the Atlantic Charter] 'abolition of empire' should be followed immediately by 'equal access for all democracies to raw materials.' " Victor Cavendish-Bentinck, the official responsible for liaison between the Foreign Office and the military services, offered the belief that Roosevelt's statements on Indochina suggested that he "is suffering from the same form of megalomania which characterised the late President Wilson and Mr. Lloyd George . . . at the end of the last war." He saw no reason for alienating the French by siding with a president "who in a year's time may be merely a historical figure."[27]

Moreover, Roosevelt's "calculated indiscretions" quickly reached de Gaulle's ears. The general's concerns about the American motivation, as he later recorded, paralleled those of the British:

A kind of messianic impulse now swelled the American spirit and oriented it toward vast undertakings. The United States, delighting in her resources, feeling that she no longer had within herself sufficient scope for her energies, wishing to help those who were in misery or bondage the world over, yielded in her turn to that taste for intervention in which the instinct for domination cloaked itself.

What bothered de Gaulle was the fact that Roosevelt's "intelligence, his knowledge, and his audacity," coupled with American power, might well allow the president to succeed. "Roosevelt meant the peace to be an American peace," and France was ordained to "recognize him as its savior and its arbiter." Spurned in his efforts to be included in wartime Pacific planning circles, de Gaulle grew increasingly frustrated and bitterly complained that "this was yet another example of the way in which he was cold shouldered and kept out of everything, his war effort ignored and his movement discouraged."[28]

De Gaulle now shifted tactics and attempted to gain active military participation in the Far Eastern war. Not only would such a role draw Free France and the Allies closer together as they fought side by side, but it would also allow de Gaulle to forestall a potential American argument that since the French had not actively assisted in the reconquest of the Far East, they had forfeited their right to return there after the war. De Gaulle later recalled his belief that "it was inconceivable that . . . the Allies would countenance the restoration of French power on territories where we had taken no part in the worldwide struggle."[29]

Since Free French forces could operate only from bases in India, Burma, or China with the consent of either the British or Americans, who had divided the Southeast Asian theater between them, de Gaulle's government again found itself in the mendicant's position. After sending out feelers during the spring and summer of 1943 about the possibility of participating in the Far Eastern conflict,[30] in September 1943 the French National Committee formally requested British permission to attach a military mission to Lord Louis Mountbatten's South East Asia Command (SEAC) at Kandy, Ceylon. The mission would ultimately take command of French forces sent to the Far East. The initial British reaction was that while such French participation might well be inevitable, it should be delayed as long as possible.[31] But the English began increasingly to have second thoughts about opposing the mission as the French, through de Gaulle's representative in London, Pierre Viénot, continued to argue that it was essential for them to give proof of their determination to participate in the Far Eastern war. After the Moscow Conference of October 1943—where it was decided not to include France in the European Advisory Commission—Alexander Cadogan, permanent undersecretary of state for foreign affairs, urged Churchill that it might be advisable to console the French by granting some kind of French representation at SEAC.

A refusal would confirm the French in their present suspicions that—and these are Cadogan's words—

> neither we nor the Americans . . . wish to see them resume sovereignty over Indo-China. This would add to their existing sense of frustration and wounded pride. Moreover, in view of the well-known American attitude towards the restoration of colonies generally, there is much to be said for the colonial powers sticking together in the Far East.[32]

But on 19 November, after a delay of two weeks, Churchill responded, "This certainly can wait."[33]

Not to be denied, however, the French continued to press the British for the military mission. In December 1943 they presented plans for the creation of a Corps Léger d'Intervention comprising approximately 500 men that would operate behind Japanese lines in Indochina.[34] The British Foreign Office was now quite inclined to accept the French participation. As Undersecretary of State Sir Maurice Peterson put it, "the longer we stave off the French requests the greater the risk that the French will put them to us in a much more unpleasant form, i.e, accompanied by political conditions."[35] The British chiefs of staff concluded that from a strictly military standpoint the French contribution to the Far Eastern war would be quite marginal, although a French mission established at Mountbatten's headquarters could serve as the nucleus of the operational headquarters that might be needed later. In any event, the chiefs did not feel that the French should participate in the military planning for the liberation of Indochina until such operations became imminent. They were quite interested, however, in the French offer of the Corps Léger d'Intervention, for it could contribute significantly to the covert activities undertaken in Indochina by the British Special Operations Executive (SOE) and the American Office of Strategic Services (OSS).[36] The French, of course, never failed to emphasize such an advantage.

A major concern of the British Foreign Office and General Staff was that if the French requests were denied, they might try to establish themselves in Chungking, where Britain would have little control over their activities. Indeed, when China finally broke diplomatic relations with Vichy in October 1943, the Free French sent former

Foreign Legion officer General Zinovi Pechkoff to Chungking as diplomatic representative. Mountbatten, originally opposed to having the French at his headquarters, began to believe by the end of 1943 that a small French mission and a limited French force in SEAC might be useful. There had been, to his mind, a tendency on the part of the Chinese to corner French interests for their own purposes, and it might be unwise to perpetuate a situation in which the sole French mission was attached to Chungking. The French assiduously sought to exploit British fears. Indeed, in the spring of 1944, de Gaulle's Committee of National Liberation warned that it would not permit the situation to slide much longer, and firmly implied that an alternative would be to transfer all French activities to China, where, in fact, the French relationship with the Chinese and with the Americans operating in China remained troubled and volatile. Nevertheless, in May 1944, Churchill directed the Foreign Office, "It would be better to delay. One can always concede."[37]

That the Foreign Office was exasperated can be seen by one official's plaintive question, "What do we do now?" Cadogan lamented, "I can only infer that the P.M. [Churchill], knowing as we all do Pres.[sic] Roosevelt's . . . sinister intentions regarding Indo-China, is careful not to do anything that might imply our recognition of French rights there."[38] Eden shared this concern and submitted his arguments directly to Churchill. He pressed for the acceptance in principle of French participation in the Far Eastern war. "The advantage," he argued, "is not only that we obtain expert local advice, but we control what the French say. Otherwise, they will run their own political warfare, uncontrolled by us, from Chungking." Seeking to play down the political ramifications of French military participation, Eden argued that the matter was essentially operational and that it need not involve political discussion of the future of the French Empire in the Far East.[39]

Eden's initiative brought a terse response from Churchill:

It is hard enough to get along in SEAC when we virtually have only the Americans to deal with. The more the French can get their finger into the pie, the more trouble they will make . . . . Before we could bring the French officially into the Indo-China area, we should have to settle with President Roosevelt. He has been more outspoken to me on that subject than on any other colonial matter and I imagine it is one of his principal war aims to liberate Indo-China from France. . . . Do you really want to . . . stir all this up at such a time as this?

Eden backed down for the moment.[40] As of July 1944, therefore, no high-level decision had been made concerning a French role in Far Eastern operations. The vexatious issue of French participation tended to fade from view as all parties became preoccupied with the invasion of Europe, the liberation of France, and the establishment of a civil administration for the nation. With the disappearance of Vichy and with the solidification of de Gaulle's position after successful visits to Washington and London in the summer of 1944, the French returned to the problem of the Far East. When René Massigli, de Gaulle's commissioner for foreign affairs, visited Eden in London that August, the first question the Frenchman raised concerned the military mission and the Corps Léger. Massigli, obviously with the intention of getting a foot in the door, suggested that if there were to be continued delays in the establishment of a permanent mission, General Roger Blaizot, as chief of the French Expeditionary Forces, Far East, should be allowed to pay a temporary visit to Mountbatten.[41] Eden, anticipating the French initiative, had already pressed the issue on behalf of the French,[42] but this time Roosevelt quashed the initiative by suggesting that the matter be deferred until the Quebec Conference, where, in fact, the subject never arose.[43]

At his meeting with Massigli in August, Eden had promised that if American consent to the French requests could not be obtained in the near future, Britain would be willing to grant a temporary visit by Blaizot to Mountbatten's headquarters. When it became apparent that the issue had not even been broached at Quebec, despite the obvious opportunity, Eden moved ahead and secured approval of the temporary visit.[44] But Eden remained "seriously concerned" about the continued American delay on the French requests, considering it an increasing source of embarrassment in Allied dealings with nearly liberated France. Moreover, as he confided to Churchill, Eden feared that if the British waited for American approval of French participation in SEAC, they ran the grave risk that the French might "throw themselves into the arms of the Americans," which would be detrimental to the general British position in the Far East. Eden concluded, "It is most desirable that they should be encouraged to work with us as regards Indo-China and that they should not be given a handle for claiming that our delay in admitting their participation in its liberation drove them to look elsewhere."[45]

In fact, the French had gone out of their way to stimulate the fear that they might be about to bolt into the American camp. In October 1944, the French leaked to the British the information that they were attempting to work through General George Marshall in Washington to gain increased participation in the Far East and that Marshall had suggested that the Blaizot mission be attached to the American command rather than to SEAC. The French indicated that while they desired to continue to work closely with the British, they were not satisfied with the very slow progress being made toward what they considered their right to share in the liberation of Indochina. The British drew the implication that unless the French were assured of more support in SEAC, they would move their center of activities to Chungking and the American theater. As British Major J. B. Sweetman put it, "They are so determined to take part in the liberation of Indo-China that they are prepared to work with anybody in order to gain their end." Indeed, in giving instructions to his representatives in the Far East, de Gaulle indicated that French policymakers would be very careful before committing themselves too completely to the British. He much preferred to work with the British, but if Britain was not prepared to take the responsibility of supporting French proposals, then de Gaulle believed that France would be well advised to wait and see what the Americans had to offer.[46] This information prodded Eden, who raised the question with Churchill once again.

Churchill had pressure from other quarters as well. Mountbatten had become convinced that the tempo of the war had been increased to such an extent that it might well be concluded by the end of 1945. He now argued that further delays in agreeing to French participation would drive them into the arms of General Joseph Stilwell in Chungking. Mountbatten argued that this would "result in General Stilwell obtaining concentrated control of Indo-China and have a disastrous effect not . . . only on the future of operational aspects of his command but on the whole British position in the Far East."[47] The British chiefs of staff also pressured Churchill to urge Roosevelt to accept the French proposals.[48] Finally, on 21 October, Churchill approved a permanent status for the Blaizot mission, although the prime minister, probably seeking to avoid Roosevelt's wrath, rationalized that there was no need to wire the president for approval. Blaizot arrived in Ceylon on 26 October—pointedly, aboard the French warship *Dumont d'Urville*.[49] Still, Churchill's concession fell far short of fully meeting the French requests. Nothing had been decided concerning the Corps Léger, and, indeed, only a day before Churchill made his decision, the French had submitted a revised series of requests providing for the participation of two French divisions in the Far East.[50]

The British remained reticent about supporting additional military requests without first securing Roosevelt's approval. Despite the optimism of some Frenchmen, however, it was quite apparent that such approval would not be forthcoming.[51] In early November, the president cautioned Undersecretary of State Edward R. Stettinius, "We must not give American approval to any French military mission . . . . It must be made clear to all our people in the Far East that they can make no decisions on political questions with the French mission or anyone else." At the end of the month, he caustically reminded Stettinius, "It should be called to the attention of our British friends that Mr. Churchill and I did not recognize the French military mission at SEAC, and further, I have made no agreement, definite or otherwise, with the British, French or Dutch to retain their Far Eastern Colonial possessions."[52] Such a statement, if ever leaked to the British, would have only confirmed their worst fears about Roosevelt's ultimate intentions and would have made them even more determined to support the French position in Indochina.

Nevertheless, for the moment, the French and British found themselves stymied. Even if London unilaterally allowed the Corps Léger to be attached to SEAC, it would not be able to operate in Indochina, as the French wished, because by the China Theater agreement of January 1942, that area had been placed in the Chinese sphere of operations, although the command was, in fact, controlled by the Americans. Subsequently, Mountbatten and Chiang Kai-shek had arrived at an oral understanding that they would both be free to attack Thailand and Indochina, which served as a supply route for Japanese forces in Burma, and that the boundaries between the two theaters would be decided by the progress of the two forces. After the Cairo Conference in the fall of 1943, the generalissimo agreed to extend the understanding to preoperational clandestine activities. But the details had remained to be worked out, and Washington characteristically dragged its feet on the matter, which became a source of considerable friction between British and American commanders in the Far East.[53]

Eden and the British Foreign Office still believed that the issue could not be treated as a purely military problem. But Churchill was reluctant to raise the issue with Roosevelt and again instructed Eden, "We had better keep this particular item till more urgent matters have been settled." In fact, only in March 1945 did Churchill finally broach the issue with Roosevelt, and only then when it became clear that General Albert C. Wedemeyer, Stilwell's successor as Chiang Kai-shek's chief of staff, refused to recognize the gentlemen's agreement between Mountbatten and Chiang Kai-shek without authority from Washington. Churchill cited to the president the importance of Indochina to Mountbatten's efforts in Burma and Malaya and suggested that both he and Roosevelt endorse an oral understanding and promote coordination between Wedemeyer and Mountbatten.[54] Roosevelt refused to bite, shrewdly recommending that Wedemeyer coordinate all Anglo-American-Chinese military operations in Indochina, regardless of their nature.[55]

While the British were apparently ready to let the matter drop, the French made several efforts after the Yalta Conference to keep alive the issue of their military participation. But direct approaches to General Wedemeyer in Chungking brought the response that he was concerned only with military matters, and this was a political question that should be referred to Washington. Yet when they appealed to Washington, the French were informed that the United States had "no useful information as to when and where we might make use of French assistance in the Pacific."[56] After Roosevelt's death, they were told that it was President Truman's policy to leave to the commanders in chief in the field matters relating to the conduct of the war.[57] By late spring of 1945, the joint chiefs of staff decided that MacArthur's main thrust would be northward for a final invasion of Japan. Therefore, American operational interest in Indochina waned, and the decision was made to turn over most of Southeast Asia to Mountbatten's SEAC command. Yet, it was only at Potsdam that Truman and Churchill, upon the advice of the combined chiefs of staff, finally agreed to divide Indochina, placing the area south of the sixteenth parallel in SEAC,[58] thus helping to pave the way for the French return following Japan's surrender.

Obviously, the issue of French military participation in the Pacific war could not be separated from the political question of whether Indochina should be returned to French control. Moreover, de Gaulle recognized that "fundamentally . . . the problem of Indochina, like the entire future of France, would be settled only in Paris." The battle for France would have to be won, and the recognition of de Gaulle's provisional government earned, before the political battle for Indochina could make any substantial headway. Moreover, since the Americans, as French Minister of Colonies René Pleven put it, "seemed totally unable to understand colonial difficulties."[59] Participation in the war would not alone salvage the French position. Sooner or later, they would have to tackle head-on Roosevelt's ideas about colonialism and, more specifically, his notions concerning the French role in Indochina.

In December 1943, after the Cairo and Teheran conferences, where Roosevelt had shared his ideas about Indochina with Chiang Kai-shek and Joseph Stalin and had received their support,[60] de Gaulle launched a direct initiative to thwart Roosevelt's scheme by announcing plans to grant Indochina a greater degree of autonomy after the war. In a speech in Algiers on 8 December, the general promised that France intended to give a new political status to those peoples within the French community who had "shown their national feeling and sense of political responsibility." He indicated that a federal organization would be implemented that would extend and protect the liberties of the various countries belonging to the union. With regard to Indochina, he pledged that the Indochinese would be given access to all public offices and that "the original imprint of Indo-China's culture and traditions would be guarded."[61]

This statement was followed in January and February by the Brazzaville Conference, an assembly of the governors of French Africa, ranking members of de Gaulle's regime, and members of the Consultative Assembly in Algiers. Although its primary function was to develop a plan for the coordination of political and economic development of the African colonies after the war, the policies recommended and the institutions proposed would necessarily affect the future of France's Far Eastern colonies as well. The conference was asked "to study what social, political, economic, and other conditions seem to you capable of being progressively applied in each of our territories in order that, through their own development and the progress of their populations, they will integrate themselves into the French community." Indeed, it was made quite apparent in the preamble to the recommendations made by the conference that "the goals of the task of civilization accomplished by France in her colonies ruled out any idea of autonomy, and possibility of evolution outside the French bloc of the empire; the eventual creation even in the distant future, of *self government* [*sic*] for the colonies is to be set aside." The French position was clear. Yet, de Gaulle's National Committee was willing to bend within this limited framework to provide for greater political participation by its colonial populations, and amidst a flood of high-sounding rhetoric the conference made some substantive recommendations for reform within the empire. As one scholar has noted, "The results of the conference, although difficult to assess, must be accounted impressive by any reasonable standard," for it advanced a comprehensive program of economic and social improvements. But most importantly, it recommended the establishment of a federal assembly that would "respect the life and the local freedom of each of the territories that constitute . . . *la fédération française.*" Furthermore, it recognized the need for the French colonies to establish their own identities. Nevertheless, although the conference presaged the end of the tired old colonial policies of "assimilation" and "association," French grandeur and empire remained entwined. As one statement issued by the conference reiterated, "access to the riches of all that bears the French name is the most certain measure of our country's return to grandeur."[62] While they were not made strictly for Roosevelt's consumption, it is most likely that the French hoped to use the proposals enunciated at Algiers and Brazzaville to their advantage when dealing with him by displaying their willingness to modify the institutional structure of the Empire. It is unlikely, however, that the French statements made much of an impression on Roosevelt, or, for that matter, on Churchill. Both were reluctant to place much stock in such statements until, as Churchill put it, "[we] see how we finish up with de Gaulle,"[63] a direct reference to the question of whether de Gaulle's National Committee should even be recognized as the government of France upon liberation.

De Gaulle's rancorous relationship with Roosevelt and Churchill certainly complicated the French situation. Not only did Roosevelt's opinion that "France would certainly not again become a first class power for at least 25 years" clash with de Gaulle's designs for greatness, but their personal dislike for each other exacerbated the situation. Roosevelt's animosity toward de Gaulle is well known. The president's frequently aired opinion that the general viewed himself as a combination of Joan of Arc and Clemenceau reflected his disdain for the general. Perhaps the low point in their relationship came in the summer of 1943, when the president angrily tried to convince Churchill that the time had come to dump de Gaulle, arguing, "I am fed up with [his] secret personal and political machinations."[64] While Churchill tried to moderate Roosevelt's outbursts, there is no doubt that he himself barely tolerated de Gaulle. Indeed, Sir Henry Pownall, chief of staff to Mountbatten's command, recorded in his diary as late as June 1944 that when de Gaulle's name arose in private conversation, the prime minister "filled the air with hate and lurid adjectives." Aware of the opposition to his movement, although his attitude was that "he was more sinned against than sinning," de Gaulle moved cautiously throughout early 1944. His most important concern necessarily remained that of obtaining recognition; other potentially explosive issues had to be deferred for the moment. As Churchill warned de Gaulle in a meeting at Marrakesh, "It behove the General to walk warily."[65]

The highlight of this crucial period for de Gaulle's government was his successful visit to Washington in July, secured through the diplomatic finesse of the British. As one observer reported, "it was very much de Gaulle's week." Amidst great ceremonial festivities, the general's public pronouncements were well received, and his impeccably affable behavior made a much better personal impression on American officials and press than had been expected. Several newspapers even commented upon the general's good humor and gentle manner.[66] But the key to success was linked to a series of meetings with Roosevelt. The president had remained critical of de Gaulle right up until the general's visit. Indeed, only a few days before the visit, Roosevelt gave his considered opinion of the Frenchman: "He's a nut!" Nevertheless, the president even had to admit later that "the visit has gone very well." In three lengthy, private meetings between the two men, Roosevelt refused to be drawn into discussions about specific issues. Instead, he effusively talked about his plans for the postwar world, indicating that he did not envision a major role for France among the great powers that would maintain the peace. In fact, France would lose some territory to the United Nations for use as military bases by the United States for maintenance of postwar security. De Gaulle later recalled that Roosevelt's "will to power cloaked itself in idealism." But, with grudging admiration, the general recognized the Roosevelt genius: "It was by light touches that he sketched in his notions, and so skillfully that it was difficult to contradict this artist, this seducer, in any categorical way." Naturally, this did not prevent de Gaulle, though taken aback, from attempting a rebuttal. He argued that incalculable dangers lurked in the postwar world if Europe were weakened, and that France must play a vital role in the reconstruction of the West. To do this, France "must recover her vigor, her self reliance and, consequently, her role. How can she do this if she is excluded from the organization of the great world powers and their decisions, if she loses her African and Asian territories—in short, if the settlement of the war definitively imposes upon her the psychology of the vanquished?" Realizing the futility of reminding Roosevelt of the American share of responsibility for the condition in which the world found itself, de Gaulle became even more convinced that "in foreign affairs, logic and sentiment do not weigh heavily in comparison with the realities of power; that what matters is what one takes and what one holds on to; that to regain her place, France must count only on herself." Roosevelt replied, "It is true that to serve France no one can replace the French people."[67] The general planned to make precisely that happen.

With regard to Indochina, de Gaulle took advantage of several opportunities to reassert his position. In one of his meetings with Roosevelt, de Gaulle apparently reiterated his intention to grant more postwar autonomy to Indochina within a federal system.[68] At a press conference, he made his intentions about Indochina quite clear. When asked whether he thought that France would retain the colony after the war, de Gaulle replied, "France is certain that she will recover intact all that belongs to her." But in a reference to the Brazzaville decisions, he added, "France is also certain that after the war and the human experiences which have been borne, the form of the French organization in the world and especially for Indochina will not be the same as before the drama that we have experienced."[69] Nevertheless, there is little doubt that de Gaulle's visit temporarily enhanced his position with Roosevelt, and the president subsequently announced that the United States had decided to consider de Gaulle's Committee of National Liberation as the temporary de facto authority for civil administration in France.[70]

As Allied forces swept through France and as de Gaulle's strong support among the French led in October to American recognition of the National Committee as the provisional government in France, France became more assertive concerning Indochina. Pleven told the press in October, "We have made an oath to reconquer Indochina just as Alsace." In anticipation of a Japanese coup in Indochina with the impending fall of the Vichy regime, de Gaulle secretly directed Gaullist leaders in Indochina to create a provisional administration under the authority of his Provisional Government.[71] Undoubtedly, secrecy was important to avoid provoking a premature Japanese military action, but it also seems likely that de Gaulle hoped to present the Americans with a fait accompli at the proper time. Yet de Gaulle maintained his flexibility, for during Massigli's visit to London in August, the general's representative agreed that France would probably be willing to follow Britain's lead in granting the joint use of bases in Indochina to others—most probably the United States or an international organization—so long as the understanding implied no relinquishment of sovereignty.[72]

In fact, in early 1944 the British had finally formulated a policy regarding the French Far Eastern possessions that would provide for continued French sovereignty on the conditions that (1) France accept the same international arrangements for mutual consultation and security as accepted by Britain; (2) France agree to the establishment of international bases at strategic points, perhaps under United States control; and (3) France give such guarantees as would allow the bases to function properly.[73] When the War Cabinet agreed to the policy, it was with the understanding that Dominions support should be obtained to persuade the United States to agree. But by the end of the summer of 1944, this had not been accomplished,[74] so the British policy remained unofficial, and the French response remained necessarily the same.

With the resurgence of France and its renewed determination regarding Indochina, and with the increasingly obvious British sympathy for the French position, by the end of 1944 Roosevelt's attitude seemed to be wavering. Certainly, statements that he made to Secretary of State Stettinius that "we have made no final decisions on the future of Indo-China," and that "I have made no agreement, definite or otherwise, with the British, French or Dutch to retain their Far Eastern Colonial possessions," did not have the old categorical ring about them. Apparently still opposed to French military participation, on 1 January he told Stettinius, "I do not want to get mixed up in any military effort toward the liberation of Indochina."[75] Yet, on 4 January, he conceded to Halifax that French saboteurs could be sent into Indochina. Moreover, several of Roosevelt's closest advisers were beginning to believe that in view of the French resurgence, "there was need for a complete review not only of the Indochina situation but of our entire French approach."[76]

As Roosevelt began the new year in moderated transition, the French started 1945 with a rush of activity. Under the direction of the minister of colonies, Pleven, an Indochina Committee began meeting to plan and orchestrate French activities concerning Indochina.[77] Veteran French diplomat Emile Naggiar, alluding to the Brazzaville policy, publicly repeated that France was ready to give Indochina "an entirely new status" that would grant the colony a large measure of autonomy. A series of government-inspired newspaper articles made it clear that while there was a need for "a readjustment of French colonial conception," France intended to remain an imperial power, and she would do so on her own responsibility.[78] At the end of January, the French declared that they planned to go forward with the integration of their colonies in to an imperial system, indicating that the individual colonies would advance toward complete equality with metropolitan France, "politically and otherwise," as soon as their development allowed.[79] On 23 March, the French Council of Ministers formally approved a statute establishing a federal government for Indochina selected from Indochinese nationals and resident Frenchmen and incorporating Indochina with other parts of the empire into a "French Union."[80] On the following day, the provisional government issued a proclamation reiterating its contention that Indochina held a special place in the French community and "would enjoy freedom in keeping with its stage of evolution and its capacities. The proclamation further made it clear that the government "considers it its duty . . . to define what shall be the status of Indochina when it has been freed from the invader."[81] Meanwhile, on 15 March, the French ambassador in Washington, Henri Bonnet, pressed Stettinius for an arrangement establishing a civil administration in Indochina upon its liberation. The approach was rebuffed over a month later, however, when Stettinius indicated that full-scale operations to liberate Indochina were not contemplated and therefore such an agreement "would serve no useful purpose."[82]

The most precise and emphatic statement of French intent, however, had come in a note directed to Washington toward the end of January 1945:

> First, France cannot admit any discussion about the principle of her establishment in Indochina. Her presence founded on agreements consistent with international law and based on the immense task carried out by her for the sake of the Indochinese population has never been disputed by any Power. The occupation of Indochina by the Japanese had not changed anything in that state of affairs. . . . [The] French Government has already decided at the Brazzaville conference the principles of the policy she means to follow in her overseas possessions. Accordingly she will determine together with the populations concerned the status of Indochina on a basis that will secure for the Union a satisfactory autonomy within the frame of the French Empire. . . . These decisions, having no international character, come solely within the competence of the French Government.[83]

As Roosevelt slowly and grudgingly retreated from his trusteeship idea, de Gaulle grew increasingly annoyed and impatient. In March, the controversy over Indochina came to a head. De Gaulle remained convinced that participation in the war against Japan was absolutely necessary to insure the return of Indochina to France after the war. Blocked in his attempts to gain formal military participation alongside the Allies, but desperately determined to get his government into the Far Eastern fight, he resorted to encouraging resistance movements and clandestine operations against the Japanese in Indochina. De Gaulle felt that after the war the French could argue that they had at least done something on their own behalf and would be able to assert their moral right to return to Indochina. Twice during 1944, Major François de Langlade, de Gaulle's representative in India, parachuted into Indochina to make contact with local authorities and to organize the local resistance. By the beginning of 1945, de Langlade had dropped at least a dozen groups into Indochina, and a *service d'action*, largely supported by Britain's SOE organization, had been established to prepare sabotage and guerrilla activities that would disrupt Japanese efforts in the event of an Allied invasion of Indochina. In the fall of 1944, after the establishment of de Gaulle's Committee as the provisional government in France, a clandestine organization, known only as the Direction Générale, Etudes et Recherches, was established in Calcutta to operate in conjunction with Force 136 of Britain's SOE.[84] In September 1944, General Eugène Mordant, since 1940 the commander of French forces in Indochina, was tapped by de Gaulle to be the secret representative of the Provisional Government to lead the resistance movement in Indochina.[85]

These developments had placed Governor-general Jean Decoux in an extremely awkward position. Ever since the collapse of metropolitan France in 1940, and the subsequent Japanese demands of 1940–41, Decoux and his colonial administration had sought to maintain a semblance of French autonomy by cooperating with and remaining subservient to the Japanese. Since the Japanese did not have the administrative or military personnel to occupy Indochina directly, they found it convenient to leave the French colonial administration and military establishment intact to run the country. Japanese bases in Indochina had been a particularly useful springboard for launching their attacks against Burma, Malaya, and Indonesia. As for Decoux, as long as the Axis tide swept along, he remained a staunch supporter of the Vichy regime, which suited his own autocratic inclinations. Yet there is little doubt that he held few illusions about the ultimate Japanese designs on Indochina, realizing that only convenience prevented them from taking over completely. Seeking to avoid provoking such a move, in 1943 Decoux contacted the Gaullist representative in Chungking, General Pechkoff, who had overall responsibility for resistance in Indochina, and urged that the Allies do nothing in Indochina that would provoke the Japanese. After the Normandy invasion and the subsequent collapse of the Vichy regime, Decoux had officially assumed full responsibility for Indochina's government. To calm the Japanese, he continued to maintain that he was interested only in maintaining the status quo. Yet, the success of the Allied drives in Europe and the Far East made it increasingly difficult to retain authority over many Frenchmen in Indochina who wished to jump on the Allied bandwagon, an idea that probably appealed to Decoux as well.

When Decoux was informed in October 1944 of Mordant's appointment as delegate general of the Gaullist resistance forces in Indochina, he was outraged. In a fit of injured pride, he fired off a dispatch to de Gaulle demanding that either he be confirmed as the legal authority in Indochina or else be allowed to resign. On 23 November, de Gaulle's Provisional Government agreed to confirm the authority conferred upon Decoux by the Vichy regime. He was instructed to remain in office until further orders were issued to him through Mordant. A new Indochina Council was established, nominally headed by Decoux, but with the real authority resting with Mordant as its vice-president and other pro-Gaullist leaders, who made certain that the admiral toed the line established in Paris. Henceforth, for all intents and purposes, Decoux was simply a figurehead.

In the meantime, clandestine activities accelerated, and plans for full-scale resistance to the Japanese moved ahead. Under Mountbatten's orders to make a "minimum of fuss," the British assisted the French in transporting personnel to SEAC from Europe, and they began to parachute arms, ammunition, and agents into Indochina. Mordant developed a plan, approved in Paris in January 1945, for the gradual withdrawal and redeployment of major French military units to areas where they could retreat to the mountains from whence they could continue a guerrilla war against the Japanese. Coupled with an outlandish exaggeration of their own capabilities, fed, no doubt, by Gaullist rhetoric, those who undertook all of these activities operated amidst considerable confusion, incredible levity, and just plain stupidity. Many of the French population openly expressed their support for the resistance and freely discussed the plans; soldiers openly collected the arms dropped in the countryside and placed them in arsenals in full view of the Japanese; a picture of de Gaulle even hung in the public offices of the French high command. To compound the situation, the Japanese apparently had broken the French code and were reading all of the French ciphers. In view of this lack of prudence, it is not surprising that the Japanese decided to take action; it is surprising only that they delayed so long before doing so.

With the successful American reconquest of the Philippines beginning in October 1944, the Japanese grew increasingly fearful that the next American move would be against Indochina in an attempt to cut off Japan from its forces in Southeast Asia. By the beginning of 1945, the Japanese high command had moved forces from South China to reinforce its garrisons in Indochina, especially in Tonkin, Laos, and Annam. Given their surveillance of French activities and their knowledge of French plans, the Japanese were able to situate troops in stategic positions to negate the anticipated French moves.[86]

Finally, on 9 March, the Japanese struck. The Japanese envoy in Saigon, Shunichi Matsumoto, declared to Decoux that since an American landing in Indochina appeared likely, Tokyo wanted to tighten the bonds of the "common defense" of Indochina. When Decoux resisted the idea, Matsumoto handed him an ultimatum containing additional Japanese demands that the French armed forces, police, and administration be placed under Japanese command. Decoux was given two hours to conform; there was no doubt that force would be used if he did not agree. Decoux, as he had done before when confronted with Japanese demands, tried to delay, suggesting that such Japanese control might be accepted if the Americans actually invaded.

This time, the Japanese refused to be put off. They responded by arresting Decoux and seizing administrative buildings, utilities, and communications centers. During the night of the ninth, they attacked police and military garrisons with lightninglike precision, and within twenty-four hours they brutally overwhelmed and interned the major part of the French armed forces. They seized General Mordant and thereby effectively beheaded the resistance movement before it could implement its plans. Only scattered units managed to avoid internment. Some fled to the mountains, while others, under the overall command of General Gabriel Sabbatier, began fighting their way toward the Chinese border. By mid-June, the remnants of the French forces finally straggled across to safety and a chilly reception from the Chinese and Americans in the area. After crossing 500 miles of rugged jungle terrain, they arrived in wretched condition, leaving behind 4,200 dead and most of their equipment.[87]

Once again, the French military forces had been caught off guard and had failed to acquit themselves satisfactorily, even though they had long anticipated such a Japanese move, and evidence collected by Gaullist intelligence gatherers had indicated that Japan would not allow the situation to persist much longer. It was a pitifully weak display of French power—a fact not lost on either the Indochinese or the French. As John T. McAllister, Jr., has noted, "Unquestionably the disappearance of its colonial authority in Indochina, in the space of a few short days in early March 1945, was for France the gravest consequence of the Japanese intervention. Once broken, its administrative control was never reestablished over all of Indochina." Ellen Joy Hammer has suggested that the diplomatic defeats of 1940 and 1941 had meant little to the Indochinese nationalists, but the sight of

French leaders and soldiers disarmed and interned made a great impression.[88] There can be little doubt that de Gaulle must bear a large share of the responsibility for this disaster. In his eagerness to have France participate militarily in the Far Eastern war in order to preserve Indochina for France, he actively encouraged the French resistance in Indochina. But, paradoxically, in doing so he provoked Japanese action that undoubtedly hastened the end of France control over the colony. In the long run, of course, it is inaccurate to argue, as Marshal Alphonse Juin did, that had the situation in Indochina been left undisturbed by the Allies until the final capitulation of the Japanese, then the Vietminh would not have been able to expand their influence after the war as they did.[89] It would have happened eventually anyway. The coup of March 1945 simply hastened the process.

On 10 March, the day following the coup, Tokyo justified its action by blaming the "utter lack of sincerity on the part of the French Indo-Chinese authorities." They argued, not untruthfully, that the French administration in Indochina had been secretly in contact with the Allies and had been preparing to attack Japanese forces in Indochina. They had ignored Japanese protests about aiding downed American pilots, and they had refused Japanese requests for closer collaboration. On the following day, the Japanese proclaimed the independence of Indochina and the elevation of their puppet, Bao-Dai, as emperor.[90]

If the Japanese coup spelled disaster for French power in the long run, there is little doubt that it was something of a political blessing for de Gaulle's government in the short run. Indeed, the embarrassment of Decoux's collaborationist government had been removed, and the Japanese action had squarely placed Indochina in the fight against Japan. These events provided de Gaulle, whose government was rapidly gaining international credibility, with another opportunity to present France's case for its return to Indochina. He could now claim that France was shedding its own blood for the liberation of its Far Eastern territory. On 14 March, the general made another of his dramatic broadcasts, urging the resisters to continue the fight and reiterating his concerns and intentions for Indochina: "Whatever the conditions of resistance in Indo-China may be, it is essential that there should be resistance. To a great extent the rapid and total victory of the United Nations in the Far East is at stake. France's honor is at stake and so is the future of Indo-China. . . . In Indo-China as everywhere else, the ordeal of this war is a boiling crucible. Our acts will be decisive."[91]

De Gaulle also pressed ahead through diplomatic channels to obtain aid for the meager French resistance in Indochina. On 12 March, even before the situation in Indochina had been clarified, the French ambassador in London, René Massigli, called on Eden and argued that the Japanese action made it more imperative than ever that the Corps Léger d'Intervention should be flown to the Far East. It would be invaluable in assisting the resistance, Massigli declared, but without making clear how the addition of some 600 men would make much difference. He suggested that if facilities and transport could be arranged in agreement with the United States, so much the better. If not, he asked that Britain itself provide the facilities. Although they took the French request under advisement, the British remained reluctant to act until Churchill had determined what Roosevelt's policy would be toward Indochina.[92]

In Washington, the French representative, Henri Bonnet, made a similar démarche on 12 March, asking for "all possible support both in material and purely military fields," including immediate tactical air support.[93] The French subsequently enlarged their requests to include a civil affairs agreement for Indochina, similar to that provided for France after the Normandy invasion. They also asked that General Blaizot be accredited to General Wedemeyer for liaison purposes.[94]

The French were told that the joint chiefs of staff would study the requests. But it is clear that the decision was not in the joint chiefs' hands. It has been argued by Wedemeyer, with some justification, that he simply did not have the resources to divert to Indochina. Yet, more aid could have been sent than was actually provided. The fact remained that Roosevelt still stood fast in his determination to avoid rendering the French military assistance in Indochina or to allow the French a military role in the defeat of Japan. As Romanus and Sunderland concluded, the United States "was most reluctant to engage in activity that might result in its being associated with or supporting French colonialism." This was made quite clear at a meeting Roosevelt held with General Wedemeyer in Washington after the Japanese coup. As Wedemeyer later recorded, "He admonished me not to give any supplies to the French forces operating in the area."[95] General Claire Chennault, whose Fourteenth Air Force operating out of southern China would have provided a large portion of any American aid sent to the French, recalled that orders from theater headquarters stated that no arms and ammunition would be provided the French under any circumstances.

> I was allowed to proceed with "normal" action against the Japanese in Indo-China provided it did not involve supplying French troops. . . . Wedemeyer's orders not to aid the French came directly from the War

Department. Apparently it was American policy then that French Indo-China would become a mandated territory after the war and would not be returned to the French. The American government was interested in seeing the French forcibly ejected from Indo-China so the problem of postwar separation from their colony would be easier.[96]

De Gaulle saw the American dilatoriness in the same light. When American Ambassador Jefferson Caffrey visited de Gaulle on 24 March, for the purpose of introducing Roosevelt's friend and special counsel, Samuel I. Rosenman, the general told Caffrey, "It seems clear now that your government does not want to help our troops in Indo-China. Nothing has yet been dropped to them by parachute." When the ambassador demurred and sought to point out the logistical problems involved, de Gaulle retorted, "No, that is not the question; the question is one of policy I assume."[97]

Nevertheless, a trickle of aid did reach the French resisters. By the end of March, Roosevelt relented and reluctantly approved air support, and Chennault's planes attempted to relieve the pressure on the retreating French by bombing and strafing the pursuing Japanese forces. It was made clear to the French, however, that American men and material would be employed in attaining the main objective of knocking out Japan. Any aid to operations in Indochina would be undertaken only "provided such action does not interfere with operations planned elsewhere." Therefore, American aid arrived late and remained minimal. As Marshall advised his field commanders, only "token assistance was appropriate." One American memo admitted that aid to Indochina "consisted of a few aerial drops, actually resulting in inconsequential assistance. It is contemplated that the same system will apply in the future."[98] The British, determined to support the French position in Indochina, did their best to supply arms by flying long missions from Calcutta. But such aid was limited by the physical constraints of distance and shortage of supplies. Moreover, the failure of the Allies to work out a jurisdictional agreement regarding theater boundaries hampered British attempts to supply French troops in what Wedemeyer regarded as Chiang Kai-shek's theater of operations.[99]

Largely rebuffed through diplomatic channels, de Gaulle sought to keep the issue alive publicly. In his emotion-packed declaration to the French people on 14 March, he criticized the Allies for their slow response to French appeals for aid, and he reminded the Allies that during the most difficult period of the Japanese advances after Pearl Harbor the National Committee had placed vital bases in the Pacific at the disposal of the Allies. He dredged up the issue of French military participation in the Far East by pointing out that "it is not [France's] fault if the forces she had long prepared to aid Indochina are not yet in line beside those of the Allies." After all, the Allies failed to make available the necessary transportation to get them there. He made it clear that the *French* resistance forces in Indochina were operating under directions from Paris. Japan had attacked the constituted *French* administration, and the Japanese in Indochina should ultimately be forced to surrender to the *French*. Still eager to have France counted among those who made some kind of military contribution to victory in the Far Eastern war, de Gaulle urged General Sabbatier to "prolong resistance on Indochinese soil whatever the difficulties." Sabbatier was ordered to remain in Indochina until the last possible moment. De Gaulle had declared that "French blood shed on the soil of Indochina would constitute an impressive claim,"[100] and now that French troops were actively engaged, although in very desperate straits, for political purposes the general was determined to keep the situation alive.

All of this, however, could not obscure the fact that French prestige had suffered another severe jolt, and that for all the pleading for aid, Roosevelt was far from becoming tied to any French military effort in Indochina, even under the most difficult circumstances created by the Japanese coup. Frustrated and irritated, and perhaps seeking to take advantage of increasing American suspicion of the Soviet Union, on 14 March de Gaulle literally erupted:

> We do not understand your [American] policy. What are you driving at? Do you want us to become, for example, one of the federated states under the Russian aegis? The Russians are advancing apace as you well know. When Germany falls they will be upon us. If the public here comes to realize that you are against us in Indochina there will be terrific disappointment and nobody knows to what that will lead. We do not want to become Communist; we do not want to fall into the Russian orbit, but I hope you do not push us into it.[101]

Stettinius appeared shaken, not only by the severity of de Gaulle's scolding, but because of the allusion to the Soviet Union, coming at a time when many in Washington had begun to reappraise the state of American-Soviet relations. During the spring of 1945, the imposition of pro-Soviet regimes in Poland and Romania confirmed the suspicions of many that the Soviets intended to carve out their own sphere of influence in Eastern Europe. The American ambassador in

Moscow, W. Averill Harriman, even warned of a "barbarian invasion of Europe" and recommended the rebuilding of Western Europe into a strong prosperous bulwark against Soviet expansionism.[102] From Paris, Jefferson Caffrey, the American representative to de Gaulle's government, frequently predicted that France would have to play a pivotal role if the Soviets were not to become the dominant power in postwar Europe.[103] But within the State Department a debate continued between the Division of European Affairs, which took basically the same position as Harriman, and the Division of Southeast Asian Affairs, which argued that the movement toward self-rule among former colonial territories was "inexorable." It had become a question of whether the United States should support French policies everywhere, including the Far East, in order to reduce French suspicions and improve Franco-American relations, or whether de Gaulle's Provisional Government should be pressured to make colonial concessions in Indochina in order to head off an inevitable outbreak of violence that might discredit all Western influence in the area.[104]

A major policy paper hammered out within the State Department during the late spring attempted to reconcile these disparate views. It concluded that "the Soviet Union offers the most perplexing problem." While it remained unclear as to the extent to which American and Soviet policies in the Far East would conflict, the report predicted that "Soviet ideology will be a rising force throughout the entire Far East." Consequently, the United States needed to harmonize as much as possible the increasing desire for freedom among the peoples of the area with the need to maintain unity among the leading allies. If care were not exercised in the formulation of policies in the area, they could "undermine the influences of the West. If such care is not taken, the consequences of such policies could be destructive to the peace and security of the area and might result in American withdrawal to a policy of isolation with its disastrous effect on our own interests and on the future peace of the world."[105]

Nevertheless, despite the growing concern in Washington about Soviet intentions, Roosevelt could not yet bring himself to abandon totally his hopes for the postwar Far East, and he quashed a proposed statement to the effect that the United States would do all that it could to aid the French resisters in Indochina.[106] True to form, Roosevelt still resisted military cooperation with the French and sought to avoid any involvement in the French cause to retake Indochina. But his trusteeship concept for Indochina, under pressure from Britain, France, and his own State Department, was clearly in disarray. Indeed, on 15 March, Roosevelt grudgingly admitted that he would be willing to allow France to retain Indochina and New Caledonia "if we can get the proper pledge from France to assume for herself the obligations of a trustee . . . with the proviso that independence was the ultimate goal."[107]

In fact, the trusteeship plan agreed upon at the Yalta Conference, as publicly announced on 3 April, allowed France and other colonial powers to place their colonies under international trusteeship on a voluntary basis. As one study has concluded, for all intents and purposes "trusteeship status for Indochina became, then a matter for French determination."[108] France, it seemed, had won its fight over the future of Indochina, barring any about-face by the new president, Harry Truman, who succeeded FDR after Roosevelt's unexpected stroke on 12 April 1945.

In the aftermath of Roosevelt's death, the French redoubled their efforts to ensure that such a reversal of policy did not occur. On 25 April, in a gesture perhaps timed to coincide with the opening of the organizational meeting of the United Nations in San Francisco, Ambassador Pechkoff reminded a news conference in Chungking about French blood being spilled for the Allied cause in the Far East: "In this conflict, the Indochinese are showing themselves faithful to the cause of France. The real 'trusteeship,' " he declared, "is in our hearts." Having been excluded from the Yalta deliberations, the French came to San Francisco in an aggressive mood, which was further exacerbated by their exclusion from many of the discussions held at the conference about major European issues. On 2 May, Georges Bidault, de Gaulle's foreign minister and leader of the French delegation, announced that the decision regarding Indochina's future would be determined by France alone. At a stormy meeting with Stettinius the following day, Bidault let loose with a barrage of pent-up anger. Asking the American to forgive the "vehemence of his tone," the Frenchmen warned that the United States must not make the mistake of pushing France into "playing the game of the little nations." On the subject of Indochina, he became even more blunt. Criticism of French colonialism that had persisted in the American press was "utter rot." Although France was committed to allowing the Indochinese people a greater participation in their government, his country had "no intention of placing Indo-China under the trusteeship system" that had been approved at Yalta. In fact, he ridiculed the voluntary provisions of the trusteeship plan because they would simply encourage independence movements among colonial peoples. Coming from the usually reserved Bidault, this kind of talk shocked Stettinius, who sought to smooth the Frenchman's ruffled feathers by assuring the foreign minister that he was "personally desirous of France being restored to her former stature." When the Frenchman reiterated the "great uncertainty and concern" in France regarding American policy toward Indochina, James C. Dunn, assistant secretary of state and a senior member of the American delegation, quickly interceded and proclaimed that "no official policy statement of this Government . . . has ever questioned even by implication French sovereignty over Indo-China."[109] When Stettinius made no move to qualify Dunn's bold statement, Bidault undoubtedly took his silence to signify approval.

In view of the increasingly apparent discord between the Americans and Soviets concerning such issues as the future of Poland and Czechoslovakia and the future of Lend-Lease aid, French support became increasingly important to the Western allies. Although there is no evidence to indicate that Bidault's outburst was timed to take advantage of such divisions (he was genuinely upset about being excluded from the Big Four discussions), there is no doubt that his stance benefited from the situation and that his vehemence had a desirable effect. That very day, Stettinius proposed that France be represented on the Big Four councils. Moreover, when he subsequently wired an account of the meeting to the State Department, he noted that "Bidault seemed relieved and has no doubt cabled Paris that he received renewed assurances of our recognition of French sovereignty over [Indochina]."[110] Indeed, Bidault should have been relieved, for Stettinius displayed little concern that comments made by the American delegation to Bidault would be interpreted by the French as statements of policy. In fact, shortly afterward, when Stettinius requested an estimate of conditions in the Far East as well as the American policies toward the area, a State Department policy paper confirmed that the question of sovereignty over Indochina had been settled. It recognized that "French policy toward Indochina will be dominated by the desire to reestablish control in order to reassert her prestige in the world as a great power." The paper concluded by stating, "The United States recognizes French sovereignty over Indochina." Only the faintest echo of the trusteeship concept could be detected in a statement that followed, almost as an afterthought, that it remained "the general policy of the United States to favor a policy which would allow colonial peoples an opportunity to prepare themselves for increased participation in their own government with eventual self-government as the goal." As George C. Herring has concluded, "The all-important question of sovereignty was settled on the spur of the moment and would not be raised again." The need for

French cooperation in Europe was assumed to be more important than securing concessions in colonial matters.[111]

At de Gaulle's request, Bidault was invited to stop in Washington on his return trip to France from San Francisco. On 17 May, Bidault met with President Truman in what the latter described as a "difficult session." By all accounts, Bidault did not raise the issue of trusteeship or Indochinese sovereignty. Instead, as de Gaulle had indicated in his request for the meeting, the question of France's "extreme desire" to have French forces participate in the war against Japan remained on French minds. The general had admitted that there would be technical difficulties involved, but he had argued that cooperation between France and the United States in the Pacific after victory in Europe "could have important political, moral, and military consequences."[112] It was in this vein that Bidault raised the issue of military participation with Truman. But the president adhered to a line suggested by the State Department. It was his policy, he said, to leave such an issue to his commander in the area. While he welcomed such Allied aid in the war against Japan, Truman reiterated that the problems of transportation and supply were enormous, a point that State Department officials pressed home again when Bidault met with them the following day.[113] Why Bidault failed to raise the issue of Indochina's sovereignty and trusteeship can only be surmised. Perhaps he believed that Stettinius's statements at San Francisco had resolved the issue to France's liking, although one would assume that he would have sought Truman's confirmation of the American position. On the other hand, he may have been unwilling to raise the prickly issue at a time when de Gaulle's antics in Europe threatened to destroy the budding rapprochement between the two states. Indeed, if France got its way over Indochina during this period, it was largely in spite of de Gaulle rather than because of any positive action taken by him.

At the time of the San Francisco Conference and Bidault's ensuing visit to Washington, major crises had exploded in Europe between de Gaulle and the Americans and in the Middle East between de Gaulle and the British. Despite Anglo-American opposition, in order to present his allies with his customary fait accompli, de Gaulle had sent troops back into the former French mandates of Syria and Lebanon, both of which had recently established their independence. Churchill had been so outraged by this action he had decided that he would not continue to defend the French position concerning Indochina. Furthermore, de Gaulle's stubborn refusal to withdraw French troops from the area of the Val d'Aosta of northwest Italy, where he proceeded with plans for territorial "adjustments," had severely tried

Truman's patience. Coming at a time when Truman was lecturing the Soviets about their actions in Eastern Europe, de Gaulle's open defiance was embarrassing to Washington. In fact, the situation became clearly dangerous when French commanders threatened to fight American troops who entered the area. Only after Truman issued an order to terminate all supplies sent to French forces did de Gaulle grudgingly concede, grumbling about having to endure yet another humiliation, which he saw as a demonstration of American "desire for hegemony, which they readily manifested and which I had not failed to discern on every occasion."[114]

Despite de Gaulle's annoying disputes with other world leaders, the momentum toward reestablishing France as a major partner in the postwar world proceeded apace. The basic position of the American government moved ever closer toward the conviction that cooperation with the colonial powers, including France, would be the best way to ensure peace in Europe as well as in the Far East. As a State Department policy paper predicted in June 1945, France would clearly encounter serious opposition to its attempt to reestablish control over Indochina after the defeat of Japan. The situation would undoubtedly be unstable, and "an increased measure of self-government would seem essential if the Indochinese are to be reconciled to continued French control." The State Department believed that while America should continue to voice its support for the right of dependent peoples to achieve increased measures of self-government, "it should avoid any course of action which would seriously impair the unity of the major United Nations."[115]

Subsequent decisions reached at the Potsdam Conference confirmed the American position. Once again, the French remained uninvited despite de Gaulle's persistent efforts to gain representation. The general's behavior concerning Italy and the Levant had used up whatever reservoir of goodwill the American and British leaders had cultivated. De Gaulle's presence at Potsdam had been viewed as a possible source of additional discord and thereby a hindrance to the progress of the conference. Consequently, his request for admission had been denied. In spite of their absence—or perhaps because of it—French interests regarding Indochina fared well. The American chiefs of staff formally approved French military participation in the Far Eastern war and agreed that French troops would be best utilized in Indochina. Already, on 15 June, de Gaulle had approved the creation of an Expeditionary Corps for the Far East. General Philippe Le Clerc, the celebrated commander of the French 2d Armored Division that had liberated Paris, was placed in charge. When Le Clerc indicated that he preferred a Moroccan assignment, de Gaulle revealed the importance of Indochina in his thinking, telling Le Clerc, "You will go to Indochina because that is more difficult."[116]

Britain's proposals for a realignment of command boundaries in Southeast Asia also met approval at Potsdam. Mountbatten's SEAC operations would henceforth include Indochina south of the Sixteenth Parallel. The Chinese remained responsible for the area north of that line, although the United States granted France the right to participate in surrender ceremonies throughout Indochina. This, of course, allowed American attention and resources to be focused upon the main task of making the final thrust against the Japanese homeland. But it also opened the door for Franco-British cooperation in reestablishing French control over the colony.[117]

The American decision to wash its hands of the Indochina issue and to accept the restoration of French sovereignty was reconfirmed when de Gaulle was finally invited for a long-sought-after, but delayed, visit to Washington in late August 1945. The record of the discussions as they related to Indochina is incomplete—indeed, most of the time spent during the three days of discussions related to European affairs. De Gaulle's account of the talks, however, suggests that Truman had abandoned any inclination to resist a French return to Indochina. According to de Gaulle, the president "admitted that the rivalry between the free world and the Soviet bloc now dominated every other international consideration." De Gaulle conceded that the "more or less 'colonial' countries" would eventually receive their independence, "though the means would inevitably be varied and gradual." He assured the president, "We have determined to forward those countries which depend on ours toward self-government. In some cases we can proceed rapidly; in others, less so. Evidently that is France's affair." The alternative, he argued, would be "a wave of xenophobia, poverty and anarchy" among those people. He implied that only the Soviet Union would be advantaged by such a situation. Truman reassured the general that the United States "offers no opposition to the return of the French army and authority in Indochina." De Gaulle's response remained true to form: "Although France need ask no permission or approval in an affair which is hers alone, I note with satisfaction the intentions you express."[118]

The general believed that the collapse of Japan effectively removed "the American veto which had kept us out of the Pacific. Indochina from one day to the next became accessible to us once again." All that remained was for France to reestablish itself physically in Indochina, and de Gaulle was determined to "waste no time returning there" and "to do so as acknowledged participants in the victory."[119] With the help of the British, French military forces began their ill-fated move back into southern Indochina in September.

The editors of *The Pentagon Papers* concluded that American policy toward Indochina "was governed . . . by the dictates of military strategy, and by British intransigence on the colonial issue." It is difficult to argue with their verdict. Yet, the record also reveals that the dogged French determination to regain control of Indochina greatly influenced British thinking and thus indirectly affected American policy. To borrow a phrase from Churchill, de Gaulle had not become the head of Free France in order to preside over the liquidation of the French Empire. Obviously, he could do little to influence substantially the course of events in the Far East until metropolitan France had been freed. Meanwhile, he opportunistically played upon the rivalries and fears of his allies and was thereby able to maximize the little leverage available to him while he gathered the strength to launch a frontal assault against Roosevelt's plans for postwar Indochina, ultimately vanquishing "the terrible indigence that had damaged our prestige" and returning there with "suitable dignity."[120]

To the end, however, the French remained little aware of the long-term futility of their efforts. As Jean Sainteny put it, after finding his warnings about rising Indochinese nationalism ignored in Paris, "Far too many of the French assume that the people of Indochina are impatiently awaiting our return and are prepared to greet us with open arms." This should not be surprising. It would have been unrealistic to expect those who had endured the ravages, deprivations, and humiliations of the war to be willing to accept less for France than she had enjoyed at the war's beginning. The same resolve and spirit that had brought victory in Europe could hardly be expected to be reconciled to accepting less in the Far East. The emotional shocks of experiencing both the depths of defeat and the pinnacle of victory did not lend themselves to a rational view of the postwar world. Even the cynical communist organ *L'Humanité* loudly proclaimed that France would "resume her place as a great world power and stand forth in the counsels of the nations in all the grandeur bestowed on her by her suffering, her struggles and her prestige." In any case, the very weakness of France at the end of the war made her even more determined to cling to every vestige of her former status. As Jean Chauvel, head of the Far Eastern Department of the French Foreign Ministry in 1945, later recalled, "We were too weak . . . and too poor to detach ourselves from the symbols of power and glory." Characteristically, therefore, at the end of the Far Eastern war, French policymakers sought to convince Washington that the United States had not made a mistake by permitting the French return. Chauvel assured Washington that French policy in Indochina

> will have certain advantages for the U.S. and Britain which therefore will insure American and British interest in the future of Indochina. We should like eventually to operate Indochina . . . not only as a lucrative business for us but [one] which also is advantageous to the other occidental powers. Furthermore, in the coming difficult period in the Far East Indochina will be the only real foothold on the Asiatic mainland for the occidental democracies.[121]

In view of the history of Indochina, France, and the United States during the next thirty years, it proved to be a most ironic statement.

Abbreviations

Cab	British Cabinet Office Records
DBFP	*Documents on British Foreign Policy, 1919–1939*
DD	*Documents Diplomatiques: Conférence de Washington, Juillet 1921–Février 1922*
DDF	*Documents Diplomatiques Français, 1932–1939*
DGFP	*Documents on German Foreign Policy, 1918–1945*
Les Evénements	*Rapport fait au nom de la commission chargée d'enquêter sur les événements en France de 1933 à 1945*
FO	British Foreign Office records
FRUS	*Foreign Relations of the United States*
IMTFE	International Military Tribunal for the Far East
JOC	*Journal Officiel de la République Française, Chambre des Députés*
MR	Map Room records, Roosevelt Library
MAE	Ministère des Affaires Etrangères records
PPF	President's Personal File, Roosevelt Library
Prem	Prime Minister's Office records
PSF	President's Secretary's File, Roosevelt Library
SD	United States Department of State decimal file
WCO	British War Cabinet Office records

Notes

1. French Interests in the Far East

1. Foreign Ministry memorandum, 21 June 1921, FMAE, E–22–1: 7, p. 81.
2. Samuel M. Osgood, "The Third French Republic in Historical Perspective," 60–61.
3. Quoted in John F. Cady, *The Roots of French Imperialism in Eastern Asia*, 107. As John Cairns has noted (*France*, 88), "nothing was so useful to imperial purpose as dead missionaries." Ferry forcefully argued, "It must be openly stated that the superior races have rights in relation to the inferior races . . . I repeat that they have rights because they have obligations—the obligation to civilize the inferior races" (Jean-Baptiste Duroselle, "Changes in French Foreign Policy since 1945," 313).
4. Raymond Betts has suggested that the Empire, like the American frontier, "did afford the space, the atmosphere, and the isolation in which self-styled men of action and energy could exercise their ambitions and fulfill their desires, could renew their lives, and could dedicate themselves to national causes" ("The French Colonial Frontier," 127).
5. Gordon Wright, *France in Modern Times*, 301. For a solid synthesis of the importance of the economic motivation for imperialism, see Christopher M. Andrew and A. S. Kanya-Forstner, *The Climax of French Imperial Expansion, 1914–1924*, 14–17.
6. Raymond F. Betts, *The False Dawn: European Imperialism in the Nineteenth Century*, 77. For more on Ferry and economic motivation for imperial conquest, see Thomas J. Power, Jr., *Jules Ferry and the Renaissance of French Imperialism*, 196–99.
7. Henri Brunschwig, *French Colonialism, 1871–1914: Myths and Realities*, 182–83. In his introduction to Brunschwig's study, Ronald Robinson agreed that French imperialism was "driven by nothing more complicated than a passion for national honour and cultural extravention" spearheaded by ambitious colonels and admirals conquering commercially insignificant territory. "The French colonel with one hand on his Gatling and the other on the proofs of his next book was no myth" (ix–x).
8. Cady, *Roots of French Imperialism*, 294–95.
9. Duroselle, "Changes in French Foreign Policy," 313.
10. Quoted in M. E. Chamberlain, *The New Imperialism*, 33.
11. Quoted in Raymond F. Betts, *Tricoleur: The French Overseas Empire*, 18.
12. Quoted in Andrew and Kanya-Forstner, *Climax of French Imperialism*, 25. For more on the colonial attitudes of Gambetta and Delcassé, see J. P. T. Bury, *Gambetta's Final Years: "The Era of Difficulties," 1877–1882*, 60–81; Charles W. Porter, *The Career of Théophile Delcassé*, 72–73, 99; and Christopher Andrew, *Théophile Delcassé and the Making of the Entente Cordiale*.
13. James J. Cook, *New French Imperialism, 1880–1910: The Third Republic and Colonial Expansion*, 10.

14. See Cook, *New French Imperialism;* Andrew and Kanya-Forstner, *Climax of French Imperialism,* 25–26; and Betts, *False Dawn,* 77.

15. Betts, *False Dawn,* 50. Andrew and Kanya-Forstner argue that public support could be aroused if it could be persuaded that the failure to acquire a colony would allow a European rival to seize it. This reflected concerns about the role of France in great-power relationships rather than inherent desire for colonial acquisition itself (*Climax of French Imperialism,* 29–32).

16. Albert Sarraut, *La mise en valeur des colonies française,* 463.

17. For the main developments of the French conquest of Indochina, see D. W. Brogan, *The Development of Modern France, 1870–1939,* 232–42; and C. G. F. Simkin, *The Traditional Trade of Asia,* 340–44.

18. Brogan, *Modern France,* 239. See also Andrew and Kanya-Forstner, *Climax of French Imperialism,* 18–23. About 72 percent of Frenchmen in Indochina were employed by the government, either as civil servants or in the military. By comparison, only 20 percent of the Dutch in Indonesia were so employed (John F. Cady, *Southeast Asia: Its Historical Development,* 548). Raymond Betts has observed that "if not always second-raters, the men who serviced the French empire were often ill-trained, often ill disposed to the people they ruled, and, generally, uninspired" (*Tricoleur,* 80).

19. Virginia Thompson, *French Indochina,* 399.

20. Betts, *Tricoleur* (see chap. 2). See also Raymond F. Betts, *From Assimilation to Association in French Colonial Policy, 1890–1914.*

21. Thompson, *French Indochina,* 217; Joseph Buttinger, *A Dragon Defiant: A Short History of Vietnam,* 68. See also Alan B. Cole, ed., *Conflict in Indo-China and International Repercussions: A Documentary History, 1945–1955,* xx.

22. For studies of the economic issues, see, for example, Brunschwig, *Myths and Realities:* Cady, *Roots of French Imperialism;* Andrew and Kanya-Forstner, *Climax of French Imperialism;* and Cook, *New French Imperialism.* The quotation is from Cady, *Southeast Asia,* 543.

23. Buttinger, *Dragon Defiant,* 65 (see also Simkin, *Traditional Trade of Asia,* 344–46); Bernard B. Fall, *The Two Viet-Nams: A Political and Military Analysis,* 27; Stephen H. Roberts, *The History of French Colonial Policy, 1870–1925,* 2:490–98.

24. Buttinger, *Dragon Defiant,* 66–68. See also Virginia Thompson, "Indo-China—France's Great Stake in the Far East," 15–22; Roger Levy et al., *French Interests and Policies in the Far East,* 22.

25. Alfred Sauvy, *Histoire économique de la France entre les deux guerres (1918–1931),* 1:304.

26. Betts, *Tricoleur,* 77; Fall, *Two Viet-Nams,* 30; Cady, *Southeast Asia,* 554; Cole, *Conflict in Indo-China,* x–xxi; and Claude A. Buss, *War and Diplomacy in Eastern Asia,* 343–46. See also Lauristan Sharp, "Colonial Regimes in Southeast Asia," 51. Banking resources in Indochina reached about 750 million francs. The Banque de l'Indochine became the most important French banking institution in the colony as well as in neighboring China. Well connected in French governing circles and partially owned by the government, it enjoyed the exclusive privilege of note issue.

27. Cady, *Southeast Asia,* 552.

28. Roberts, *French Colonial Policy,* 2:497–98.

29. Virginia Thompson and Richard Adloff (*The French Pacific Islands,* 238–39) suggest that the French annexation may have been motivated by a desire to punish natives who had killed and eaten a number of French sailors. They place the number of convicts at a more modest figure of 20,000 (241) than Douglas L. Oliver (*The Pacific Islands,* 324; cited in the text).

30. Oliver, *Pacific Islands,* 324–27. By 1938, New Caledonia still supplied 6 percent of the world's production of chrome and 8 percent of its nickel.

31. Ibid., 329; C. Hartley Grattan, *The Southwest Pacific since 1900*, 405-6; Glenn Barclay, *A History of the Pacific*, 134–36; and Lewis S. Feuer, "End of Coolie Labor in New Caledonia," 264.

32. Grattan, *Southwest Pacific*, 405; Oliver, *Pacific Islands*, 326. The French colonists' attitude was undoubtedly enhanced by New Caledonia's contribution to the French war effort between 1915 and 1918, when the island contributed 2,170 men to the Pacific Battalion that served on the western front. Nearly one-fourth of them died during the hostilities (Thompson and Adloff, *French Pacific Islands*, 251).

33. Grattan, *Southwest Pacific*, 411. The archipelagoes included the Society Islands comprising Tahiti, the Marquesas, the Tuamotus, the Gambiers, the Australes, and Clipperton Island off the coast of southern Mexico.

34. Ibid., 411–12.

35. W. P. Morrell, *The Great Powers in the Pacific*, 18, 22.

36. Oliver, *Pacific Islands*, 245–52.

37. Quoted in Akira Iriye, *Across the Pacific: An Inner History of American–East Asian Relations*, 35.

38. For the development of French interests in China, see Cady, *Roots of French Imperialism;* Herbert Ingram Priestley, *France Overseas: A Study of Modern Imperialism*, 102–8; and Kenneth Scott Latourette, *The Development of China*, 168–69, 183–85.

39. This examination of French economic interests in China is based largely on Chiming Hou, *Foreign Investment and Economic Development in China, 1840–1937;* C. F. Remer, *Foreign Investments in China*, 619–36; and Levy et al., *French Interests*, 17–40 (see esp. Levy et al., *French Interests*, 18–26, on China, Indochina, and France). Prior to 1914, China enjoyed a favorable balance of trade with France because of French imports of silk (Francis E. Hyde, *Far Eastern Trade, 1860–1914*, 190).

40. Jeffrey J. Clarke's "Nationalization of War Industries in France, 1936–1937: A Case Study" (413) discusses the commerce in the automotive industry.

41. Even as late as 1938, however, it was estimated that France still held 23 percent of China's foreign debt, ranking behind only Britain and the United States. For a breakdown of French loans to China's government, see Levy et al., *French Interests*, 26–33. On France's substantial interests in other railways in China, see Remer, *Foreign Investments in China*, 622–23, and for exports to Yunnan, see Remer, 630–31. For an estimate of the monopolistic value of the Yunnan Railway, see William Burton, "French Imperialism in China," 428–33.

42. Levy et al., *French Interests*, 39.

43. For a discussion of the French protection of Catholic missionaries in China, see Paul A. Cohen, "Christian Missions and Their Impact to 1900," 10:552–53; Pat Barr, *To China with Love: The Life and Times of Protestant Missionaries in China, 1860–1900*, 68–70; Kenneth Scott Latourette, *A History of Christian Missions in China*, 306–13; Latourette, *Development of China*, 162–63; Henri Bruschwig, *La colonisation française*, 134–36; and Cady, *Roots of Imperialism*.

44. Bernard Auffray, *Pierre de Margerie (1861–1942) et la vie diplomatique de son temps*, 207; Tine-yee Kuo, "Self-strengthening: The Pursuit of Western Technology," 10:520; Levy, *French Interests*, 11–13; Paul Clay Sorum, *Intellectuals and Decolonization in France*, 21.

45. Meron Medzini's *French Policy in Japan during the Closing Years of the Tokugawa Regime* is the best study of early French contacts with Japan (176).

46. Edwin O. Reischauer, *The United States and Japan*, 11; Ernst L. Presseisen, *Before Aggression: Europeans Prepare the Japanese Army*, 136–37, 67.

47. Michio Nagai, "Westernization and Japanization: The Early Meiji Transformation of Education," 47–53.

48. See Medzini, *French Policy in Japan*, 50–51; Levy et al., *French Interests*, 41, 42, 44–45. Both before and after the war, France tended to "buy far and sell near." Consequently, its largest trade deficits were with Japan and the United States. On the other hand, trade with Japan was not large enough to rank it among France's ten most important trading partners (Sauvy, *Histoire économique de la France*, 1:302–3.

49. See Ian Nish, *A Short History of Japan*, 117–18; and Tom Kemp, *The French Economy, 1913–1939: The History of a Decline*, 21. As one observer noted, as of 1936 French investment was so small that Japanese sources did not list them separately (Buss, *War and Diplomacy in Eastern Asia*, 353). For a breakdown of French foreign investment around the turn of the century, see Theodore Zeldin, *France, 1848–1945*, vol. 2, *Intellect, Taste and Anxiety*, 119. Japan did not rank among the top forty nations in which the French invested.

50. E. W. Edwards, "The Japanese Alliance and the Anglo-French Agreement of 1904," 19–27; and Ian Nish, *The Anglo-Japanese Alliance: The Diplomacy of Two Island Empires, 1894–1907*, 26–35.

51. With the encouragement of France a similar agreement was negotiated between Japan and Russia, for the French were concerned that an agreement between Paris and Tokyo might endanger the Franco-Russian alliance. For the complex negotiations undertaken, see E. W. Edwards, "The Far Eastern Agreements of 1907," 340–55; and Nish, *Anglo-Japanese Alliance*, 359–63.

52. Alfred Sauvy has described well the dislocations in France's foreign trade caused by the war. A prewar economic equilibrium based on imports of raw materials being paid for by exports of finished goods and return on capital investment had been destroyed. Much French wealth overseas had been sold to finance the war effort (or, as in the case of Russia, had been simply repudiated), and France had ceased to be one of the bankers of the world. This situation was further complicated by the twin issues of reparations and interallied debts. Suavy concluded that the postwar period "required therefore the reconstitution of foreign exchanges on a new basis" (*Histoire économique de la France*, 1:295–96). Prior to the war, France had supplied over 20 percent of international investment capital. After the war, it became necessary for France to become a net-capital importer to finance postwar reconstruction (Derek Aldcroft, *From Versailles to Wall Street, 1919–1929*, 239).

53. Betts, *Tricoleur*, 74. Some 205,000 colonial subjects died in battle during the war (Sorum, *Intellectuals and Decolonization in France*, 25). The war also generated a new sense of assertiveness among many colonial troops, who began to challenge French authority when they returned home. See William B. Cohen, ed., *Robert B. Delavignette on the French Empire: Selected Writings*, 10.

54. The survey information is from Sorum, *Intellectuals and Decolonization in France*, 25. J. P. T. Bury recounts the one-vote empire-building mandate in *France, 1814–1940*, 168; and Betts's *Tricoleur* (33) tells of the great-power view.

2. VERSAILLES AND AFTER

1. See Sauvy, *Histoire économique*, 2:19–39, 440–43; and François Bédarida, "Des réalités de la guerre aux mirages de la prosperité (1913–1930)," in *Histoire du peuple français: Cent ans d'esprit républicain*, 279–97, for the impact of the Great War.

2. Stephen A. Schuker, *The End of French Predominance in Europe: The Financial Crisis of 1924 and the Adoption of the Dawes Plan*, 5. For other recent analyses of the security and reparations issues, see Walter A. McDougall, *France's Rhineland Diplomacy, 1914–1924: The Last Bid for a Balance of Power in Europe;* Marc Trachtenberg, *Reparation in World Politics: France and European Economic Diplomacy, 1916–1923;* Denise Artaud, *La question des detted interalliées*

et la reconstruction de l'Europe, 1917–1929, 2 vols; Arno J. Mayer, *Politics and Diplomacy of Peacemaking: Containment and Counterrevolution at Versailles, 1918–1919*, 178–87. Sally Marks neatly sums up the debate in "The Myth of Reparations," 231–55. See also Pierre Renouvin, *Le traité de Versailles*, 12–15; and René Albrecht-Carrié, *Britain and France: Adaptations to a Changing Context of Power*, 398–400.

3. Japanese cabinet memo quoted in Charles E. Neu, *The Troubled Encounter: The United States and Japan*, 85.

4. Arthur L. Link, *Wilson the Diplomatist: A Look at His Major Foreign Policies*, 114. For the related Japanese diplomatic activities during the war, see Ian Nish, *Japanese Foreign Policy, 1869–1942*, 95–118; Ian Nish, *Alliance in Decline: A Study in Anglo-Japanese Relations, 1908–1923*, chaps. 7–12; Madeleine Chi, *China Diplomacy, 1914–1918*; O. Edmund Clubb, *Twentieth-Century China*, 82–83; and Neu, *Troubled Encounter*, 85–97.

5. Harold S. Quigley and George H. Blakeslee, *The Far East: An International Survey*, 216–17.

6. Chi, *China Diplomacy*, 86, 143; and Peter Lowe, *Great Britain and Japan, 1911–1915: A Study of British Far Eastern Policy*, 208–11. Also see Chi, *China Diplomacy*, 39, 86–87. The British foreign secretary's admonition to Britain's embassy in Tokyo probably reflected well the French attitude: "It would be madness to quarrel with the Japanese while the war lasts; our proper course is to lie low" (38).

7. Nish, *Alliance in Decline*, 202–11; Briand to Regnault (Tokyo), 25 Feb. 1917, Archives of the Ministère des Affaires Etrangères (hereafter cited as MAE, followed by the series and dossier / volume), E62.11 / 35.

8. Regnault (Tokyo) to Foreign Ministry, 8 Feb. 1917, MAE, E62.11 / 35. Briand believed that the agreement would increase the chances of persuading Japan to agree to increase its involvement in the war and thus hasten its end. Briand to French Ambassadors in London, Petrograd, Washington, Rome, and Tokyo, 10 Feb. 1917, MAE, E65.11 / 35.

9. See a report by Felecien Challaye, Apr. 1918, MAE, E22.1 / 5.

10. Chi, *China Diplomacy*, 129; Pichon to Jusserand (Washington), 12 June 1918, MAE, 62.2 / 8; Pichon to French Ambassadors in London, Rome, Washington, 27 May 1918, MAE, E24.1 / 35.

11. Roy Watson Curry, *Woodrow Wilson and Far Eastern Policy, 1913–1921*, 258–61.

12. See Bapst (Tokyo) to Foreign Ministry, 31 Dec. 1919, MAE, E62.1 / 6; FO minute by R. Macleay, 12 Feb. 1919, Foreign Office (hereafter cited as FO), 608, vol. 211, no. 1841; Balfour (Paris) to Lord Curzon, 8 May 1919, FO 608, no. 4318. See also H. W. V. Temperley, ed., *A History of the Paris Peace Conference*, 3:738–40, 5:123–26.

13. Lou Tseng-Tsiang (Paris) to Clemenceau (President of Council of Three), 4 May 1919, FO 608, vol. 210, no. 9213; FO minute by Macleay, 12 Feb. 1919, FO 608, vol. 211, no. 1841; Balfour (Paris) to Lord Curzon, 8 May 1919, FO 608, no. 4318; Temperley, *Paris Peace Conference*, 3:755–57, 5:141–43, 249–50; and Pierre Renouvin, *La Question d'extrême-orient*, 308–10.

14. Quoted in Arthur Walworth, *Wilson and His Peacemakers: American Diplomacy at the Paris Peace Conference, 1919*, 359–76. For the main lines of the American-Japanese contretemps, see Curry, *Wilson and Far Eastern Policy*, 249–73; Link, *Wilson the Diplomatist*, 114. As a rule, the Japanese did not play a significant role in discussions related to Europe, rarely speaking and usually concerning only issues directly affecting Japanese interests (Russell H. Fifield, *Woodrow Wilson and the Far East: The Diplomacy of the Shantung Question*, 115). Consequently, when they vigorously pursued their Shantung aims, their words probably had maximum impact. See also Nish, *Japanese Foreign Policy*, 120–22. For the debate within the Council of Four during April 1919, see Howard Elcock, *Portrait of a Decision: The Council of Four and the Treaty of Versailles*, 230–37. Paul Birdsall's account of the "Japanese strategy,"

in *Versailles, Twenty Years After,* 83–115, is still worth studying, as is Harold Nicolson, *Peacemaking, 1919,* 144–47.

15. Foreign Office memorandum. (Political Intelligence Department), 16 Feb. 1919, FO 608, vol. 124, no. 2841.

16. On the Clemenceau-Saionji history, see British Delegation minute, 18 July 1919, FO 608, vol. 210, no. 15692. Clemenceau is quoted in Fifield, *Wilson and the Far East,* 241. Clearly, the German question remained uppermost in Clemenceau's mind. As he told General Henri Mordacq, "Yes, we have won the war, and not without difficulty. But now we have got to win the peace, and it may well be more difficult still" (quoted in J. Hampden Jackson, *Clemenceau and the Third Republic,* 188). Winning the peace, he believed, could not be done by diverting one's attention to such far-off matters as Shantung. On the other hand, there is some evidence that he was glad to see Japan get its claim, for that would make it easier for France when its turn came (Jackson, *Clemenceau,* 195).

17. Quoted in Temperley, *Paris Peace Conference,* 3:506.

18. Fifield (*Wilson and the Far East,* 242) points out that Clemenceau was little impressed by the analogy posed by one Frenchman who wrote to him arguing that Shantung had an importance to China comparable to Normandy's importance to France.

19. On the Shantung issue, see Paul Mantoux, *Paris Peace Conference, 1919; Proceedings of the Council of Four (March 24–April 18);* Lord Maurice Hankey, *The Supreme Control of the Paris Peace Conference, 1919.* Lord Hankey is quoted in Fifield, *Wilson and the Far East,* 290. Temperley (*Paris Peace Conference,* 5:147) provides an example. Wilson, although doubting the validity of the wartime Sino-Japanese treaties, had to agree. See also Fifield, *Wilson and the Far East,* 254n, 294, and, on the Clemenceau-Wilson exchange, 253–54.

20. Probably for the same reason, Clemenceau rejected a subsequent Chinese proposal that they sign the Treaty of Versailles with "reservations." Clemenceau judged that "a Treaty which was signed with reservations was not a treaty" (quoted in Fifield, *Wilson and the Far East,* 329).

21. Ibid., 142.

22. Pichon note, 17 Mar. 1919, MAE, E22.1 / 6. See also note pour le Ministre, 1 Apr. 1919, MAE, E24.1 / 35.

23. Berthelot to French Legation (Peking), 23 Feb. 1919, MAE, E22.1 / 5.32; Foreign Ministry memorandum to l'Administrateur Directeur de la Banque de l'Indochine (Paris), n.d., MAE, E22.1 / 6.

24. Pichon to Boppe (Peking), 28 May 1919, MAE, E62.2 / 8.

25. Clemenceau to Lou Tseng-Tsiang (Chinese Delegation), 14 May 1919, FO 608, vol. 209, no. 10033.

26. Renouvin, *La Question d'extrême-orient,* 314–16; Clubb, *Twentieth-Century China,* 84–87; and Walworth, *Wilson and His Peacemakers,* 373–75.

27. See Boppe (Peking) to Foreign Ministry, 24 May 1919, MAE, E62.2 / 8; and Pichon to Peking, 28 May 1919, MAE, E62.2 / 8. Boppe, the French ambassador in Peking, suspected that the Japanese had been responsible for the rumor so that some of the Chinese wrath would be diverted against the West.

28. Bapst (Tokyo) to Pichon, 31 Dec. 1919, MAE, E24.1 / 36.

29. See *Journel Officiel de la République Français, Chambre des Députés* (hereafter cited as *JOC*) for the debate regarding the treaty. In most cases, when debate turned to the clauses related to overseas issues, as on 17 September, when Henry Simon, minister of colonies, defended the treaty, Africa received most of the attention. Summaries of many of the debates can be found in George Grahame (Paris) to FO, FO 608, vol. 125.

30. See, for example, Pierre Miquel, *La Paix de Versailles et l'opinion publique français;* and George Bernard Noble, *Policies and Opinions at Paris, 1919.*

31. Foreign Ministry note to l'Administrateur Directeur de la Banque de l'Indochine (Paris), n.d., MAE, E22.1 / 6.

32. Pierre-Etienne Flandin, *Politique française, 1919–1940,* 127.

33. A. P. Thornton, *Imperialism in the Twentieth Century,* 194.

34. Schuker, *End of French Predominance,* 5, 6. See also Jacques Bariéty, *Les Relations franco-allemandes après la première guerre mondiale.*

35. Sally Marks, *The Illusion of Peace: International Relations in Europe, 1918–1933,* 29.

36. For more on the Anglo-American discussions, see Nish, *Alliance in Decline;* and Thomas H. Buckley, *The United States and the Washington Conference, 1921–1922,* 127–28.

37. For the most comprehensive studies of the conference, see Buckley, *United States and the Washington Conference;* John Chalmers Vinson, *The Parchment Peace: The United States Senate and the Washington Conference, 1921–1922;* A. Whitney Griswold, *The Far Eastern Policy of the United States,* 269–304; and Robert H. Van Meter, Jr., "The Washington Conference of 1921–1922: A New Look," 603–24. A useful contemporary account is Raymond Leslie Buell, *The Washington Conference.* Specific facets of the conference and the attitudes of the other powers involved are discussed in Harold Sprout and Margaret Sprout, *Toward a New Order of Sea Power: American Naval Power and the World Scene, 1918–1922,* 118–292; William R. Braisted, *The United States Navy in the Pacific, 1909–1922;* Stephen Roskill, *Naval Policy between the Wars,* Vol. I, *The Period of Anglo-American Antagonism, 1919–1929,* 300–330; Nish, *Alliance in Decline;* William Roger Louis, *British Strategy in the Far East, 1919–1939,* 79–108; Akira Iriye, *After Imperialism: The Search for a New Order in the Far East, 1921–1931,* 1–22; Yamoto Ichihashi, *The Washington Conference and After;* Asada Sadao, "Japan's 'Special Interests' and the Washington Conference, 1921–1922," 62–70; Noel H. Pugach, "American Friendship for China and the Shantung Question at the Washington Conference, 67–86"; and Donald S. Birn, "Open Door Diplomacy at the Washington Conference of 1921–1922: The British and French Experience," 297–319.

38. Fifield, *Wilson and the Far East,* 360–61; Pugach, "American Friendship for China and the Shantung Question at the Washington Conference"; and Buckley, *United States and the Washington Conference,* 157–66. Japan finally agreed to withdraw its troops from the area and return the Kiaochow territory to China in return for future considerations protecting Japanese economic interests there.

39. Although it is beyond the scope of this study, the general French position at the conference is still widely neglected and misunderstood. A thorough examination of French attitudes, concerns, and policies needs to be undertaken. The general correspondence between the French delegation and the Quai d'Orsay can be followed in the *Documents diplomatiques: Conférence de Washington, Juillet 1921–Février 1922* (hereafter cited as *DD*). Little is revealed, however, about the considerations that went into the policy decisions relayed to the French delegation. Unfortunately, the Foreign Ministry archives are not much more revealing; there is a paucity of internal memoranda. An intensive investigation into the archives of the several ministries involved is needed to reconstruct the whole story. French positions and correspondence with the American delegation and Secretary of State Charles Evans Hughes, who chaired the proceedings, can be found in *Foreign Relations of the United States* (hereafter cited as *FRUS*) *1921,* vol. 1, and *1922,* vol. 1. Records of the proceedings of the plenary sessions and major committees can be found in Senate Committee on Foreign Relations, *Conference on the Limitation of Armament: Subcommittees.* For French correspondence and relations with Britain during the period, see *Documents on British Foreign Policy, 1918–1945* (hereafter cited as *DBFP*), 1st ser., vol. 14. The Unpublished British Foreign Office Papers, FO 371, and Cabinet Conclusions (hereafter cited as Cab) 30 help to fill in the gaps in the published record. The sense of British distrust of French intentions is clearly revealed. The best treatment of French activities related to the conference can be found in

Georges Suarez, *Briand: Sa vie—son oeuvre*, vol. 5, *L'Artisan de la paix, 1918–1923*, 239–312; and Buckley, *United States and the Washington Conference*. On the French attitude about the Five Power Treaty on naval limitations, see Sprout and Sprout, *Toward a New Order of Sea Power*; and Birn, "Open Door Diplomacy." Léon Archimbaud, *La Conférence de la Washington* provides a contemporary defense of French arguments for land forces and submarines, though based frequently upon fictional accounts.

40. Louis Aubert memorandum, 14 July 1921, MAE, B24.9 / 80. All quotations in the ensuing two paragraphs also come from this source.

41. Quoted in J. Néré, *The Foreign Policy of France from 1914 to 1945*, 273. After his return from Washington, Briand admitted to the Chamber that he had attended the conference in order to gain a hearing for the "special situation of France" in Europe and the reasons that compelled her to maintain a strong army—an army she could afford to reduce only if her dangers were shared by her allies. Hardinge (Paris) to FO, 7 Dec. 1921, FO 371, 6981, W12770 / 247 / 17. Briand had continued to make such familiar points since the conference had been called; see Suarez, *Briand*, 211–13.

42. Néré, *Foreign Policy of France*, 274; *DD*, 207. At a meeting of the Committee on the Limitation of Armament a couple of days later, Briand returned to the charge: "When the enemy is at the door, when one saw one's country torn asunder, 600,000 homes destroyed, factories leveled to the ground, thousands of peasants living in holes, the soil itself laid to waste, when through the streets passed 2,000,000 of crippled men and under the ground lay 1,500,000 dead, that was not a platonic situation and one did not discuss aspirations but realities." The French assembly had given him "a very explicit mandate; France might agree to any reduction of armament, if her safety were guaranteed. If she were alone, she could agree to nothing" (*Conference on the Limitation of Armament*, 248).

43. Buckley, *United States and the Washington Conference*, 106–7. As luck would have it, shortly after the beginning of the disarmament discussions opened in Washington, the Chamber of Deputies took up the issue of the government's naval budget proposal for 1922. The debate between the navy supporters on the right and the opponents of increased military spending on the left, who criticized all of the existing admirals who "navigate in the corridors of the rue Royale," drew even more attention to the question of France's naval status. See *JOC* for the debates that opened on 5 December in the Chamber of Deputies.

44. Quoted in Buckley, *United States and the Washington Conference*, 110. See also de Bon's arguments in Sarraut (Washington) to Briand, 15 Dec. 1921, *DD*, no. 70, 53–54; Sarraut (Washington) to Bonnevay (Garde des Sceaux), 16 Dec. 1921, *DD*, no. 72, 61–62; and Balfour (Washington) to FO, 16 Dec. 1921, FO 371, 5626, A9373 / 18 / 45. Sarraut also warned Hughes that "on naval questions [France] . . . cannot disappear as a naval and colonial power, agreeing to be swept from the surface of the seas and letting its naval force be cut up bit by bit." Sarraut (Washington) to Bonnevay, 20 Dec. 1921, *DD*, no. 82, 74.

45. Hughes to Briand (London), 16 Dec. 1921, *DD*, 55. See also Hughes to Herrick (Paris), 16 Dec. 1921, *FRUS, 1921*, 1:130–33. Briand (London) to Hughes, 19 Dec. 1921, *DD*, no. 78, 71. See also Briand (Paris) to French Ambassadors in London, 23 Dec. 1921, *DD*, no. 85, 78; and Briand (London) to Sarraut, 17 Dec. 1921, *DD*, no. 73, 63–64. The French Ambassador in Washington, Jules Jusserand, argued, "France simply demanded the minimum indispensable to the defense of its colonies . . . ." Sarraut (Washington) to Bonnevay, 20 Dec. 1921, *DD*, nos. 82, 75.

46. Sarraut defined the French position precisely: "As for French naval policy, it is clear. In no way does she aim at England or any other friendly country: we have coasts and colonies to defend and communications to secure and we only seek satisfaction of our needs and submarines." Sarraut (Washington) to Briand, 24 Dec. 1921, *DD*, no. 90, 83. On

Anglo-French misunderstandings concerning the submarine issue, see Birn, "Open Diplomacy at the Washington Conference," 312–16.

47. Buckley, *United States and the Washington Conference*, 133–34; Nish, *Alliance in Decline*, 374. The French *Documents Diplomatiques* are largely silent about the Far Eastern negotiations.

48. Suarez, *Briand*, 5:295–96.

49. See Buckley, *United States and the Washington Conference*, 145–56.

50. See *Conference on the Limitation of Armament*, 1062–64; and Cab 30, vol. 14, 106.

51. *Conference on the Limitation of Armament*, 1066–74.

52. Wellesley to FO, 17 Nov. 1921, FO 371, 6645, F4231 / 833 / 10. Winston Churchill, Britain's colonial secretary, expressed his uncompromising hostility to the surrender of Wie-hai-wei, although Balfour, Britain's chief delegate to the conference, believed that the territory was useless except as a sanatorium. See also Curzon to Balfour (Washington), 6 Dec. 1921, FO 371, 6645, F4461 / 833 / 10 for the foreign secretary's opposition to such an action. Wellesley minuted the dispatch, "France had clearly tried to force the pace to secure the good graces of the U.S."

53. Sarraut (Washington) to Bonnevay, 17 Dec. 1921, DD, no. 74, 64; Jacques Chastenet, *Histoire de la Troisième République*, vol. 5, *Les années d'illusions*, 89.

54. *Le Temps*, 7 Feb. 1922. During the debate regarding capital ship limits and the role of submarines, *Le Temps* generally promoted the government's position. See, for example, its analysis on 19 December. *L'Echo de Paris* of 19 December asserted the French right to maintain proper fleet strength and opposed French sacrifice for the sake of international disarmament. *Le Matin* on the same day concluded, "The submarine is a defensive arm. To deprive us of it would be to place us in a position of being unable to defend our naval ports or even the French coast."

55. Poincaré is quoted in Jules Laroche, *Au Quai d'Orsay: Avec Briand et Poincaré, 1913–1926*, 146. On the difficulties of Briand, see, for example, the criticism of Jean le Cour Grandmaison, *JOC*, 24 Mar. 1922, who argued that the whole history of the conference was a tale of blunders by the French government, which was "unprepared, ill-informed, ignorant of the program of the conference." Every nation except France, Grandmaison claimed, had benefited from the conference. Many French naval officers actively condemned the treaty. See Birn, "Open Diplomacy at the Washington Conference," 318. Consequently, the tough ratification battle was won only in July 1923, well after the other major signatories had ratified the treaties and well after the French public had tired of the whole affair.

56. Nish, *Alliance in Decline*, 391.

57. Dorothy Borg's *American Policy and the Chinese Revolution, 1925–1928* remains the best treatment of China and the great power involvement there during the late 1920s. See also Robert T. Pollard, *China's Foreign Relations, 1917–1931;* Wesley Fishel, *The End of Extraterritoriality in China;* and Iriye, *After Imperialism*.

58. Borg, *American Policy and the Chinese Revolution*, 413. See also Paul A. Varg, "The Missionary Response to the Nationalist Revolution," 326.

59. As wishful thinking, see, for example, Briand to Fleuriau (Peking), 30 Dec. 1921, MAE, E22.1 / 7; and Tambrun (Military Attaché, Peking) to Minister of War, 8 Dec. 1920, MAE, E22.1 / 6. For the "Soviet initiative," see Iriye, *After Imperialism*, 25–122. Several dispatches and memoranda in MAE exemplify the concern over Indochina.

60. See William J. Duiker, *The Rise of Nationalism in Vietnam, 1900–1941*.

61. On the complaints against the French legation, see the report by Felicien Challaye, Apr. 1919, MAE, E22.1 / 5. Fleuriau, the chief representative in Peking, held this view of

the Chinese government. Fleuriau (Minister Plenipotentiary, Peking) to Briand, 9 Sept. 1921, MAE, E22.1 / 7.

62. Voruz is quoted in F. S. G. Piggott, *Broken Thread: An Autobiography*, 168–69. The Foreign Ministry report, "Situation generale en Chine depuis cinq derniers années," June 1921, MAE, E22. 1 / 7, illustrates the view of Japan and its frustrated designs on China. The ambassador is quoted from Henry (Tokyo) to Foreign Ministry, 23 Dec. 1920, MAE, E62.2/8.

63. See Bapst (Tokyo) to Foreign Ministry, 23 Dec. 1920, MAE, E62.2 / 8; de Lapomarede (Military Attaché, Tokyo) to Minister of War, 30 Nov. 1920, MAE, E62.2 / 8; and Ministry of War to Foreign Minister, 17 Jan. 1920, MAE, E62.2 / 8. For an analysis of Japan's favorable postwar impression of France, see Felicien Challaye, "Premier Rapport sur Japon, 1919," Apr. 1919, MAE, E62.1 / 6, which concluded that "never has France been so popular, so much esteemed, so much admired."

64. Claudel (Tokyo) to Poincaré, 8 Feb. 1922, MAE, E62.2 / 8; and Claudel (Tokyo) to Foreign Ministry, 18 Mar. 1922, MAE, E62.2 / 8.

65. Claudel (Tokyo) to Poincaré, 8 Feb. 1922, MAE, E62.2 / 8.

66. Buckley, *United States and the Washington Conference*, 190; *Le Temps*, 26 Feb. 1922.

67. See Iriye, *After Imperialism*.

68. Christopher Thorne, *The Limits of Foreign Policy: The West, the League, and the Far Eastern Crisis of 1931–1933*, 41.

3. THE MANCHURIAN CRISIS: FROM MUKDEN TO SHANGHAI

1. Robert J. C. Butow, *Tojo and the Coming of the War*, 31–32. For surveys of the pre-1931 Chinese developments and relations with Japan, see Butow, chap. 2; Harold M. Vinacke, *A History of the Far East in Modern Times*, 6th ed., 437–61; James C. Thomson, *While China Faced West*; Iriye, *After Imperialism*, 227–99; and Pollard, *China's Foreign Relations*. See also Dorothy Borg, *American Policy and the Chinese Revolution, 1925–1928*.

2. For the background to Japan's initiative in 1931, see James B. Crowley, *Japan's Quest for Autonomy: National Security and Foreign Policy, 1930–1938*; Sadako N. Ogata, *Defiance in Manchuria: The Making of Japanese Foreign Policy, 1931–1932*; Takehiko Yoshihashi, *Conspiracy at Mukden: The Rise of the Japanese Military*; Nish, *Japanese Foreign Policy*, chap. 8; and Butow, *Tojo*, 16–34. For a brief summary, see Crowley's excellent essay, "A New Deal for Japan and Asia," in *Modern East Asia: Essays in Interpretation*, ed. James B. Crowley, 238–44. For an important study of the military planning and politics behind the incident and the subsequent campaign, see Mark R. Peattie, *Ishiwara Kanji and Japan's Confrontation with the West*, 87–139.

3. Robert H. Ferrell, "The Mukden Incident: September 18–19, 1931," 66–72.

4. For more on the Japanese developments and the Mukden incident, see Thorne, *The Limits of Foreign Policy*, 131–32; and Ogata, *Defiance in Manchuria*, 53–69.

5. It seems clear that Chiang ordered Chinese forces in Manchuria not to resist, hoping to deprive the Japanese of an excuse to advance further while he continued to focus his attention on eliminating Mao Tse-tung's communist forces (Thorne, *Limits of Foreign Policy*, 126; and Warren I. Cohen, *America's Response to China: An Interpretive History of Sino-American Relations*, 2d ed., 126).

6. Nish, *Japanese Foreign Policy*, 178–79.

7. For the details of the League's action and Japan's response, see Sara R. Smith, *The Manchurian Crisis, 1931–1932: A Tragedy in International Relations*. See also Crowley, *Japan's Quest for Autonomy*, 122–59.

8. See Alfred Sauvy, "The Economic Crisis of the 1930s in France," 21–24; and Nathanael Greene, *From Versailles to Vichy: The Third French Republic, 1919–1940*, 50–54; Raymond J. Sontag, *A Broken World, 1919–1939*, 242–43.

9. Osgood, "The Third French Republic," 68.

10. Greene, *From Versailles to Vichy*, 135. The *ambiance générale* of the times in France can best be appreciated in Alexander Werth, *The Twilight of France*; and Jacques Debu-Bridal, *L'Agonie de la Troisième République, 1929–1939*. The best surveys of the political developments of the period are Edouard Bonnefous, *Histoire politique de la Troisième République*, vol. 5, *La République en danger: des Ligues au Front Populaire (1930–1936)*; and Jacques Chastenet, *Histoire de la Troisième République*, vol. 6, *Déclin de la Troisième, 1931–1938*. Two recent studies are Philippe Bernard and Henry Dubief, *The Decline of the Third Republic, 1914–1938*, trans. Anthony Forster; and Julian Jackson, *The Politics of Depression in France, 1932–1936*. For the Cartel des Gauches, see Michel Soulié, *La vie politique d'Edouard Herriot*, 351–417. Herriot's own view of the period can be traced in his memoirs, *Jadis*, vol. 2, *D'une guerre à l'autre, 1914–1936*, 265–365. Characteristically, Herriot, who played a leading role during the period, either in opposition or as premier, ignored the Far Eastern developments. His attention regarding foreign affairs remained riveted on the issues of debt, disarmament, and security. As he recorded in his journal, "My preoccupation is reconciling national interests with the necessities of international politics" (*Jadis* 2:305).

11. Thorne, *Limits of Foreign Policy*, 78–79 n. 4.

12. Ibid., 78.

13. Werth (*Twilight of France*, 7) describes Briand's condition in October. For the details of his decline, see Suarez, *Briand*, vol. 6. Herriot is quoted in Thorne, *Limits of Foreign Policy*, 78. The Barros statement is from *Office without Power: Secretary-General Sir Eric Drummond, 1919–1933*, 341.

14. Hugh R. Wilson, *Diplomat between Wars*, 253. The quotation on Massigli is from Gilbert (Geneva) to Sec. St., 7 Nov. 1931, *FRUS, 1931*, 3:388. See also Richard D. Challener, "The French Foreign Office: The Era of Philippe Berthelot," in *The Diplomats, 1919–1939*, ed. Gordon A. Craig and Felix Gilbert, 65–85. On Léger, see R. F. Wigram memorandum (Paris), 10 Oct. 1931, FO 371, 15492, F5689 / 1391 / 10; Tyrrell (Paris) to Vansittart, 10 Oct. 1931, *Documents on British Foreign Policy, 1919–1939* (hereafter cited as *DBFP*) 2d ser., 8:746; and Gilbert (Geneva) to Sec. St., 7 Nov. 1931, *FRUS, 1931*, 3:388.

15. R. F. Wigram memorandum (Paris), 10 Oct. 1931, FO 371, 15492, F5689 / 1391 / 10.

16. Anthony Adamthwaite, *France and the Coming of the Second World War, 1936–1939*, 138; and Sir Willmott Lewis, quoted in the 20 Jan. 1932 *London Times*, is quoted in Constantine Brown, "French Policy in the Far East," 288.

17. Campbell (Paris) to FO, 13 July 1933, FO 371, 17301, W8901 / 2301 / 17; and Sir Francis Lindley (Tokyo) to FO, 24 Sept. 1931, FO 371, 15489, F5120 / 1391 / 10; and Castle (Undersec. St.) memorandum, 12 Oct. 1931, *FRUS, 1931*, 3:155.

18. Quoted in Thorne, *Limits of Foreign Policy*, 7. For a summary of French press reaction, see 137, 174–75; and Armin Rappaport, *Henry L. Stimson and Japan, 1931–1933*, 20, 63.

19. *La Lumière*, 6 Feb. 1932; and Thorne, *Limits of Foreign Policy*, 175.

20. Patteson (Geneva) to Marquess of Reading, 23 Sept. 1931, *DBFP*, 2d ser., 8:677. Reading to Lindley (Tokyo), 24 Sept. 1931, *DBFP*, 2d ser., 8:679.

21. Vansittart to Tyrrell (Paris), 6 Oct. 1931, *DBFP*, 2d ser., 8:714–15. For Massigli's account, see Tyrrell (Paris) to Vansittart, 10 Oct. 1931, FO 371, 15492, F5689 / 1391 / 10.

22. McKillop minute on Lindley (Tokyo) to FO, 24 Sept. 1931, FO 371, 15489, F5128 / 1391 / 10.

23. Tyrrell (Paris) to FO, 10 Oct. 1931, FO 371, 15492, F5689 / 1391 / 10.

24. Pierre Laval's refusal in February 1932 to answer in the Chamber of Deputies a question about such an agreement undoubtedly helped to fuel additional rumors. A Laval supporter subsequently revealed that while no agreement existed, informal staff conversations had occurred. See Brown, "French Policy in the Far East," 288.

25. Thorne, *Limits of Foreign Policy*, 47.

26. Brown, "French Policy in the Far East," 337–38. For more on this, see Rappaport, *Stimson*, 78 n. 145; in regard to the scholarship, see Rappaport, 20.

27. Quoted in Dorothy Borg, *The United States and the Far Eastern Crisis of 1933–1938*, 9; and Henry L. Stimson and McGeorge Bundy, *On Active Service in Peace and War*, 235–36. For summaries of the American position during the early phases of the crisis, see Borg, *United States and Far Eastern Crisis*, 1–9; Robert H. Ferrell, *American Diplomacy in the Great Depression: Hoover-Stimson Foreign Policy, 1929–1933*, chaps. 8–10; Neu, *Troubled Encounter*, 134–38; Cohen, *America's Response to China*, 126–35; and Rappaport, *Stimson*.

28. Louis, *British Strategy in Far East*, 189–92; and Stimson and Bundy, *On Active Service*, 237–38.

29. Secretary of State Stimson memorandum, 2 Jan. 1932, *FRUS, 1932*, 3:2–3.

30. See Briand to French Ambassador (London), n.d., in Wellesley memorandum, 7 Jan. 1932, *DBFP*, 2d ser., 9:87. See also memorandum by Secretary Stimson, 5 Jan. 1932, *FRUS, 1932*, 3:4–5.

31. Secretary of State Stimson memorandum, 7 Jan. 1932, *FRUS, 1932*, 3:10–11; and Victor Wellesley memorandum, 7 Jan. 1932, *DBFP*, 2d ser., 9:87.

32. Edge (Paris) to Sec. St., 11 Jan. 1932, *FRUS, 1932*, 3:22.

33. Geoffrey Warner, *Pierre Laval and the Eclipse of France*, 52–53.

34. Ibid.

35. For these developments, see David Bergamini, *Japan's Imperial Conspiracy*, 457–69. For another view, see Crowley, *Japan's Quest for Autonomy*, 159–68.

36. Quoted in Thorne, *Limits of Foreign Policy*, 209.

37. For public reaction, see ibid., 210–25. For British reaction, see Reginald Bassett, *Democracy and Foreign Policy: A Case History, The Sino-Japanese Dispute, 1931–1933*, chaps. 8–10. For American reaction, see Rappaport, *Stimson*, 114–15.

38. Crowley, *Japan's Quest for Autonomy*, 166–67.

39. See Rappaport, *Stimson*, 127–28; Crowley, *Japan's Quest for Autonomy*, 162–63; and Ogata, *Defiance in Manchuria*, 143.

40. For an excellent account of the debate between London and Washington concerning Shanghai, see Thorne, *Limits of Foreign Policy*, 247–66; and Louis, *British Strategy in the Far East*, 185–99.

41. See Stimson and Bundy, *On Active Service*, 243–54; Rappaport, *Stimson*, 141; and Ferrell, *American Diplomacy in the Great Depression*, 184–93.

42. Crowley, *Japan's Quest for Autonomy*, 165.

43. Ferrell, *American Diplomacy in the Great Depression*, 186; Borg, *United States and Far Eastern Crisis*, 15; and Thorne, *Limits of Foreign Policy*, 213–14.

44. Crowley, *Japan's Quest for Autonomy*, 160; and Ferrell, *American Diplomacy in the Great Depression*, 187. The negotiations can be followed in *DBFP*, 2d ser., 10:190–409.

45. *L'Ere Nouvelle*, 28 Jan. 1932.

46. Thorne, *Limits of Foreign Policy*, 215. Herriot is quoted in *L'Ere Nouvelle*, 28 Jan. 1932; Pertinax's remark is quoted in Rappaport, *Stimson*, 124. The statement from *Le Temps* is from 30 Jan. 1932.

47. *Le Temps*, 28 Feb. 1932. The paper criticized China's attempts to involve the League in the crisis. See, for example, 1 Feb. 1932. Pertinax's comments are from *L'Echo de Paris*, 5 Mar. 1932.

48. Thorne, *Limits of Foreign Policy*, 232.

49. Admiralty to FO, 1 Jan. 1932, FO 371, 16144, F717 / 1 / 10; and French Embassy to Sec. St., 1 Feb. 1932, *FRUS, 1932*, 3:175.

50. See French Ministry for Foreign Affairs memorandum to British Embassy (Paris) in Tyrrell (Paris) to FO, 1 Feb. 1932, FO 371, 16143, F705 / 1 / 10; Tyrrell (Paris) to FO, 30 Jan. 1932, FO 371, 16143, F6901 / 1 / 10; and Undersecretary Castle, memorandum, 1 Feb. 1932, *FRUS, 1932* 3:157.

51. French Embassy to Dept. of State, 1 Feb. 1932, *FRUS, 1932*, 3:174; Tyrrell (Paris) to Simon, 2 Feb. 1932, *DBFP*, 2d ser., 9:302–3.

52. Stimson, memorandum, 1 Feb. 1932, *FRUS, 1932*, 3:288; and Vansittart to Patterson (Geneva), 16 Feb. 1932, *DBFP*, 2d ser., 9:445.

53. Stimson, memorandum, 18 Feb. 1932, *FRUS, 1932*, 3:374–75.

54. Thorne, *Limits of Foreign Policy*, 256.

55. Stimson, memorandum, 10 Mar. 1932, *FRUS, 1932*, 3:552–53.

56. Joseph Paul-Boncour, *Entre deux guerres: souvenirs sur la Troisième République*, 2:203.

57. Quoted in Thorne, *Limits of Foreign Policy*, 262.

58. See *JOC*, 9 Feb. 1932.

59. The quotations are from Thorne, *Limits of Foreign Policy*, 260–61.

60. Ibid., 10, 247, 261; and Borg, *United States and Far Eastern Crisis*, 14.

61. See, for example, documents in *FRUS, 1932*, 3:157, 174, 428. Some observers speculated that the basis of such an agreement consisted of French moral support in Manchuria in return for Japanese support of a French free hand in penetrating the Chinese provinces of Kwangsi and Yunnan bordering Indochina. See C. F. Garstin (Harbin) to Lampson (Peking), 23 Jan. 1932, FO 371, 16161, F3000 / 1 / 10; and Handley-Derry (Yunnanfu) to Lampson (Peking), 18 Feb. 1932, *DBFP*, 2d ser., 9:539. See also Brown, "French Policy in the Far East," for an example of contemporary journalistic speculation about such an implicit understanding.

62. See, for example, Scott minute on Ingram (Peking) to FO, 14 Sept. 1932, FO 371, 16177, F6748 / 1 / 10; and Orde minute on Lindsay (Washington) to FO, 23 Mar. 1932, FO 371, 16162, F2153 / 1 / 10.

63. Thorne, *Limits of Foreign Policy*, 175, 215.

64. See, for example, Castle, 1 Feb. 1932, *FRUS, 1932*, 3:157; Claudel to Dept. of State, 1 Feb. 1932, *FRUS, 1932*, 3:174; Stimson, memorandum 24 Feb. 1932, *FRUS, 1932*, 3:429; and Ingram (Peking) to Simon, 29 Jan. 1932, *DBFP*, 2d ser., 9:228.

65. See Stimson, memoranda, 9 Feb. and 2 Mar. 1932, *FRUS, 1932*, 3:429, 493.

66. Vansittart, memorandum, 22 Feb. 1932, FO 371, 16151, F1640 / 1 / 10.

67. Vansittart, memorandum, 12 Feb. 1932, FO 371, 16245, F1400 / 1 / 10. The initial Japanese approach had been made to Marshal Joseph Joffre when he toured the Far East in 1922. Although intrigued with the idea, he ultimately recommended against it.

68. Tyrrell (Paris) to FO, 7 Mar. 1932, FO 371, 16156, F2250 / 1 / 10.

4. The Manchurian Crisis: Manchukuo and Beyond

1. Thorne, *Limits of Foreign Policy*, 214. *Le Temps* echoed these sentiments by arguing that the creation of an independent Manchukuo surprised nobody, that the province had been definitely lost by China, and that the League Commission of Inquiry would be forced to recognize the fait accompli. See 20 Feb. 1932.

2. See de Fleuriau (London) to Vansittart memorandum, 24 Feb. 1932, FO 371, 16153, F1875 / 1 / 10. See also the attached minutes by Roberts and McKillop.

3. For an analytical summary of these problems and their effect on Far Eastern questions, see Thorne, *Limits of Foreign Policy*, chap. 9.

4. Ogata, *Defiance in Manchuria*, 165–66.

5. See Rapport de la délégation française à Genève, 9 July 1932, *Documents diplomatiques français, 1930–1936* (hereafter cited as *DDF*), 1st ser., 1:9 n.

6. Ibid., 7–9.

7. Ibid., 7n.

8. De Martel (Tokyo) to Herriot, 19 July 1932, *DDF*, 1st ser., 1:56 and note.

9. Reynaud (Harbin) to Herriot, 8 Aug. 1932, *DDF*, 1st ser., 1:158.

10. Berthelot procès-verbal, 7 Sept. 1932, *DDF*, 1st ser., 1:275–78.

11. Herriot to de Martel (Tokyo), 11 and 12 July 1932, *DDF*, 1st ser., 1:56–57. If the approach made by Araki was considered by the Quai d'Orsay, no record of it or the response has come to light.

12. Quoted in Rappaport, *Stimson*, 166.

13. The full text of Stimson's address can be found in *FRUS, 1932*, 1:575–83.

14. For a summary of press reaction, see Rappaport, *Stimson*, 170–73.

15. Jules Henry (Washington) to Herriot, 10 Aug. 1932, *DDF*, 1st ser., 1:163–67.

16. Rappaport, *Stimson*, 173–74; and Thorne, *Limits of Foreign Policy*, 275.

17. Walter E. Edge (Paris) to Sec. St., 19 Sept. 1932, *FRUS, 1932*, 4:265–66.

18. Note de la direction politique, 11 Sept. 1932, *DDF*, 1st ser., 1:302–5.

19. Henry (Washington) to Herriot, 17 Sept. 1932, *DDF*, 1st ser., 1:343.

20. Henry (Washington) to Herriot, 19 Sept. 1932, *DDF*, 1st ser., 1:350–52. Similarly, Massigli at Geneva reported that Hugh Wilson, the American minister to Switzerland, had linked the Far Eastern and German issues. See Massigli (Geneva) to Herriot, 22 Sept. 1932, *DDF*, 1st ser., 1:360.

21. Edge (Paris) to Sec. St., 8 Sept. 1932, *FRUS, 1932*, 4:234–35.

22. Edge (Paris) to Sec. St., 10 Sept. 1932, *FRUS, 1932*, 4:239–40, 295, 298–99.

23. Sabine Jessner, *Edouard Herriot: Patriarch of the Republic*, 122–24.

24. Edouard Herriot, "An International Drama," *International Conciliation* 290 (May 1933): 232.

25. See Atherton (Paris) to Sec. St., 25 Aug. 1932; and Edge (Paris) to Sec. St., 19 Sept. 1932, *FRUS, 1932*, 4:207, 265.

26. Wilden (Peking) to Herriot, 22 Sept. 1932, *DDF*, 1st ser., 1:257–58. In an astute bit of prognostication, Wilden warned that statements being made in Japan forebode an eventual attempt to force a union of Oriental peoples under the direction of Japan that would seek "to render Asia to the Asiatic" and exclude Westerners and their civilization.

27. Adrien de Lens (Tokyo) to Herriot, 23 Sept. 1932, *DDF*, 1st ser., 1:378–80.

28. Report by George H. Blakeslee to Hornbeck, quoted in Rappaport, *Stimson*, 212.

29. Thorne, *Limits of Foreign Policy*, 270. As Thorne notes, however, no trace of such instructions exists in the Quai d'Orsay archives, if indeed they were ever issued. In fact, there seems to have been little contact between Claudel and his government during the Commission's labors.

30. De Martel (Tokyo) for Claudel to Herriot, 9 July 1932, *DDF*, 1st ser., 1:6.

31. Quoted by Blakeslee in Rappaport, *Stimson*, 220.

32. Wilden (Peking) to Herriot, 3 Sept. 1932, *DDF*, 1st ser., 1:261.

33. The entire 100,000-word, ten-chapter report may be read in League of Nations, *The Report of the Commission of Inquiry of the League of Nations into the Sino-Japanese Dispute, 1932*. The essence of the report is best summarized in Thorne, *Limits of Foreign Policy*, 283–84.

34. Ogata, *Defiance in Manchuria*, 172.

35. These developments can be followed in Thorne, *Limits of Foreign Policy*, 328–36; and Rappaport, *Stimson*, 183–99.

36. See, for example, Massigli (Geneva) to Herriot, 23 Sept. 1932, *DDF*, 1st ser., 1:376–77; and Claudel (Washington) to Herriot, 14 Oct. 1932, *DDF*, 1st ser., 1:436.

37. Note du Département, 18 Nov. 1932, *DDF*, 1st ser., 2:22–26.

38. See de Lens (Tokyo) to Herriot, 8 Nov. 1932, *DDF*, 1st ser., 1:674–76; and Edge (Paris) to Sec. St., 19 Sept. 1932, FRUS, 1932, 4:265.

39. Castle memorandum, 22 Nov. 1932, *FRUS, 1932*, 4:360–61.

40. Ibid., 360.

41. Gilbert (Geneva) to Sec. St., 8 Dec. 1932, *FRUS, 1932*, 4:399–400; and Bassett, *Democracy and Foreign Policy*, 294–95.

42. See Massigli (Geneva) to Herriot, 9 and 12 Dec. 1932, *DDF*, 1st ser., 2:211–12, 242–43. For more on the Assembly debate, see Bassett, *Democracy and Foreign Policy*, chap. 13; and Thorne, *Limits of Foreign Policy*, 331–34.

43. Massigli (Geneva) to Herriot, 12 Dec. 1932, *DDF*, 1st ser., 2:242–43.

44. Barros, *Office without Power*, 378–79.

45. Paul-Boncour to Wilden (Peking), 27 Dec. 1932, *DDF*, 1st ser., 2:311–12.

46. Note du Service français de la Société des Nations (hereafter cited as SDN), 10 Jan. 1933, *DDF*, 1st ser., 2:410.

47. Note de la sous-direction d'Asie-Océanie, 15 Jan. 1933, *DDF*, 1st ser., 2:444–49.

48. For a summary of prevailing press opinion at the turn of the year, see Edge (Paris) to Sec. St., 5 Jan. 1933, *FRUS, 1933*, 3:13–14. See also Wigram (Paris) memorandum, 8 Jan. 1933, *DBFP*, 2d ser., 11:209–10.

49. Hornbeck memorandum, 9 Jan. 1933, *FRUS, 1933*, 3:27; and Wigram memorandum, 8 Jan. 1933, *DBFP*, 2d ser., 11:209–10.

50. Cot (sous-secrétaire d'etat à la présidence du Conseil) to Paul-Boncour, 15 Jan. 1933, *DDF*, 1st ser., 2:450. Three days later, Hugh Wilson, American representative to Switzerland and delegate to the Disarmament Conference at Geneva, made a similar approach to Massigli. See Note de la délégation française à la Conférence du désarmament (Geneva), 18 Jan. 1933, *DDF*, 1st ser., 2:467–68. Wilson took pains to emphasize that the United States did not intend to substitute itself for the League in finding a solution. When asked, he refused to reveal whether Washington would support the League should the latter adopt the Lytton report.

51. Claudel (Washington) to Paul-Boncour, 21 Jan. 1933, *DDF*, 1st ser., 2:493.

52. On Stimson, see Claudel (Washington) to Paul-Boncour, 10 Feb. 1933, *DDF*, 1st ser., 2:606. See also the French delegation's cables sent from Geneva, in *DDF*, 1st ser., 2:471, 501, 562, 573, 592, 605.

53. De Lens (Tokyo) to Paul-Boncour, 6 Jan. 1933, *DDF*, 1st ser., 2:362–64. See also de Lens (Tokyo) to Paul-Boncour, 24 Jan. 1933, *DDF*, 1st ser., 2:501. De Lens (Tokyo) to Paul-Boncour, 14 Feb. 1933, *DDF*, 1st ser., 2:623. From Peking came word that the Chinese, so close to receiving a favorable decision from the League, were equally disinclined to compromise. Therefore, any other avenue to a settlement, such as a Franco-British mediation, appeared inopportune. See Wilden (Peking) to Paul-Boncour, 16 Feb. 1933, *DDF*, 1st ser., 2:645–47. De Lens (Tokyo) to Paul-Boncour, 24 Feb. 1933, *DDF*, 1st ser., 2:687.

54. Massigli (Geneva) to Paul-Boncour, 24 Feb. 1933, *DDF*, 1st ser., 2:688.

55. These developments can be followed in Bonnefous, *La République en danger*, 125–44; and Maurice Baumont, *La Faillite de la paix*, vol. 1, *De Rothondes à Stresa (1918–1935)*, 419–27. See *Le Temps*, 29 Feb. 1933.

56. The quotation is from the Note de la sous-direction d'Asie-Océanie, 6 Mar. 1933, *DDF*, 1st ser., 2:740–41. For more on the abortive arms embargo, see Christopher Thorne,

"The Quest for Arms Embargoes: Failure in 1933," 129–49. On Matsuoka's visit to Berlin, see François-Poncet (Berlin) to Paul-Boncour, 10 Mar. 1933, *DDF,* 1st ser., 2:786–87. The evolution of German-Japanese relations can be followed in Ernst L. Pressiesen, *Germany and Japan: A Study in Totalitarian Diplomacy, 1933–1941,* 25–54; and James William Morley, ed., *Deterrent Diplomacy: Japan, Germany, and the USSR, 1935–1940,* 9–23.

57. De Fleuriau (London) to Paul-Boncour, 8 Mar. 1933, *DDF,* 1st ser., 2:761.

58. Borg, *United States and Far Eastern Crisis,* 22, 36–37; and Thorne, *Limits of Foreign Policy,* 328–29, 371–74. See also Wilden (Peking) to Paul-Boncour, 4 June 1933, *DDF,* 1st ser., 3:654.

59. These issues and negotiations can be followed in Jean-Baptiste Duroselle, *Politique étrangère de la France: La décadence, 1932–1939,* chap. 2; and Néré, *Foreign Policy of France,* 111–16.

60. For domestic developments, see Bonnefous, *République en danger,* 142–59.

61. De Martel (Tokyo) to Paul-Boncour, 28 Mar. 1933, *DDF,* 1st ser., 3:102–4; Wilden (Peking) to Paul-Boncour, 3 Mar. 1933, *DDF,* 1st ser., 3:413–14. On the Chinese appeals, see, for example, Wilden (Peking) to Paul-Boncour, 28 Apr. 1933, *DDF,* 1st ser., 3:354–55. Baudet is supported in Wilden (Peking) to Paul-Boncour, 5 May 1933, *DDF,* 1st ser., 3:425–26.

62. Paul-Boncour to Representatives in Peking, Tokyo, London, Washington, 29 Apr. 1933, *DDF,* 1st ser., 3:375.

63. The quotations are from Paul-Boncour to French Delegation at the Disarmament Conference (Geneva), 19 May 1933, *DDF,* 1st ser., 3:524. Paul-Boncour had made a démarche to the Americans in April, when he expressed similar concerns about the fate of the international peacekeeping machinery should Japan be permitted to tear up treaties. But he had no solution to offer, and he received no encouragement from the American representative. See Marriner (Paris) to Sec. St., 22 Apr. 1933, *FRUS, 1933,* 3:286. See also Hornbeck, memorandum, 2 May 1933, *FRUS, 1933,* 3:301–2.

64. Note de la sous-direction d'Asie-Océanie, 31 May 1933, *DDF,* 1st ser., 3:605. The note cautioned that the conflict had brought the Japanese face-to-face with the Russians for the first time since 1905, a development that could have uncertain consequences.

65. For the best treatments of Japanese developments during the 1933–37 period, see Crowley, *Japan's Quest for Autonomy,* chaps. 4 and 5; and Shimada Toshihiko, "Designs on North China, 1933–1937," trans. James B. Crowley, in *The China Quagmire: Japan's Expansion on the Asian Continent, 1933–1941,* ed. James William Morley. See also the selections concerning Japan in Dorothy Borg and Shumpei Okamoto, eds., *Pearl Harbor as History: Japanese-American Relations, 1931–1941.*

66. For these developments, see *DDF,* 1st ser., 3:629–30, 637, 725–27, 749–51, 811–13.

67. On the ambiguity surrounding the statement of doctrine, see Borg, *United States and Far Eastern Crisis,* 55–76. The quotation from the Far Eastern Department is from Note de la sous-direction d'Asie-Océanie, 20 Apr. 1934, *DDF,* 1st ser., 6:307–10. From Tokyo, Ambassador Fernand Pila wired that the declaration reflected the continuing influence of the military in Japan's governing circles. See Pila (Tokyo) to Barthou, 21 Apr. 1934, *DDF,* 1st ser., 6:316. Pila also believed that it represented a continuation of Japan's determination to deal with China "tête à tête" in order to assure itself a preponderant position in that country (Pila [Tokyo] to Barthou, 23 Apr. 1934, *DDF,* 1st ser., 6:332). See also Note du Département, 27 Apr. 1934, *DDF,* 1st ser., 6:361–69; and for the French view of the legality of the Japanese action, see idem., 367–69. The second quotation is from Barthou to Ambassadors in Washington and London, 24 Apr. 1934, *DDF,* 1st ser., 6:343. See also Barthou to de Laboulaye (Washington), 28 Apr. 1934, *DDF,* 1st ser., 6:375.

68. See Borg, *United States and Far Eastern Crisis*, 79–80, on Washington's statement. A week before the American statement to Japan, William Phillips of the State Department had hinted to French Ambassador de Laboulaye that Washington would not be willing to do much beyond making such a statement. See Phillips memorandum, 24 Apr. 1934, *FRUS, 1934*, 3:132–33. The quotation is from de Laboulaye (Washington) to Barthou, 30 Apr. 1934, *DDF*, 1st ser., 6:381–82.

69. Communication du Département to Japanese Embassy (Paris), 3 May 1934, *DDF*, 1st ser., 6:403. On the U.S. policy, see Hull to Grew (Tokyo), 12 May 1934, *FRUS, 1934*, 3:176–77.

70. Note de la sous-direction d'Asie-Océanie, 2 Oct. 1933, *DDF*, 1st ser., 4:470–71.

71. See *DDF*, 2d ser., 1:315, 553, 708–10; and *DDF*, 2d ser., 2:23–24.

72. See Flandin (Paris) to Pila (Tokyo), 10 Mar. 1936, *DDF*, 2d ser., 1:487; Pila (Tokyo) to Flandin, 14 Mar. 1936, *DDF*, 2d ser., 1:553; and Note du Département, 30 Mar. 1936, *DDF*, 2d ser., 1:708–9.

73. The Far Eastern Department's note is from 30 Mar. 1936, *DDF*, 2d ser., 1:709–10; Henry, in Washington, wrote to Flandin, 20 May 1936, *DDF*, 2d ser., 2:347–50.

74. For the reasons behind the Japanese action, see Crowley, *Japan's Quest for Autonomy*, 303–6; Delbos to Kammerer (Tokyo), 25 Nov. 1936, *DDF*, 2d ser., 4:48; Kammerer (Tokyo) to Delbos, 20 Nov. 1936, *DDF*, 2d ser., 4:2; and Kammerer (Tokyo) to Delbos, 2 Dec. 1936, *DDF*, 2d ser., 4:105–6.

75. Delbos to French Ambassadors in Tokyo, London, Washington, et al., 9 Dec. 1936, *DDF*, 2d ser., 4:189.

76. See Mast (Tokyo) to Daladier (Minister of National Defense), 10 Dec. 1936, annexed to Kammerer (Tokyo) to Delbos, 14 Dec. 1936, *DDF*, 2d ser., 4:240–44, and 4:234.

77. Pila (Tokyo) to Flandin, 18 May 1936, *DDF*, 2d ser., 2:335–40. Notes de la sous-direction d'Asie-Océanie, 28 Sept. 1936 and 21 Dec. 1936, *DDF*, 2d ser., 3:429, 4:302–3, show the French alarm and determination regarding the interests of France in the Far East. It was Henry in Tokyo who exclaimed over the contradictions (to Delbos, 28 Apr. 1937, *DDF*, 2d ser., 5:604–10).

78. Sabbatier (Peking) to Daladier (Minister of National Defense), 30 June 1937, *DDF*, 2d ser., 6:251–55.

5. OPPORTUNITY LOST: THE SINO-JAPANESE CONFLICT THROUGH THE BRUSSELS CONFERENCE

1. Henry (Tokyo) to Delbos, 9 July 1937, *DDF*, 2e, 6:345; Bullitt (Paris) to Sec. St., 13 July 1937, *FRUS, 1937*, 3:153.

2. United States State Department memorandum, 13 July 1937, SD 793.94 / 8780. See also Hornbeck (Political Advisor for Far Eastern Affairs) to Hull, 13 July 1937, SD 793.94 / 8777; Bingham (London) to Sec. St., 15 July 1937, SD 793.94 / 8746; and Bullitt (Paris) to Sec. St., 15 July 1937, *FRUS, 1937*, 3:173. On 23 July, the Japanese thanked the French for their concern, but they bluntly stated that the intrusion of third parties into the already-confused situation in China would only complicate matters further. See Delbos to French Representatives, 24 July 1937, *DDF*, 2e, 6:463; and Bullitt (Paris) to Sec. St., 24 July 1937, *FRUS, 1937*, 3:254.

3. Note de la sous-direction de la SDN, 14 July 1937, *DDF*, 2e, 6:381–82; Delbos to Corbin (London), 13 July 1937, *DDF*, 2e, 6:370; and Bullitt (Paris) to Sec. St., 15 July 1937, *FRUS, 1937*, 3:173–74.

4. Bullitt (Paris) to Sec. St., 30 July 1937, *FRUS, 1937,* 4:2.

5. On the risks to France, see Note de la sous-direction de la SDN, 14 July 1937, *DDF,* 2e, 6:381–82; and Delbos to Corbin (London), 13 July 1937, *DDF,* 2e, 6:370. Delbos's advice on the League is quoted in Bullitt (Paris) to Sec. St., 15 July 1937, *FRUS, 1937,* 3:174.

6. Delbos to Corbin (London), 13 July 1937, *DDF,* 2e, 6:370; and Note de la sous-direction de la SDN, 14 July 1937, *DDF,* 2e, 6:382.

7. Foreign Office memorandum, 29 July 1937, FO 371, 21002, F4764 / 1420 / 10.

8. Bullitt (Paris) to Sec. St., 26 Aug. 1937, *FRUS, 1937,* 3:475–77. Delbos believed that an early resolution of the conflict was imperative. If it dragged on, the chances appeared great that the Far East would ultimately become dominated by either the fascists or the Bolsheviks. Either outcome would be detrimental to the interests and ideals of the Western democracies. France was willing to participate in whatever approach Britain or the United States might advocate, "even though it might involve the use of force."

9. Enclosure in Eden to Lloyd Thomas (Paris), 30 Aug. 1937, FO 371, 20955, W16299 /23 / 41.

10. Bullitt (Paris) to Sec. St., 2 Sept. 1937, SD 793.94 / 9871. For the American attitude during the period immediately following the outbreak of the conflict, see Borg, *United States and Far Eastern Crisis,* 283–96.

11. Harrison (Geneva) to Sec. St., 21 Sept. 1937, SD 793.94 / 10183. Addressing the League Assembly on the same day, Stanley M. Bruce, the Australian high commissioner, apparently with the approval of France and Britain, broached the possibility of organizing a conference that would include those states that had interests in the Pacific basin. See Hull memorandum, 23 Sept. 1937, Cordell Hull Papers, container 57, Library of Congress, Washington, D.C. See also United Kingdom Delegation (Geneva) to FO, 22 Sept. 1937, FO 371, 20956, F6774 / 9 / 10, and 6 Oct. 1937, FO 371, 21015, F8543 / 6799 / 10; Harrison (Geneva) to Sec. St., 28 Sept. 1937, *FRUS, 1937,* 4:29–30; and Bradford A. Lee, *Britain and the Sino-Japanese War, 1937–1939,* 53. A chief concern of the British was the possibility of embarrassing the United States by attempting to involve it in a conference before Washington was ready to assume such a role.

12. Note de la sous-direction de la SDN, 26 Sept. 1937, *DDF,* 2e, 6:867–68.

13. Henry (Tokyo) to Delbos, 12 Sept. 1937, *DDF,* 2e, 6:761–62.

14. First and Second Reports Adopted by the League of Nations Assembly, 6 Oct. 1937, in *FRUS: Japan, 1931–1941,* 1:394, 396.

15. For some of the problems related to organizing the conference, see Nicholas R. Clifford, *Retreat from China: British Policy in the Far East, 1937–1941,* 38. See Wilson (Paris) to Sec. St., 16 Oct. 1937, SD 852.00 / 6696. Léger generally tended to view the Far Eastern developments pessimistically. See, for example, Bullitt's impression of Léger's views very early in the crisis in his memorandum, to Hull, 13 July 1937, *FRUS, 1937,* 3:153. In mid-August, Léger complained to Bullitt that he saw "no possibility whatsoever" of stopping what appeared to be shaping up as a long war.

16. On the Japanese activity and France's situation, see Grew (Tokyo) to Sec. St., 31 Aug. 1937, SD 793.94 / 9815; and Wilson (Paris) to Sec. St., 29 Sept. 1937, SD 793.94 / 10323. For an estimate of Indochina's defenses, see Hogg (Saigon) to Eden, 20 Sept. 1937, FO 371, 20695, C7320 / 240 / 17.

17. See note attached to Note de la sous-direction d'Asie-Océanie, 5 Oct. 1937, *DDF,* 2e, 7:39.

18. Ibid., 38–41.

19. The record of this meeting has apparently been destroyed. See the editor's note on Note de la sous-direction d'Asie-Océanie, 3 Dec. 1937, *DDF,* 2e, 7:598. For the best esti-

mates of the debate, see Wilson (Paris) to Sec. St., 19 Oct. 1937, SD 794.94111 / 81; and Delbos to Henry (Tokyo), 25 Oct. 1937, DDF, 2e, 7:226.

20. The quotation is from Note de la sous-direction d'Asie-Océanie, 3 Dec. 1937, DDF, 2e 7:598. As Delbos put it to Ambassador Charles-Arsène Henry in Tokyo, "superior considerations" made it imperative for France to balance its sympathies for China, while at the same time safeguarding its interests in the Far East without appearing to favor Japan (Delbos to Henry [Tokyo], 28 Oct. 1937, DDF, 2e, 7:598). See also Delbos to French Representatives, 8 Nov. 1937, DDF, 2e, 7:357. Earlier in the conflict, the government had planned to ward off Japanese irritation by explaining that France had no control over the sale of such arms by private enterprise. But since a large percentage of French munitions and aircraft production had been nationalized, it was difficult to hide behind such a subterfuge. See Bullitt (Paris) to Sec. St., 23 Aug. 1937, SD 793.94 / 963; and Bullitt (Paris) to Sec. St., 26 Aug. 1937, FRUS, 1937, 3:477.

21. Wilson (Paris) to Sec. St., 19 Oct. 1937, SD 793.94111 / 81. See Alexander Cadogan's minute attached to the dispatch from Sir Eric Phipps in Paris to the Foreign Office, 27 Oct. 1937, FO 371, 20979, F8531 / 130 / 10. See also Cabinet Committee on British Shipping in the Far East, Cab 27 / 634, FES (37) Series; Grew (Tokyo) to Sec. St., 1 Nov. 1937, FRUS, 1937, 4:136; and Craigie (Tokyo) to Eden, 2 Nov. 1937, FO 371, 20979, F8989 / 130 / 10. See draft of Cadogan's instructions attached to Phipps (Paris) to Eden, 20 Oct. 1937, FO 371, 20979, F8232 / 130 / 10. On the situation vis-à-vis the United States, see Jules Henry (Washington) to Delbos, 22 Oct. 1937, DDF, 2e, 7:216. See also Welles to Bullitt (Paris), 22 Oct. 1937, FRUS, 1937, 3:632. Only on October 21 had Premier Camille Chautemps confirmed to Bullitt the French decision to halt the transit of arms. Bullitt (Paris) to Sec. St., 22 Oct. 1937, SD 793.9411 / 83.

22. Delbos to French Representatives, 8 Nov. 1937, DDF, 2e, 7:307; Bullitt (Paris) to Sec. St., 23 Oct. 1937, SD 793.94111 / 84; and Bullitt (Paris) to Sec. St., 23 Oct. 1937, FRUS, 1937, 3:638.

23. Bullitt (Paris) to Sec. St., 22 Oct. 1937, SD 793.94111 / 83. For similar statements made by Delbos, see Bullitt to Sec. St., 23 Oct. 1937, SD 793.94111 / 84; and Phipps (Paris) to Eden, 26 Oct. 1937, FO 371, 20979, F8531 / 130 / 10. In Washington, Chargé d'Affaires Henry conveyed a message to the president through Welles in which he indicated that the possibility of a Japanese attack against Indochina was not a "remote contingency." See Welles memorandum, 10 Nov. 1937, in President's Secretary's File (hereafter cited as PSF), Box 41, folder (France, 1933–1939), Franklin D. Roosevelt (hereafter FDR) Library, Hyde Park, New York.

24. For the full text of the speech, see FRUS: Japan, 1931–1941, 1:379–83. For the debate concerning Roosevelt's intent, see, for example, Dorothy Borg, "Notes on Roosevelt's 'Quarantine' Speech"; Borg, United States and Far Eastern Crisis, 380–86; and John McVickar Haight, Jr., "Franklin D. Roosevelt and a Naval Quarantine of Japan."

As Haight has written, "Dailies from left to right rejoiced that now if France suffered attack she could count upon direct American aid" ("France and the Aftermath of Roosevelt's 'Quarantine' Speech," 285). Perhaps La Lumière, a moderate weekly of the Left, best reflected, some of the ambivalence of the press. It cautioned that past experience "teaches us not to abandon ourselves prematurely to the hope of a sudden and total turn of the attitude taken until now by the Americans." On the other hand, the newspaper contended that Roosevelt's speech had sounded the alarm to the American people that "isolation is morally and technically impossible" (see La Lumière, 8 Oct. 1937).

25. Jules Henry (Washington) to Delbos, 7 Oct. 1937, DDF, 2e, 7:60–62. Henry confided to Jay Pierepont Moffat, chief of the Division of European Affairs at the State Department, that he considered Roosevelt's speech "designed to educate American opinion to

realize the dangers of isolation but that France would be making a terrible mistake if it based any policy on its implementation" (see 14 Oct., Moffat Papers, vol. 39, Houghton Library, Harvard University, Cambridge, Massachusetts).

26. Jules Henry (Washington) to Delbos, 26 Oct. 1937, *DDF*, 2e, 7:243–44. Henry tempered his zeal, however, with a reminder that Hull still had not openly advocated joint international action to halt such aggression.

27. Delbos to Henry (Tokyo), 25 Oct. 1937, *DDF*, 2e, 7:226; Phipps (Paris) to Eden, 26 Oct. 1937, FO 371, 20979, F8531 / 130/10. The British Foreign Office was clearly exasperated by the French decision. Even after the French modified their position, Nigel Ronald of the Far Eastern Department, fulminated, "I am afraid it is only too clear that we are not likely to get the French to budge an inch from the pusillanimous attitude which they have taken up." See also Ronald's minute on Phipps's dispatch.

28. Bullitt (Paris) to Sec. St., 23 Oct. 1937, SD 793.94111 / 84.

29. Presseisen, *Germany and Japan*, 132–33; Note de la sous-direction d'Asie-Océanie, 31 Dec. 1937, *DDF*, 2e, 7:809; and Grew (Tokyo) to Sec. St., 22 Oct. 1937, SD 793.94 Conference / 83. See also Lee, *Britain and Sino-Japanese War*, 62; and Clifford, *Retreat from China*, 40. Even before invitations were sent out, the French and American ambassadors in Tokyo received a strong inkling of the Japanese position, when, in response to the Westerners' urging, the Japanese foreign minister replied that "the pressure of public opinion in this country would probably require the government to refuse." Hirota is quoted in Grew (Tokyo) to Sec. St., 22 Oct. 1937, SD 793.94 Conference / 83. For the American efforts and reaction to the Japanese refusal, see Borg, *United States and Far Eastern Crisis*, 412.

30. Nancy Harvison Hooker, ed., *The Moffat Papers: Selections from the Diplomatic Journals of Jay Pierrepont Moffat, 1919–1943*, 161; and Bullitt (Paris) to R. Walton Moore, 3 Nov. 1937, R. Walton Moore Papers, FDR Library, Hyde Park, New York. In characteristic Bullitt style, he added, "If you want a different attitude in Paris, I can raise hell and produce one, but obviously only on instruction."

31. Davis (Brussels) to Sec. St., 3 Nov. 1937, SD 793.94 Conference / 172. See also Hooker, *Moffat Papers*, 165. John McVickar Haight writes that at this meeting "Delbos took a stand against any appeasement" and actively argued for more positive steps ("France and Roosevelt's 'Quarantine' Speech," 295). The British, who had met with Davis that morning, believed the American position to be inadequate, and the next day the American delegate was "put straight" about the British attitude. If Roosevelt were to do anything, it could not be done halfheartedly. It would be useless, for example, to apply sanctions unless they were effective and accompanied by preparations for war. See Oliver Harvey, *The Diplomatic Diaries of Oliver Harvey, 1937–1940*, 55–56; and Anthony Eden, *The Memoirs of Anthony Eden, Earl of Avon*, vol. 1, *Facing the Dictators*, 608–9.

32. For the text of the keynote speeches, see U.S. Department of State, *The Conference of Brussels, November 3–24, 1937*, Conference series 37, 24–31. See also Note de la sous-direction d'Asie-Océanie, 31 Dec. 1937, *DDF*, 2e, 7:810, for a summary of the main points of the speeches; Hooker, *Moffat Papers*, 168–70; and Davis (Brussels) to Sec. St., 7 Nov. 1937, *FRUS, 1937*, 4:162–64.

33. For the best records of this meeting, see Note du Ministre, 6 Nov. 1937, *DDF*, 2e, 7:346–49; United Kingdom Delegation (Brussels) to Foreign Office, 8 Nov. 1937, FO 371, 21016, F9291 / 6799 / 10; Norman R. Davis Papers, container 5, folder Nine Power Conference, Library of Congress, Washington, D.C.; Hooker, *Moffat Papers*, 168–70; and Davis (Brussels) to Sec. St., 7 Nov. 1937, *FRUS, 1937*, 4:162–64.

34. Delbos to Henry (Washington), 9 Nov. 1937, *DDF*, 2e, 7:364; Davis Papers, container 5, folder Nine Power Conference; Davis to Sec. St., 6 Nov. 1937, *FRUS, 1937*, 4:157–58; and Davis Papers, container 5, folder Conversations and Memoranda, October–December 1937.

35. Haight, "France and Roosevelt's 'Quarantine' Speech," 298; Borg, *United States and Far Eastern Crisis*, 423-24.

36. Henry (Washington) to Delbos, 7 Nov. 1937, *DDF*, 2e, 7:355-57.

37. Bullitt (Paris) to Sec. St., 8 Nov. 1937, SD 793.94111 / 89.

38. See Welles to Bullitt (Paris), 9 Nov. 1937, *FRUS, 1937*, 4:170-71. This account of Roosevelt's meeting with Henry is nearly impossible to recognize as a report on the same meeting that Henry wrote about. One might expect differences of nuance when two diplomats describe the same event, but this difference extends far beyond shading. What Roosevelt actually had in mind is unclear, though he approved Welles's account.

39. Delbos to Henry (Washington), 9 Nov. 1937, *DDF*, 2e, 7:364-65.

40. Bullitt (Paris) to Sec. St., 8 Nov. 1937, *FRUS, 1937*, 4:168.

41. Bullitt (Paris) to Sec. St., 10 Nov. 1937, *FRUS, 1937*, 4:172-73. In a following telegram, Bullitt emphasized the "deadly seriousness" of Chautemps. He concurred that it was unwise to say anything "unless we intend to back up all the implications of our words with an extremely big stick" (Bullitt [Paris] to Sec. St., 10 Nov. 1937, *FRUS, 1937*, 4:174-75). Bullitt elaborated upon his view about the Far East in a direct communication with the president a couple of weeks after the conference ended, saying that in his opinion, "We have large emotional interests in China, small economic interests, and no vital interests. . . . The far-off bugaboo of complete Japanese domination of Asia and an eventual attack seems to be no base whatsoever for present-day policy. The Japanese will have their hands full with China and the Soviet Union and their one hope will be to avoid war with us. I think, therefore, that for the foreseeable future we should watch events in the Far East but not participate in them if we can avoid participation" (Bullitt [Paris] to FDR, 7 Dec. 1937, Bullitt Papers, FDR Library, Hyde Park, New York).

42. This debate can be followed best in Note du Ministre (Brussels), 6 Nov. 1937, *DDF*, 2e, 7:346-48; Hooker, *Moffat Papers*, 170-71; Eden (Brussels) to Foreign Office, 4 Nov. 1937, FO 371, 21016, F9071 / 6799 / 10; Bullitt (Paris) to Sec. St., 6 Nov. 1937, *FRUS, 1937*, 4:162-64; and draft of telephone conversation with Bullitt, 6 Nov. 1937, Davis Papers, container 5, folder Conversations and Memoranda, October–December 1937. Even as late as 8 November, after Delbos had returned to Paris and after the second invitation had been sent to Tokyo, Delbos phoned Bullitt to express his concern about the possibility that France might be left off the committee.

43. For descriptions of the meetings of 10 November, see the unpublished Moffat Papers, 10 Nov. 1937, vol. 39, and the incomplete edited version in Hooker, *Moffat Papers*, 174-78. Some amplification may be gained from Davis (Brussels) to Sec. St., 11 Nov. 1937, *FRUS, 1937*, 4:177-78; and Eden (Brussels) to Foreign Office, 10 Nov. 1937, FO 371, 21017, F9473 / 6799 / 10. C. W. Orde of the British Foreign Office minuted Eden's dispatch, "It is interesting to find France taking up the same position as ourselves and Holland. The next move is surely with the U.S. Gov't. [*sic*]." See also Haight, "France and Roosevelt's 'Quarantine' Speech," 300-301.

44. Memorandum of conversation, 10 Nov. 1937, in Moffat Papers, vol. 39. Eden was speaking for himself at this point. Chamberlain had already warned him, saying, "On no account will I impose sanctions." Moreover, Eden's own department was divided about the question of sanctions. See Lee, *Britain and Sino-Japanese War*, 72-74.

45. In fact, Davis was being urged by the State Department to continue the conference as long as possible. Davis Papers, 10 and 12 Nov. 1937, container 4.

46. For this meeting, see Hooker, *Moffat Papers*, 177-78; and memorandum of conversation, 10 Nov. 1937, in Moffat Papers, vol. 39.

47. See Welles to Bullitt (Paris), 9 Nov. 1937, *FRUS, 1937*, 4:170-71.

48. Davis (Brussels) to Sec. St., 10 Nov. 1937, *FRUS, 1937*, 4:175-77; and Hooker, *Moffat Papers*, 174-75. A paraphrase of this document can be found in Davis Papers, container 4. Davis supported a plan that would exert financial pressure on Japan, while at the same time doing nothing to damage China's military effort. For the best treatment of the debate concerning policy within the American delegation and Davis's apparent change of heart, see Borg, *United States and Far Eastern Crisis*, 423-25.

49. Davis (Brussels) to Sec. St., 14 Nov. 1937, *FRUS, 1937*, 4:184-85; Haight, "France and Roosevelt's 'Quarantine' Speech," 300.

50. Davis to Sec. St., 14 Nov. 1937, FRUS, 1937, 4:184.

51. Henry (Washington) to Delbos, 10 Nov. 1937, *DDF*, 2e, 7:369-70.

52. Henry (Washington) to Delbos, 11 Nov. 1937, *DDF*, 2e, 7:390-92. See also Welles, memorandum, 10 Nov. 1937, Davis Papers, container 5, folder Nine Power Conference; and British Delegation (Brussels) to Foreign Office, 11 Nov. 1937, FO 371, 21017, F9488 / 6799 / 10.

53. Record of Meeting on 11 Nov. 1937, Davis Papers, container no. 5, folder Nine Power Conference. Delbos did reiterate his belief that it was "useless to expect that moral pressure would have any effect on Japan." See also Hull to Davis (Brussels), 12 Nov. 1937, *FRUS, 1937*, 4:180-81. For a full treatment of the debate among American policymakers at this point, see Borg, *United States and Far Eastern Crisis*, 428-32. Moffat is quoted by Hooker (*Moffat Papers*, 181-82). As Moffat admitted to his diary, "My personal preoccupation is to prevent at any costs the involvement of the United States in hostilities anywhere, and to that end to discourage any formation of a common front of the democratic powers" (Hooker, 183).

54. Department of State, *Conference of Brussels*, 53-54, 55-63; and Hooker, *Moffat Papers*, 180-81. See also U.K. Delegation (Brussels) to Foreign Office, 13 Nov. 1937, FO 371, 21017, F9625 / 6799 / 10. For the Quai d'Orsay's rather unrevealing account of these developments, see Note de la sous-direction d'Asie-Océanie, 31 Dec. 1937, *DDF*, 2e, 7:811-12.

55. Department of State, *Conference of Brussels*, 65-67.

56. Hull to Davis (Brussels), 12 Nov. 1937, *FRUS, 1937*, 4:181.

57. Davis (Brussels) to Sec. St., 14 Nov. 1937, *FRUS, 1937*, 4:184-85; Hull to Davis (Brussels), 15 Nov. 1937, *FRUS, 1937*, 4: 187-88; Hull to Davis (Brussels), 16 Nov. 1937, *FRUS, 1937*, 4:193; and Davis (Brussels) to Sec. St., 17 Nov. 1937, *FRUS, 1937*, 4:201.

58. Delbos to Corbin (London), 16 Nov. 1937, *DDF*, 2e, 7:430-31.

59. See editors' note, ibid., 431.

60. Eden to Phipps (Paris), 13 Nov. 1937, FO 371, 20959, F9591 / 9 / 10; Henry (Tokyo) to Delbos, 13 Nov. 1937, *DDF*, 2e, 7:415; and Naggiar (Peking) to Delbos, 11 Nov. 1937, *DDF*, 2e, 7:389-90.

61. Corbin (London) to Delbos, 18 Nov. 1937, *DDF*, 2e, 7:447; and Vansittart, memorandum, 18 Nov. 1937, FO 371, 21017, F9829 / 6799 / 10. Eden initialed the memorandum and apparently agreed with Vansittart's response.

62. Corbin (London) to Delbos, 19 Nov. 1937, *DDF*, 2e, 7:456-57; and Eden, memorandum, 19 Nov. 1937, FO 371, 21017, F9865 / 6799 / 10. Rather lamely, Eden again tried to raise the point that French insistence upon being included on any mediation committee, should such a group be established, would hamper its chances for success because all the others would then want to be included. Corbin reiterated the large French interests in the Far East as the basis for its demand for inclusion. The matter was dropped at that point. For more on the British machinations to mediate the struggle without French involvement, see Lee, *Britain and Sino-Japanese War*, 75-76.

63. Haight, "France and Roosevelt's 'Quarantine' Speech," 303. Henry had wired the previous day that congressional concern about getting dragged into war had resulted in the

introductions of two constitutional amendments into the Senate, both restricting the president's power to declare war. The French chargé correctly judged that such amendments had little chance of being adopted, but they might be used as a barometer of the American mood. See Henry (Washington) to Delbos, 17 Nov. 1937, *DDF*, 2e, 7:440.

64. *JOC*, 19 Nov. 1937, 2469–70. Delbos's private comment on the destiny of mankind is quoted in Haight, "France and Roosevelt's 'Quarantine' Speech," 304.

65. Phipps (Paris) to Eden, 20 Nov. 1937, FO 371, 21018, F9859 / 6799 / 10.

66. Department of State, *Conference of Brussels*, 76–77; Hooker, *Moffat Papers*, 187; and Report of the Fourth Plenary Meeting, 22 Nov. 1937, FO 371, 21018, F9964 / 6799 / 10.

67. Davis (Brussels) to Sec. St., 21 Nov. 1937, *FRUS*, *1937*, 4:224; *Le Temps*, 15 Nov. 1937; and *L'Echo de Paris*, 13 and 17 Nov. 1937.

68. For analyses of the discussions culminating in the final report, see Borg, *United States and Far Eastern Crisis*, 437–38; and Lee, *Britain and Sino-Japanese War*, 76–77. For the text of the final speeches and the documents, see Department of State, *Conference of Brussels*, 69–80.

69. *L'Oeuvre*, 13 Nov. 1937.

70. On Jules Henry's consistent cautions, see, for example, Henry (Washington) to Delbos, 11 Oct. 1937, *DDF*, 2e, 7:100–101; Robert Dallek, *Franklin D. Roosevelt and American Foreign Policy, 1932–1945*, 151–53.

71. Attention-grabbing European events included Italy's announcement just prior to the conference that it would join the Anti-Comintern Pact and Lord Halifax's meeting with Hitler on 19 November.

72. Leon Booth's "Brussels Conference and the Conflict with Japan" (257) is an example of the Brussels-Munich arguments. Eden's remark is from *Facing the Dictators*, 613.

73. See John E. Dreifort, *Yvon Delbos at the Quai d'Orsay: French Foreign Policy during the Popular Front, 1936–1938*, 141–50.

74. Herbert Feis, *The Road to Pearl Harbor: The Coming of the War between the United States and Japan*, 16.

6. The Deepening Far Eastern Dilemma
and the Search for Allies, 1938–1939

1. Presseisen, *Germany and Japan*, 134–42; and John P. Fox, *Germany and the Far Eastern Crisis, 1931–1938*, 259–90. See also John Hunter Boyle, *China and Japan at War, 1937–1945: The Politics of Collaboration*, 69–70. For an account of the negotiations as they were pieced together at the time, see Henry (Tokyo) to Delbos, 24 Jan. 1938, *DDF*, 2e, 8:56–59. For a French analysis of Berlin's motives for assuming the role of mediator, see Lamarle (Berlin) to Delbos, 20 Jan. 1938, *DDF*, 2e, 8:15–20.

2. See Bullitt (Paris) to Sec. St., 6 Dec. 1937, *FRUS*, *1937*, 3:769; Bullitt (Paris) to Sec. St., 5 Jan. 1938, *FRUS*, *1938*, 3:5.

3. Note by Sabbatier (Peking), 15 Dec. 1937, *DDF*, 2e, 7:708–13.

4. Naggiar (Shanghai) to Delbos, 2 Jan. 1938, *DDF*, 2e, 7:817–18. General Iwani Matsui, head of the Japanese forces in China, admitted to Naggiar that he expected the fighting to continue for another two or three months, until Chiang Kai-shek's government had been eliminated from the scene.

5. Lacoste (Peking) to Naggiar (Shanghai), 11 Jan. 1938, *DDF*, 2e, 7:874.

6. Henry (Tokyo) to Delbos, 5 Jan. 1938, *DDF*, 2e, 7:822. On Tokyo's intentions, see Henry (Tokyo) to Delbos 7 Jan. 1938, *DDF*, 2e, 7:849. The quotation is from Henry (Tokyo) to Delbos, 10 Jan. 1938, *DDF*, 2e 7:854.

7. Henry (Tokyo) to Delbos, 16 Jan. 1938, *DDF*, 2e, 7:935–36. For the internal machinations of the Konoye regime during this critical period, see Crowley, *Japan's Quest,* 358–78.
8. Henry (Tokyo) to Delbos, 18 Jan. 1938, *DDF*, 2e, 8:5–6.
9. See U.K. Delegation (Geneva) to FO, 28 Jan. 1938, FO 371, 22101, F1215 / 78 / 10.
10. See Cranborne, U.K. Delegation (Geneva) to FO, 31 Jan. 1938, FO 371, 22101, F1266 / 78 / 10, and 10 and 14 May 1938, FO 371, 22102, F4984, 5234 / 78 / 10; and U.K. Delegation (Geneva) to FO, 30 Sept. 1938, *DBFP*, 3d ser., 8:110–11.
11. Georges Taboulet, "La France et l'Angleterre face au conflit sino-japonais (1937–1939)," 123–24; and Arthur N. Young, *China and the Helping Hand, 1937–1945*, 50, 72, 138, 440.
12. For a summary of the foreign credits arranged, see Young, *Helping Hand*, 441.
13. Ibid., 208; and Taboulet, "La France et l'Angleterre," 136.
14. Young, *Helping Hand*, 49, 51–52; Acting Sec. of War (Johnson) to Sec. St., 15 June 1938, *FRUS, 1938*, 3:601.
15. Young, *Helping Hand*, 50; and Taboulet, "La France et l'Angleterre," 137.
16. Taboulet, "La France et l'Angleterre," 137, 138. See also Delbos to Henry (Tokyo), 13 Nov. 1937, *DDF*, 2e, 7:419.
17. On only two occasions did Tokyo raise the issue of arms. See Henry (Tokyo) to Delbos, 3 Dec. 1937 and 12 Jan. 1938, *DDF*, 2e, 7:904. For the memo to Delbos, see Note de la sous-direction d'Asie-Océanie, 28 Feb. 1938, *DDF*, 2e, 8:557.
18. Note de la sous-direction d'Asie-Océanie, 28 Feb. 1938, *DDF*, 2e, 8:558; Lagarde (Geneva) to Foreign Affairs Ministry, 1 Feb. 1938, *DDF*, 2e, 8:165–67; and Note de la sous-direction d'Asie-Océanie, 22 Mar. 1938, *DDF*, 2e, 9:31–32.
19. On developments in Washington, see Henry (Washington) to Delbos, 30 Jan. 1938, *DDF*, 2e, 8:148–49. On the Chinese, see Lagarde (Geneva) to Foreign Affairs Ministry, 2 Feb. 1938, *DDF*, 2e, 8:182–83.
20. Note de la sous-direction d'Asie-Océanie, 21 Apr. 1938, *DDF*, 2e, 9:453–54.
21. See Charles-Arsène Henry (Tokyo) to Bonnet, 30 May 1938, *DDF*, 2e, 9:943–44. For a sampling of the press attacks, see Craigie (Tokyo) to FO, 16 June 1938, FO 371, 22109, F7414 / 84 / 10. *Kokumin shimbun,* which tended to be more virulent than other papers, compared France to a "thief during a fire," taking advantage of the situation for itself. The unsubstantiated press allegations covered a variety of issues, including arms transit, military advisers, and railway loans.
22. Bonnet to Henry (Tokyo), 1 June 1938, *DDF*, 2e, 9:979–80. Bonnet made the same point to the Japanese ambassador in Paris, indicating that such press attacks "could only make it more difficult for us to pursue a policy of balance and impartiality" (Bonnet to Henry [Tokyo], 2 June 1938, *DDF*, 2e, 9:1000).
23. Boyle, *China and Japan at War*, 147. For the peace talks initiated during the summer, only to flounder in August, see 156–60.
24. Henry (Tokyo) to Bonnet, 10 June 1938, *DDF*, 2e, 10:1–3.
25. Henry (Tokyo) to Bonnet, 19 June 1938, *DDF*, 2e, 10:100–102.
26. Bonnet to Henry (Tokyo), 18 June 1938, *DDF*, 2e, 10:91–92.
27. Henry (Tokyo) to Bonnet, 20 June 1938, *DDF*, 2e, 10:109–10.
28. See Craigie (Tokyo) to FO, 13 July 1938, FO 371, 22109, F8489 / 84 / 10.
29. Bonnet to Henry (Tokyo), 29 June 1938, *DDF*, 2e, 10:215–17.
30. Henry (Tokyo) to Bonnet, 3 July 1938, *DDF*, 2e, 10:265–67, details the meeting with Ugaki. On the gradual cessation of the press attacks, see Craigie (Tokyo) to FO, 13 July 1938, FO 371, 22109, F8489 / 84 / 10; and Grew (Tokyo) to Sec. St., 11 July 1938, *FRUS, 1938*, 3:218–20.

31. Wilson (Paris) to Sec. St., 2 Mar. 1938, *FRUS, 1938*, 3:113; Bullitt (Paris) to Sec. St., 4 Apr. 1939, *FRUS, 1939*, 3:747; and American Consul (Yunnanfu) to Sec. St., 30 Mar. 1938, SD 893.24 / 395.

32. See Communication de l'Ambassade du Japon à Paris au Département, 28 Oct. 1938, *DDF*, 2e, 12:386–87. See also Henry (Tokyo) to Bonnet, 28 Oct. 1938, *DDF*, 2e 12:403–5. Henry speculated that the renewed pressure reflected indecision in Tokyo concerning the China conflict. He argued that Konoye sought to keep the militants in line by the anti-French campaign and that Paris should do whatever possible to help the Japanese premier restrain his opponents.

33. Note de la sous-direction d'Asie-Océanie, 15 Nov. 1938, *DDF*, 2e, 12:566–67; and Henry (Tokyo) to Foreign Ministry, 26 Oct. 1938, *DDF*, 2e, 12:405. See also Wilson (Paris) to Sec. St., 29 Oct. 1938, *FRUS, 1938*, 3:351–52; Grew (Tokyo) to Sec. St., 2 Nov. 1938, *FRUS, 1938*, 3:607; Craigie (Tokyo) to Halifax, 4 Nov. 1938, *DBFP*, 3d ser., 8:184; and Wilson (Paris) to Sec. St., 7 Nov. 1938, *FRUS, 1938*, 3:374–75.

34. Wilson (Paris) to Sec. St., 16 Nov. 1938, *FRUS, 1938*, 3:609–10. Of course, the record is replete with Chinese expressions of concern about difficulties with the French government regarding the shipment of munitions. See, for example, Wilson (Paris) to Sec. St., 5 Apr. 1938, *FRUS, 1938*, 3:135–36. Cordell Hull's remark is from Memorandum of Conversation, 22 Nov. 1938, Hull Papers, container 58. Foreign observers confirmed the slackening of shipments around that time. See Palmer (Saigon) to Sec. St., 23 Nov. 1938, SD 65G. / 11251 / 6; and Johnson (Chungking) to Sec. St., 25 Nov. 1938, SD 893.24 / 500.

35. Quoted by Clark Kerr (Shanghai) to FO, 21 Apr. 1939, FO 371, 22921, C8244 / 249 / 17.

36. Southard (Hong Kong) to Sec. St., 11 Feb. 1939, SD 851G.1561 / 2. Although observers believed that some of the congestion resulted from French restrictions, for the most part it reflected the increased demands placed on the system and inefficiency at the harbor. See Jarvis (Shanghai) to Sec. St., 13 Jan. 1939, SD 793.94 / 14722 for a good outline of the Indochinese facilities and their use for the transit of goods; see also Donovan (Hong Kong) to Sec. St., 24 May 1939, SD 851G.1561 / 6.

37. Bullitt (Paris) to Sec. St., 6 Feb. 1939, SD 740.00 / 568. Daladier's promise to let China have everything that France could spare must be considered in view of the fact that on the same day he indicated his intention of ordering more than 200 planes from the United States. See Orville Bullitt, ed., *For the President, Personal and Secret: Correspondence between Franklin D. Roosevelt and William C. Bullitt*, 311. The fact remained that France, in the midst of its own emergency rearmament program, had little to spare for China.

38. Bullitt (Paris) to Sec. St., 22 Feb. 1939, SD 893.24 / 539. This apparently represented a change in Mandel's position, which had been described by one official of the Far Eastern section of the Quai d'Orsay in November 1938 as being exceedingly cautious, for fear of providing Japan a pretext to act against France. See attachment to Wilson (Paris) to Sec. St., 9 Nov. 1938, SD 893.24 / 501.

39. The quotation is from Robert (Canton) to Asst. Chief of Staff, G-2, 27 Sept. 1938, SD 793.94 / 14268. Corbin's admission is cited in Grew Papers (Harvard University), 28 June 1938, Conversations, vol. 4, 1937–1939.

40. For the substance of the concern and debate regarding Hainan and the other neighboring islands in the South China Sea, see FO 371, file 287 / 10. See also Bullitt (Paris) to Sec. St., 21 June 1938, SD 793.94 / 13280; and Palmer (Saigon) to Sec. St., 29 June 1938, SD 793.94 / 13510.

41. For developments surrounding the French occupation of the Paracels, see *DDF*, 2e, 10:128, 133, 141, 147, and 12:350; Craigie (Tokyo) to FO, 8 July 1938, FO 371, 22137, F7296 / 287 / 10; FO Memorandum, 4 July 1938, FO 371, 22137, F7160 / 287 / 10; and

Report by the CID Chiefs of Staff Subcommittee, "Islands in the South China Seas: Strategic Importance and Japanese Encroachment," Annex II to Phipps (Paris) to FO, 15 Mar. 1938, FO 371, 22175, F2965 / 956 / 61. London believed that it would be better to have the French occupy the islands than the Japanese, although the British remained skeptical about the military value of the atolls.

42. Lee, *Britain and Sino-Japanese War*, 274; Feis, *Road to Pearl Harbor*, 18; and Bergamini, *Japan's Imperial Conspiracy*, 699.

43. Bergamini, *Japan's Imperial Conspiracy*, 699–700; and Taboulet, "La France et l'Angleterre," 141.

44. Bullitt (Paris) to Sec. St., 11 Feb. 1939, *FRUS, 1939*, 3:104–5. Bonnet argued that the Franco-Japanese Treaty of 1907 had pledged both powers to respect Chinese territorial integrity and that this promise had been violated (Bonnet to Henry [Tokyo], 10 Feb. 1939, *DDF*, 2e, 14:163).

45. Henry (Tokyo) to Bonnet, 14 Feb. 1939, *DDF*, 2e, 14:195; Grew (Tokyo) to Sec. St., 15 Feb. 1939, SD 793.94 / 14761; and Cab 23, vol. 97, 7(39)4, 15 Feb. 1939, 255–56. Henry warned that the Japanese press rabidly favored the permanent occupation of Hainan and might well influence government action.

46. Bullitt (Paris) to Sec. St., 16 Feb. 1939, *FRUS, 1939*, 3:110.

47. Note du sous-directeur d'Europe (Hoppenot), 12 Feb. 1939, *DDF*, 2e, 14:186; and Bullitt (Paris) to Sec. St., 11 Feb. 1939, *FRUS, 1939*, 3:104–5. Some French officials suspected that the Japanese action might have been partly provoked by France's rejection in January of Masayuki Tani as ambassador to Paris because of his alleged anti-French statements earlier. See Grew (Tokyo) to Sec. St., 15 Feb. 1939, SD 793.94 / 14761. Others, such as Henry, had long anticipated that whenever the military wished to act, it would take Hainan and that Japan's civilian leaders would be powerless to prevent it. See Henry (Tokyo) to Bonnet, 23 Nov. 1938, *DDF*, 2e, 12:724.

48. Grew (Tokyo) to Sec. St., 15 Feb. 1939, SD 793.94 / 14761. See also Note du sous-directeur d'Europe (Hoppenot), 12 Feb. 1939, *DDF*, 2e 14:186. On the French and British, see Grew (Tokyo) to Sec. St., 15 Feb. 1939, SD 793.94 / 14761.

49. Henry (Tokyo) to Bonnet, 31 Mar. 1939, *DDF*, 2e, 15:331–32. For background to the Spratly Islands developments, see *DDF*, 2e, 9, nos. 333, 338, 473; 10, nos. 162, 397, 433; and 15, no. 222; and French Foreign Ministry to Phipps, 14 Mar. 1938, in Phipps (Paris) to FO, 15 Mar. 1938, FO 371, 22175, F2965 / 956 / 61. See also Taboulet, "La France et l'Angleterre," 128–29.

50. Sec. St. (Washington) to Grew (Tokyo), 31 Mar. 1939, *FRUS, 1939*, 3:113; and Craigie (Tokyo) to FO, 19 Apr. 1939, FO 371, 23567, F5201 / 874 / 23. Discussions had gone on in Paris in the aftermath of the occupation of Hainan about the advisability of sending a naval contingent to the islands, but for unclear reasons the step was not taken. See Bonnet to Campinchi (Minister of the Navy), 27 Feb. 1939, *DDF*, 2e, 14:400–401.

51. Bullitt (Paris) to Sec. St., 1 and 6 Apr. 1939, *FRUS, 1939*, 3:113–15. In Tokyo, Henry was convinced that the initiative had been taken by the Japanese Foreign Ministry rather than the navy in an effort to silence Foreign Minister Arita's rabid critics. Henry (Tokyo) to Bonnet, 5 Apr. 1939, *DDF*, 2e, 15:400.

52. Bonnet to Henry (Tokyo), 3 Apr. 1939, *DDF*, 2e, 15:360. See also Bullitt (Paris) to Sec. St., 6 Apr. 1939, *FRUS, 1939*, 3:114; and Grew (Tokyo) to Sec. St., 8 Apr. 1939, SD 851G.014 / 15.

53. Grew (Tokyo) to Sec. St., 8 Apr. 1939, SD 851G.014 / 15; and Henry (Tokyo) to Bonnet, 5 Apr. 1939, *DDF*, 2e, 15:400. Renzo Sawada, Japan's vice-minister for foreign affairs, rationalized the action on the grounds that France too thoroughly supported Britain's

anti-Japanese policy, thereby reflecting the extremist journalistic influence, Henry believed, upon Japanese policymakers at the foreign ministry.

54. See Annex II to Phipps (Paris) to FO, 15 Mar. 1938, FO 371, 22175, F2965 / 956 / 61.

55. Grew (Tokyo) to Sec. St., 8 Apr. 1939, SD 851G.014 /15.

56. See Phipps (Paris) to FO, 15 Mar. 1938, FO 371, 22175, F2965 / 956 / 61. See also Lee, *Britain and Sino-Japanese War,* 176–77; and Craigie (Tokyo) to FO, 18 Apr. 1939, FO 371, 23567, F5837 / 874 / 23.

57. Memorandum by Hamilton, 11 Apr. 1939, SD 851G.014 / 18; Sec. St. to Japanese Ambassador (Horinouchi), 17 May 1939, *FRUS, Japan: 1931–1941,* 2:280–81; and Georges Bonnet, *Défense de la Paix,* vol. 2, *Fin d'une Europe,* 106.

58. Cosme (Chungking) to Bonnet, 21 Mar. 1939, *DDF,* 2e, 15:137–38; and Koo (Paris) to Foreign Ministry, 4 Apr. 1939, *DDF,* 2e, 15:376–77. On the inadvisability of China's entry, see Bonnet to Corbin (London), 7 Apr. 1939, *DDF,* 2e, 15:500–501; Corbin (London) to Bonnet, 14 Apr. 1939, *DDF,* 2e, 15:648–49; Note de la sous-direction d'Asie-Océanie (Chauvel), 18 Apr. 1939, *DDF,* 2e, 15:704–5; and Bonnet to Cosme (Peking), 24 Apr. 1939, *DDF,* 2e, 15:788.

59. Bonnet to Henry (Tokyo), 10 Feb. and 3 Apr. 1939, *DDF,* 2e, 14:164 and 15:360; Bonnet to Knobel (Shanghai), 20 Feb. 1939, *DDF,* 2e, 14:256–57; Bonnet to Corbin (London), 13 Mar. 1939, *DDF,* 2e, 14:563; and Bullitt (Paris) to Sec. St., 16 Feb. 1939, *FRUS, 1939,* 3:110; see also Peck (Chungking) to Sec. St., 8 Feb. 1939, *FRUS, 1939,* 3:739. One memo circulated through the Foreign Ministry by the political division advocated removing all restrictions on arms transit. Note de la Direction politique, 31 Mar. 1939, *DDF,* 2e, 15:340.

60. Bonnet to Henry (Tokyo), 8 Apr. 1939, *DDF,* 2e, 15:510. For the type and amount of raw materials exported from Indochina to Japan, see Committee of Imperial Defence (Defence Plans [Policy] Sub-Committee), "Situation in the Far East," in FO 371, 20952, F4772 / 9 / 10; and Walsh (Saigon) to FO, 17 Mar. 1939, FO 371, 22921, C4157 / 249 / 17. On the 27 April prohibition, see Walsh (Saigon) to FO, 20 May 1939, FO 371, 22921, C7743 / 249 / 17.

61. Bonnet to Corbin (London), 14 Apr. 1939, *DDF,* 2e, 15:631.

62. Bullitt (Paris) to Sec. St., 18 Apr. 1939, SD 793.94 / 14902; Bullitt (Paris) to Sec. St., 3 May 1939, *FRUS, 1939,* 3:534–35; Memorandum by Moffat, 19 Apr. 1939, *FRUS, 1939,* 3:529–30. The quote is from Ronald (London) to Phipps (Paris), 24 Apr. 1939, FO 371, 23567, F3732 / 982 / 23.

63. A summary of the French note can be found in Memorandum by Welles, 21 July 1939, *FRUS, 1939,* 3:541–43.

64. Neu, *Troubled Encounter,* 161.

65. Lee, *Britain and Sino-Japanese War,* 151; Butow, *Tojo and the Coming of the War,* 120; and Boyle, *China and Japan at War,* 192. For the text of the Japanese statement, see *FRUS, Japan: 1931–1941,* 1:477–81. The policy statement also reflected a tactical change in dealing with the Chinese Nationalists and was not simply directed at the Western powers. See Yoshitake Oka, *Konoe Fumimaro: A Political Biography,* trans. Shumpei Okamoto and Patricia Murray, 79–80.

66. Dallek, *Roosevelt and American Foreign Policy,* 193; William L. Langer and S. Everett Gleason, *The Challenge to Isolation, 1937–1940,* 42–45.

67. Saint-Quentin (Washington) to Bonnet, 6 Nov. 1938, *DDF,* 2e, 12:474–75.

68. Bonnet to Saint-Quentin (Washington), 9 Nov. 1938, *DDF,* 2e, 12:494–96. See also Bonnet, *Fin d'Europe,* 104–5. See also Wilson (Paris) to Sec. St., 10 Nov. 1938, SD 751.62 / 495.

69. Wilson (Paris) to Sec. St., 7 Nov. 1938, *FRUS, 1938,* 3:374–75. French representatives in China were especially strident in their advocacy of a vigorous response to Japan's actions. Guillaume Georges-Picot, chargé d'affairs in Chungking, placed the crisis in a larger context: Western submissiveness in the face of Japanese assertiveness "is in the eyes of the Chinese and all the peoples of the Far East an admission of impotence of the democracies and a tribute to Japanese power" (Georges-Picot [Chungking] to Knobel [Shanghai], 28 Nov. 1938, *DDF,* 2e, 12:839). Emile Naggiar, the well-respected French ambassador in Shanghai, also pressed for a strong defense of the letter as well as the substance of Western rights in the area. He submitted, however, that if the Americans refused to act, then France might be better advised to reach an accommodation with Tokyo by reviving the Franco-Japanese Treaty of 1907, which provided for respecting each other's rights and territory on the Asian continent (Naggiar [Shanghai] to Bonnet, 17 and 25 Nov. 1938, *DDF,* 2e, 12:629–30 and 796–97); and Robert Luc, interview with author, 22 Feb. 1982.

70. Corbin (London) to Bonnet, 11 Nov. 1938, *DDF,* 2e, 12:535–36; Memorandum by Cadogan, 11 Nov. 1938, FO 371, 22144, F12062 / 575 / 10; Lee, *Britain and Sino-Japanese War,* 161–63; and Clifford, *Retreat from China,* 94–96.

71. Chamberlain's hope is from Record of Anglo-French Conversations, 24 Nov. 1938, *DBFP,* 3d ser., 3:308–9. For the Foreign Office report, see Memorandum, 16 Nov. 1939, FO 371, 22176, F12923 / 4727 / 61.

72. Langer and Gleason, *Challenge to Isolation,* 43–44; Clifford, *Retreat from China,* 96; F. C. Jones, *Japan's New Order in East Asia: Its Rise and Fall, 1937–1945,* 138–39; and Craigie (Tokyo) to Japanese Minister for Foreign Affairs, 14 Jan. 1939, *DBFP,* 3d ser., 8:403–5.

73. Saint-Quentin (Washington) to Bonnet, 3 Jan. 1939, *DDF,* 2e, 13:489.

74. Note de la sous-direction d'Asie-Océanie (Chauvel), 9 Jan. 1939, *DDF,* 2e, 13: 584–85.

75. Henry (Tokyo) to Bonnet, 11 Jan. 1939, *DDF,* 2e, 13:604–5; and Bonnet to Henry (Tokyo), 14 Jan. 1939, *DDF,* 2e, 13:650–51. See also *DBFP,* 3d ser., 8:394–96.

76. Samuel Rosenman, ed., *The Public Papers and Addresses of Franklin D. Roosevelt,* 8: 1–4; and Robert A. Divine, *The Reluctant Belligerent: American Entry into World War II,* 56.

77. On the State Department and public opinion, see Saint-Quentin (Washington) to Bonnet, 16 and 25 Dec. 1938, *DDF,* 2e, 13:314–15, 412–13; Saint-Quentin (Washington) to Bonnet, 6 Jan. 1939, *DDF,* 2e, 13:545. See also 516–20, 551.

78. For the debate, see Dallek, *Roosevelt and American Foreign Policy,* 179–92; and Divine, *Reluctant Belligerent,* 56–63.

79. See Dallek, *Roosevelt and American Foreign Policy,* 172–75; and Saint-Quentin (Washington) to Bonnet, 30 Jan. 1939, *DDF,* 2e, 13:825. For more on the Monnet purchasing mission, see Jean Monnet, *Memoirs,* trans. Richard Mayne, 118–23; and John McVickar Haight, Jr., *American Aid to France, 1938–1940,* chap. 4. See also Saint-Quentin (Washington) to Bonnet, 3 Feb. 1939, *DDF,* 2e, 14:46–47.

80. Saint-Quentin (Washington) to Bonnet, 5 Mar. 1939, *DDF,* 2e, 14:473. The French ambassador found some hope a couple of days later, when Roosevelt told the press that the neutrality laws "had not served the cause of peace" and that the United States would be stronger without them. Saint-Quentin (Washington) to Bonnet, 8 Mar. 1939, *DDF,* 2e, 14:512. In fact, Saint-Quentin read far too much into what amounted to a very cautious response by the president to a very leading question. See Rosenman, ed., *Public Papers of Roosevelt,* 18:154–55.

81. Dallek, *Roosevelt and American Foreign Policy,* 184.

82. The battle over the revision of the neutrality legislation can best be followed in Robert A. Divine, *The Illusion of Neutrality,* chap. 8. See also Wayne S. Cole, *Roosevelt and*

the Isolationists, 1932–1945, 312–19; Divine, *Reluctant Belligerent*, 57–63; Dallek, *Roosevelt and American Foreign Policy*, 179–92; and Langer and Gleason, *Challenge to Isolation*, 136–47.

83. Saint-Quentin (Washington) to Bonnet, 17 Mar. 1939, *DDF*, 2e, 15:44; Saint-Quentin (Washington) to Bonnet, 21 Mar. 1939, *DDF*, 2e, 15:142; Bonnet to Saint-Quentin (Washington), 10 Apr. 1939, *DDF*, 2e, 15:524; and Saint-Quentin (Washington) to Bonnet, 10 Apr. 1939, *DDF*, 2e, 15:532–33. The quotations are from Saint-Quentin, 21 Mar., Bonnet, 10 Apr., and Saint-Quentin, 10 Apr., respectively.

84. Peter Lowe, *Great Britain and the Origins of the Pacific War: A Study of British Policy in East Asia, 1937–1941*, 52–62; and Lee, *Britain and Sino-Japanese War*, chap. 6.

85. Ian Hamill, *The Strategic Illusion: The Singapore Strategy and the Defence of Australia and New Zealand, 1919–1942*, 290–98; and N. H. Gibbs, *Grand Strategy*, vol. 1, *Rearmament Policy*, 421–28.

86. For the best discussion of these conversations, see Gibbs, *Grand Strategy*, 1:667–76; and William Gregory Perett, "French Naval Policy and Foreign Affairs, 1930–1939," 407–46. Jean-Baptiste Duroselle has cogently commented that one must "admire the ease with which Gamelin used the terms 'it is necessary,' 'it will be necessary,' without indicating by what means one would realize the goals" (*La Décadence, 1932–1939*, 436).

87. For Daladier's statement to Phipps, see Phipps (Paris) to Halifax, 9 Apr. 1939, *DBFP*, 3d ser., 5:152. Bonnet's statement is cited in Phipps (Paris) to Halifax, 10 Apr. 1939, *DBFP*, 3d ser., 5:160. Perett cites the naval staff paper ("French Naval Policy," 434). Odend'hal's statement appears in Cab 20, vol. 160, AFC (J.) 17, 45. For the best discussion of these conversations, see Gibbs, *Grand Strategy*, 1:667–76; and Perett, "French Naval Policy," 406–46. The conversations can be followed in great detail in Cab 20, which includes reports and notes of the meetings from March through August. See also FO 371, file 281 / 17.

88. Perett, "French Naval Policy," 437. Some delay also resulted from the interest of the British commander-in-chief, Admiral Sir Percy Noble, in having an American warship visit Singapore during the talks to impress the Japanese. Both the Admiralty and the Foreign Office discouraged the proposal for fear of adverse reaction in the United States. See Dankwerts (Admiralty) to FO, 13 June 1939, FO 371, 23549, F5790 / 2742 / 61. For the best study of the Tientsin crisis that erupted on 14 June, see Lee, *Britain and Sino-Japanese War*, 174–204.

89. The Report of the Franco-British Staff Conversations at Singapore is in FO 371, 23549, F7285 / 2742 / 61. A summary can be found in Gibbs, *Grand Strategy*, 1:429–30. See also Duroselle, *La Décadence*, 466–67, and Jean Decoux, *A la barre de l'Indochine: Histoire de mon Gouvernement Général (1940–1945)*. The participants devoted considerable attention to the importance of maintaining Thailand's neutrality in the event of war with Japan because of its strategic importance in the area.

90. In July, Britain did decide to send air and ground reinforcements to Singapore (Lee, *Britain and Sino-Japanese War*, 171).

91. Phipps (Paris) to Halifax, 16 and 17 June 1939, *DBFP*, 3d ser., 9:192–93 contains Bonnet's concerns. Bührer is quoted in Adamthwaite, *France and the Coming of the Second World War*, 329.

92. Wilson (Paris) to Sec. St., 16 Nov. 1938, *FRUS, 1938*, 3:610.

93. Jean Chauvel, *Commentaire*, 1:44, 51.

94. Note de la sous-direction de la SDN, 14 July 1937, *DDF*, 2e, 6:382. Shortly after the outbreak of fighting in China, Ambassador Bullitt reported, "The French Government faced by its troubles in Europe is somewhat loath to take any active part with regard to matters in the Far East" (Bullitt [Paris] to Sec. St., 13 July 1937, *FRUS, 1937*, 3:153).

95. The "European preoccupation of France" frequently surfaced during the meetings at Geneva. See, for example, U.K. Delegation (Geneva) to FO, 28 Jan. 1938, FO 371, 22101, F1215 / 78 / 10. For Léger's statements, see Wilson (Paris) to Sec. St., 16 Oct. 1937, SD 852.00 / 6636. The issue of fascism is in Memorandum of Conversation (Brussels), 10 Nov. 1937, Davis Papers, container 5, folder Nine Power Conference. Delbos's remarks to Phipps are reflected in Phipps (Paris) to FO, 20 Jan. 1938, FO 371, 22106, F811 / 84 / 10.

96. Bullitt (Paris) to Sec. St., *FRUS, 1939*, 3:698.

97. Bullitt (Paris) to Sec. St., 5 Jan. 1938, *FRUS, 1938*, 3:5. As Daladier indicated to Bullitt, neither France nor England had sufficient forces to "distribute them over the earth." Therefore, it was necessary to concentrate their forces in Europe and to "sacrifice whatever it might be necessary to sacrifice in the Far East" (Bullitt [Paris] to Sec. St., 13 Feb. 1939, SD 851.248 / 139).

98. See Naggiar (Peking) to Delbos, 17 July 1937, *DDF*, 2e, 6:419, for an expression of this concern. See also Davies (Moscow) to Sec. St., 25 Oct. 1937, SD 793.94 / 11400.

99. See, for example, Mandel's concern in Bullitt (Paris) to Sec. St., 15 Sept. 1938, *FRUS, 1938*, 3:290.

100. Many observers in the Far East, upon reflection, believed that the Japanese actions had probably been planned for some time and were not necessarily related to the Czech crisis, although it was undoubtedly useful to them. See, for example, Johnson (Chungking) to Sec. St., 27 Oct. 1938, SD 793.94 / 14216; and Grew (Tokyo) to Sec. St., 28 Oct. 1938, *FRUS, 1938*, 3:347–48.

101. Campbell (Paris) to FO, 17 Aug. 1939, FO 371, 23531, F9075 / 6457 / 10.

102. For issues surrounding the effect of the Anti-Comintern Pact, see *DDF*, 2e, 13, no. 28; 14, nos. 127, 279; 15, no. 61; and FO 371, file 456. On the specific issue of the Japanese and the Russians, the Japanese warned several times that if the Western powers concluded an alliance with the Soviet Union, Japan would have to reconsider her position with regard to her relations with Germany and Italy. See Craigie (Tokyo) to FO, 30 Mar. 1939, FO 371, C4445 / 421 / 63; and Grew (Tokyo) to Sec. St., 18 May 1939, *FRUS, Japan: 1939–1941*, 2:2.

103. Grew (Tokyo) to Sec. St., 16 May 1939, *FRUS, 1939*, 3:38; and Bullitt (Paris) to Sec. St., 23 May 1939, *FRUS, 1939*, 3:38–39.

104. Chauvel is quoted in Campbell (Paris) to FO, 10 Aug. 1939, FO 371, 23530, F8729 / 6457 / 10. Chauvel was one who believed that Japan's threat to reconsider its relations with Germany might have been a bluff. Campbell (Paris) to FO, 11 Aug. 1939, FO 371, 23530, F8821 / 6457 / 10. The whole Far Eastern situation was complicated during the summer of 1939 by a crisis between Japan and the Western powers concerning the Tientsin concessions. See Lee, *Britain and Sino-Japanese War*, chap. 7.

105. Bonnet to Corbin (London), 26 Aug. 1939, *DDF*, 2e, 19:23. See also Bonnet to Henry (Tokyo), 27 Aug. 1939, *DDF*, 2e, 19:63.

106. Phipps (Paris) to FO, 25 and 28 Aug. 1939, FO 371, 23562, F9450, F9599 / 456 / 23.

107. See FO Minutes on Phipps (Paris) to FO, 25 Aug. 1939, FO 371, 23562, F9450 / 456 / 23. See also Note de la sous-direction d'Asie, 28 Aug. 1939, *DDF*, 2e, 19:132.

108. The Wonderland analogy is from a minute by Ronald on Campbell (Paris) to Sargent (London), 11 Aug. 1938, FO 371, 21592, C8578 / 13 / 17. Pratt's hunting imagery is in a minute by Sir John Pratt, 20 Dec. 1937, FO 371, 20961, F11289 / 9 / 10.

7. Policy Adrift: September 1939–June 1940

1. Dooman (Tokyo) to Sec. St., 12 Sept. 1939, *FRUS, 1939*, 3:68–69. Alexis Léger suggested to the British on 2 September, on the eve of the French declaration of war in

Europe, that the time might be right for a joint démarche to Japan, perhaps leading to a Western mediation of the Sino-Japanese war and a warming of Western relations with Japan. The British responded negatively, correctly surmising that Japan would probably follow an independent policy regarding China. Moreover, such a Franco-British approach, which might be interpreted as abandoning China, risked the loss of American goodwill, "which is at least as necessary to us in the Far East as it is in Europe." See Phipps (Paris) to FO, 3 Sept. 1939, and FO to Phipps, 5 Sept. 1939, FO 371, 23444, F9790 / 69 / 10.

2. Crowley, "New Deal for Japan and Asia," 256; Craigie (Tokyo) to FO, 5 Sept. 1939, FO 371, 23562, F9932 / 456 / 23; and Dooman (Tokyo) to Sec. St., 12 Sept. 1939, *FRUS, 1939*, 3:64–69.

3. Crowley, "New Deal for Japan and Asia," 256; and Hata Ikuhiko, "The Japanese-Soviet Confrontation, 1935–1939," in *Deterrent Diplomacy: Japan, Germany, and the USSR, 1935–1940*, ed. James William Morley, 129–77; see *FRUS, 1939*, 3:558–76 for the text and discussion of the American notice to terminate the treaty of 1911.

4. Iriye, *Across the Pacific*, 207–8.

5. Quoted in Dooman (Tokyo) to Sec. St., 5 Sept. 1939, *FRUS: Japan, 1931–1941*, 2:9. See also Hull, *Memoirs*, 1:718.

6. Craigie (Tokyo) to FO, 6 Sept. 1939, FO 371, 23460, F9869 / 82 / 10; Minute by Dening on Ashley Clark memorandum, 14 Sept. 1939, FO371, 23558, F10176 / 347 / 23; Minute by Brenan, 14 Sept. 1939, FO 371, 23460, F10193 / 87 / 10. Brenan recommended that Washington be informed that Britain intended to withdraw its troops from North China immediately "unless assured of effective American support in keeping them there." See also Sir Llewellyn Woodward, *British Foreign Policy in the Second World War*, 2:88.

7. Hull, *Memoirs*, 1:719. See also Hull memorandum, 7 Sept. 1939, *FRUS: Japan, 1931–1941*, 2:12–14. On the Japanese response, see Langer and Gleason, *Challenge to Isolation*, 297.

8. Bullitt (Paris) to Sec. St., 11 Sept. 1939, SD 79394 / 15369. The British had more realistically emphasized that a clash between Western and Japanese forces in the Tientsin area might be imminent and that no real support could be expected from the United States in that area, which had no American interests.

9. Phipps (Paris) to FO, 11 Sept. 1939, FO 371, 23460, F10109 / 87 / 10. In Paris, apparently Ambassador Bullitt actively encouraged such an approach to the State Department. Phipps to FO, 13 Sept. 1939, FO 371, 23460, F10151 / 87 / 10. R. V. Howe of the British Foreign Office agreed that it would be worthwhile to "force the U.S. Govt. [*sic*] into the open," but he was far less optimistic than the French about the possibility of any practical support from Washington. See Howe's minute on Phipps's dispatch. Dening caustically commented, "It is a pity that the French cannot rid themselves of the idea that we can buy Japan off, and 'come to an understanding.' We have nothing to offer which is ours to give. Japan on the other hand has much that she can take without asking our permission, and in the last resort it is only America which can make her pause" (Minute by Dening on Ashley Clark minute, 14 Sept. 1939, FO 371, 23558, F10176 / 347 / 23).

10. Halifax to Craigie (Tokyo), 15 Sept. 1939, FO 371, 23460, F10109 / 87 / 10; and Halifax to Phipps (Paris), 16 Sept. 1939, FO 371, 23460, F10133 / 87 / 10.

11. Halifax to Phipps (Paris), 16 Sept. 1939, FO 371, 23460, F10133 / 87 / 10.

12. French aide-mémoire, 20 Sept. 1939, Hull Papers, container 58. See also Léger to Phipps, 17 Sept. 1939, FO 371, 23460, F10257 / 87 / 10. The French note added that France would make it clear to Japan that the French withdrawal would be for purely military—and only temporary—reasons. France did not intend to surrender its treaty rights in the area.

13. Lothian (Washington) to FO, 16 Sept. 1939, FO 371, 23460, F10246 / 87 / 10. Dening at the Foreign Office argued that it would be wiser to make "a dignified and orderly

withdrawal for reasons of our own" rather than be forced "to beat a hurried and undignified retreat." See Dening's minute on Lothian's dispatch.

14. See Hull, memorandum, 15 Sept. 1939, *FRUS: Japan, 1931–1941*, 2:15–19; Hull, *Memoirs*, 1:721; and Hornbeck and State Department memorandum to French Embassy, 27 Sept. 1939, *FRUS, 1939*, 3:266–67.

15. Bullitt (Paris) to Sec. St., 30 Sept. 1939, *FRUS, 1939, 3:272*.

16. For Léger's argument, see Bullitt (Paris) to Sec. St., 20 Oct. 1939, *FRUS, 1939, 3:294*. For Chauvel's, see Phipps (Paris) to FO, 30 Sept. 1939, FO 371, 23461, F10598 / 87 / 10.

17. British Embassy to Department of State, 20 Oct. 1939, *FRUS, 1939*, 3:291–92; see Bullitt (Paris) to Sec. St., 14 Nov. 1939, *FRUS, 1939*, 3:318; Campbell (Paris) to FO, 24 Oct. 1939, FO 371, 23461, F11237 / 87 / 10; and Levy et al., *French Interests*, 141.

18. Bullitt (Paris) to Sec. St., 14 Nov. 1939, *FRUS, 1939*, 3:318–19. Ambassador Henry in Tokyo affirmed that the policy of his government was to go very "softly" with Japan. It could not afford to do anything else (Grew Papers, 16 Oct. 1939, Conversations: vol. 5, 1939–1940).

19. For Léger's attitude, see Campbell (Paris) to Howe (FO), 16 Nov. 1939, FO 371, 23462, F11986 / 87 / 10. The confused situation at Haiphong and the French orders can best be followed in Reed (Hanoi) to Sec. St., 3 Oct. 1939, *FRUS, 1939*, 3:272–75; Reed (Hanoi) to Sec. St., 22 and 27 Oct. 1939, SD 851G.1561 / 7 and 893.24 / 652; Meyer (Yunnanfu) to Sec. St., 20 Oct. 1939, SD 893.24 / 632; and Hornbeck memorandum, 9 Oct. 1939, *FRUS, 1939*, 3:762. One notable example of such Chinese bungling occurred at the Foo Shing assembly plant, where trucks were assembled for transshipment. Because of a disinclination to keep track of the large number of accessories, 400 steel cab bodies were simply mislaid and were found only after weeks of searching (Reed [Hanoi] to Sec. St., 22 Oct. 1939, SD 851G.1561 / 7).

20. Hornbeck, memorandum, 9 Oct. 1939, *FRUS, 1939*, 3:762. See Hull-Bullitt (Paris) correspondence, 9–14 Sept. 1939, *FRUS, 1939*, 3:757–59.

21. Bullitt (Paris) to Sec. St., 14 Sept. 1939, *FRUS, 1939*, 3:759.

22. Quoted in Crowley, "New Deal for Japan and Asia," 256. Earlier, on 20 October, the Japanese foreign minister had made a statement undoubtedly directed at Paris and London: "The Japanese resolve for this new order is . . . a thing of iron which nothing can shake. . . . The key to the adjustment in the relations with Britain and France is the full understanding by them of the design" (quoted in Craigie [Tokyo] to FO, 21 Oct. 1939, FO 371, 23562, F11161 / 456 / 23).

23. For the text of the Japanese note, see Nomura to Henry, 30 Nov. 1939, FO 371, 24673, F955 / 57 / 10; and Grew (Tokyo) to Sec. St., 20 Dec. 1939, SD 751.94/93. A summary is included in Bullitt (Paris) to Sec. St., 13 Dec. 1939, *FRUS, 1939*, 3:769–72.

24. The French response is contained in Grew (Tokyo) to Sec. St., 20 Dec. 1939, SD 751.94 / 93. See also Bullitt (Paris) to Sec. St., 13 Dec. 1939, *FRUS, 1939*, 3:769–72; and Craigie (Tokyo) to FO, 28 Dec. 1939, FO 371, 23462, F13084 / 87 / 10. Chauvel also issued a public statement that the Japanese charge about the "transit via Indo-China of arms, ammunition, and war supplies destined for China is false." Quoted in Bullitt (Paris) to Sec. St., 4 Dec. 1939, *FRUS, 1939*, 3:768.

25. See Grew (Tokyo) to Sec. St., 20 Dec. 1939, SD 751.94 / 93.

26. Bullitt (Paris) to Sec. St., 13 Dec. 1939, *FRUS, 1939*, 3:771.

27. See Sec. St. to Bullitt (Paris), 2 Dec. 1939, *FRUS, 1939*, 3:717; Johnson (Chungking) to Sec. St., 8 and 27 Dec. 1939, *FRUS, 1939*, 3:327–28 and 718–19; Bullitt (Paris)

to Sec. St., 30 Nov. 1939, *FRUS, 1939,* 3:716; and Cabinet Conclusions, 9 Dec. 1939, Cab 66, WP(39)152, p. 16.

28. Bullitt (Paris) to Sec. St., 30 Nov. 1939, *FRUS, 1939,* 3:716; and Bullitt (Paris) to Sec. St., 1 Dec. 1939, *FRUS, 1939,* 3:90–91.

29. In fact, it was rumored that in order to offset the loss of the Nanning route, the French might be willing to pour as much as 80 million francs into the expansion of railway facilities and 16 million francs into the construction of a new road from Haiphong to Laokay, the point at which the railway crossed into China. Peck (Chungking) to Sec. St., 3 Dec. 1939, *FRUS 1939,* 3:767; and Johnson (Chungking) to Sec. St., 8 Dec. 1939, *FRUS, 1939,* 3:328. No evidence has been found to suggest that these projects were actually initiated. Indeed, it is improbable that France, with its budget already strained by the war in Europe, would commit such resources to Indochina.

30. For accounts of these attacks, see Greenway (Shanghai) to FO, 5 and 9 Jan. 1940, FO 371, 24672, F175 / F310 / 51 / 10; and Davidson (Kunming), 1 and 3 Feb. 1940, FO 371, 24672, F753 / F813 / 51 / 10.

31. Grant (Air Ministry) to FO, 16 Mar. 1940, FO 371, 24319, C4263 / 166 / 17. One observer described the general Japanese attitude toward foreign interests in the following manner: "I am engaged in robbing my neighbor and burning his house; naturally I couldn't help looting and destroying the contents of the room you have rented in the house: it is most unreasonable of you to complain." See Ashley Clarke minute on Craigie (Tokyo) to FO, 7 Feb. 1941, FO 371, 27908, F627 / 86 / 23.

32. For the Japanese note, see attachment to Ashley Clarke, memorandum, 18 Jan. 1940, FO 371, 24666, F459 / 43 / 10. See also Bullitt (Paris) to Sec. St., 15 Jan. 1940, *FRUS, 1940,* 4:262–63.

33. Bullitt (Paris) to Sec. St., 15 Jan. 1940, *FRUS, 1940,* 4:263–65.

34. Hull to Grew (Tokyo), 27 Jan. 1940, *FRUS, 1940,* 4:279; and Hornbeck, memorandum, 20 Jan. 1940, *FRUS, 1940,* 4:268–69.

35. Ashley Clarke, memorandum, 6 Feb. 1940, FO 371, 24666, F873 / 43 / 10.

36. Jonathon G. Utley, *Going to War with Japan, 1937–1941,* 76–79; John E. Wiltz, *From Isolation to War, 1931–1941,* 105; Cole, *Roosevelt and Isolationists,* 346–54; and Langer and Gleason, *Challenge to Isolation,* 577–78. See also Clifford, *Retreat from China,* 135.

37. Ashley Clarke, memorandum, 12 Feb. 1940, FO 371, 24672, F1151 / 51 / 10; and Campbell (Paris) to FO, 9 Feb. 1940, FO 371, 24672, F1050 / 51 / 10.

38. Ashley Clarke, memorandum, 21 Feb. 1940, FO 371, 24672, F1300 / 51 / 10.

39. Campbell (Paris) to FO, 9 Feb. 1940, F0 371, 24672 / F1050 / 51 / 10.

40. Levy et al., *French Interests,* 142, and Grew Papers, 9 May 1940, Conversations: vol. 5, 1939–1940. See also Grew (Tokyo) to Sec. St., 28 Jan. 1940, *FRUS, 1940,* 4:280, for an earlier view of Japanese concern about such obstructions.

41. For the best summaries of the Japanese démarche and French response, see Campbell (Paris) to FO, 27 Feb. 1940, FO 371, 24672, F1442 / 51 / 10; and Ashley Clarke, memorandum, 29 Feb. 1940, FO 371, 24672, F1459 / 51 / 10.

42. Memorandum of conversation with Roché by Ashley Clarke, 8 Mar. 1940, FO 371, 24673, F1749 / 57 / 10.

43. Bullitt (Paris) to Sec. St., 3 May 1940, *FRUS, 1940,* 4:320.

44. On the one-month agreement, see Campbell (Paris) to FO, 22 Apr. 1940, FO 371, 24325, C6065 / 6065 / 17. On the French-Japanese-Soviet matters, see Bullitt (Paris) to Sec. St., 12 Apr. 1940, SD 740.0011 / European War 1939 / 2167; and Grew Papers, 9 May 1940, Conversations: vol. 5, 1939–1940.

45. See Ashley Clarke, memorandum of conversation with Roché, 10 Apr. 1940, FO 371, 24651, F2540 / 5 / 10. Craigie (Tokyo) to FO, 13 Apr. 1940, FO 371, 24651, F2733 / 5 / 10; Campbell (Paris) to FO, 14 Apr. 1940, 24651, F2730 / 5 / 10; and Brenan's minute on Craigie to FO, 29 Apr. 1940, FO 371, 24651, F3033 / 5 / 10.

46. Mandel revealed his thoughts to Georges Catroux at a meeting between the two men before the latter departed Paris to assume his post as governor-general of Indochina in August 1939 (Georges Catroux, *Deux actes du drame Indochinois: Hanoi: Juin 1940–Dien Bien Phu: Mars–Mai 1954*, 6–8).

47. Phipps (Paris) to FO, 22 Oct. 1939, FO 371, 22932, C17126 / 797 / 17; Phipps (Paris) to FO, 19 May 1938, FO 371, 21595, C4643 / 36 / 17; and General Maurice Gamelin, *Servir*, vol. 3, *La Guerre (September 1939–19 Mai 1940)*, 476.

48. John M. Sherwood, *Georges Mandel and the Third Republic*, 219–20.

49. Levy et al., *French Interests*, 137–38; Ellen Joy Hammer, *The Struggle for Indochina, 1940–1955*, 15–16; and Phipps (Paris) to FO, 22 Oct. 1939, FO 371, 22932, C17126 / 797 / 17.

50. Paul Auphan and Jacques Mordal, *The French Navy in World War II*, 22, 31, 194 (the Churchill quotation appears on 30), and Henri La Masson, *The French Navy*, 1:40. Not considered one of the plums of the French navy, the Far Eastern command had been turned down by others before Decoux accepted it in January 1939.

51. Hammer (*Struggle for Indochina*, 16) cites the French general's estimates. On inter-Allied planning, see Walsh (Saigon) to FO, 10 Jan. 1940, FO 371, 24319, C1064 / 166 / 17; and Clauson (FO) to Strang (FO), 6 Mar. 1940, FO 371, 24325, C3771 / 3652 / 17; and Harvey (Paris) to FO, 21 Mar. 1940, 24325, C4456 / 3652 / 17. Bührer's praise of Mandel is quoted in Sherwood (*Mandel*, 221). *Le Petit Parisien* paid tribute to Mandel's efforts by stating that he, "at a time when many talked without acting, had acted without talking" (quoted in Phipps [Paris] to FO, 22 Oct. 1939, FO 371, 22932, C17126 / 797 / 17).

52. Some observers even believed that prior to the conclusion of the Nazi-Soviet Pact a military revolt might have occurred if the government had failed to align itself more closely with Berlin. See Private Papers of Lord Inverchapel (Sir Archibald Clark Kerr), FO 800, 2, 39 / 35, 201, Public Record Office.

53. Hosoya Chihiro, "The Tripartite Pact, 1939–1940," in *Deterrent Diplomacy: Japan, Germany, and the USSR, 1935–1940*, 191–95; and Hosoya Chihiro, "The Japanese-Soviet Neutrality Pact," in *The Fateful Choice: Japan's Advance into Southeast Asia, 1939–1941*, ed. James William Morley, 19–30; and Arnold Toynbee and Virginia M. Toynbee, eds., *The Initial Triumph of the Axis*, 566.

54. Akira Iriye, "Japan's Policies toward the United States," in *Japan's Foreign Policy, 1868–1941: A Research Guide*, ed. James William Morley, 452.

55. Akira Iriye persuasively argues that it is misleading to view Japan's road to the Pacific War as though it were a straight line, reflecting a logically determined decision by its leaders. See "Japan's Policies," 456.

56. See, for example, Ashley Clarke, memorandum of conversation with Louis Roché of the French Embassy in London, 14 Sept. 1939, FO 371, 23558, F10176 / 347 / 23.

57. *Le Temps*, 7 Feb. 1940. On Daladier's statements, see Campbell (Paris) to FO, 2 Mar. 1940, FO 371, 24672, F1538 / 51 / 10; Murphy (Paris) to Sec. St., 27 Mar. 1940, *FRUS, 1940*, 4:302–5; and Levy et al., *French Interests*, 143.

58. On Daladier's focus, see Murphy (Paris) to Sec. St., 27 Mar. 1940, *FRUS, 1940*, 4:303. On Chauvel, see Bullitt (Paris) to Sec. St., 1 Dec. 1939, *FRUS, 1939*, 3:90. On another occasion, Chauvel lamented that almost nobody in Paris knew anything about the Far East and that those who believed that they knew the situation displayed only a superficial knowledge and advocated impractical solutions. Bullitt (Paris) to Sec., St., 28 Nov. 1939, *FRUS, 1939*, 3:88.

59. See Grew (Tokyo) to Sec. St., 31 Oct. 1939, *FRUS, 1939*, 3:307; and Grew Papers, 16 Oct. 1939, Conversations: vol. 5, 1939–1940.

8. BOWING TO THE FORCE MAJEURE: JAPAN'S ADVANCE INTO INDOCHINA

1. As General Shunroka Hata, the Japanese war minister, and a moderate in military circles, declared, "We should not miss the present opportunity or we shall be blamed by posterity" (quoted in Langer and Gleason, *Challenge to Isolation*, 603).

2. By establishing air bases in Indochina, the Japanese would also bring themselves within striking distance of the newly completed Burma Road, the only other significant supply route for Chiang Kai-shek's forces.

3. It must have given Tani particular satisfaction to issue such a statement. A notorious Francophobe, he had only a few months earlier been refused by the French government when he sought official reception as Japan's ambassador to Paris.

4. International Military Tribunal for the Far East (hereafter cited as IMTFE), 6713. See also Levy et al., *French Interests*, 150–51; Jones, *Japan's New Order*, 221; and Toynbee and Toynbee, *Initial Triumph of the Axis*, 583. To add force to their demands, the Japanese began moving their army in China's Kwangsi province into position along the Indochinese border. Units of the Japanese navy were dispatched to maneuver in the Gulf of Tonkin.

5. Craigie (Tokyo) to FO, 21 June 1940, FO 371, 24719, F3429 / 3429 / 61. See also memorandum of conversation between Saint-Quentin and Stanley Hornbeck (Adviser on Political Relations), 20 June 1940, *FRUS, 1940*, 4:29; Georges Catroux, *New York Times*, 2 Aug. 1945, and Catroux, *Deux actes du drame Indochinois*, 58.

6. "Catroux Defends Indochina Regime," *New York Times*, 7. No State Department memorandum concerning this conversation has ever been found, but other documentation confirms its substance. See the record of a conversation between Saint-Quentin and Hornbeck on the following day, 20 June, in *FRUS, 1940*, 4:29. See also Paul Baudouin, *The Private Diaries of Paul Baudouin*, trans. Sir Charles Petrie, 146; François Charles-Roux, *Cinq mois tragiques au affaires étrangères (21 mai–1 novembre 1940)*, 71; Jean Chauvel, *Commentaire*, 1:232; Langer and Gleason, *Challenge to Isolation*, 598; Reed (Hanoi) to Sec. St., 17 June 1940, *FRUS, 1940*, 4:25–26; and Catroux, *Deux actes du drame Indochinois*, 54–55.

7. Hornbeck, memorandum, 20 June 1940, *FRUS, 1940*, 4:29; and Catroux, *Deux actes du drame Indochinois*, 55.

8. "Catroux Defends," *New York Times*, 2 Aug. 1945, and FO to Consul General (Saigon), 29 June 1940, FO 371, 24328, C7405 / 7327 / 17.

9. See B. E. F. Gage, FO memorandum, 19 July 1940, FO 371, 24719, F3526 / 3429 / 61. At a meeting on the twenty-seventh with Admiral Sir Percy Noble, commander-in-chief of Britain's Far Eastern forces, Decoux became convinced that British naval forces would not be sent to defend Indochina. Catroux, *Deux actes du drame Indochinois*, 70.

10. Quoted in note from Francefort (Free French Mission in London) to FO, 17 June 1944, FO 371, 41723, F2894 / 66 / 61.

11. Catroux indicated that all freight shipped to China would be prohibited and that he would agree to the establishment of a Japanese control commission provided that it operated in a "discreet" manner. Grew (Tokyo) to Sec. St., 20 June 1940, *FRUS, 1940*, 4:31; and Catroux, *Deux actes du drame Indochinois*, 58–61.

12. "Catroux Defends," *New York Times*. The letter is quoted in Adrienne Doris Hytier, *Two Years of French Foreign Policy, Vichy, 1940–1942*, 215. For other rationalizations sent to his superiors, see Catroux, *Deux actes du drame Indochinois*, 62–66.

13. Baudouin, *Private Diaries*, 146; Jean Decoux, *A la barre de l'Indochine: Histoire de mon Gouvernement Général (1940–1945)*, 66. Catroux's independence had become increasingly obvious. In a series of telegrams sent to Vichy after 20 June, he petulantly asserted his need to be "free to judge and to act."

14. See Decoux, *A la barre de l'Indochine*, 55–58; and Gage, memorandum, 19 July 1940, FO 371, 24719, F356 / 3429 / 61.

15. For more on this, see Chauvel, *Commentaire*, 1:230–31; and Biddle (Bordeaux) to Sec. St., 20 June 1940, *FRUS, 1940*, 4:30. Chauvel surmised that dispatches between Catroux and de Gaulle may have been intercepted. But more likely, Catroux's tendency to seize the bit worried Rivière that such a decree would be "interpreted as an encouragement to dissidence."

16. For discussions of the nature and depth of Anglophobia in France at the time of its defeat, see Samuel M. Osgood, "Le mythe de 'la perfide Albion' en France, 1919–1940," 18–20; and P. M. H. Bell, "The Breakdown of the Alliance in 1940," in *Troubled Neighbors: Franco-British Relations in the Twentieth Century*, ed. Neville Waites, 200–227.

17. See Charles de Gaulle, *The Complete War Memoirs of Charles de Gaulle*, 83–84.

18. Quoted in Henderson (Saigon) to FO, 20 June 1940, FO 371, 24327, C7343 / 7327 / 17.

19. Catroux is quoted from Henderson (Saigon) to FO, 27 June 1940, FO 371, 24328, C7405 / 7327 / 17. The following day, 28 June, Catroux further revealed his attitude when he met with Admiral Noble. He indicated that he planned to obey outwardly the orders of the Pétain government, while still seeking British support. See Noble to Admiralty, 28 June 1940, FO 371, 24328, C7405 / 7327 / 17. For the meeting with Noble, see also Decoux, *A la barre de l'Indochine*, 42–48; Charles-Roux, *Cinq mois*, 72.

20. Quoted in Hammer, *Struggle for Indochina*, 18. For an opposite viewpoint, see Maurice Martin du Gard, *La Carte Impériale: Histoire de la France outre-mer, 1940–1945*, 420.

21. FO to Henderson (Saigon), 29 June 1940, FO 371, 24328, C7405 / 7327 / 17. Admiral Noble reported that Catroux seemed encouraged by the British promises of aid, but Noble doubted whether the governor-general would be able to resist pressure from Pétain's government. See also Gage memorandum, 19 July 1940, FO 371, 24719, F3526 / 3429 / 61.

22. On this early response, see Henderson (Saigon) to FO, 20 June 1940, FO 371, 24327, C7343 / C7380 / 7327 / 17. Hammer (*Struggle for Indochina*, 19) describes the political loyalties. Furthermore, by 10 July, it was reported that morale among military officers had deteriorated badly and that defeatism was rampant because of the inertia caused by the Catroux-Decoux controversy. See minute by Gage, 19 July 1940, FO 371, 24719, F3526 / 3429 / 61. It was also rumored that Catroux feared reprisals against his family in France if he did not resign. It seems unlikely, however, that this kind of pressure could have influenced him too much, considering his subsequent allegiance to de Gaulle's movement and the fact that his son had already left for London.

23. Catroux (Cairo) to de Schompre (Singapore) through Lampson (Cairo) to FO, 24 Dec. 1940, FO 371, 24722, F5739 / 3429 / 61. See also Lampson (Cairo) to FO, 26 Nov. 1940, FO 371, 24721, F5402 / 3429 / 61. Apparently, de Schompre, headquartered at Singapore as de Gaulle's representative in the Far East, later advocated an insurrection against Decoux's pro-Vichy regime. Catroux torpedoed the idea.

24. Minute by Dening on Craigie (Tokyo) to FO, 2 Sept. 1940, FO 371, 24719, F4126 / 3429 / 61. From Tokyo, the British ambassador, Sir Robert Craigie, urged that everything possible be done to prevent an uprising in favor of the French National Committee in London.

25. As one British official put it, "We should all naturally prefer that General de Gaulle should keep quiet about Indo-China" (Minute by J. C. Sterndale Bennett, 20 Dec. 1940, FO 371, 24723, F5616 / 3429 / 61). At the end of the year, the British Far Eastern Committee reported that it had been preoccupied with the problem of encouraging resistance to further Japanese encroachments. "In Indo-China this has meant refraining from any subversive movement in favor of de Gaulle in the hope that either the constituted authorities or the army independently would feel strong enough to withstand Japanese demands." War Cabinet, W.P. (40)484, 18 Dec. 1940, "Report by the Far Eastern Committee," in FO 371, 24711, F5683 / 143 / 61.

26. Quoted in Levy et al., French Interests, 155.

27. "Catroux Defends," New York Times; and Decoux, A la barre de l'Indochine, 68–71.

28. IMTFE, 6886, 6713–14. See also Baudouin, Private Diaries, 187; and Charles-Roux, Cinq mois, 250. On the following day, Colonel Naotake Sato, Nishihara's subordinate and temporary replacement, made similar demands to Decoux. This action was probably not coordinated with Tokyo, for later reports say that upon his return on 10 August, Nishihara quickly banished the impetuous Sato back to the Canton Army. It is conceivable that intramilitary politics may have led Sato to attempt to undercut his superior and garner some glory for himself. In any event, Decoux put him off by indicating that he would have to refer such matters to Vichy. Some analysts believe that Tokyo was interested in dealing directly with Vichy in any case. See Jones, Japan's New Order, 225. See also Decoux, A la barre de l'Indochine, 94–95; and Francefort (London) to FO, 17 June 1944, FO 371, 41723, F2844 / 66 / 61.

29. Baudouin, Private Diaries, 187–88. Baudouin also suggested that it was the form rather than the substance of the Japanese demands to which the French government objected.

30. Chauvel, Commentaire, 1:238–39.

31. Ibid., 236; Baudouin, Private Diaries, 199–200; Henry Lémery, D'Une République à l'autre: Souvenirs de la melée politique, 1894–1944, 253–58.

32. Bührer's basic arguments were put forth in a memorandum that he submitted to Pétain on 7 August. He believed that Japan's long war in China had revealed serious weaknesses in the Japanese military. In an area that favored the defense, the French army would equal what Japan could muster for an invasion. Moreover, he still hoped for, indeed, anticipated, American and especially British intervention. General X [Jules Bührer], Aux heures tragiques de l'Empire, 1938–1941, 262–65. Decoux is from A la barre de l'Indochine, 98.

33. Robert Murphy, Diplomat Among Warriors, 75.

34. Baudouin, Private Diaries, 200. See also Chauvel, Commentaire, 1:239.

35. Charles-Roux, Cinq mois, 251–52; and Dunn (Adviser on Political Relations) to Welles, 6 Aug. 1940, FRUS, 1940, 4:64–65.

36. Baudouin, Private Diaries, 199–201.

37. Charles-Roux, Cinq mois, 254; see also Toynbee and Toynbee, Initial Triumph of the Axis, 615.

38. Baudouin, Private Diaries, 203.

39. Charles-Roux, Cinq mois, 254; and Murphy (Vichy) to Sec. St., 17 Aug. 1940, FRUS, 1940, 4:80–81.

40. Shortly after sending the new instructions to Henry, Baudouin called Murphy to inform him of the French action and to point out that the temporary nature of the Japanese occupation could be better insured if the United States would make a démarche to that effect in Tokyo. See Baudouin, Private Diaries, 204–5; and Murphy (Vichy) to Sec. St., 17 Aug. 1940, FRUS, 1940, 4:80–81.

41. Charles-Roux, *Cinq mois*, 254–55 (the quotation is from 255); and Grew (Tokyo) to Sec. St., 7 Aug. 1940, *FRUS, 1940*, 4:68. See also Baudouin, *Private Diaries*, 204.

42. Charles-Roux, *Cinq mois*, 255–56 (Welles is quoted on 255). See also Langer and Gleason, *Undeclared War*, 12.

43. Charles-Roux, *Cinq mois*, 257. Charles-Roux generally supported Baudouin's viewpoint, cognizant that Indochina was incapable of resisting a determined Japanese attack by itself. For more on Henry's anxiety, see a French Intelligence estimate of the negotiations as included in Spagent (Shanghai) to Morgenthau (Sec. of Treasury), Morgenthau Diaries, Book 308, FDR Library, Hyde Park, New York.

44. Tokyo sought to have Germany put pressure on Vichy to accede to Japan's demands. But, unwilling to offer the quid pro quo of a tripartite pact sought by the Germans, Tokyo found Berlin inclined to lend only lukewarm support for its demands. See Presseisen, *Germany and Japan*, 256; and Jones, *Japan's New Order*, 227.

45. Baudouin, *Private Diaries*, 218–20. Decoux and General Martin were confident that they could resist a Japanese attack. Martin had the distinct impression that the Japanese army, in position along the Indochinese frontier, wanted to create an incident that would have halted the negotiations entirely. See General Martin's testimony in *Procès du Maréchal Pétain*, 277; and Decoux, *A la barre de l'Indochine*, 101–2.

46. IMTFE, 6396–99; Baudouin, *Private Diaries*, 223–24; and Charles-Roux, *Cinq mois*, 258.

47. See Spagent (Shanghai) to Morgenthau (Sec. of Treasury), 21 Sept. 1940, Morgenthau Diaries, Box 308. See also Decoux, *A la barre de l'Indochine*, 103.

48. Testimony of General Martin, *Procès de Pétain*, 277; and Decoux, *A la barre de l'Indochine*, 103, 107–8; and Baudouin, *Private Diaries*, 235.

49. Hull to Grew (Tokyo), 3 Sept. 1940, *FRUS: Japan, 1931–1941*, 2:291–92. On the State Department's actions, see Matthews (Vichy) to Sec. St., 5 Sept. 1940, *FRUS, 1940*, 4:100–101; and Hull to Matthews, 9 Sept. 1940, *FRUS, 1940*, 4:104–6. See also Langer and Gleason, *Challenge to Isolation*, 14. Henry-Haye's conversation with Hull is recounted in Hull, *Memoirs*, 1:904.

50. Charles-Roux, *Cinq mois*, 259–60. In fact, Decoux had sent a military purchasing mission to Washington for the purpose of acquiring fighter aircraft, proposing that twenty could be sent immediately from the Philippines. Spagent (Shanghai) to Morgenthau (Sec. of Treasury), Morgenthau Diaries, Book 308.

51. Matthews (Vichy) to Sec. St., 19 Sept. 1940, *FRUS, 1940*, 4:134.

52. Charles-Roux, *Cinq mois*, 260–61.

53. Decoux, *A la barre de l'Indochine*, 109–10; and Baudouin, *Private Diaries*, 243–44; Matthews (Vichy) to Sec. St., 22 Sept. 1940, *FRUS, 1940*, 4:141.

54. Francefort to FO, 17 June 1944, FO 371, 41723, F2894 / 66 / 61; and Decoux, *A la barre de l'Indochine*, 111–12.

55. Hull, *Memoirs*, 1:906.

56. For the text of the agreement, see IMTFE, 6954; see also Decoux, *A la barre de l'Indochine*, 112; Reed (Hanoi) to Sec. St., 22 Sept. 1940, *FRUS, 1940*, 4:141–42.

57. David Bergamini argues that the Japanese attack resulted from initiatives taken by Major General Tominaga Kyoji, a special General Staff emissary to the negotiations, and that Tojo's disciplinary action was only symbolic, as Hirohito quickly reassigned the instigators to important posts. He also suggests that the Indochinese forces resisted "stoutly" (*Japan's Imperial Conspiracy*, 727–28). Certainly, few French observers viewed the resistance so favorably. Although Robert Butow rather casually dismisses the incident as an exchange of fire caused by difficult communications, he more persuasively argues that Tokyo was truly embarrassed by the incident. Consequently, Tojo's disciplinary action was consistent

with his determination to control the army and therefore meant to be taken seriously. See Butow, *Tojo and the Coming of the War*, 193–94.

58. Baudouin, *Private Diaries*, 250.

59. Sterndale Bennett, in a minute of 5 Feb. 1941, FO 371, 27760, F540 / 9 / 61, wrote of the loss of Indochina. The description of Japan's ambiguous punctiliousness is from an account given by Captain René Jouan, Decoux's naval chief of staff to Admiral Noble in Singapore, 26 Dec. 1940, FO 371, 27761, F1094 / 9 / 61. On the difficult economic negotiations, see Levy et al., *French Interests*, 175–76; and FO 371, file 74 / 61.

60. C. in C. China to Admiralty, 26 Feb. 1941, FO 371, 27762, F1435 / 9 / 61. It was hoped, too, that the reestablishment of commercial relations between Indochina and the Dutch East Indies, interrupted since the Franco-German armistice of 1940, might allow both colonies to coordinate their economic policies and improve their resistance to Japanese demands.

61. FO memorandum, 6 Jan. 1941, attached to C. in C. China to Admiralty, 29 Dec. 1941, FO 371, 24722, F5765 / 3429 / 61. See also Cadogan's minute of 2 January, recounting a conversation with de Gaulle about the issue. For more on the decision to limit Gaullist propaganda, see FO memorandum, 21 Feb. 1941, FO 371, 27761, F1160 / 9 / 61. Undoubtedly, as the prospect of an early Axis victory receded and as the effect of British trade restrictions upon the staggering Indochinese economy became apparent, Decoux may have found that his early anti-British attitude may have been too hasty.

62. Chester L. Cooper, *The Lost Crusade: America in Vietnam*, 38; see Department of State Press Release, 23 Sept. 1940, *FRUS: Japan, 1931–1941*, 2:297; and Hull, *Memoirs*, 2:906–7.

63. Craigie (Tokyo) to FO, 24 Jan. 1941, FO 371, 27760, F398 / 9 / 61. Craigie added, "The United States Government seems in fact to have drawn an imaginery [*sic*] line north of Singapore and of parts of the Netherlands East Indies, but south of Indo-China, and to be ready to act decisively only when Japan crossed this line." Cadogan in London found American policy "a little puzzling," as the Americans seemed to "accept the inevitability of the march of events" (Cadogan to Butler [Washington], 14 Jan. 1941, FO 371, 28108, F142 / 5 / 40). Cadogan was responding to a comment by Stanley Hornbeck to the British ambassador in Washington, indicating that he had "made it clear that the United States regards Japan's absorption of Indo-China as inevitable."

64. Hamilton (Chief of Division of Far Eastern Affairs), memorandum, 17 July 1941, *FRUS, 1941*, 4:325. The Americans received coldly a French purchasing mission from Indochina that arrived in Washington about the time of the French collapse. See Francefort to FO, 17 June 1944, FO 371, 41723, F2894 / 66 / 61. The Americans and British both feared that such munitions, especially one hundred aircraft on the French island of Martinique that the French wanted permission to send to Indochina, would fall into Japanese hands. The French were caught in a vicious circle. Without such weapons, Indochina could not be successfully defended, but the British and Americans believed that the acquisition of the arms might precipitate a Japanese attack and result in Japan's acquiring them. For more on this issue, see, for example, memorandum of Welles's conversation with Henry-Haye, 20 Oct. 1940, PSF: France: 1940, FDR Library, Hyde Park, New York; Butler (Washington) to FO, 25 Dec. 1940, FO 371, 24711, F5732 / 193 / 61; Minute by Ashley Clarke, 15 Jan. 1941, on Craigie (Tokyo) to FO, 8 Jan. 1941, FO 371, 27759, F83 / 9 / 61; and Charles-Roux, *Cinq mois*, 265–66.

65. Samuel Eliot Morison, *History of the United States Naval Operations in World War II*, vol. 3, *The Rising Sun in the Pacific, 1931–April 1942*, 61. For more on the Thai attitude and machinations during the period, see Josiah Crosby, the British representative in Bangkok, *Siam: The Crossroads*.

66. Francefort to FO, 17 June 1944, FO 371, 41723, F2894 / 66 / 71; undated, unsigned French memorandum, in FO 371, 27762, F2515 / 9 / 61. For more concerning the Indochina-Thailand conflict, see Hytier, *Two Years*, 209–13; Charles-Roux, *Cinq mois*, 264–65; and Martin du Garde, *La Carte Impériale*, 435–39.

67. For the Indochina-Japan trade negotiations and agreement, see FO file 74 / 61. For the main points of the agreement, see Craigie (Tokyo) to FO, 7 May 1941, FO 371, 27783, F3862 / 74 / 61. For analyses of the agreement and Japanese mediation, see Butler to Halifax (Washington), 28 Mar. 1941, FO 371, 28131, F2390 / 246 / 10; and Craigie (Tokyo) to FO, 27 Jan. 1941, FO 371, 27760, F458 / 9 / 61. For the agreement, see IMTFE, 6721.

68. Joseph C. Grew, *Ten Years in Japan*, 378; C. in C. China to Admiralty, 13 May 1941, FO 371, 27762, F4045 / 9 / 61. The cat-and-mouse imagery is from a minute by Ashley Clarke, 20 May 1941, FO 371, 27763, F4045 / 9 / 61.

69. In fact, Chauvel had anticipated such a move as early as April, when a Soviet-Japanese nonaggression pact had been concluded. He correctly surmised that Stalin, confronted with deteriorating relations with Hitler, had decided to protect himself in the Far East by diverting Japan toward the south. See Leahy (Vichy) to Sec. St., 13 and 16 Apr. 1941, *FRUS, 1941*, 4:941, 953–54.

70. For the Japanese ultimatum, see IMTFE, 6723. See also Jones, *Japan's New Order*, 260. The Darlan-Leahy communication is recorded in Leahy (Vichy) to Sec. St., 1 Aug. 1941, PSF: Safe: France, FDR Library, Hyde Park, New York. When Leahy pressed Darlan about the decision, the Frenchman became "much annoyed." He "bitterly resented" American criticism of French policy when the United States had done nothing to restrain Japan. "It is always the same story. The United States is too late." As for Japanese trustworthiness, how could they be any worse than the British of Mers-El-Kebir?

71. Konoye's message is noted in Halifax (Washington) to FO, 28 July 1941, FO 371, 27766, F7446 / 9 / 61; and 19 July 1941, 27763, F6473 / 9 / 61. For a summary of the accession to Japanese demands and what followed, see Hytier, *Two Years*, 325–26, and Jones, *Japan's New Order*, 260–63. For a firsthand account of the Japanese occupation, see Henderson (Saigon) to FO, 17 Sept. 1941, FO 371, 27767, F13264 / 9 / 61. Apparently, Indochinese officials were not consulted, but merely informed of the Japanese terms after Vichy had accepted them. Moreover, arguing that satisfaction had not been achieved when American assistance had been sought earlier, Vichy did not consult with Washington. William Leahy, the American ambassador in Vichy, incredulously wired, "It would appear that the Marshal does not consider the Indochina agreement a surrender of any French rights of sovereignty." Leahy to Welles, 18 Sept. 1941, PSF: Diplomatic: France, 1941, FDR Library.

72. Johnson (Chungking) to Sec. St., 24 July 1940, *FRUS, 1940*, 4:407.

73. Feis, *Road to Pearl Harbor*, 57.

9. THE QUEST FOR SYMBOLS OF POWER AND GLORY: FRANCE AND THE ALLIED FAR EASTERN WAR

1. De Gaulle, *Memoirs*, 160.

2. On the U.S.–Indochina connection at this time, see Akira Iriye, *The Cold War in Asia: A Historical Introduction*, 54–58. See also Langer and Gleason, *Undeclared War;* and Gordon W. Prange, *At Dawn We Slept: The Untold Story of Pearl Harbor*. For treatments of American policy, see Lloyd C. Gardner, *Approaching Vietnam: From World War II through Dienbienphu;* Walter Lafeber, "Roosevelt, Churchill, and Indochina: 1942–1945," 1275–95; Edward R. Drachman, *United States Policy toward Vietnam, 1940–1945;* Gary R. Hess, "Franklin Roosevelt and Indochina," 353–68; William Roger Louis, *Imperialism at Bay:*

The United States and the Decolonization of the British Empire, 1941–1945; Christopher Thorne, "Indochina and Anglo-American Relations, 1942–1945," 73–96; and George C. Herring, "The Truman Administration and the Restoration of French Sovereignty in Indochina," 97–177.

3. Charles de Gaulle, Discours et messages, 1940–1946, 1:3.

4. De Gaulle, Memoirs, 3. Jean-Baptiste Duroselle has noted de Gaulle's overwhelming aspiration to revive France's greatness. "The need was to 'resume a place in the first rank' and 'maintain it.' " ("Changes in French Foreign Policy," 335). The response of the Empire to de Gaulle's call for support was mixed. Generally, those colonies furthest from the battlefields and those with the strongest British influence found the most nerve and sided with the Free French, while the others cast their lot with Pétain's Vichy government.

5. De Gaulle to Cadogan (Foreign Office), 20 Jan. 1941, FO 371, 27760, F338 / 9 / 61. See also de Gaulle to Catroux (Cairo), 25 Jan. 1941, in FO 371, 27758, F271 / 8 / 61; and de Schompre (Singapore) to de Gaulle, 26 Jan. 1941, FO 371, 27758, F456 / 9 / 61. For Britain's concern and attitude, see Craigie (Tokyo) to FO, 9 Jan. 1941, FO 371, 27759, F30 / 9 / 61; minute by B. E. F. Gage, 21 Jan. 1940, FO 371, 27760, F303 / 9 / 61; and Ashley Clarke, memorandum, 4 Mar. 1941, FO 371, 27762, F1624 / 9 / 61. As one Foreign Office official put it, "We should all naturally prefer that General de Gaulle should keep quiet about Indo-China" (minute by J. C. Sterndale Bennett, 20 Dec. 1940, FO 371, 24723, F5616 / 3429 / 61).

6. See, for example, de Gaulle's appeal of 7 Feb. 1941: "The time has come to bring home to all Frenchmen in imperial territories which have not yet joined in the fight against Germany and Italy . . . the urgency of their duty to participate in the war." The general was careful to avoid mentioning Indochina and instead pitched his appeal to Africa, but he made certain that Gaullist representatives in the Far East received copies of the message. He declared that "the hour is ripe for action and any kind of cooperation with the enemy . . . would be read by the world at large as a fresh and final renunciation." See de Gaulle to French Representatives in Somerville-Smith (Spears Mission) to Mack (Foreign Office), 7 Feb. 1941, FO 371, 28462, Z851 / 881 / 17.

7. Quoted in Drachman, United States Policy, 36.

8. Churchill's stance is quoted in a minute by W. H. B. Mack, 27 May 1942, FO 371, 31884, Z4292 / 14 / 17. Mack was reviewing the contradictory nature of commitments made by mid-1942. See also Morton (Prime Minister's Office) to Mack, 30 June 1942, FO 371, 32041, Z7718 / 880 / 17. Eden is quoted in an enclosure in Hull to Roosevelt, 14 Jan. 1944, FRUS, 1944, 3:772.

9. De Gaulle, Memoirs, 211–13. As Dorothy Shipley White put it, "unofficial America was indifferent, and official Washington was frigid" (Seeds of Discord: De Gaulle, Free France and the Allies, 264). Finally, in November 1941, Roosevelt agreed to extend the benefits of Lend-Lease to Free France because "the defense of the territories rallied to Free France was vital for the defense of the United States." For the best discussion of the Pleven mission, see White, Seeds of Discord, 263–75; and Milton Viorst, Hostile Allies: FDR and Charles de Gaulle, 68–70.

10. Quoted in minute by Mack, 27 May 1942, FO 371, 31884, Z4292 / 14 / 17.

11. Declaration by de Gaulle, 8 Dec. 1941, in FO 371, 28604, Z10415 / 10384 / 17. Admiral d'Argenlieu was ordered to offer to the Allies all facilities that French bases at New Caledonia, Tahiti, and the New Hebrides could offer. De Gaulle to Free Representatives, 9 Dec. 1941, FO 371, 28604, Z10384 / 10384 / 17. A similar offer had been made to the American government just a week before Pearl Harbor, after Washington, obviously expecting some overt Japanese move, had requested air bases from the French. De Gaulle had used the occasion to note, "Should the occasion arise [that] the French National Committee

would attach importance to Free French Forces cooperating in particular in the deliverance of Indo-China." Commissariat National aux Affaires Etrangères (London) to Free French Representatives, 1 Dec. 1941, FO 371, 28604, Z10384 / 10384 / 17.

12. Free French Representative (Washington) to de Gaulle, 26 Feb. 1942, FO 371, 31883, Z1693 / 14 / 17. Meanwhile, Roosevelt had instructed his representative in Vichy, Admiral Leahy, to use every occasion to reassure Marshal Pétain and General Weygand that one of his "greatest wishes is to see France reconstructed in the post-war period in accordance with its splendid position in history." He added, "the word 'France' in the mind of the President includes the French colonial empire." He warned, however, that it would be "wholly logical and wholly simple" for the United States to regard as a hostile act any steps that would give aid and comfort to the enemy at home or in the colonies. Franklin Delano Roosevelt, memorandum to Leahy (Vichy), 20 Jan. 1942, PSF: France: 1942, FDR Library, Hyde Park, New York.

13. The State Department rationalized its position by arguing that it did not want to give Vichy the slightest pretext to cede bases in North Africa to the Axis. Free French Representative (Washington) to de Gaulle, 26 Feb. 1942, FO 371, 31883, Z1693 / 14 / 17.

14. De Gaulle to French Representatives, 5 Mar. 1942, FO 371, 31883, Z1693 / 14 / 17.

15. For a summary of these pronouncements, see Enclosure in Hull to Roosevelt, 7 Jan. 1944, *FRUS, 1944*, 3:770–72.

16. Christopher Thorne, *Allies of a Kind: The United States, Britain and the War against Japan, 1941–1945*. The quotation is from p. 715; see also pp. 592–95, 629; and James MacGregor Burns, *Roosevelt: The Soldier of Freedom*, 543.

17. Thorne, *Allies of a Kind*, 546, 637; and Gardner, *Approaching Vietnam*, 48. On Secretary of State Hull's opposition to the trusteeship plan for Indochina, see his *Memoirs*, 2:598–99.

18. Dallek, *Roosevelt and American Foreign Policy*, 429. Gardner, *Approaching Vietnam*, 22–31. Walter Lafeber has concluded, "FDR's anti-colonialism was firmly rooted in the determination to protect American spheres of interest with military force" ("Roosevelt, Churchill, and Indochina," 1285).

19. The quotation is from Roosevelt to Sec. State, 24 Jan. 1944, *FRUS, 1944*, 3:773. At the Casablanca Conference, Roosevelt reproached Murphy for his statement, indicating that Murphy "overdid things a bit . . . pledging the United States Government to guarantee the return to France of every part of her empire. Your letter may make trouble for me after the war" (quoted in *Diplomat among Warriors*, 168).

20. FO minutes on Ismay (War Cabinet Offices) to Mack, 12 Feb. 1942, FO 371, 31883, Z1286 / 14 / 17. In theory, the Pacific War Council, composed of two groups, one meeting in London and the other in Washington, was an advisory body that undertook to coordinate the views of the Far Eastern Allied governments on the general conduct of the war against Japan. In practice, the former group met infrequently, since the bulk of the fighting was carried out by the Americans, while the latter body tended to serve merely as a sounding board for Roosevelt. Roosevelt regarded the council as a forum in which he "could keep everybody happy by telling stories and doing most of the talking" (quoted in R. M. Younger, *Australia and the Australians: A New Concise History*, 617).

21. Ismay (WCO) to Mack, 22 Jan. 1942, FO 371, 31882, Z681 / 14 / 17; Eden minute, 19 Feb. 1942, on Ismay (WCO) to Mack, 12 Feb. 1942, FO 371, 31883, Z1286 / 14 / 17; FO memo., ibid; and Eden to de Gaulle, 4 Mar. 1942, included in FO 371, 31883, Z1286 / 14 / 17. See also minute by Rumbold on Strang minute, 8 Sept. 1942, FO 371, 35921, F4871 / 1422 / 61.

22. Minute by V. F. W. Cavendish-Bentinck, 15 Sept. 1943, FO 371, 35921, F4871 / 1422 / 61. Cavendish-Bentinck went on to warn, "If we do not afford them an opportu-

nity for doing so agitation and ill feeling will grow, and eventually we may be driven to set up some body that may be more inconvenient than a London Pacific Council." Churchill's opinion is from Churchill minute on Campbell (Washington) to FO, 14 Oct. 1943, FO 371, 35921, F5379 / 1422 / 61. When Cadogan broached the issue again a few days later, Churchill shot back, "No action yet." See Cadogan to Prime Minister, 21 Oct. 1943, ibid. Pierre Viénot, the London representative of the French National Committee, was warned to "go slowly in these matters and not try to rush the Americans." After all, there was still plenty of time. Sargent, memorandum, 2 Dec. 1943, FO 371, 35921, F5906 /1422 /61.

23. Campbell (Washington) to FO, 14 Oct. 1943, and Ashley Clarke minute, 18 Oct. 1943, FO 371, 35921, F5379 / 1422 / 61. See also, Stettinius (Washington) to FDR, memorandum, 29 Oct. 1943, PSF: France, FDR Library, Hyde Park, New York.

24. Minute by Cavendish-Bentinck, 15 Sept. 1943, FO 371, 35921, F4871 / 1422 / 61.

25. Memorandum of 8th meeting of the Pacific War Council, 20 May 1942, Map Room Files: Pacific War Council: March 1942–April 1944, FDR Library, Hyde Park, New York. If Roosevelt sought a sympathetic hearing, except from the British he got it. The Chinese foreign minister, T. V. Soong, pitched in with the comment that France had exploited their nation but had never done anything to educate the Indochinese or to encourage them to aspire to self-government.

26. Memorandum of 25th meeting of the Pacific War Council, 9 Dec. 1942, ibid. Undoubtedly, his frustration with Vichy's collaboration with Germany stiffened his attitude. At a meeting of the council in July, he sarcastically noted, "The problem of French neutrality is rapidly approaching *reductio ad absurdum*." Memorandum of 16th meeting of the Pacific War Council, 29 July 1942. It should be noted that Roosevelt began promoting his trusteeship proposal as early as May 1942, nearly a year before some students of the problem, notably Lafeber, would have it occurring ("Roosevelt, Churchill, and Indochina," 1279). Hess, in "Roosevelt and Indochina," 355, argues that Roosevelt first took up the issue of the trusteeship for Indochina in January 1943. To foreign observers, the signals coming from Washington must have been quite confusing. On 24 May, just four days after Roosevelt's comments to the Pacific War Council, Hull indicated in a press conference that the general policy of the State Department was the ultimate restoration of France to all of its territories. Only strategic considerations would alter the policy. Matthews (Washington) to FO, 24 May 1942, FO 371, 31884, Z4330 / 14 / 17. In September 1942, Undersecretary of State Sumner Welles added to the confusion when he told R. K. Law, the British parliamentary undersecretary of state, that since no other state was competent to handle the administration during the trusteeship period, the French would have to be kept on so long as they recognized that they were merely trustees for the ultimate independence of Indochina. Law memorandum in Halifax (Washington) to FO, 9 Sept. 1942, FO 371, 31314, U778 / 27 / 70. For additional insight regarding Roosevelt's attitude about the French colonies, see Elliott Roosevelt's account of a conversation with his father during the Casablanca Conference in early 1943. Roosevelt confessed, "I'm by no means sure in my own mind that we'd be right to return France her colonies *at all, ever,* without first obtaining in the case of each individual colony some sort of pledge . . . of just what was planned, in terms of each colony's administration." He reminded his son, "Don't think for a moment, Elliott, that Americans would be dying in the Pacific tonight, if it hadn't been for the shortsighted greed of the French and the British and the Dutch. Shall we allow them to do it all, all over again?" (Elliott Roosevelt, *As He Saw It*, 114–15).

27. Eden to Churchill, 15 June 1942, FO 371, 30653, Z5574 / 31 / 45; and Scott's minute of 17 June attached. Scott's minute prompted Eden to respond, "It may be that we can only look for either (1) isolation or (2) big business from America after the war. This

may be too gloomy a view. I hope so." See Eden's minute of 17 June, ibid.; Minute by Cavendish-Bentinck on Halifax (Washington) to FO, 17 Dec. 1943, FO 371, 35921, F6656 / 1422 / 61.

28. De Gaulle, *Memoirs,* 392; and Peake (British Mission to French National Committee) to Mack, 4 July 1942, FO 371, 31966, Z5560 / 115 / 17. Peake reported that at the end of his tirade de Gaulle "subsided into a subdued mutter about how hostile life was to him in general."

29. De Gaulle, *Memoirs,* 625.

30. See Peake (British Mission to French National Committee) to Strang, 5 Mar. 1943, FO 371, 35921, F1422 / 1422 / 61. The British Foreign Office, realizing de Gaulle's motivations for gaining a foothold in Indochina, but also cognizant that the Americans had their own plans for the colony, thought de Gaulle's plans "pretty fantastic." See Hogg's minute, ibid.

31. Minute by Strang, 8 Sept. 1943, FO 371, 35921, F5608 / 1422 / 61.

32. Cadogan to Churchill, 3 Nov. 1943, FO 371, 35921, F5608 / 1422 / 61. W. H. B. Mack observed, "It is difficult to find convincing reasons in favour of a negative attitude towards the French requests." Minute by Mack, ibid.

33. Quoted in Foulds minute, 22 Dec. 1943, FO 371, 35921, F6814 / 1422 / 61. Again, on 17 December, Churchill ordered, "We should adopt a negative and dilatory attitude." Peterson (FO) to Ismay (WCO, Chiefs of Staff Committee), 11 Mar. 1944, FO 371, 31719, F1294 / 9 / 61.

34. Secretariat, Comite de Défense Nationale (Algiers), memorandum, 10 Dec. 1943, in FO 371, 31719, F9 / 9 / 61. The CLI eventually comprised some 1,200 men, specialists in various skills and Indochinese languages who were to be dispersed in small groups throughout strategic areas of Indochina as cadres for an expanded resistance later. Peter M. Dunn, *The First Vietnam War,* 28–29.

35. Peterson to General Ismay (WCO, Chiefs of Staff Committee), 11 Mar. 1944, FO 371, 41719, F1294 / 9 / 61.

36. WCO to Ashley Clarke, 19 Apr. 1944, FO 371, 41719, F1911 / 9 / 61. For the CLI connection with the SOE, see Charles Cruickshank, *SOE in the Far East,* 122–36.

37. See Cruickshank on the British concerns regarding Chungking. Thorne, in *Allies of a Kind,* discusses the Pechkoff mission (349). See also General G. Sabbatier, *Le Destin de l'Indochine: Souvenirs et documents, 1941–1951,* 69. As J.-B. Duroselle has put it, the Free French influence with Chiang's government had remained "most slight" ever since de Gaulle had sent an intermediary to China in 1940 to obtain recognition. Even after Pearl Harbor and de Gaulle's declaration of war on Japan, Chiang recognized Free France only as a "political movement." "Chinese ambitions on Indochina . . . manifested themselves clearly in 1942 and 1943" (*L'Abîme, 1939–1945,* 502–3). Regarding Mountbatten, see FO memorandum, 22 Nov. 1942, FO 371, 35921, F6782 / 1422 / 61; and Peterson (FO) to General Hastings Ismay (WCO, Chiefs of Staff Committee), 11 Mar. 1944, FO 371, 41719, F1294 / 9 / 61. Mountbatten expressed his fear several times. The French warning of 1944 is discussed in Keswick (SEAC) to Dening, 17 Mar. 1944, FO 371, 41719, F1394 / 9 / 61. On the French-Chinese-American relationships, see Archimedes L. A. Patti, *Why Vietnam? Prelude to America's Albatross,* 61–147. Churchill's remark is from WCO to FO, 4 May 1944, FO 371, 41723, F2223 / 66 / 61.

38. See Young minute, 11 May 1944, and Cadogan minute, 12 May 1944, ibid. In his diary that night, Cadogan wrote, "Why does P.M. want to drive France further and further away from us?" (*The Diaries of Sir Alexander Cadogan, 1938–1945,* ed. David Dilks, 628).

39. Eden to Churchill, 18 May 1944, FO 371, 41723, F2223 / 66 / 61.

40. Churchill to Eden, 21 May 1944, FO 371, 41719, F2502 / 9 / 61; and Eden to Churchill, 1 June 1944, FO 371, 41719, F2703 / 9 / 61.

41. See Viorst, *Hostile Allies*, chap. 11; Arthur L. Funk, *Charles De Gaulle: The Crucial Years, 1943-1944*, chap. 6; and Record of Massigli-Eden meeting, 24 Aug. 1944, FO 371, 46305, F4028 / 66 / 61.

42. The foreign secretary had prompted the British chiefs of staff to request the combined chiefs of staff in Washington to give their assent to the French proposals regarding the military mission and the CLI. Eden memorandum, 13 Aug. 1944, FO 371, 43724, F3789 / 66 / 61. When no response had been received from Washington by the time Massigli arrived in London, Eden, hoping to give the Frenchman a positive response before he left, directed Lord Halifax in Washington to indicate again Britain's desire to agree to the French proposals. Hull to Roosevelt, 26 Aug. 1944, *FRUS, 1944*, 3:774-75; and Matthews, memorandum, 26 Aug. 1944, *FRUS, The Conference at Quebec, 1944*, 247-49.

43. Roosevelt to Hull, 28 Aug. 1944, *FRUS, The Conference at Quebec, 1944*, 251-52; editor's note on Matthews memorandum, 29 Aug. 1944, ibid., 253; and Eden to Churchill, 7 Oct. 1944, FO 371, 41720, F4681 / 9 / 61. When informed of Roosevelt's determination to defer the matter to the Quebec Conference, the French were surprisingly amenable. See minute by Peterson, 13 Sept. 1944, FO 371, 41720 / 9 / 61. Apparently, the issue also did not arise during Churchill's visit to Hyde Park a few days later.

44. Foulds minute on Dening (SEAC) to FO, 30 Sept. 1944, FO 371, 41720, F4495 / 9 / 61. When Blaizot and his staff arrived at SEAC headquarters at the end of October, it was clear that they had brought with them the nucleus of a force headquarters and were determined to make their temporary visit a permanent one. Dening (SEAC) to FO, FO 371, 41720, F5011 / 9 / 61.

45. Eden to Churchill, 8 Oct. 1944, FO 371, 41720, F4681 / 9 / 61.

46. Major J. B. Sweetman to FO, 12 Oct. 1944, FO 371, F4780 / 66 / 61. Sweetman had been in Paris and had conferred with Colonel Jean Escarra, political adviser on Far Eastern affairs, Jacques Soustelle, head of the French information service, and Colonel Passy, head of de Gaulle's intelligence service as well as several others. Concerning de Gaulle's statement, see Colonel G. F. Taylor to Sterndale Bennett, 5 Oct. 1944, FO 371, 43724, F4682 / 66 / 61.

47. See Dening (SEAC) to FO, 30 Sept. 1944, FO 371, 41720, F4495 / 9 / 61; and Sterndale Bennett to Dening (SEAC), 23 Oct. 1944, FO 371, 41720, F4930 / 9 / 61. The French kept the pressure on Mountbatten by refusing to keep SOE fully informed of their own clandestine activities in Indochina. Dening (SEAC) to FO, 7 Sept. 1944, FO 371, 41720, F4119 / 9 / 61.

48. See Sterndale Bennett to Dening (SEAC), 25 Oct. 1944, FO 371, 41720, F4930 / 9 / 61. In a subsequent note by the imperial chief of staff on 5 November, the COS position was clearly stated:

From the political point of view there are strong reasons for encouraging French participation in operations in the Far East, and more particularly in the liberation of Indo-China, so far as this can be done without interference with operations on the Western Front and without real interference with the movement of our own troops in the Far East. Apart from the question of future French co-operation in Far Eastern reconstruction, it is to our advantage to do what we can to assist the French in restoring confidence in their army and its efficiency as the best safeguard against the establishment once more at some future date of a hostile power within range of London.

See FO 371, 41721, F5301 / 9 / 61.

49. Sterndale Bennett to Dening (SEAC), 23 Oct. 1944, FO 371, 41720, F4920 / 9 / 61; and War Office to Henderson (FO), 14 Dec. 1944, FO 371, 41721, F5953 / 9 / 61.

50. See A. M. Brossin de Saint-Didier (Chief of French Military Mission, Washington), memorandum, 20 Oct. 1944, in note by General Sir Alan Brooke (Chief of Imperial General Staff), 5 Nov. 1944, FO 371, 41721, F5301 / 9 / 61. See also Stettinius (Washington) to FDR, 15 Nov. 1944, PSF: Indochina, FDR Library. The French wanted one division attached to the American command and the other to SEAC, although they stipulated that both divisions should be used in the liberation of Indochina. The British chiefs of staff indicated that for logistical reasons they would not be able to use such forces before 1946. The American attitude was similar, although the United States gave tacit approval to organize the two divisions in the south of France so long as it did not interfere with other allied operations. For more on the dispute between the Americans and French regarding the Blaizot mission and other military and clandestine activities proposed by the French, see Patti, *Why Vietnam?*, 18–21.

51. Berle to Roosevelt, 21 Oct. 1944, PSF: Diplomatic: France: 1944–1945, FDR Library, Hyde Park, New York.

52. Roosevelt to Stettinius, 3 Nov. 1944, *FRUS, 1944*, 3:780; and Roosevelt to Stettinius, 24 Nov. 1944, PSF: Safe: Indochina, FDR Library, Hyde Park, New York.

53. See Charles F. Romanus and Riley Sunderland, *Stilwell's Mission to China*, 380–81; and Patti, *Why Vietnam?*, 122–23.

54. The quotation is from Churchill to Eden, 11 Oct. 1944, FO 371, 41720, F4681 / 9 / 61. Churchill instructed Eden, "Pray draft a telegram to the President at your leisure!" For more on the boundary and jurisdictional dispute, see Eden to Churchill, 8 Oct. 1944, FO 371, 41720, F4681 / 9 / 61; FO to Washington, 16 Nov. 1944, FO 371, 41721, F5303 / 9 / 61; and Eden, undated memorandum, FO 371, 41720, F4348 / 9 / 61. The summary is based on Churchill to Roosevelt, 17 Mar. 1945, in Francis Loewenheim, Harold D. Langley, and Manfred Jonas, eds., *Roosevelt and Churchill: Their Secret Wartime Correspondence*, 677.

55. Roosevelt to Churchill, 22 Mar. 1945, ibid., 680–83. Roosevelt ultimately got his way when it was decided that Mountbatten would operate in Chiang's theater only by prearrangement. Charles F. Romanus and Riley Sunderland, *United States Army in World War II: China-Burma-India Theater*, vol. 3, *Time Runs Out in CBI*, 260; and General Albert C. Wedemeyer, *Wedemeyer Reports!*, 270–71. This decision was reaffirmed by President Truman on 14 April, shortly after he assumed office. Harry S. Truman, *Memoirs*, vol. 1, *Year of Decisions*, 34–35.

56. On Wedemeyer's policy, see Atcheson (Chungking) to Sec. St., 24 Feb. 1945, *FRUS, 1945*, 7:55–56. The quotation is from Leahy, 17 Mar. 1945, memorandum, in *The Pentagon Papers: The Defense Department History of United States Decision Making on Vietnam*, 4 vols., ed. Mike Gravel, 1:14.

57. Grew (Acting Sec. of St.), memoranda, 18 and 19 May 1945, *FRUS, 1945*, 4:689, 692. For more on the French requests culminating with a message from de Gaulle on 15 May 1945, see Grew to Truman, 16 May 1945, *FRUS, 1945*, 6:307–8; and French Embassy (Chungking) to United States Embassy (Chungking), 10 Jan. 1945, *FRUS, 1945*, 6:295–96. See also Atcheson (Chungking) to Sec. St., 24 Feb. 1945, *FRUS, 1945*, 7:55–56.

58. Truman to Hurley (Chungking), 1 Aug. 1945, *FRUS, 1945*, 7:143. See also COS to Truman and Churchill, 24 July 1945, *FRUS: Conference of Potsdam*, 1465. The initiative for taking up the matter again apparently came from the British. See COS, memorandum, 22 July 1945, ibid., 1319. For more on the Anglo-American dispute regarding the theater command, see Thorne, *Allies of a Kind*, 300–301, 454, 522–23; and Louis Allen, *The End of the War in Asia*, 117–20.

59. De Gaulle, *Memoirs*, 626. Plevin is quoted in Morton (Prime Minister's Office) to Bourdillon (FO), 31 May 1943, FO 371, 36229, Z6398 / 486 / 69. For more on de Gaulle's

efforts to secure official recognition of his committee as a provisional government for France, see René Massigli, *Une comédie des erreurs 1943–1956*, chaps. 1, 2.

60. See *FRUS: Conferences at Cairo and Teheran, 1943*, 325, 485, 509–10; and *The Diaries of Edward R. Stettinius, Jr., 1943–1946*, ed. Thomas M. Campbell and George C. Herring, 38–40. During his return voyage from Yalta, Roosevelt met with reporters and revealed some of the substance of his discussions at Cairo and Teheran, indicating that both Chiang Kai-shek and Stalin had agreed with his scheme for Indochina. Chiang had indicated that China did not want Indochina: "It is no help to us. . . . They would not assimilate into the Chinese people." But the generalissimo had said that it should not be returned to the French. Roosevelt's trusteeship plan, which he had suggested at the time, included a French member, one or two Indochinese, and a Chinese and a Russian, and maybe a Filipino and an American. Their task would be to educate the Indochinese for self-government. The president pointed out, however, that it had taken the United States fifty years to prepare the way for Philippine independence. Stalin had liked the idea, too. But, Roosevelt lamented, "it would only make the British mad." Therefore, he had decided to "keep quiet just now" (Rosenman, *Public Papers of FDR*, vol. 13, *Victory and the Threshold of Peace*, 562–63). Perhaps to assuage Churchill's sensitivities about the issue, Roosevelt had told the prime minister, "If Great Britain and America are to police the world, they must have the right to select the police stations." In any case, France "should not be allowed . . . to let down the world a second time." Harold Macmillan, *War Diaries: Politics and War in the Mediterranean*, 318.

61. Drachman, *United States Policy*, 53.

62. D. Bruce Marshall, *The French Colonial Myth and Constitution-making in the Fourth Republic*, 107–10. For an excellent treatment of the Brazzaville Conference, see 102–15.

63. Quoted in WCO to FO, 12 June 1944, FO 371, 41719, F2718 / 9 / 61.

64. Roosevelt's plan for the limited future of France is from Minutes of president's meeting with JCS, 15 Nov. 1943, *FRUS: Cairo and Tehran, 1943*, 195. For the comment to Churchill, see Roosevelt to Churchill, 17 June 1943, *FRUS, 1943*, 2:160. A month earlier, the president had wired Churchill that de Gaulle's "course and attitude is well nigh intolerable" (ibid., 8 May 1943, 111). Roosevelt confided to his son in 1943, "I can't imagine a man I would distrust more" (Roosevelt, *As He Saw It*, 73). For more on the the de Gaulle-Roosevelt relationship, see Viorst, *Hostile Allies;* and White, *Seeds of Discord*. On occasion, the issues of de Gaulle and Indochina even strained the normally good relationship between Churchill and Roosevelt. After the Cairo Conference, for example, when the prime minister expressed his disbelief that Chiang Kai-shek had no designs on Indochina, Roosevelt exploded, "Winston, this is something which you are just not able to understand. You have 400 years of acquisitive instinct in your blood and you just don't understand how a country might not want to acquire land somewhere if they can get it. A new period has opened in the world's history, and you will have to adjust to it" (Campbell and Herring, eds., *Diaries of Stettinius*, 40).

65. Sir Henry Pownall, *Chief of Staff: The Diaries of Lieutenant-General Sir Henry Pownall*, vol. 2, *1940–1944*, ed. Brian Bond, 174. For more on the volatile relationship between these two "pachyderms," as A. J. P. Taylor labeled them, see François Kersaudy, *Churchill and De Gaulle;* and Duroselle, *L'Abîme*. See also A. Duff Cooper (Algiers) in Halifax to Roosevelt, 12 Feb. 1944, Map Room Files: Naval Aide's Files: France and the Free French, 1942–1945, FDR Library, Hyde Park, New York. It is he who reveals de Gaulle's aggrieved self-perception and refers to Churchill's warning to de Gaulle. For more about the debate concerning the recognition of de Gaulle's committee as the official director of France's war effort, see Dallek, *Roosevelt and American Foreign Policy*, 406–9.

66. Campbell (Washington) to FO, 16 July 1944, FO 371, 41958, Z4578 / 1555 / 17. For discussions of de Gaulle's visit, see Viorst, *Hostile Allies*, 307–9; Kersaudy, *Churchill and*

De Gaulle, 360–62; Dallek, *Roosevelt and American Foreign Policy*, 461–63; de Gaulle, *Memoirs*, 569–77; and Warren F. Kimball, ed., *Churchill and Roosevelt: The Complete Correspondence*, 3:237–40.

67. Kersaudy quotes Roosevelt's "He's a nut!" (*Churchill and De Gaulle*, 361). De Gaulle's *Memoirs*, 573–75, contain the remaining account of their meetings.

68. Drachman, *United States Policy*, 53.

69. De Gaulle, *Discours et Messages*, 418; Drachman, *United States Policy*, 53–54; and Hull to Acting American Representative to the French Committee of National Liberation at Algiers (Chapin), 11 July 1944, *FRUS, 1944*, 3:724–25.

70. Roosevelt to Churchill, 10 July 1944, in Kimball, *Churchill and Roosevelt* 3:236; Viorst, *Hostile Allies*, 209; Herbert Feis, *Roosevelt, Churchill, and Stalin: The War They Waged and the Peace They Sought*, 321–22. De Gaulle was still not completely out of the woods in his relationship with Roosevelt and Churchill. Anthony Eden later recalled that at the Quebec Conference in September each of them went "off in turn on a tirade against de Gaulle" (*The Memoirs of Anthony Eden, Earl of Avon*, vol. 2, *The Reckoning*, 553).

71. Plevin, originally reported in *France Libre*, 13 Oct. 1944, is quoted in FO 371, 41935, Z7099 / 819 / 17. On de Gaulle's secret planning, see Record of Eden-Massigli meeting, 24 Aug. 1944, FO 371, 46305, F4028 / 66 / 61; Général Mordant, *Au service de la France en Indochine*, 91–92; Sabbatier, *Le destin de l'Indochine*, 69; Decoux, *A la barre de l'Indochine*, 306; and Claude de Boisanger, *On pouvait éviter la guerre de l'Indochine: Souvenirs, 1941–1945*, 83–86.

72. Record of Eden-Massigli meeting, 24 Aug. 1944, FO 371, 46305, F4028 / 66 / 61. De Gaulle had struck a similar note a few days earlier, when he indicated that while he hoped a formula for maintaining postwar peace could be found, he shrewdly maintained that "such a solution must benefit the common interest of all nations against aggression and must not be adopted at the detriment of the sovereignty of one or another nation" (extract from *France*, 15 Aug. 1944, in FO 371, 41958, Z5297 / 1555 / 17).

73. War Cabinet Paper W.P. (44)111, 16 Feb. 1944, in FO 371, 41723, F980 / 66 / 61; Cab 25 (44), 24 Feb. 1944, in War Cabinet to FO, 24 Feb. 1944, FO 371, 41723, F1075 / 66 / 61; and FO memorandum, 3 Aug. 1944, FO 371, 41724, F3789 / 66 / 61.

74. FO memorandum, 3 Aug. 1944, FO 371, 41724, F3789 / 66 / 61.

75. This series of quotations is from Roosevelt to Stettinius, 3 Nov. 1944, *FRUS, 1944*, 3:780; Roosevelt to Stettinius, 24 Nov. 1944, PSF: Safe: Indochina, FDR Library, Hyde Park, New York; and Roosevelt to Stettinius, 1 Jan. 1945, *FRUS, 1945*, 6:293. He added on the first of January that "from both the military and civil point of view action at this time is premature."

76. See, for example, Harry Hopkins, quoted in Lafeber, "Roosevelt, Churchill, and Indochina," 1291. See also Gardner, *Approaching Vietnam*, 47–50, for more on Roosevelt's changing views and the pressures on him.

77. Philippe Devillers, *Histoire du Viêt-Nam de 1940 à 1952*, 118; and Chauvel, *Commentaire*, vol. 2, *D'Alger à Berne (1944–1952)*, 173.

78. Cooper (Paris) to FO, 27 Jan. 1945, FO 371, 46304, F730 / 11 / 61; French Press and Information Service release, 19 Jan. 1945, in Halifax (Washington) to FO, 29 Jan. 1945, FO 371, 46304, F875 / 11 / 61; and Bonnet, *Quai d'Orsay*, 386. Naggiar was attending a conference held at Hot Springs to deal with Pacific problems. Although he attended as a private citizen representing France, it is most likely that he had gained prior approval for his statement.

79. Caffrey (Paris) to FO, 20 Jan. 1945, *FRUS, 1945*, 4:667.

80. Cooper (Paris) to FO, 25 Mar. 1945, FO 371, 45306, F1943 / 11 / 61. Jean de la Roché, a prominent spokesman in the United States for the French Ministry of Foreign

Affairs, wrote that the new French colonial policies had rendered Roosevelt's trusteeship plan outmoded. Drachman, *United States Policy*, 55.

81. Declaration of the Provisional French Government, 24 Mar. 1945, in Cole, ed. *Conflict in Indo-China*, 57.

82. Bonnet (Washington) to Sec. St., 12 Mar. 1945, *FRUS, 1945*, 6:299–300; and Stettinius to Bonnet, 20 Apr. 1945, *FRUS, 1945*, 6:306–7.

83. French Embassy (Chungking) to American Embassy (Chungking), 20 Jan. 1945, *FRUS, 1945*, 6:294–95. The French note added that the occupation of Indochina was no different from the Japanese invasion of Malaya, the East Indies, or Burma. Consequently, it was implied, French possessions should not be treated any differently after the war than those of Britain and the Netherlands. The note reiterated that "France intends to take part in the liberation of those of her territories that have been momentarily torn away from her by the enemy."

84. See Chauvel, *Commentaire*, 2:36; Devillers, *Histoire du Viêt-Nam*, 114–15; F. S. V. Donnison, *British Military Administration in the Far East, 1943–1946*, 403; and Cruickshank, *SOE in Far East*, 126, 130–31. Additionally, a Free French military mission led by Jean Escarra had been established at Kunming in 1943, and it had maintained contact with Gaullist sympathizers in Indochina. See Jean Sainteny, *Histoire d'une paix manquée*, 22–26.

85. Devillers, *Histoire du Viêt-Nam*, 117–18; and Patti, *Why Vietnam?*, 37–39.

86. For firsthand accounts of the wartime developments in Indochina and the background to the Japanese coup of March 1945, see Decoux, *A la barre de l'Indochine*, 298–324; Sabbatier, *Le Destin de l'Indochine*, chaps. 4–6; Mordant, *Service en Indochine*, chaps. 1 and 2; and de Boisanger, *On pouvait éviter la guerre d'Indochine*. See also Maréchal Alphonse Juin, *Mémoires*, 2:107–9; Chauvel, *Commentaire*, 2:36–37; Patti, *Why Vietnam?*, 38–41; and André Gaudel, *L'Indochine Française en face du Japon*. For secondary accounts, consult Devillers, *Histoire de Viêt-Nam*, 144–48; Hammer, *Struggle for Indochina*, 34–42; Donald Lancaster, *The Emancipation of French Indochina*, 96–105; Joseph Buttinger, *Vietnam: A Dragon Embattled*, vol. 1, *From Colonialism to the Viet-Minh*, 238–50, 278–84; F.-C. Jones, Hugh Berton, and B. R. Pearn, et al., *Survey of International Affairs*, vol. 6, *The Far East, 1942–1946*, 24–32; Allen, *End of War in Asia*, 96–109; and R. Harris Smith, *OSS: The Secret History of American's First Central Intelligence Agency*, 320–28.

87. For detailed accounts of the Japanese coup and the plight of the French resisters, see Decoux (*A la barre de l'Indochine*, 324–36), who roundly condemned the activities of the Gaullist resistance forces in Indochina and Calcutta; Mordant, *Au service de la France*, 132–47; de Boisanger, who was Decoux's diplomatic counselor, *On pouvait éviter la Guerre d'Indochine*, 87–110; and Sainteny, *Histoire d'une paix manquée*, 14–43. Sainteny was a resistance leader who commanded one of the independent French intelligence groups that had been established along the frontier of China and Indochina. His group, Mission 5, was based in Kunming and like other groups attempted to maintain liaison with the French resisters in Indochina, gather information for the Allies, and provide aid for downed Allied pilots. See pp. 22, 27. See also Devillers, *Histoire du Viêt-Nam*, 123; Patti, *Why Vietnam?*, 72–78, 88–95; Lancaster, *Emancipation of Indochina*, 105–6; and J. Lee Ready, *Forgotten Allies*, vol. 2, *The Asian Theater*, 197–99.

88. John T. McAllister, Jr., *Vietnam: The Origins of Revolution*, 114; and Hammer, *Struggle for Indochina*, 41.

89. Juin, *Mémoires*, 2:108.

90. Jones et al., *Survey: Far East*, 33; and Chauvel, *Commentaire*, 2:173. Prince Norodom Sihanouk of Cambodia quickly declared his country's independence on 13 March, and a month later the Laotian king, Sisavang Vong, followed suit. Patti, *Why Vietnam?*, 73.

91. De Gaulle, *Discours et messages*, 532–34; and quoted in Cooper (Paris) to FO, 16 Mar. 1945, FO 371, 46305, F1657 / 11 / 61.

92. Eden to Cooper (Paris), 12 Mar. 1945, FO 371, 46305, F1563 / 11 / 61. The resistance organization in Indochina had informed de Gaulle's government in July 1944 that the essential condition for effective resistance was that a minimum of five to six hundred specially trained French officers and men familiar with Indochina should be parachuted into Indochina. This had led to the formation in North Africa of the CLI. By 15 February 1945, the arrangements had finally been made for its departure to India. The British High Command, however, countermanded its approval, citing the need to consult with the combined chiefs of staff. There the matter had rested until the Japanese coup. It is unfortunate that in his memoirs of the period, *Une comédie des erreurs*, Massigli includes little about Far Eastern matters. See further, both Massigli and Chiefs of Staff (45), 75th meeting, 22 Mar. 1945, FO 371, 46305, F1883 / 11 / 61.

93. Bonnet (Washington) to Sec. St., 12 Mar. 1945, *FRUS, 1945*, 6:297–99; and Dunn (Asst. Sec. St.), memorandum, 19 Mar. 1945, ibid., 301–3.

94. Acheson (Acting Sec. St.) to Caffrey (Paris), 19 Mar. 1945, *FRUS, 1945*, 6:301.

95. Romanus and Sunderland, *Time Runs Out in CBI*, 259–60; and Wedemeyer, *Wedemeyer Reports!*, 340.

96. Claire Lee Chennault, *Way of a Fighter*, 342. See also Sainteny, *Histoire d'une paix manquée*, 36–37; and Dunn, *First Vietnam War*, 94–104.

97. Caffrey (Paris) to Sec. St., 24 Mar. 1945, *FRUS, 1945*, 6:302.

98. Chennault, *Way of a Fighter*, 342; Sec. St. to Bonnet (Washington), 4 Apr. 1945, *FRUS, 1945*, 6:303; and Sabbatier, *Le Destin de l'Indochine*, 206. Directions to this effect had been issued to Wedemeyer by Admiral Leahy on 18 March. Dunn, memorandum, 19 Mar. 1945, *FRUS, 1945*, 6:302. The American memorandum is quoted in Dunn, *First Vietnam War*, 99.

99. Romanus and Sunderland, *China-Burma-India Theater*, 3:260; and Chennault, *Way of a Fighter*, 342, discuss the actual provision of aid and the Chiang complication.

100. De Gaulle, *Discours et messages*, 532–34, 855. De Gaulle sought to use the Indochinese situation to counter increasing criticism of his government at home by emphasizing the need for unity. See Claude Mauriac, *The Other de Gaulle: Diaries, 1944–1954*, 106–7; Sabbatier cites his orders from de Gaulle in *Le Destin de l'Indochine*, 193. Seeking to minimize the effect of Japan's coup upon indigenous Indochinese nationalist leadership, de Gaulle also offered a vague form of local autonomy on a federal basis. For more on the French attempts to address the issue of colonial policy toward Indochina at that point, see Marshall, *French Colonial Myth*, 134–38.

101. De Gaulle's statement is in Caffrey (Paris) to Sec. St., 13 Mar. 1945, *FRUS, 1945*, 6:300.

102. Quoted in Herring, "Truman Administration and French Sovereignty," 101. Harriman also warned, "There is every indication the Soviet Union will become a 'World Bully' wherever their interests are involved unless we take issue with their present policy. When they turn their attitude in that direction this policy will reach into the Pacific and China as well." (quoted in Dunn, *First Vietnam War*, 82–83).

103. Steven P. Sapp, "The United States, France and the Cold War: Jefferson Caffrey and American-French Relations, 1944–1949," 20–21, 69–72. Caffrey repeatedly cautioned that if the aggressive French Communist Party won the forthcoming elections, "the entire continent of Europe might fall into the Russian orbit."

104. Ibid., 100–103. For an excellent analysis of the divisions within the State Department by a participant, see Abbot Low Moffat's testimony before Congress published in

Senate Committee on Foreign Relations, *Causes, Origins, and Lessons of the Vietnam War: Hearings*, 92d Cong., 2d sess., 1973, 172-77.

105. "An Estimate of Conditions in Asia and the Pacific at the Close of the War in the Far East and the Objectives and Policies of the United States," enclosure in Acting Secretary of State (Grew) to Secretary of War (Stimson), 28 June 1945, *FRUS, 1945*, 6:556-58, 567-68, 577-80.

106. Stettinius to Roosevelt, 16 Mar. 1945, and Leahy to Stettinius, 17 Mar. 1945, in *Pentagon Papers*, 1:12-13; *Diaries of Edward Stettinius*, 304-5. Soon thereafter, however, Roosevelt ordered the American air forces in China to aid the French, provided that such operations did not impede operations against Japan. Lafeber, "Roosevelt, Churchill, and Indochina," 1293. For the limited nature of such aid, see Chennault, *Way of a Fighter*, 342; and *Pentagon Papers*, 1:13.

107. Taussig (Advisor on Carribean Affairs), memorandum, 15 Mar. 1945, *FRUS, 1945*, 1:124. For more on Roosevelt's wavering, see Thorne, *Allies of a Kind*, 628-31.

108. *Pentagon Papers*, 1:2, 14-15. What exactly transpired at Yalta regarding trusteeships, if anything, remains something of a mystery. Although Roosevelt apparently intended to raise the issue of a trusteeship for Indochina, the record is devoid of any official discussion of the matter. Roosevelt did reveal something of his attitude in a private conversation with Stalin, when he indicated that de Gaulle had asked for ships to transport French troops to Indochina. Roosevelt's response was that no ships were available; the implication was that as far as he was concerned, they would never be available. *FRUS: Conferences at Malta and Yalta, 1945*, 770. See also Diane Shaver Clemens, *Yalta*, 249; and Louis, *Imperialism at Bay*, chap. 29.

109. The quotations from Pechkoff and Bidault are from Patti, *Why Vietnam?*, 117. The exchange shared by Stettinius, Bidault, and Dunn is quoted in Herring, "Truman Administration and French Sovereignty," 104-5. See also Grew (Acting Sec. St.) to Caffrey (Paris), 9 May 1945, *FRUS, 1945*, 6:307.

110. See Grew (Acting Sec. St.) to Caffrey (Paris), 9 May 1945, *FRUS, 1945*, 6:307. While Bidault may not have been overtly playing the "Soviet card," de Gaulle remained willing to do so. At a meeting with Caffrey on 5 May, the general pessimistically predicted that after the war the United States and the Soviet Union would be the only two real forces in the world. He added, "I would much rather work with the USA than any other country. . . . If I cannot work with you I must work with the Soviets even if it is only for a while and even if in the long run they gobble us up too" (quoted in Caffrey [Paris] to Acting Secretary of State [Grew], 5 May 1945, *FRUS, 1945*, 4:686).

111. Department of State Policy Paper, 22 June 1945, *FRUS, 1945*, 6:568. For an excellent discussion of the issues of international supervision of trusteeships and self-government versus independence at the San Francisco Conference, see Louis, *Imperialism at Bay*, 512-47. For the most part, the French took a back seat and allowed the British to defend the position of the colonial powers. Herring, "Truman Administration and French Sovereignty," 105.

112. De Gaulle to Truman, 15 May 1945, *FRUS, 1945*, 6:308-9.

113. Truman, *Memoirs*, 1:240; and Matthews (Director of Office of European Affairs) to State-War-Navy Coordinating Committee, memorandum, 23 May 1945, *FRUS, 1945*, 1:310. Perhaps to allay American suspicions about French motives, Bidault indicated that French troops could be used anywhere in the Pacific war.

114. De Gaulle, *Memoirs*, 873-77. See Truman's account in Truman, *Memoirs*, 1:241-43. See also, Herbert Feis, *Between War and Peace: The Potsdam Conference*, 128-35; and Sapp, "Jefferson Caffrey and American-French Relations," 44-69.

115. Department of State Policy Paper, 22 June 1945, *FRUS, 1945*, 6:557–58.

116. On the participants invited to Potsdam, see Feis, *Between War and Peace*, 128–38. Some doubt also existed whether Stalin could be induced to accept a French presence. De Gaulle's exchange with Le Clerc is from de Gaulle's *Memoirs*, 926.

117. Herring, "Truman Administration and French Sovereignty," 109.

118. De Gaulle, *Memoirs*, 906–11. De Gaulle could not resist taking one last swipe at American policy by reminding Truman that the implementation of French policies would be "hampered by the arrangements our allies are making without consulting us first." The official American record of the discussions contains no reference to Indochina, and Truman's own memoirs are silent about the meetings. In response to questions about Indochina's future at a subsequent press conference, de Gaulle announced, "The position of France in Indochina is very simple. France intends to recover its sovereignty over Indochina." See de Gaulle, *Discours et Messages*, 1:605.

119. De Gaulle, *Memoirs*, 926.

120. *Pentagon Papers*, 1:2; and de Gaulle, *Memoirs*, 931.

121. Sainteny, *Histoire d'une paix manquée*, 47. *L'Humanité* is quoted in Christopher Thorne, *The Issue of War: States, Societies, and the Far Eastern Conflict of 1941–1945*, 299. See also p. 201. For more on the attitudes about the empire of the other major parties, see Marshall, *French Colonial Myth*, 236–71. Other parties, if they paid any attention to the colonial issue in 1945, generally supported the retention of colonies. As the MRP Congress statement of 1945 declared, "France will only be a great power so long as our flag continues to fly in all the overseas territories" (R. E. M. Irving, *The First Indochina War*, 144–46). Chauvel's quoted remark is from *Commentaire*, 2:175; his statement on French policy in Indochina is from Caffrey (Paris) to Sec. St., 16 Aug. 1945, *FRUS, 1945*, 4:704–5.

Bibliography

Unpublished Primary Material

Government Archives

France
Ministère des Affaires Etrangères (MAE). Quai d'Orsay, Paris.
Ser. B: Amérique (1918–1940)
Ser. E: Asie-Océanie (1918–1929)
Ser. Y: Internationale (1918–1940)
Ser. Z: Europe (1918–1940)
Ser. Conférence de la Paix 1914–1931
Great Britain
Foreign Office (FO). Public Record Office, London.
FO 371: General Correspondence, Political
FO 425: Confidential Print Series: Western Europe
FO 432: Confidential Print Series: France (1934–1939)
FO 436: Confidential Print Series: Far East (1937–1945)
FO 608: Correspondence 1919–1920
FO 800: Private Collections: Ministers and Officials (including papers of Alexander Cadogan, Archibald Clark Kerr, George Nathaniel Lord Curzon, Edward Lord Halifax, Samuel Hoare, Orme Sargent, Robert Cecil Viscount Cranborne, and R. F. Wigram)
Cabinet Conclusions (Cab). Public Record Office, London.
Cab 23: Minutes to 1939
Cab 24: Documents and Memoranda to 1939
Cab 27: Committee Records
Cab 29: Anglo-French Staff Conversations (1939)
Cab 66: War Cabinet Memoranda from 1939
Prime Minister's Office (Prem). Public Record Office, London.
Prem 1: Correspondence and Papers
Prem 3: Operational Papers
United States
Department of State Decimal File (SD), National Archives, Washington, D.C.
Files 65G, 462, 500A, 701, 711, 741, 751G, 752, 760F, 762, 770, 793, 800, 851, 852, 860, 871, 893, 894, 898, and 951

International
International Military Tribunal for the Far East (IMTFE).
   Papers, Journal, Exhibits, and Judgment. National Archives Microfilm, T918. 39 rolls.
   Washington, D.C.

Franklin D. Roosevelt Library, Hyde Park, New York

Map Room File (MR), 1941–1945
Official File (OF), 1933–1945
President's Personal File (PPF), 1933–1945
President's Secretary's File (PSF), 1933–1945
Press Conferences, 1933–1945

Private Papers

Stanley Baldwin (Cambridge University Library)
Adolf Berle (Franklin D. Roosevelt Library)
Alexander Cadogan (FO 800, Public Record Office)
Archibald Clark Kerr (Lord Inverchapel) (FO 800, Public Record Office)
Edouard Daladier (Foundation Nationales des Sciences Politiques)
Norman H. Davis (Library of Congress)
W. Cameron Forbes (Library of Congress)
Joseph C. Grew (Houghton Library, Harvard University)
Edward Halifax (FO 800, Public Record Office)
Maurice Hankey (Churchill College Library, Cambridge University; and FO 800, Public
   Record Office)
Samuel Hoare (Cambridge University Library)
Cordell Hull (Library of Congress)
General Frank R. McCoy (Library of Congress)
J. Pierrepont Moffat (Houghton Library, Harvard University)
R. Walton Moore (Franklin D. Roosevelt Library, Hyde Park, New York)
Henry Morgenthau, Jr. (Franklin D. Roosevelt Library, Hyde Park, New York)
Eric Phipps (Churchill College Library, Cambridge University)
William Phillips (Houghton Library, Harvard University)
Orme Sargent (FO 800, Public Record Office)
Arthur Sweetser (Library of Congress)
R. F. Wigram (FO 800, Public Record Office)

Interviews and Correspondence

Bidault, Suzanne. Interview with the author, Paris, 18 July 1974.
Bonnet, Georges. Interview with the author, Paris, 11 August 1969.
Bonnet, Henri. Interview with the author, Paris, 30 August 1969.
———. Letter to author, 23 March 1972.
Corbin, Charles. Interview with the author, Paris, 25 August 1969.
Eden, Sir Anthony. Letter to author, 23 May 1972.
Luc, Robert. Interview with author, Wichita, Kansas, 22 February 1982.
———. Letter to author, 5 May 1982.
Murphy, Robert. Interview with author, New York, 9 June 1977.

PUBLISHED PRIMARY MATERIAL

Government Documents

Belgium
Ministère des Affaires Etrangères. *Documents diplomatiques belges, 1920–1940.* 5 vols. Brussels: Palais des Académies, 1964–66.
France
Assemblée Nationale. *Les Evénements survenus en France de 1933 à 1945: Témoinages et documents recueillis par la Commission d'Enquête Parlementaire.* 9 vols. Paris: Presses Universitaires de France, 1947–54.
Haute Cour de Justice. *Procès du Maréchal Pétain.* Paris: Imprimerie des Journaux Officiels, 1945.
Journal Officiel de la République Française. Chambre des Députés. Débats parlementaires. Paris: Imprimerie des Journaux Officiels.
Journal Officiel de la République Française. Sénat. Débats parlementaires. Paris: Imprimerie des Journaux Officiels.
Ministère des Affaires Etrangères. *Documents diplomatiques: Conférence de Washington, Juillet 1921–Février 1922.* Paris: Imprimerie Nationale, 1923.
Documents diplomatiques français, 1932–1939. 1st ser. (1932–36). Paris: Imprimerie Nationale, 1964–86.
Documents diplomatiques français, 1933–1939. 2d ser. (1936–39). Paris: Imprimerie Nationale, 1964–84.
Le Livre jaune français: Documents diplomatiques, 1938–1939. Paris: Imprimerie Nationale, 1939.
Ministère des Relations Extérieures. *Les Archives du Ministère des Relations Extérieures depuis les origines.* 2 vols. Paris: Imprimerie Nationale, 1985.
Germany
Documents on German Foreign Policy, 1918–1945. Series D. Washington, D.C.: U.S. Government Printing Office, 1949–64.
Great Britain
Documents on British Foreign Policy, 1919–1939. Edited by E. L. Woodward, Rohan Butler, W. N. Medlicott et al. Ser. 1–3. London: Her Majesty's Stationery Office, 1947–82.
League of Nations
Official Journal, 1931–1938. Geneva: League of Nations, 1931–38.
Official Journal, Special Supplements. Nos. 169, 177. Geneva: League of Nations.
The Report of the Commission of Inquiry of the League of Nations into the Sino-Japanese Dispute, 1932. Geneva: League of Nations, 1932.
United States
Congress. Senate. Committee on Foreign Relations. *Causes, Origins, and Lessons of the Vietnam War.* Hearings. 92d Cong., 1st sess., May 9–11, 1972.
Congress. Senate. *Conference on the Limitation of Armament.* 67th Cong., 2d sess., 1921–22. Washington, D.C.: U.S. Government Printing Office, 1922.
Department of State. *The Conference of Brussels, November 3–24, 1937.* Conference Series 37. Washington, D.C.: U.S. Government Printing Office, 1938.
Foreign Relations of the United States: Diplomatic Papers, 1919–1945. Washington, D.C.: U.S. Government Printing Office, 1942–69.
Papers Relating to the Foreign Relations of the United States: Japan, 1931–1941. 2 vols. Washington, D.C.: U.S. Government Printing Office, 1943.

Other Documentary Sources

Cole, Alan B., ed. *Conflict in Indo-China and International Repercussions: A Documentary History, 1945–1955.* Ithaca, N.Y.: Cornell University Press, 1956.

Kimball, Warren F., ed. *Churchill and Roosevelt: The Complete Correspondence.* 3 vols. Princeton, N.J.: Princeton University Press, 1984.

Gravel, Mike, ed. *The Pentagon Papers: The Defense Department History of United States Decision Making on Vietnam.* 4 vols. Boston: Beacon, 1971.

Mantoux, Paul. *Paris Peace Conference, 1919: Proceedings of the Council of Four, March 24–April 18.* Translated by John Boardman Whitton. Foreword by Jacques Freymond. Geneva: Droz, 1964.

Rosenman, Samuel I., ed. *The Public Papers and Addresses of Franklin D. Roosevelt.* 13 vols. New York: Harper, 1950.

Survey of International Affairs. Published annually for the Royal Institute for International Affairs, Oxford: Oxford University Press.

Newspapers

La Dépêche de Toulouse
L'Echo de Paris
L'Ere Nouvelle
Je Suis Partout
London Times
La Lumière
Matin
New York Times
L'Oeuvre
Le Populaire
Sunday Times (London)
Le Temps

Memoirs, Published Diaries, and Personal Journals

Argenlieu, Thierry d'. *Souvenirs de Guerre.* Paris: Librairie Plon, 1973.

Baeyens, Jacques. *Au bout de Quai: Souvenirs d'un retraité des postes.* Paris: Fayard, 1975.

Baudouin, Paul. *The Private Diaries of Paul Baudouin.* Translated by Sir Charles Petrie. Foreword by Sir Malcolm Muggeridge. London: Eyre & Spottiswoode, 1948.

Bidault, Suzanne. *Par une porte etre baíllée.* Paris: La Table Ronde, 1972.

Boisanger Claude de. *On Pouvait éviter la guerre d'Indochine: Souvenirs, 1941–1945.* Paris: Libraire d'Amérique et d'Orient, 1977.

Blum, John Morton. *From the Morgenthau Diaries.* Vol. 2, *Years of Urgency, 1938–1941.* Boston: Houghton Mifflin, 1965.

Bonnet, Georges. *Défense de la Paix.* Vol. 2, *Fin d'une Europe.* Geneva: Les Editions du Cheval Ailé, 1948.

———. *Le Quai d'Orsay sous trois républiques, 1870–1961.* Paris: Librairie Arthème Fayard, 1961.

Bührer, General Jules [General X, pseud.]. *Aux heures tragiques de l'Empire, 1938–1941.* Paris: Office Colonial d'Edition, 1947.

Bullitt, Orville, ed. *For the President, Personal and Secret: Correspondence between Franklin D. Roosevelt and William C. Bullitt.* Boston: Houghton Mifflin, 1972.

Cadogan, Sir Alexander. *The Diaries of Sir Alexander Cadogan.* Edited by David Dilks. New York: G. P. Putnam's Sons, 1971.

Catroux, Général Georges. *Deux actes du drame Indochinois: Hanoi: Juin 1940–Dien Bien Phu: Mars–Mai 1954*. Paris: Plon, 1958.

Charles-Roux, François. *Cinq mois tragiques aux affaires étrangères (21 Mai–1 Novembre 1940)*. Paris: Librairie Plon, 1949.

Chauvel, Jean. *Commentaire*. 2 vols. Paris: Fayard, 1971–72.

Chennault, Claire L. *Way of a Fighter*. New York: G. P. Putnam's Sons, 1949.

Craigie, Sir Robert. *Behind the Japanese Mask*. London: Hutchinson, 1946.

Crosby, Josiah. *Siam: The Crossroads*. London: Hollis and Carter, 1945.

Decoux, Admiral Jean. *A la barre de l'Indochine: Histoire de mon gouvernement général (1940–1945)*. Paris: Librairie Plon, 1949.

De Gaulle, Charles. *The Complete War Memoirs of Charles de Gaulle*. New York: Simon and Schuster, 1964.

———. *Discours et messages, 1940–1946*. Paris: Librairie Plon, 1946.

Eden, Anthony. *The Memoirs of Anthony Eden, Earl of Avon*. Vol. 1, *Facing the Dictators*. Boston: Houghton Mifflin, 1962.

———. *The Memoirs of Anthony Eden, Earl of Avon*. Vol. 2, *The Reckoning*. Boston: Houghton Mifflin, 1965.

Fischer, Louis. *Men and Politics: An Autobiography*. New York: Duell, Sloan and Pearce, 1941.

Flandin, Pierre-Etienne. *Politique française, 1919–1940*. Paris: Les Editions Nouvelles, 1947.

Forrestal, James. *The Forrestal Diaries*. Edited by Walter Millis. New York: Viking, 1951.

Gamelin, Général Maurice. *Servir*. 3 vols. Paris: Librairie Plon, 1947.

Grew, Joseph C. *Ten Years in Japan*. New York: Simon and Schuster, 1944.

———. *Turbulent Era: A Diplomatic Record of Forty Years, 1904–1945*. Edited by Walter Johnson. 2 vols. Boston: Houghton Mifflin, 1952.

Hankey, Maurice Lord. *The Supreme Control at the Paris Peace Conference, 1919*. London: George Allen and Unwin, 1963.

Harvey, Oliver. *The Diplomatic Diaries of Oliver Harvey, 1937–1940*. Edited by John Harvey. London: Collins, 1970.

Herriot, Edouard. *Jadis*. Vol. 2, *D'une guerre à l'autre, 1914–1936*. Paris: Flammarion, 1952.

Hooker, Nancy Harvison, ed. *The Moffat Papers: Selections from the Diplomatic Journals of Jay Pierrepont Moffat, 1919–1943*. Cambridge, Mass.: Harvard University Press, 1956.

Hornbeck, Stanley K. *The United States and the Far East: Certain Fundamentals of Policy*. Boston: World Peace Foundation, 1942.

Hull, Cordell. *The Memoirs of Cordell Hull*. 2 vols. New York: Macmillan, 1948.

Juin, Maréchal Alphonse. *Mémoires*. 2 vols. Paris: Arthème Fayard, 1959–60.

Laroche, Jules. *Au Quai d'Orsay: Avec Briand et Poincaré, 1913–1926*. Paris: Hachette, 1957.

Lémery, Henry. *D'Une République a l'autre: Souvenirs de la mêlée politique, 1894–1944*. Paris: La Table Ronde, 1964.

Macmillan, Harold. *War Diaries: Politics and War in the Mediterranean, January 1943–May 1945*. New York: St. Martin's Press, 1984.

Marchand, Général Jean. *Le drame Indochinois*. Paris: J. Peyronnet & Cie, 1953.

Martin du Gard, Maurice. *La Carte Impériale: Histoire de la France outre-mer, 1940–1945*. Paris: Editions André Bonne, 1949.

Massigli, René. *Une comédie des erreurs, 1943–1956*. Paris: Librairie Plon, 1978.

Mauriac, Claude. *The Other de Gaulle: Diaries, 1944–1954*. New York: John Day, 1970.

Monnet, Jean. *Memoirs*. Translated by Richard Mayne. Garden City, N.Y.: Doubleday, 1978.

Mordant, Général. *Au service de la France en Indochine, 1941–1945*. Saigon: Edition IFOM, 1946.

Murphy Robert D. *Diplomat among Warriors*. Garden City, N.Y.: Doubleday, 1964.

Patti, Archimedes L. A. *Why Vietnam? Prelude to America's Albatross.* Berkeley: University of California Press, 1980.
Paul-Boncour, Joseph. *Entre deux guerres: Souvenirs sur la Troisième République.* 3 vols. Paris: Librairie Plon, 1945–46.
Phillips, William. *Ventures in Diplomacy.* Boston: Beacon, 1952.
Piggott, Major-General F. S. G. *Broken Thread: An Autobiography.* Aldershot: Gale & Polden, 1950.
Pownall, Sir Henry. *Chief of Staff: The Diaries of Lieutenant-General Sir Henry Pownall.* Edited by Brian Bond. 2 vols. Hamden, Conn.: Archon, 1974.
Sabbatier, General G. *Le destin de l'Indochine: Souvenirs et documents, 1941–1951.* Paris: Librairie Plon, 1952.
Saint-Aulaire, Comte de. *Confession d'un vieux diplomate.* Paris: Flammarion, 1953.
Sainteny, Jean. *Histoire d' une paix manquée.* Paris: Librairie Fayard, 1967.
Sautot, Henri. *Grandeur et décadence du Gaullisme dans le Pacifique.* London: F. W. Cheshire, 1949.
Stettinius, Edward R., Jr. *The Diaries of Edward R. Stettinius, Jr., 1943–1946.* Edited by Thomas M. Campbell and George C. Herring. New York: New Viewpoints, 1975.
Stimson, Henry L. *The Far Eastern Crisis.* New York: Harper, 1936.
Truman, Harry S. *Memoirs.* Vol. 1, *Year of Decisions.* New York: Doubleday, 1955.
Varillon, Pierre. *Marins héroiques.* Paris: Amiot-Dumont, 1950.
Wedemeyer, General Albert C. *Wedemeyer Reports!* New York: Henry Holt, 1958.
Welles, Sumner. *The Time for Decision.* New York: Harper, 1944.
Wellesley, Sir Victor. *Diplomacy in Fetters.* London: Hutchinson, 1944.
Wilson, Hugh R. *Diplomat between Wars.* New York: Longmans, Green, 1941.

Historical Studies

Adamthwaite, Anthony. *France and the Coming of the Second World War, 1936–1939.* London: Frank Cass, 1977.
Abrams, L., and D. J. Miller. "Who Were the French Colonists? A Reassessment of the *Parti Colonial*, 1890–1914." *Historical Journal* 19 (1976): 685–725.
Albertini, Rudolf von. *Decolonization: The Administration and Future of the Colonies, 1919–1960.* Garden City, N.Y.: Doubleday, 1971.
Albertini, Rudolf von. With Albert Wirz. *European Colonial Rule, 1880–1940: The Impact of the West on India, Southeast Asia, and Africa.* Westport, Conn.: Greenwood, 1982.
Albrecht-Carrié, René. *Britain and France: Adaptations to a Changing Context of Power.* Garden City, N.Y.: Doubleday, 1970.
Aldcroft, Derek. *From Versailles to Wall Street, 1919–1929.* Berkeley: University of California Press, 1977.
Aldred, Francis K. "The Brussels Conference: A Study of Efforts during 1937 to Formulate a Joint Anglo-American Far Eastern Policy." Ph.D. diss., University of Virginia, 1967.
Allen, Louis. *The End of the War in Asia.* London: Hart-Davis, MacGibbon, 1976.
Andrew, Christopher. *Théophile Delcassé and the Making of the Entente Cordiale.* London: Macmillan, 1968.
Andrew, Christopher M., and A. S. Kanya-Forstner. *The Climax of French Imperial Expansion, 1914–1924.* Stanford, Calif.: Stanford University Press, 1981.
Archimbaud, Léon. *La Conférence de Washington.* Paris: Payot, 1923.
Asada, Sadao. "Japan's Special Interests and the Washington Conference, 1921–1922." *American Historical Review* 67 (1961): 62–70.
Artaud, Denise. *La question des dettes interalliées et la reconstruction de l'Europe, 1917–1929.* 2 vols. Paris: Librairie Honore Champion, 1978.

Auffray, Bernard. *Pierre de Margerie (1861–1942) et la vie diplomatique de son temps.* Paris: Librairie C. Klincksiek, 1976.

Auphan, Paul, and Jacques Mordal. *The French Navy in World War II.* Annapolis: U.S. Naval Institute, 1959.

Baker, Ray Stannard. *Woodrow Wilson and World Settlement.* 2 vols. 1922. Reprint. Gloucester, Mass.: Peter Smith, 1960.

Barclay, Glen. *A History of the Pacific.* New York: Taplinger Publishing Co., 1978.

Bariéty, Jacques. *Les Relations franco-allemandes après la première guerre mondiale.* Paris: Editions Pedone, 1977.

Barr, Pat. *To China with Love: The Life and Times of Protestant Missionaries in China, 1860–1900.* London: Secker & Warburg, 1972.

Barros, James. *Office without Power: Secretary-General Sir Eric Drummond, 1919–1933.* New York: Oxford University Press, 1979.

Bassett, Reginald. *Democracy and Foreign Policy: A Case History: The Sino-Japanese Dispute, 1931–1933.* London: Longmans, Green, 1952.

Baumont, Maurice. *La faillite de la paix.* Vol. 1, *De Rothondes à Stresa (1918–1935).* Paris: Presses Universitaires de France, 1967.

Bédarida, François. "Des réalités de la guerre aux mirages de la prosperité (1913–1930)." In *Histoire du peuple français: Cent ans d'esprit républicain,* edited by Jean Marie Mayeur et al. Paris: Nouvelle librairie de France, 1964.

Bell, P. M. H. "The Breakdown of the Alliance in 1940." In *Troubled Neighbours: Franco-British Relations in the Twentieth Century,* edited by Neville Waites. London: Weidenfeld, 1971.

Bergamini, David. *Japan's Imperial Conspiracy.* New York: William Morrow, 1971.

Bernard, Philippe, and Henri Dubief. *The Decline of the Third Republic, 1914–1938.* Translated by Anthony Forster. London: Cambridge University Press, 1985.

Betts, Raymond F. *The False Dawn: European Imperialism in the Nineteeth Century.* Minneapolis: University of Minnesota Press, 1975.

———. "The French Colonial Frontier." In *From the Ancien Regime to the Popular Front,* edited by Charles K. Warner. New York: Columbia University Press, 1967.

———. *From Assimilation to Association in French Colonial Theory, 1890–1914.* New York: Columbia University Press, 1961.

———. *Tricoleur: The French Overseas Empire.* London: Gordon & Cremonesi, 1978.

———. *Uncertain Dimensions: Western Overseas Empires in the Twentieth Century.* Minneapolis: University of Minnesota Press, 1985.

Binoche, Jacques. "La politique extrême-orientale française et les relations franco-japonaises de 1919 à 1939." *Revue française d'histoire outre-mer* 284–85, no. 2–3 (1989): 531–43.

Birdsall, Paul. *Versailles Twenty Years After.* New York: Reynal, 1941.

Birn, Donald S. "Open Door Diplomacy at the Washington Conference of 1921–1922: The British and French Experience." *Comparative Studies in Society and History* 12 (July 1970): 297–319.

Blatt, Joel. "The Parity That Meant Superiority: French Naval Policy towards Italy at the Washington Conference, 1921–1922, and Interwar French Foreign Policy." *French Historical Studies* 12 (Fall 1981): 233–48.

Bonnefous, Edouard. *Histoire politique de la Troisième République.* Vol. 5, *La République en danger: Des Ligues au Front Populaire (1930–1936).* Paris: Presses Universitaires de France, 1962.

Booth, Leon. "The Brussels Conference and the Conflict with Japan." *World Affairs* 135 (1972): 240–59.

Borg, Dorothy. *American Policy and the Chinese Revolution. 1925–1928.* New York: American Institute of Pacific Relations and Macmillan, 1947.

———. "Notes on Roosevelt's 'Quarantine' Speech." *Political Science Quarterly* 72 (September 1957): 405–33.

———. *The United States and the Far Eastern Crisis of 1933–1938.* Cambridge, Mass.: Harvard University Press, 1964.

Borg, Dorothy, and Shumpei Okamoto, eds. *Pearl Harbor as History: Japanese-American Relations, 1931–1941.* New York: Columbia University Press, 1973.

Boyle, John Hunter. *China and Japan at War, 1937–1945: The Politics of Collaboration.* Stanford, Calif.: Stanford University Press, 1972.

Braisted, William Reynolds. *The United States Navy in the Pacific, 1909–1922.* Austin: University of Texas Press, 1971.

Brogan, D. W. *The Development of Modern France, 1870–1939.* Rev. ed. New York: Harper & Row, 1966.

Brown, Constantine, "French Policy in the Far East." *Asia* 32 (May 1932): 284–89, 335–38.

Brunschwig, Henri. *La Colonisation française.* Paris: Calmann-Levy, Editeurs, 1949.

———. *French Colonialism, 1871–1914: Myths and Realities.* Translated by W. G. Brown, New York: Frederick A. Praeger, 1966.

Buckley, Thomas H. *The United States and the Washington Conference, 1921–1922.* Knoxville: University of Tennessee Press, 1970.

Buell, Raymond Leslie. *The Washington Conference.* New York: Appleton, 1922.

Burns, James MacGregor. *Roosevelt: The Soldier of Freedom.* New York: Harcourt Brace Jovanovich, 1970.

Burns, Richard Dean, and Edward M. Bennett. *Diplomats in Crisis: United States-Chinese-Japanese Relations, 1919–1941.* Santa Barbara, Calif.: ABC-Clio, 1974.

Burton, William. "French Imperialism in China." *Current History* 39 (January 1934): 428–43.

Bury, J. P. *France, 1814–1940.* New York: A. S. Barnes and Co., Inc., 1962.

———. *Gambetta's Final Years: "The Era of Difficulties," 1877–1882.* London: Longman, 1982.

Buss, Claude A. *War and Diplomacy in Eastern Asia.* New York: Macmillan, 1941.

Butow, Robert J. C. *Tojo and the Coming of the War.* Princeton, N.J.: Princeton University Press, 1961.

Buttinger, Joseph. *A Dragon Defiant: A Short History of Vietnam.* New York: Praeger, 1972.

———. *Vietnam: A Dragon Embattled.* Vol. 1, *From Colonialism to the Viet-Minh.* New York: Praeger, 1967.

Cady, John F. *The Roots of French Imperialism in Eastern Asia.* Ithaca, N.Y.: Cornell University Press, 1954.

———. *Southeast Asia: Its Historical Development.* New York: McGraw-Hill, 1964.

Cairns, John C. *France.* Englewood Cliffs, N.J.: Prentice-Hall, 1965.

Callahan, Raymond. "The Illusion of Security: Singapore, 1919–1942." *Journal of Contemporary History* 9 (April 1974): 69–92.

Catroux, Georges. "Catroux Defends Indochina Regime." *New York Times.* 2 August 1945, 7.

Cerny, Philip G. *The Politics of Grandeur: Ideological Aspects of de Gaulle's Foreign Policy.* London: Cambridge University Press, 1980.

Challener, Richard D. "The French Foreign Office: The Era of Philippe Berthelot." In *The Diplomats, 1919–1939,* edited by Gordon A. Craig and Felix Gilbert. New York: Atheneum, 1965.

Chamberlain, M. E. *The New Imperialism.* London: Historical Association, 1970.

Chastenet, Jacques. *Historie de la troisième république*. Vol. 5, *Les années d'illusions, 1918–1931*. Paris: Librairie Hachette, 1960.

———. *Histoire de la troisième république*. Vol. 6, *Declin de la troisième, 1931–1938*. Paris: Librairie Hachette, 1962.

Chi, Madeleine. *China Diplomacy, 1914–1918*. Cambridge, Mass.: East Asian Research Center, 1970.

Chihiro, Hosoya. "The Japanese-Soviet Neutrality Pact." In *The Fateful Choice: Japan's Advance into Southeast Asia, 1939–1941*, edited by James William Morley. New York: Columbia University Press, 1980.

———. "The Tripartite Pact, 1939–1940." In *Deterrent Diplomacy: Japan, Germany, and the USSR, 1935–1940*, edited by James William Morley. New York: Columbia University Press, 1976.

Clarke, Jeffrey J. "The Nationalization of War Industries in France, 1936–1937." *Journal of Modern History* 49 (September 1977): 411–30.

Clemens, Diane Shaver. *Yalta*. New York: Oxford University Press, 1970.

Clifford, Nicholas R. *Retreat from China: British Policy in the Far East, 1937–1941*. Seattle: University of Washington Press, 1967.

Clubb, O. Edmund. *Twentieth-Century China*. 3d ed. New York: Columbia University Press, 1978.

Cohen, Paul A. "Christian Missions and Their Impact to 1900." In *The Cambridge History of China*, edited by John K. Fairbank, Vol. 10, London: Cambridge University Press, 1978.

Cohen, Warren I. *America's Response to China: An Interpretive History of Sino-American Relations*. 2d ed. New York: John Wiley, 1980.

Cohen, William B. "The Lure of Empire: Why Frenchmen Entered the Colonial Service." *Journal of Contemporary History* 4 (January 1969): 103–16.

Cohen, William B., ed. *Robert Delavignette on the French Empire: Selected Writings*. Translated by Camille Garnier. Chicago: University of Chicago Press, 1977.

Cole, Wayne S. *Roosevelt and the Isolationists, 1932–1945*. Lincoln: University of Nebraska Press, 1983.

Cook, James J. *New French Imperialism, 1880–1910: The Third Republic and Colonial Expansion*. Hamden, Conn.: Archon, 1973.

Cooper, Chester L. *The Lost Crusade: America in Vietnam*. New York: Dodd, Mead, 1970.

Crowley, James B. *Japan's Quest for Autonomy: National Security and Foreign Policy, 1930–1938*. Princeton, N.J.: Princeton University Press, 1966.

———. "A New Deal for Japan and Asia: One Road to Pearl Harbor." In *Modern East Asia: Essays in Interpretation*, edited by James B. Crowley. New York: Harcourt, Brace and World, 1970.

Cruickshank, Charles. *SOE in the Far East*, New York: Oxford University Press, 1983.

Curry, Roy Watson. *Woodrow Wilson and Far Eastern Policy, 1913–1921*. 1957. Reprint. New York: Octagon, 1968.

Dallek, Robert. *Franklin D. Roosevelt and American Foreign Policy, 1932–1945*. New York: Oxford University Press, 1979.

Debu-Bridel, Jacques. *L'agonie de la Troisième République, 1929–1939*. Paris: Editions du Bateau Ivre, 1948.

DePorte, A. W. *De Gaulle's Foreign Policy, 1944–1946*. Cambridge, Mass.: Harvard University Press, 1968.

Devillers, Philippe. *Histoire du Viêt-Nam de 1940 à 1952*. Paris: Editions de Seuil, 1952.

Dingman, Roger. *Power in the Pacific: The Origins of Naval Arms Limitation, 1914–1922*. Chicago: University of Chicago Press, 1976.

Divine, Robert A. *The Illusion of Neutrality*. Chicago: University of Chicago Press, 1962.

———. *The Reluctant Belligerent: American Entry into World War II*. New York: John Wiley, 1965.

Donnison, F. S. V. *British Military Administration in the Far East, 1943–1946*. London: Her Majesty's Stationery Office, 1956.

Dower, J. W. *Empire and Aftermath: Yoshida Shigeru and the Japanese Experience, 1878–1954*. Cambridge, Mass.: Harvard University Press, 1979.

Drachman, Edward R. *United States Policy toward Vietnam, 1940–1945*. Rutherford, N.J.: Fairleigh Dickinson University Press, 1970.

Dreifort, John E. *Yvon Delbos at the Quai d'Orsay: French Foreign Policy during the Popular Front, 1936–1938*. Lawrence: University Press of Kansas, 1973.

Duiker, William J. *The Rise of Nationalism in Vietnam, 1900–1941*. Ithaca, N.Y.: Cornell University Press, 1976.

Dunn, Peter M. *The First Vietnam War*. New York: St. Martin's, 1985.

Duroselle, Jean-Baptiste. *L'Abîme, 1939–1945*. Paris: Imprimerie Nationale, 1982.

———. "Changes in French Foreign Policy since 1945." In *In Search of France*, edited by Stanley Hoffmann et al. Cambridge, Mass.: Harvard University Press, 1963.

———. *France and the United States from the Beginnings to the Present*. Translated by Derek Coltman. Chicago: University of Chicago Press, 1978.

———. *Historie diplomatique de 1919 à nos jours*. Paris: Dalloz, 1971.

———. *Politique étrangère de la France: La décadence, 1932–1939*. Paris: Imprimerie Nationale, 1979.

———. *La Politique extérieure de la France de 1914 à 1945*. Paris: Centre de Documentation Universitaire, 1965.

Edwards, E. W. "The Far Eastern Agreements of 1907." *Journal of Modern History* 26 (December 1954): 340–55

———. "The Japanese Alliance and the Anglo-French Agreement of 1904." *History* 42 (February 1957): 19–27.

Elcock, Howard. *Portrait of a Decision: The Council of Four and the Treaty of Versailles*. London: Eyre Methuen, 1972.

Fairbank, John K., ed. *Missionary Enterprise in China and America*. Cambridge, Mass.: Harvard University Press, 1974.

Fall, Bernard B. *The Two Viet-Nams: A Political and Military Analysis*. 2d ed. New York: Frederick A. Praeger, 1967.

Feis, Herbert. *Between War and Peace: The Potsdam Conference*. Princeton, N.J.: Princeton University Press, 1960.

———. *The Road to Pearl Harbor: The Coming of the War between the United States and Japan*. Princeton, N.J.: Princeton University Press, 1950.

———. *Roosevelt, Churchill, and Stalin: The War They Waged and the Peace They Sought*. Princeton, N.J.: Princeton University Press, 1957.

Ferrell, Robert H. *American Diplomacy in the Great Depression: Hoover-Stimson Foreign Policy, 1929–1933*. New Haven, Conn.: Yale University Press, 1957.

———. "The Mukden Incident: September 18–19, 1931." *Journal of Modern History* 27 (March 1955): 66–72.

Feuer, Lewis S. "End of Coolie Labor in New Caledonia." *Far Eastern Survey* 15 (28 August 1946): 264–67.

Fifield, Russell H. "Secretary Hughes and the Shantung Question." *Pacific Historical Review* 23 (November 1954): 373–85.

———. *Woodrow Wilson and the Far East: The Diplomacy of the Shantung Question*. 1952. Reprint. Hamden, Conn.: Archon, 1965.

Fishel, Wesley R. *The End of Extraterritoriality in China.* 1952. Reprint. New York: Octagon, 1974.

Flood, E. Thaddeus. "The 1940 Franco-Thai Border Dispute and Phibuum Sonkhraam's Commitment to Japan." *Journal of Southeast Asian History* 10 (September 1969): 304–25.

Fox, John P. *Germany and the Far Eastern Crisis, 1931–1938.* London: Oxford University Press, 1982.

Funk, Arthur L. *Charles de Gaulle: The Crucial Years, 1943–1944.* Norman: University of Oklahoma Press, 1959.

Garrett, Clark W. "In Search of Grandeur: France and Vietnam, 1940–1946," *Review of Politics* 29 (July 1967): 303–23.

Gaudel, André. *L'Indochine française en face du Japon.* New York: AMS, 1975.

Gardner, Lloyd C. *Approaching Vietnam: From World War II through Dienbienphu, 1941–1954.* New York: W. W. Norton, 1988.

Gibbs, N. H. *Grand Strategy.* Vol. 1, *Rearmament Policy.* London: Her Majesty's Stationery Office, 1976.

Girardet, Raul. *L'Idée coloniale en France de 1871 à 1962.* Paris: La Table Ronde, 1972.

Graebner, Norman A. Introduction to *Diplomats in Crisis: United States-Chinese-Japanese Relations, 1919–1941,* edited by Richard Dean Burns and Edward M. Bennett. Santa Barbara, Calif.: ABC-Clio, 1974.

Grattan, C. Hartley. *The Southwest Pacific since 1900.* Ann Arbor: University of Michigan Press, 1963.

Greene, Nathanael. *From Versailles to Vichy: The Third French Republic, 1919–1940.* New York: Thomas Y. Crowell, 1970.

Grimal, Henri. *Decolonization: The British, French, Dutch and Belgian Empires, 1919–1963.* Boulder, Colo.: Westview, 1978.

Griswold, A. Whitney. *The Far Eastern Policy of the United States.* New York: Harcourt, Brace, 1938.

Haight, John McVickar, Jr. *American Aid to France, 1938–1940.* New York: Atheneum, 1970.

———. "France and the Aftermath of Roosevelt's 'Quarantine' Speech." *World Politics* 14 (January 1962): 283–306.

———. "Franklin D. Roosevelt and a Naval Quarantine of Japan." *Pacific Historical Review* 40 (May 1971): 203–26.

Hamill, Ian. *The Strategic Illusion: The Singapore Strategy and Defence of Australia and New Zealand, 1919–1942.* Singapore: Singapore University Press, 1981.

Hammer, Ellen Joy. *The Struggle for Indochina, 1940–1955.* Stanford, Calif.: Stanford University Press, 1954.

Harrison, James Pinckney. *The Endless War: Fifty Years of Struggle in Vietnam.* New York: Free Press, 1982.

Herriot, Edward. "An International Drama." *International Conciliation* 290 (May 1933): 228–32.

Herring, George C. "The Truman Administration and the Restoration of French Sovereignty in Indochina." *Diplomatic History* 1 (Spring 1977): 97–117.

Hess, Gary R. "Franklin Roosevelt and Indochina." *Journal of American History* 59 (September 1972): 353–68.

Hou, Chi-ming. *Foreign Investment and Economic Development in China, 1840–1937.* Cambridge, Mass.: Harvard University Press, 1965.

Hyde, Francis E. *Far Eastern Trade, 1860–1914.* London: Adams & Charles Black, 1973.

Hytier, Adrienne Doris. *Two Years of French Foreign Policy: Vichy, 1940–1942.* Paris: Librairie E. Droz, 1958.

Ichihashi, Yamoto. *The Washington Conference and After.* Stanford, Calif.: Stanford University Press, 1928.

Ikuhiko, Hata. "The Japanese-Soviet Confrontation, 1935–1939." In *Deterrent Diplomacy: Japan, Germany, and the USSR, 1935–1940,* edited by James William Morley. New York: Columbia University Press, 1976.

Iriye, Akira. *Across the Pacific: An Inner History of American-East Asian Relations.* New York: Harcourt, Brace & World, 1967.

———. *After Imperialism: The Search for a New Order in the Far East, 1921–1931.* Cambridge, Mass.: Harvard University Press, 1965.

———. *The Cold War in Asia: A Historical Introduction.* Englewood Cliffs, N.J.: Prentice-Hall, 1974.

———. "Japan's Policies toward the United States." In *Japan's Foreign Policy, 1868–1941: A Research Guide,* edited by James W. Morley. New York: Columbia University Press, 1974.

———. *Power and Culture: The Japanese-American War, 1941–1945.* Cambridge, Mass.: Harvard University Press, 1981.

Irving, R. E. M. *The First Indochina War: French and American Policy, 1945–1954.* London: Croom Helm, 1975.

Jackson, J. Hampden. *Clemenceau and the Third Republic.* London: Hodder & Stoughton, 1959.

Jackson, Julian. *The Politics of Depression in France, 1932–1936.* London: Cambridge University Press, 1985.

Jenkins, E. H. *A History of the French Navy: From Its Beginnings to Modern Day.* London: MacDonald and Jane's, 1973.

Jessner, Sabine. *Edouard Herriot: Patriarch of the Republic.* New York: Haskell House, 1974.

Jones, F. C. *Japan's New Order in East Asia: Its Rise and Fall, 1937–1945.* London: Oxford University Press, 1954.

Jones, F. C., Hugh Barton, and B. R. Pearn. *Survey of International Affairs.* Vol. 6, *The Far East, 1942–1946.* London: Oxford University Press, 1955.

Keesing, Felix M. *The South Seas in the Modern World.* New York: John Day, 1941.

Kemp, Tom. *The French Economy, 1913–1939: The History of a Decline.* London: Longman, 1972.

Kennedy, Paul. *Strategy and Diplomacy, 1870–1945.* London: George Allen & Unwin, 1983.

———. *The Rise and Fall of the Great Powers: Economic Change and Military Conflict from 1500 to 2000.* New York: Random House, 1987.

Kersaudy, François. *Churchill and De Gaulle.* New York: Atheneum, 1982.

Kuo, Ting-yee. "Self-strengthening: The Pursuit of Western Technology." In *The Cambridge History of China,* edited by John K. Fairbank. Vol. 10. London: Cambridge University Press, 1978.

LaFeber, Walter. "Roosevelt, Churchill, and Indochina, 1942–1945." *American Historical Review* 80 (December 1975): 1275–95.

Laffey, John F. "Roots of French Imperialism in the Nineteenth Century: The Case of Lyon." *French Historical Studies* 6 (April 1969): 78–92.

La Masson, Henri. *The French Navy.* Garden City, N.Y.: Doubleday, 1969.

Lancaster, Donald. *The Emancipation of French Indochina.* London: Oxford University Press, 1961.

Langer, William L., and S. Everett Gleason. *The Challenge to Isolation, 1937–1940.* New York: Harper, 1952.

———. *The Undeclared War, 1940–1941.* New York: Harper, 1953.

Latourette, Kenneth Scott. *A History of Christian Missions in China.* 1929. Reprint. New York: Paragon, 1970.

———. *The Development of China.* Boston: Houghton Mifflin, 1946.

Lee, Bradford A. *Britain and the Sino-Japanese War, 1937–1939*. Stanford, Calif.: Stanford University Press, 1973.

Levy, Roger et al. *French Interests and Policies in the Far East*. New York: Institute of Pacific Relations, 1941.

Link, Arthur S. *Wilson the Diplomatist: A Look at His Major Foreign Policies*. Baltimore, Md.: Johns Hopkins University Press, 1957.

Louis, William Roger. *British Strategy in the Far East, 1919–1939*. London: Oxford University Press, 1971.

———. *Imperialism at Bay: The United States and the Decolonization of the British Empire, 1941–1945*. New York: Oxford University Press, 1978.

Lowe, Peter. *Great Britain and Japan, 1911–1915: A Study of British Far Eastern Policy*. New York: St. Martin's Press, 1969.

———. *Great Britain and the Origins of the Pacific War: A Study of British Policy in East Asia. 1937–1941*. New York: Oxford University Press, 1977.

Lowenheim, Francis, Harold D. Langley, and Manfred Jonas, eds. *Roosevelt and Churchill: Their Secret Wartime Correspondence*. New York: Saturday Review, 1975.

Lu, David J. *From the Marco Polo Bridge to Pearl Harbor: Japan's Entry into World War II*. Washington, D.C.: Public Affairs Press, 1961.

McAllister, John T., Jr. *Vietnam: The Origins of Revolution*. New York: Alfred A. Knopf, 1970.

McDougall, Walter A. *France's Rhineland Diplomacy, 1914–1924: The Last Bid for a Balance of Power in Europe*. Princeton, N.J.: Princeton University Press, 1978.

Marks, Sally. *The Illusion of Peace: International Relations in Europe, 1918–1933*. New York: St. Martin's Press, 1976.

———. "The Myth of Reparations." *Central European History* 17 (September 1978): 231–55.

Marshall, D. Bruce. *The French Colonial Myth and Constitution-making in the Fourth Republic*. New Haven, Conn.: Yale University Press, 1973.

Mayer, Arno J. *Politics and Diplomacy of Peacemaking: Containment and Counterrevolution at Versailles, 1918–1919*. New York: Alfred A. Knopf, 1967.

Medzini, Meron. *French Policy in Japan during the Closing Years of the Tokugawa Regime*. Cambridge, Mass.: Harvard University Press, 1971.

Miquel, Pierre. *La Paix de Versailles et l'opinion publique française*. Paris: Flammarion, 1972.

Morison, Samuel Eliot. *History of the United Naval Operations in World War II*. Vol. 3, *The Rising Sun in the Pacific, 1931–April 1942*. Boston: Little, Brown, 1948.

Morley, James William, ed. *The China Quagmire: Japan's Expansion on the Asian Continent, 1933–1941*. New York: Columbia University Press, 1983.

———. *Deterrent Diplomacy: Japan, Germany, and the USSR, 1935–1940*. New York: Columbia University Press, 1976.

———. *The Fateful Choice: Japan's Advance into Southeast Asia, 1939–1941*. New York: Columbia University Press, 1980.

———. *Japan's Foreign Policy, 1868–1941: A Research Guide*. New York: Columbia University Press, 1974.

Morrell, W. P. *The Great Powers in the Pacific*. London: Historical Association, 1963.

Myers, Ramon H., and Mark R. Peattie, eds. *The Japanese Colonial Empire, 1895–1945*. Princeton, N.J.: Princeton University Press, 1984.

Nagai, Michio. "Westernization and Japanization: The Early Meiji Transformation of Education." In *Tradition and Modernization in Japanese Culture*, edited by Donald H. Shively. Princeton, N.J.: Princeton University Press, 1971.

Néré J. *The Foreign Policy of France from 1914 to 1945*. London: Routledge & Kegan Paul, 1975.

Neu, Charles E. *The Troubled Encounter: The United States and Japan.* New York: John Wiley, 1975.

Nicolson, Harold. *Peacemaking, 1919.* 1933. Reprint. New York: Grosset & Dunlap, 1965.

Nish, Ian. *Alliance in Decline: A Study in Anglo-Japanese Relations, 1908–1923.* London: Athlone, 1972.

——— . *The Anglo-Japanese Alliance: The Diplomacy of Two Island Empires, 1894–1907.* London: Athlone, 1966.

——— . *Japanese Foreign Policy, 1869–1942.* London: Routledge & Kegan Paul, 1977.

——— . *A Short History of Japan.* New York: Frederick A. Praeger, 1968.

Noble, George Bernard. *Policies and Opinions at Paris, 1919.* New York: Macmillan, 1935.

Norton, Henry K. "Foreign Office Organization: A Comparison of the British, French, German, and Italian Foreign Offices with that of the State Department of the United States of America." *Annals of the American Academy of Political and Social Sciences (Supplement)* 143 (May 1929): 1–86.

Ogata, Sadako N. *Defiance in Manchuria: The Making of Japanese Foreign Policy, 1931–1932.* Berkeley: University of California Press, 1964.

Oka, Yoshitake. *Konoe Fumimaro: A Political Biography.* Translated by Shumpei Okamoto and Patricia Marray. Tokyo: University of Tokyo Press, 1983.

Oliver, Douglas L. *The Pacific Islands.* Rev. ed. Garden City, N.Y.: Doubleday, 1961.

Osborne, Milton E. *The French Presence in Cochinchina and Cambodia: Rule and Response (1859–1905).* Ithaca, N.Y.: Cornell University Press, 1969.

Osgood, Samuel M. "Le Mythe de 'la perfide Albion' en France, 1919–1940." *Cahiers d'Histoire* 20 (1975): 5–20.

——— . "The Third French Republic in Historical Perspective." In *Statesmen and Statecraft of the Modern West,* edited by Gerald N. Grob. Barre, Mass.: Barre, 1967.

Peattie, Mark R. *Ishiwara Kanji and Japan's Confrontation with the West.* Princeton, N.J.: Princeton University Press, 1975.

Pedrazzani, J. M. *Le France en Indochine: De Catroux à Sainteny.* Paris: Arthaud, 1972.

Persell, Stuart Michael. *The French Colonial Lobby, 1889–1938.* Stanford, Calif.: Hoover Institution, 1983.

Perett, William Gregory. "French Naval Policy and Foreign Affairs, 1930–1939." Ph.D. diss., Stanford University, 1977.

Pollard, Robert T. *China's Foreign Relations, 1917–1931.* 1933. Reprint. New York: Arno, 1970.

Porter, Charles W. *The Career of Théophile Delcassé.* Philadelphia: University of Pennsylvania Press, 1936.

Power, Thomas F., Jr. *Jules Ferry and the Renaissance of French Imperialism.* 1944. Reprint. New York: Octagon, 1977.

Prange, Gordon W. *At Dawn We Slept: The Untold Story of Pearl Harbor.* New York: McGraw-Hill, 1981.

Presseisen, Ernst L. *Before Aggression: Europeans Prepare the Japanese Army.* Tucson: University of Arizona Press, 1965.

——— . *Germany and Japan: A Study in Totalitarian Diplomacy, 1933–1941.* The Hague: Martinus Nijhoff, 1958.

Priestley, Herbert Ingram. *France Overseas: A Study of Modern Imperialism.* 1938. Reprint. New York: Octagon, 1966.

Pugach, Noel H. "American Friendship for China and the Shantung Question at the Washington Conference." *Journal of American History* 64 (June 1977): 67–86.

Quigley, Harold S., and George H. Blakeslee. *The Far East: An International Survey.* Boston: World Peace Foundation, 1938.

Rappaport, Armin. *Henry L. Stimson and Japan, 1931–1933*. Chicago: University of Chicago Press, 1963.

Ready, J. Lee. *Forgotten Allies*. Vol. 2, *The Asian Theater*. Jefferson, N.C.: McFarland, 1985.

Reischauer, Edwin O. *The United States and Japan*. 3d ed. Cambridge, Mass.: Harvard University Press, 1965.

Remer, Charles F. *Foreign Investments in China*. 1933. Reprint. New York: Howard Fertig, 1968.

Renouvin, Pierre. *La question d'extrême-orient, 1840–1940*. Paris: Librairie Hachette, 1946.

———. *Le traité de Versailles*. Paris: Flammarion, 1969.

Roberts, Stephen H. *The History of French Colonial Policy, 1870–1925*. 2 vols. 1929. Reprint. Hamden, Conn.: Archon, 1963.

Romanus, Charles F., and Riley Sunderland. *United States Army in World War II: China-Burma-India Theater*. Vol. 3, *Time Runs Out in CBI*. Washington, D.C.: Office of the Chief of Military History, Department of the Army, 1959.

Roosevelt, Elliott. *As He Saw It*. New York: Duell, Sloan and Pearce, 1946.

Roskill, Stephen. *Naval Policy between the Wars*. Vol. 1, *The Period of Anglo-American Antagonism, 1919–1929*. London: Collins, 1968.

Sadao, Asada. "Japan's 'Special Interests' and the Washington Naval Conference, 1921–1922." *American Historical Review* 67 (October 1961): 62–70.

Sapp, Steven P. "The United States, France and the Cold War: Jefferson Caffrey and American-French Relations, 1944–1949." Ph.D. diss., Kent State University, 1978.

Sarraut, Albert. *La mise en valeur des colonies français*. Paris: Payot, 1923.

Sauvy, Alfred. "The Economic Crisis of the 1930s in France." *Journal of Contemporary History* 4 (October 1969): 21–35.

———. *Histoire économique de la France entre les deux guerres (1918–1931)*. 2 vols. Paris: Librairie Arthème Fayard, 1965.

Schaller, Michael. *The U.S. Crusade in China, 1938–1945*. New York: Columbia University Press, 1979.

Schroeder, Paul W. *The Axis Alliance and Japanese-American Relations, 1941*. Ithaca, N.Y.: Cornell University Press, 1958.

Schuker, Stephen A. *The End of French Predominance in Europe: The Financial Crisis of 1924 and the Adoption of the Dawes Plan*. Chapel Hill: University of North Carolina Press, 1976.

Sellen, Robert W. "Comparative Perspectives on Indochina during World War II: The French Viewpoint, 1940–1945." Paper presented at the annual meeting of the American Historical Association, San Francisco, 19 December 1978.

Shai, Aron. "Was There a Far Eastern Munich?" *Journal of Contemporary History* 9 (July 1974): 161–69.

Sharp, Lauriston. "Colonial Regimes in Southeast Asia." *Far Eastern Survey* 15 (17 February 1946): 45–53.

Sherwood, John M. *Georges Mandel and the Third Republic*. Stanford, Calif.: Stanford University Press, 1970.

Simkin, C. G. F. *The Traditional Trade of Asia*. London: Oxford University Press, 1968.

Smith, R. Harris. *OSS: The Secret History of America's First Central Intelligence Agency*. Berkeley: University of California Press, 1972.

Smith, Sara R. *The Manchurian Crisis, 1931–1932: A Tragedy in International Relations*. New York: Columbia University Press, 1948.

Sontag, Raymond J. *A Broken World, 1919–1939*. New York: Harper & Row, 1971.

Sorum, Paul Clay. *Intellectuals and Decolonization in France*. Chapel Hill: University of North Carolina Press, 1977.

Soulié, Michel. *La vie politique d'Edouard Herriot*. Paris: Armand Colin, 1962.

Spotswood, Rogers D. "Japan's Southward Advance as an Issue in Japanese-American Relations, 1940–1941." Ph.D. diss., University of Washington, 1974.

Sprout, Harold, and Margaret Sprout. *Toward a New Order of Sea Power: American Naval Power and the World Scene, 1918–1922*. Princeton, N.J.: Princeton University Press, 1940.

Stimson, Henry L., and McGeorge Bundy. *On Active Service in Peace and War*. New York: Harper, 1947.

Suarez, Georges. *Briand: Sa vie—son oeuvre*. Vol. 5, *L'Artisan de la paix, 1918–1923*. Paris: Librairie Plon, 1941.

Taboulet, Georges. "La France et l'Angleterre face au conflit sino-japonais (1937–1939)." *Revue d'Histoire Diplomatique* 88 (January–June 1974): 112–44.

Temperley, H. W. V., ed. *A History of the Paris Peace Conference*. 6 vols. London: Institute of International Affairs, 1920–24.

Thompson, Virginia. *French Indochina*. New York: Macmillan, 1937.

——— . "Indo-China—France's Great Stake in the Far East." *Far Eastern Survey* 6 (20 January 1937): 15–22.

Thompson, Virginia, and Richard Adloff. *The French Pacific Islands*. Berkeley: University of California Press, 1971.

Thomson, James C. *While China Faced West*. Cambridge, Mass.: Harvard University Press, 1969.

Thorne, Christopher. *Allies of a Kind: The United States, Britain, and the War against Japan*. New York: Oxford University Press, 1978.

——— . "Indochina and Anglo-American Relations, 1942–1945." *Pacific Historical Review* 45 (February 1976): 73–96.

——— . *The Issue of War: States, Societies, and the Far Eastern Conflict of 1941–1945*. New York: Oxford University Press, 1985.

——— . *The Limits of Foreign Policy: The West, the League, and the Far Eastern Crisis of 1931–1933*. New York: G. P. Putnam's Sons, 1972.

——— . "The Quest for Arms Embargoes: Failure in 1933." *Journal of Contemporary History* 5, no. 4 (1970): 129–49.

Thornton, A. P. *Imperialism in the Twentieth Century*. Minneapolis: University of Minnesota Press, 1978.

Toshihiko, Shimada. "Designs on North China, 1933–1937." In *The China Quagmire: Japan's Expansion on the Asian Continent, 1933–1941*. Translated by James B. Crowley and edited by James William Morley. New York: Columbia University Press, 1983.

Toynbee, Arnold, and Veronica M. Toynbee, eds. *The Initial Triumph of the Axis*. London: Oxford University Press, 1958.

Trachtenberg, Marc. *Reparation in World Politics: France and European Economic Diplomacy, 1916–1923*. New York: Columbia University Press, 1980.

Utley, Jonathon G. *Going to War with Japan, 1937–1941*. Knoxville: University of Tennessee Press, 1985.

Van Meter, Robert H., Jr. "The Washington Conference of 1921–1922: A New Look." *Pacific Historical Review* 64 (November 1977): 603–24.

Varg, Paul A. "The Missionary Response to the Nationalist Revolution." In *The Missionary Enterprise in China and America*, edited by John K. Fairbank. Cambridge, Mass.: Harvard University Press, 1974.

Varenne, Alexandre. "Indo-China in the Path of Japanese Expansion." *Foreign Affairs* 17 (October 1938): 164–71.

Vinacke, Harold M. *A History of the Far East in Modern Times*. 6th ed. New York: Appleton-Century-Crofts, 1964.

Vinson, John Chalmers. *The Parchment Peace: The United States Senate and the Washington Conference, 1921–1922.* Athens: University of Georgia Press, 1955.

Viorst, Milton. *Hostile Allies: FDR and Charles de Gaulle.* New York: Macmillan, 1965.

Walworth, Arthur. *Wilson and His Peacemakers: American Diolomacy at the Paris Peace Conference, 1919.* New York: W. W. Norton, 1986.

Warner, Charles K., ed. *From the Ancien Regime to the Popular Front.* New York: Columbia University Press, 1969.

Warner, Geoffrey. *Pierre Laval and the Eclipse of France.* London: Eyre & Spottiswood, 1968.

Werth, Alexander. *The Twilight of France.* New York: Harper & Brothers, 1942.

Wheeler, Gerald E. *Prelude to Pearl Harbor: The United States Navy and the Far East, 1921–1931.* Columbia: University of Missouri Press, 1963.

White, Dorothy Shipley. *Seeds of Discord: De Gaulle, Free France, and the Allies.* Syracuse, N.Y.: Syracuse University Press, 1964.

Wiltz, John E. *From Isolation to War, 1931–1941.* New York: Thomas Y. Crowell, 1968.

Woodburn Kirby, Major-General S. *The War against Japan.* 5 vols. London: Her Majesty's Stationery Office, 1957–69.

Woodward, Sir Llewelyn. *British Foreign Policy in the Second World War.* 5 vols. London: Her Majesty's Stationery Office, 1970–76.

Wright, Gordon. *France in Modern Times.* 2d ed. Chicago: Rand McNally, 1974.

Yoshihashi, Takehiko. *Conspiracy at Mukden: The Rise of the Japanese Military.* New Haven, Conn.: Yale University Press, 1963.

Young, Arthur N. *China and the Helping Hand, 1937–1945.* Cambridge, Mass.: Harvard University Press, 1963.

Younger, R. M. *Australia and the Australians: A New Concise History.* New York: Humanities, 1970.

Zeldin, Theodore. *France, 1848–1945.* Vol. 2, *Intellect, Taste and Anxiety.* Oxford: Oxford University Press, 1977.

Periodicals Screened

American Historical Review; American Political Science Review; Asia; Cahiers d'Histoire; Central European History; Comparative Studies in Society and History; Current History; Diplomatic History; European Studies Review; Far Eastern Survey; Foreign Affairs; French Historical Studies; History; History Today; International Affairs; International Conciliation; Journal of American History; Journal of Contemporary History; Journal of Modern History; Journal of Southeast Asian Studies; Pacific Historical Review; Pacific History; Political Science Quarterly; Revue des Deux Mondes; Revue française d'histoire outre-mer; Revue Historique; Revue d'Histoire de la Deuxieme Guerre Mondiale; Revue d'Histoire Diplomatique; Revue d'Histoire Moderne et Contemporaine; Western Society for French History Proceedings; World Affairs; World Politics.

Index

MYOPIC GRANDEUR
was composed in 10.5/12 Bembo on a Xyvision system
with Linotron 202 output
by BookMasters, Inc.;
printed by sheet-fed offset on 50-pound, acid-free,
Glatfelter Natural Smooth stock,
Smyth sewn and bound over .088″ binders boards
in ICG Arrestox B cloth
and wrapped with dust jackets printed on 80-pound stock
by Braun-Brumfield, Inc.;
text designed by Diana Gordy;
jacket designed by Will Underwood;
and published by
THE KENT STATE UNIVERSITY PRESS
Kent, Ohio 44242